AAUG MONOGRAPH SERIES: NO. 9

THE ARAB WORLD: A HANDBOOK

Hassan S. Haddad
Basheer K. Nijim
editors

with a foreword by
Ibrahim Abu-Lughod

Medina Press
Wilmette, Illinois
1978

First Published in the United States of America by

Medina Press
P.O. Box 125
Wilmette, IL 60091

LCC: 78-70237

ISBN 0-914456-19-9 (clothbound edition)
ISBN 0-914456-20-2 (paperback edition)

Hassan S. Haddad is Professor and Chairman of the Department of History and Political Science at St. Xavier College, Chicago.

Basheer K. Nijim is Professor and Head of the Department of Geography at the University of Northern Iowa, Cedar Falls, Iowa.

CONTENTS

CONTRIBUTORS OF RESOURCE PAPERS

Algeria	Mahfoud Bennoune, Department of Anthropology, University of Algiers, Algeria.
Bahrain	Emile and Mary Nakhleh, Mount St. Mary's College, Emmitsburg, Maryland.
Iraq	Ayad al-Qazzaz, Department of Sociology, University of California, Sacramento, California.
Jordan	Jamil. E. Jreisat, Department of Political Science, University of South Florida, Tampa, Florida.
Kuwait	Naseer Aruri, Department of Political Science, Southern Massachusetts University, North Dartmouth, Massachusetts.
Lebanon	William Haddad, Department of Political Science, Illinois State University, Normal, Illinois.
Mauritania	Samir Zoghby, Library of Congress, Washington, D.C.
Morocco	Henry Munson, Department of Anthropology, University of Chicago, Chicago, Illinois.
Palestine	Ibrahim Abu-Lughod, Department of Political Science, Northwestern University, Evanston, Illinois.
Somalia	Said Samatar, Department of History, Northwestern University, Evanston, Illinois.
Sudan	Carolyn and Richard Lobban, Department of Anthropology and Geography, Rhode Island College, Providence, Rhode Island.
Tunisia	Basheer Chourou, University of Tunis, Tunisia.

PICTURE CREDITS

Introduction to Geography, p. 4, B. K. Nijim; 5, b, c, B. K. Nijim, a, d, Denis Baly; 8, 10, B. K. Nijim.
Algeria, 36, 37, 38, 41, United Nations.
Bahrain, 46, Aramco World Magazine; 47, Arab Information Center.
Djibouti, 50, 52, Alain Nogues-Sygma.
Egypt, 58, 63, Egypt Tourist Office; 61, 62, H. S. Haddad.
Iraq, 68, 71, H. S. Haddad; 69, Abdeen Jabara; 70, B. K. Nijim.
Jordan, 74, 76, 79, Jordan Ministry of Tourism.
Kuwait, 84, Aramco World; 86, 87, Kuwait Airlines.
Lebanon, 90, 92, 95, H.S. Haddad; 94, Abdeen Jabara.
Libya, 100, 101, 104, Libya Dept. of Information.
Mauritania, 108, 109, United Nations.
Morocco, 112, 114, 117, 120, Moroccan Tourist Office.
Oman, 122, 125, 126, Oman Ministry of Information.
Palestine, 131, 135, J. Allen Carr; 136, 139, Abdeen Jabara; 138, Aramco World.
Qatar, 140, 142, Qatar Ministry of Information.
Saudi Arabia, 149, 150, 154, Saudi Arabia, Ministry of Information; 156, Aramco World.
Somalia, 160, United Nations; 162, Rouleau-Sygma.
Sudan, 168, 169, Carolyn Fluehr-Lobban; 172, Kuwait Airlines.
Syria, 176, 178, 181, 182, H. S. Haddad; 179, Arab Information Center.
Tunisia, 186, 188, 189, Tunisian Tourist Office.
United Arab Emirates, 196, 197, 198, 199, U.A.E. Ministry of Information.
Yemen Arab Republic, 204, 206, Abdeen Jabara; 208, Arab Information Office.
Yemen, PDR, 212, Carolyn Fluehr-Lobban; 214, PDRY Information Ministry.

Line Drawings by H. S. Haddad except pp. 124 and 128: Penny Williams, Aramco World Magazine.

FOREWORD

For more than a decade the Association of Arab-American University Graduates (AAUG) has been contributing to the growth of knowledge about Arab culture, society and institutions by means of its varied publications. The Association commissioned this volume of essays on the Arab world to provide the general reader with a handy yet scholarly reference guide to all Arab countries and thereby hopefully to dispel commonly held misconceptions about the identity of the Arab world or the Arab people.

Students and scholars of the Middle East are aware that most writings on the Arab region have tended to subsume discussions of the Arabs or the Arab world under the rubric of the Middle East or the Islamic world. And when Arabs or the Arab world are specifically addressed, more frequently than not such discussions are attenuated. They tend to generalize from some Arab countries to the rest of the Arab world or they simply discuss Arab inhabitants of one particular area and assume that to be valid for other Arabs. Thus the reader of books dealing with the Middle East or the Islamic world sometimes is led to confuse the identity of Arabs with other Middle Eastern people such as Persians, Turks or other Muslims and unconsciously assumes that either all Arabs are Muslims or all Muslims are Arabs.

This volume is therefore important in several respects: First, each essay is a scholarly, factual portrayal of an Arab country's history, geography, politics, economy, etc. Second, the editors have provided some important general comments that help in establishing the links—historical, political, and cultural—that make it possible for the reader to appreciate the unity of the Arab world as a cultural region. And finally, the volume constitutes an important beginning in establishing the study of Arab society, culture, and institutions as an independent academic endeavor, free from the stranglehold of either Middle East or Islamic studies.

Scholars and political propagandists alike continue to argue as to who is and what makes an Arab. While this volume does not concern itself explicitly with this kind of argument, implicitly it provides an answer which is accepted by the Arabs themselves. Using a long historical and cultural perspective, this volume tends to accept as the decisive criteria for inclusion a common linguistic and cultural identity of the Arab people. It furthermore accepts self-definition as another criteria for including specific countries in its coverage. Thus membership in the League of Arab States, which is restricted by its Charter to self-defined Arab States, constitutes the Association's perspective on the identity of the Arab States comprehended in this volume. In the light of both criteria, it was imperative to include a discussion of Palestine and the Palestinian people despite the fact that Palestine is not an independent Arab State. The long historical connection of Palestine with the Arab world, and the fact that the Palestinians are Arabs, are obvious justifications for including a discussion of Palestine and the Palestinians. In that sense, this volume is indeed unique; since the dismemberment of Palestine in 1948, Palestine ceased to be treated in Western literature as part of the Arab *patrie.* Yet in the Arab world itself, this has not been the case. Arabs and Palestinians alike consider Palestine to be an integral part of the Arab world severed by Zionist colonialism, and both assume that the Palestinian Arabs constitute an important component of the Arab nation. While the reader will have an appreciation of the basic facts pertaining to Palestine additionally, he/she will have a better appreciation of the factors underlying the conflict between the Arab world and Israel.

This volume is appearing at an important juncture in human history. It will be evident to the reader that the Arab people and the Arab States are making important strides in their attempt to revamp their institutions and consolidate their social, economic and political gains. On the other hand, the West and the United States in particular are becoming more alert to the unique importance of the Arab world to the world community. Without question, our understanding of the reality, problems and achievements of the Arab world and its potential contribution to the new international economic and political order is enhanced considerably by reading this volume. The active community of AAUG scholars who contributed the individual chapters, led ably by the distinguished editors and supported by the Officers of the Association, deserve our gratitude.

September 1978

Ibrahim Abu-Lughod
Northwestern University

PREFACE

The first stated objective of the Association of Arab-American University Graduates (AAUG) is the "dissemination of accurate scientific, cultural and educational information about the Arab World." Realizing the dire need for a book of basic information about the Arab World to serve the general reader and the student, the AAUG commissioned this work to partially fill the information gap about an area which is steadily growing in cultural, political and economic importance, yet remains generally obscured by misconceptions and prejudices.

Defining the scope of a study, or identifying its limits, often is not an easy task. In our case the task was not difficult. For a common denominator we chose membership in the Arab League as the determining criterion, a criterion which is unambiguous and which is readily ascertained. As of September, 1978, the Arab League had twenty-two members.

The use of a date in the last sentence emphasizes the relevance of time. When the League was founded in March 1945 it had seven members. The subsequent withdrawal of European colonial powers resulted in a rapid increase in membership, the last one of which was Djibouti in September, 1977. One of the members, Palestine, represented by the Palestine Liberation Organization, is unique in that presently it does not exercise control over its own territory.

The body of this Handbook has two main parts: an introduction to the Arab World and a treatment of each of the twenty-two component members. The first part consists of a geographical introduction and an historical introduction to the Arab World as a whole. Both treatments are novel in that there does not exist in the literature an examination of this region, as here defined, as a whole. In the second part of the Handbook each country is considered in a separate chapter, and this part is followed by an appendix of statistical information presented graphically, a chronological table, a guide to further reading, and an index. It is hoped that the non-specialist reader, for whom the Handbook is primarily intended, will profit from the various parts. It is hoped that the specialist will also gain some benefit.

The text is enhanced by the use of maps, pictures and line drawings to add a dimension of visual appreciation of the variety of human types, cultures and landscapes in the Arab World. On the maps no attempt was made to distinguish between boundaries in terms of status.

After consulting with specialists as well as with students the editors chose to employ commonly used spellings of names of persons and places rather than adhere to a strict system of transliteration.

The co-editors are indebted to the authors of manuscripts which became invaluable resource papers for several of the country chapters. They are also appreciative of the assistance they received from the following: Sandra Heller, typing; Annette Blum, Larry Larsen and David Hansen, map work; Germana Nijim and Safia Haddad, editorial assistance; Dorothy White and Rhea Wehrmeister for assisting in the early stages of preparation, Helen Hatab for her help in the search for pictures, and Michael Skibo for his able assistance in the production of this volume.

September 1978 — The Editors

AN INTRODUCTION TO THE GEOGRAPHY OF THE ARAB WORLD

The Arab World stretches from the Atlantic coast of northern Africa in the west to beyond the Arabian (Persian) Gulf in the east, a distance of some 5000 miles. Its area is 5.25 million square miles, and its population is about 150 million. By comparison, the forty-eight United States stretch 2650 miles from San Francisco to New York, comprise three million square miles, and contain about 215 million people. In terms of area most of the Arab World is sparsely populated desert. The relatively small areas of well-watered highlands and river valleys have high population densities, and today at least ten urban concentrations have populations of over a million each. There are twenty-two members of the League of Arab States. Each is a separate political unit, though they share a common language and a common heritage, and they cooperate in certain economic and political activities.

PHYSICAL GEOGRAPHY

Climate

The Arab World is dominated by dry conditions. Even places which may be classified as humid rather than arid have a water supply problem sometime during the year. Much of the region is dominated by what is known as the subtropical high pressure. This high pressure is generally found 20° to 30° of latitude north and south of the equator on eastern sides of ocean basins, thus affecting the western sides of continents. High pressure means descending and diverging air. Since in order for rain to come down air must go up; high pressure areas have a very low possibility of rain. This prevailing pressure condition is the main cause of deserts in southwestern United States, northern Chile, southwestern Africa, interior and western Australia, and of course the Sahara and adjacent parts of southwest Asia.

The northern part of the Arab World reaches the southern fringes of areas affected by midlatitude low pressure systems. In the Arab World these conditions are experienced, if at all, only in winter when the global pressure and wind patterns shift southwards because of the southward movement of the sun's vertical rays. The result is a wet winter and a dry

THE ARAB WORLD

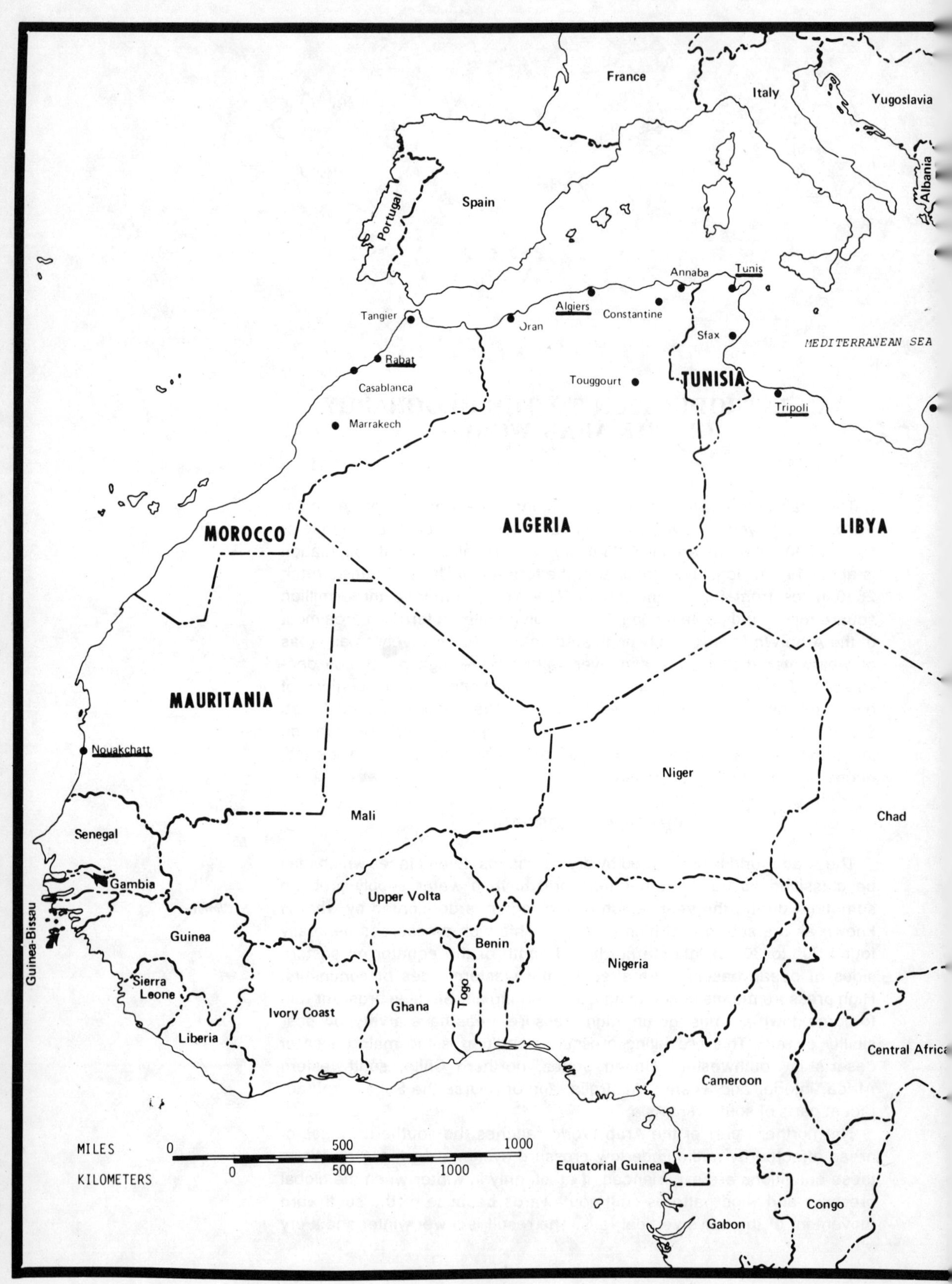

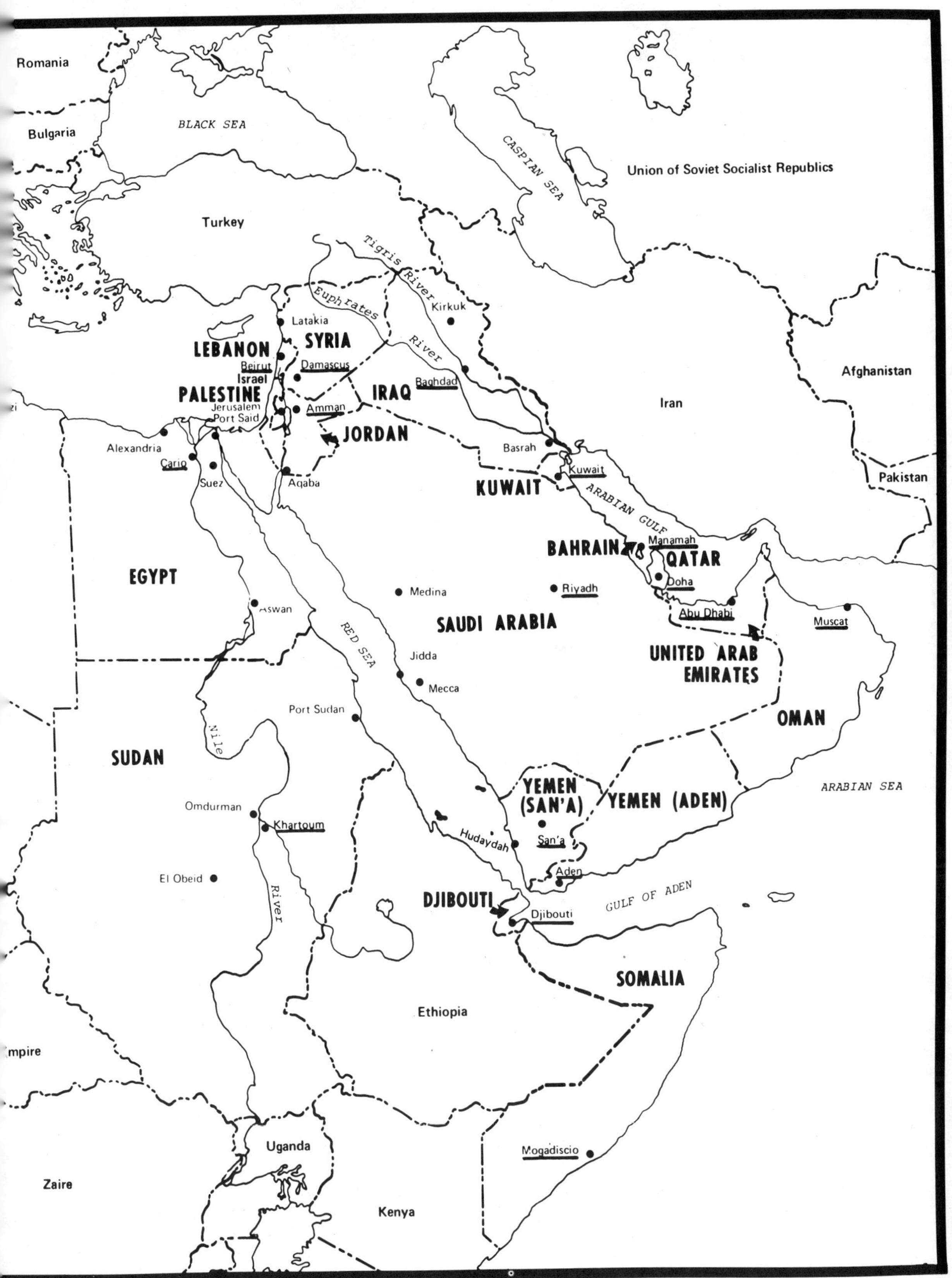
Romania
Bulgaria
BLACK SEA
CASPIAN SEA
Union of Soviet Socialist Republics
Turkey
Tigris River
Euphrates River
Kirkuk
Latakia
LEBANON
SYRIA
Beirut
Damascus
Israel
PALESTINE
Jerusalem
Port Said
IRAQ
Baghdad
Amman
JORDAN
Iran
Afghanistan
Pakistan
Alexandria
Cario
Suez
Aqaba
Basrah
Kuwait
KUWAIT
ARABIAN GULF
BAHRAIN
Manamah
QATAR
Doha
EGYPT
Medina
Riyadh
Aswan
SAUDI ARABIA
Abu Dhabi
Muscat
RED SEA
Jidda
Mecca
UNITED ARAB EMIRATES
OMAN
Port Sudan
Nile
SUDAN
YEMEN (SAN'A)
YEMEN (ADEN)
ARABIAN SEA
Omdurman
Khartoum
Hudaydah
San'a
Aden
El Obeid
River
DJIBOUTI
Djibouti
GULF OF ADEN
SOMALIA
Ethiopia
Uganda
Mogadiscio
Zaire
Kenya

Sand dunes in Saudi Arabia. Such cresentic dunes are shaped by the prevailing wind.

summer, just as is experienced in southern California. This type of seasonal precipitation pattern is known as the Mediterranean type of climate and is found in such northern parts of the Arab World as northern Morocco, Algeria and Tunisia, and in the eastern Mediterranean borderlands. Beyond the eastern Mediterranean, low pressure systems reach southeastwards in the Tigris-Euphrates lowland, and for some distance southeastwards over the Red Sea along the western edge of the Arabian peninsula.

Mountains

The orographic, or mountain, factor has the effect of increasing the difference between wet and dry areas in terms of the amount of precipitation received. Air may be forced to rise against the highlands, thus enhancing the possibility of rain. In northwest Africa (Morocco, Algeria, Tunisia), for instance, if there were no Atlas Mountains then the rainfall received would spread over a larger area to the interior (and in fact total amounts would be less), so that no place would receive much rain and, consequently, desert conditions would reach from the Sahara all the way to the sea coast, as is true of Egypt and most of Libya. Other important mountain systems are the Lebanon Mountains and extensions into Syria, and the Zagros Mountains in western Iran. Iran is not part of the Arab World, but the rain on the Zagros ranges contributes important runoff into Iraq. A similar role is played by the highlands of eastern and southern Turkey. Orographically induced or enhanced rain is also found along the plateau edge of western Arabia, especially in the south in the two Yemens, where the rainy season is summer, with a dry winter, because of a monsoonal effect similar to that experienced in Ethiopia and India. In both eastern Libya along the Mediterranean and in extreme eastern Arabia in Oman the highlands are known as the Jabal al-Akhdar (the Green Mountain), a descriptive term which reflects the sharp distinction in vegetation cover between the uplands and adjacent areas. (In Oman, however, rather than referring specifically to vegetation, this name may relate to limestone as opposed to volcanic outcrops. The porous limestone contains life-supporting springs.)

Drainage

Given the prevailing aridity, reliable sources of water have become immensely important, be they springs or rivers. Examples of the former are oases. Of much greater importance are the river valleys, and paramount among these are the Nile and Tigris-Euphrates river systems.

The Nile starts in the Lake Victoria basin in eastern Africa and flows northwards through Uganda, Sudan and Egypt. In Sudan it is joined at the capital city of Khartoum by the Blue Nile, coming from the Ethiopian highlands. In terms of volume of water, the Blue Nile is more important

a

The Arab World has a wide variety of landscapes. A mesa (a) at the fringes of the Sahara Desert in Morocco south of the Atlas Mountains. On the other side of the Arab World another kind of desert surface is formed of old lava flow (b), a scene near the Syrian-Jordanian border. Mountain landscapes are not unusual in the Arab World. A rugged mountain scene in the Lebanon (c) displays snow-capped peaks; in Morocco (d) where the mountain meets the desert, there is enough water to support a village.

b

c

d

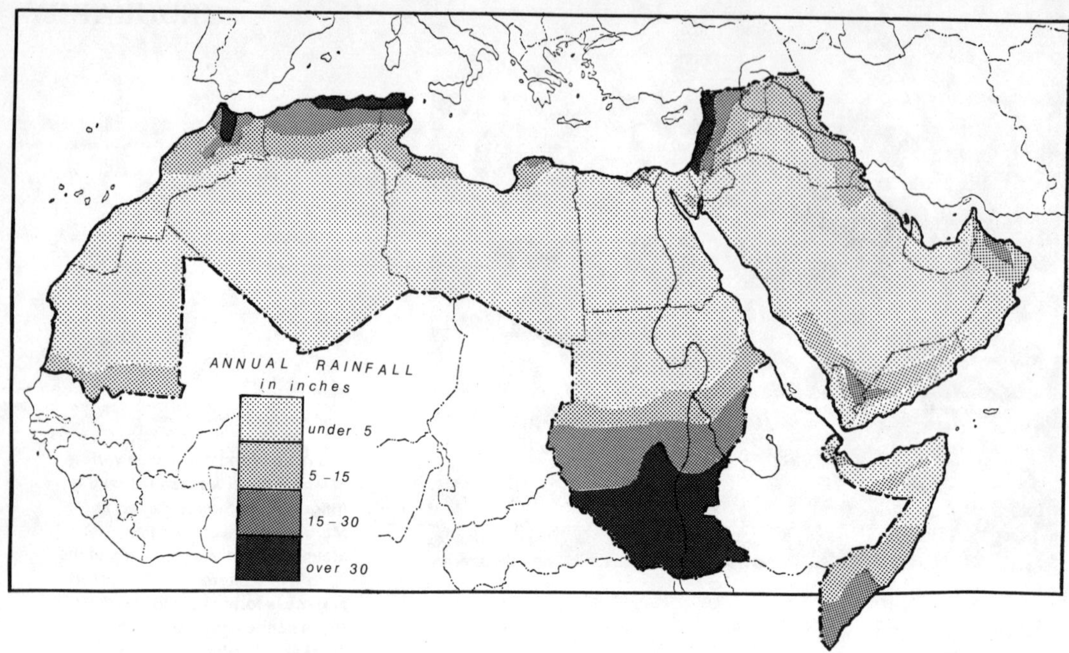

Nile River

than the White Nile (the main channel upstream, or southwards, from Khartoum), accounting for about sixty percent of the annual discharge. The Ethiopian highlands are the source of two other tributaries, the Sobat and the Atbara, and the sharply seasonal monsoon rains are reflected in the flow of all three rivers. As a result, the Nile itself, downstream (northwards) from Khartoum, has a markedly seasonal flow, with a maximum occurring early in September and a minimum in mid-May. It is this seasonal maximum flow which has resulted, until about 1970, in the famous annual floods in Egypt. The floods have been eliminated by the completion of the mammoth High Dam project, four miles upstream (south) of the city of Aswan. This dam is also known as the Aswan High Dam, to distinguish it from the Aswan Dam which was first built in 1902 and then raised twice, in 1912 and 1934.

The High Dam is the latest in a series of efforts, over thousands of years, to maximize the use of Nile water. At first, simple means brought waters directly from the river to adjacent fields, especially in spring and early summer when the river flow was at its lowest. Later, more elaborate barrages and weirs made it possible for long canals to carry water for several miles, using gravity flow. But the problem of an excess of water in the fall and a shortage in spring-summer still remained. Reservoir dams enabled the storage of water during the flood season for release during the low discharge season. The construction of several such dams in the Nile system allowed for overyear, as well as seasonal, storage—water from wet years could be stored for use during dry years. But the annual volume of river flow can vary greatly, and so, with ever expanding demand, it became desirable to have enough storage facilities to accommodate discharge changes over a period of many years. This need resulted in the principle known as century storage, proposed in the 1930s. The intent was to construct a series of projects throughout the basin in a coordinated way so that there would still be enough water for customary use even if the river discharge were at a one-hundred-year minimum. Projects were to be constructed in Sudan, Uganda and Ethiopia, but following the overthrow of the Egyptian monarchy in 1952, the new government preferred to minimize its dependence on the goodwill of upstream countries by embarking on the High Dam project.

The enormity of the High Dam undertaking is illustrated by the fact that the volume of material needed for the dam was 17 times the volume of the Great Pyramid. To Egypt the Nile is very much a lifeline, for climatically the country is a desert. In fact, a good deal of Egypt's foreign policy, especially with countries to the south, has been related to a concern about the flow of the Nile.

Tigris and Euphrates Rivers

The Tigris and Euphrates are as important to Iraq as the Nile is to Egypt, and their combined valley, Mesopotamia, has witnessed a succession of civilizations and empires for over five thousand years. The Euphrates is more akin to the Nile than the Tigris, in that its last permanent tributary, the Khabur River, is a long distance from the mouth. The Khabur in fact joins the Euphrates in Syria, 75 miles above (northwest of) the Iraqi border. The Tigris, on the other hand, receives several tributaries from the Zagros Mountains as far downstream as its mouth. In contrast with the Nile valley, the flood season in Mesopotamia is in March and April, following the melting of winter snow on the Turkish and Iranian highlands. Like the Nile, the Mesopotamian rivers, especially the Euphrates, have become the subject of international negotiations for purposes of regulation and use.

Other, smaller, river systems are found in the Arab World, such as along the northwestern slopes of the Moroccan Atlas (the Sebou, Oum er-Rhbia, and Tensift rivers), the northern slopes of the Algerian Atlas (the Chelif) and eastwards into northern Tunisia (the Medjerda). The Orontes in northwest Syria, the Litani in Lebanon, and the Jordan in Jordan and Palestine are also prominent. The great importance of a continuous source of water in a region of prevailing aridity is illustrated by the Jordan River. This river looms large in the minds of many people because of the historical and religious associations, and most individuals are quite disappointed when they first see it and discover that it is hardly more than a creek which can be forded in some places. Between the Sea of Galilee and the Dead Sea (both of which are in fact very small lakes) the straight line distance is only 65 miles, which is about half as long as one of the branches of the Nile delta. The meandering Jordan, though, takes 200 miles to cover the distance.

The Jordan River during the dry season just before it empties into the Dead Sea. Very little water is left after water upstream is diverted for irrigation.

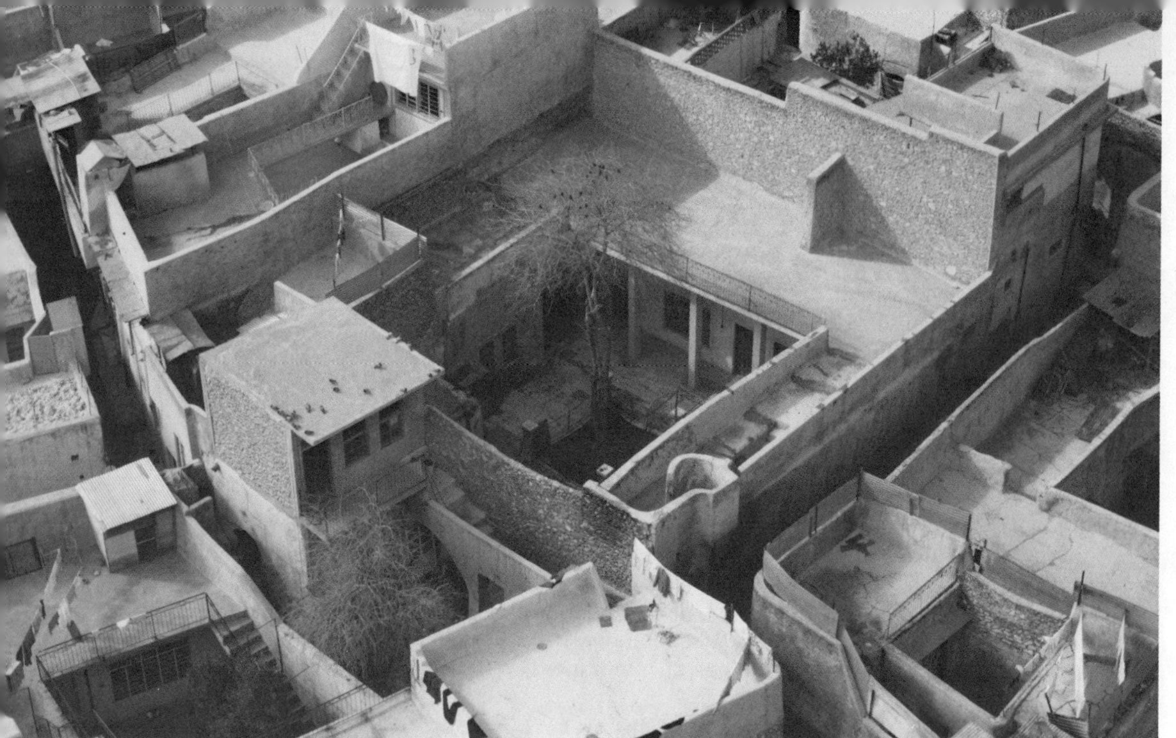

Old, pre-automobile urban pattern is typical of many cities and towns in the Arab World. This scene is in Mosul in northern Iraq

POPULATION AND SETTLEMENT

The Arab World's population is a youthful one—in 1977 about 44 percent of the total were under 15 years old. Life expectancy at birth is about 55 years, and only 3 or 4 percent of the population is over 64 years old. Birth and death rates are about 42 and 14 per thousand respectively, giving an annual rate of natural increase of 2.8 percent. The population will thus double in 25 years if these rates are maintained, reaching 281 million by the year 2000.

Population Distribution

When applied to the Arab World, the concept of average population density is not only of little help, but it is misleading as well. Differences between settled and unsettled areas are so great that in many countries it is possible to stand with one foot in a cultivated field and with the other in the desert. Egypt is a striking, though not the only, example. Whereas the presence of water may not necessarily mean the presence of human settlement, human settlement is found only where there is a water supply. It is not surprising, therefore, that in the Maghrib (northwest Africa) concentrations are heaviest on the northern and northwestern sides of the Atlas mountain system. In Libya there are two regional concentrations, centered on Tripoli in the west and on Benghazi in the east. In Egypt population is strongly associated with the Nile. In Sudan population is also strongly associated with the White Nile, Blue Nile, and the Atbara River. However, south of Khartoum there is an increase in rainfall amount, so that pastoral activity is widespread and not limited to river valleys. In southern Sudan summer is the rainy season and winter is dry, the opposite of the Mediterranean seasonal pattern. Somalia is an arid and semiarid country with a widely scattered pastoral population. In the Arabian peninsula, Yemen (San'a) stands out as having the greatest concentrations of settled population. Here the edge of the Arabian plateau reaches ten thousand feet above sea level and receives enough rain for settled agriculture to be carried out. In central Arabia there is a belt, northwestwards from Riyadh, of a relatively numerous population associated with a reliable spring water supply. High densities are found along the eastern Mediterranean borderlands, in

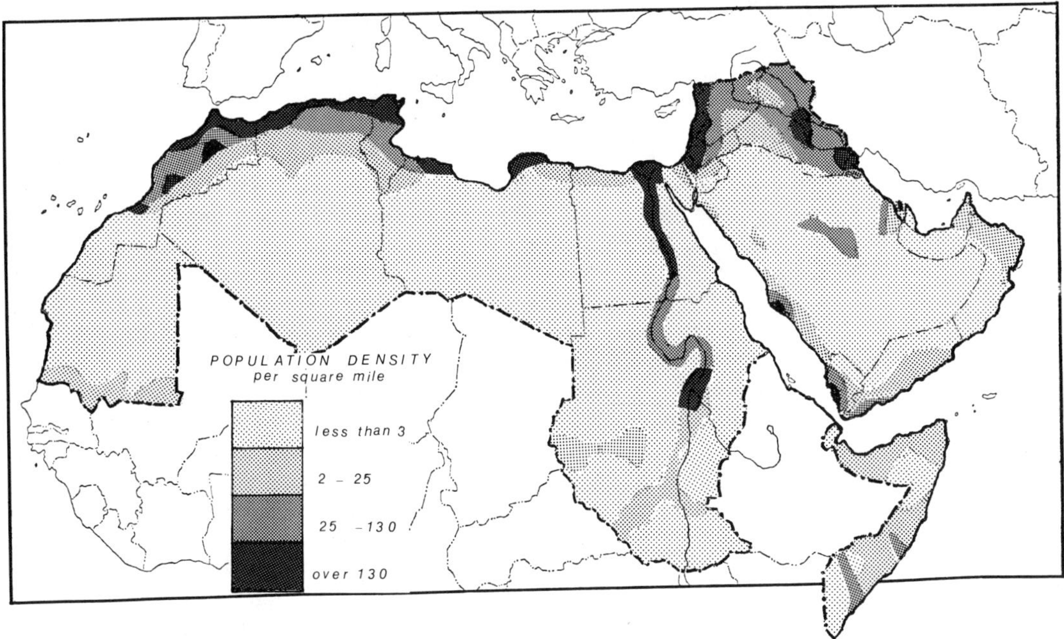

western Syria, Lebanon, Israeli-occupied Palestine and western Jordan. The Tigris-Euphrates valleys also have high population concentrations, though settlement between the two rivers is not continuous.

Fertile Crescent

The concept of the Fertile Crescent, as originally used, applies to an agricultural region stretching in an arc from the Nile in Egypt to Mesopotamia, and passing through the eastern Mediterranean borderlands. The two ends of the Crescent are climatically dry, but agriculture is possible because of the reliable river water supply. The terrain is level, so that cultivation is not difficult, though flooding is a perennial problem. The central part of the Crescent has a Mediterranean climate, thus making rainfed agriculture possible. However, land use is hampered by a mountainous and rough terrain. Because level land, such as the Beqa' valley in Lebanon, is at a premium, the demand has led to its creation through terracing. Terracing is very expensive in terms of labor, both in construction and maintenance. Until the advent of motorized transport, movement between Mesopotamia and the Nile was along the arch of the Crescent: up the Euphrates to northern Syria, then southwards through Damascus and Palestine. Thus Palestine witnessed the passage of the conquering forces of Assyrians, Babylonians, Persians, Egyptians, Greeks, Crusaders, Turks, French and British. This Crescentic path was made even more important by the presence of a rough broken lava desert in southern Syria and northern and eastern Jordan, a surface that was virtually impenetrable even to the camel. Not surprisingly, to inhabitants of Palestine Mesopotamia was perceptually to the north. The automobile, truck, and later the airplane enabled direct movement from Amman to Baghdad.

Cities

About forty percent of the Arabs live in cities, and the proportion increases every day. However, in this respect, as in so many others, there are great differences from place to place. The least urban country is Oman, where it is estimated that five percent of the population is urban. The other extreme is Bahrain, where seventy-eight percent of the population are urban. Absolute values should be kept in mind. In Egypt the urban figure of forty-five percent means about 18 million persons, or about as many people as there are in all of Morocco, the second most populous country in the Arab World after Egypt.

City life is not new to the Arab World. In fact, the worldwide "competition" for being the oldest continually inhabited urban site is dominated by Arab cities, notably Damascus, Aleppo and Jericho. Commerce has always been an essential and prominent feature of Arab and Middle Eastern livelihood. The world's oldest known port is Jbeil (Byblos), 20 miles north of Beirut. The historic and characteristic importance of urbanism preceded the industrial revolution by centuries and millennia, and this fact reflects and illustrates the diversity of Arab World environments and livelihoods, for commerce would not have developed to such an extent in a pre-industrial setting if the setting were largely homogeneous. Damascus, for instance, served as a "desert port" and became the focus for the exchange of goods, on the one hand between agricultural areas to the west and pastoral areas to the east, and on the other between the Nile Valley and Palestine in one direction and Mesopotamia in another. Other factors contributing to the prominence of cities are: location at intersections of main transportation routes (whether land or sea), strategic locations for tribal and communal strongholds (Jerusalem, originally Jebus of the Jebusites, is an example), centers of political control and conquest (whether local or imperial), and foci of religious activity and diffusion. Today, Cairo, with about 7 million people, is the largest urban area not only in the Arab World, but in the whole Mediterranean region and in all of Africa. Other Arab cities whose urban areas contain a million or more people are Casablanca, Rabat-Sale, Algiers, Tunis, Alexandria, Giza, Beirut, Damascus, Baghdad, and possibly greater Amman.

Urbanization is associated with the movement not only of goods and services, but of course of people as well. Migration is both a national and international process, and its tempo has been accelerating. Its basic cause is simple enough: conditions are perceived to be better elsewhere than at home, enough to tip the balance in favor of moving. Movement is dominantly rural to urban, and in some cases it is hierarchical, in that there is a flow from smaller to larger cities. Often migration consists of entire families. Specific factors contributing to migration include: lack of social amenities in the countryside, non-ownership of agricultural land, attraction of development complexes, mining activity, government projects (such as irrigation or attempts to stimulate growth

The first urban centers in history were founded in the Arab World. Remains of ancient cities attract tourists and archeologists. The Roman Forum at Jarash in Jordan

in neglected areas), improvement in communication and thus a heightened awareness of opportunities elsewhere, oil-generated and supported development projects, and political and military happenings, such as the Israeli occupation of Arab lands. Whereas migration may lead to an alleviation of population pressure in the areas of origin, often what results is a transplanting of population pressure to urban areas, with the associated sprouting of shantytowns. Other consequences include: traditional roots gradually give way to a security based on occupation, wealth and social status; source areas are deprived of substantial numbers of economically active individuals, though this loss is partially compensated by the return flow of remittances; dual economies develop, "modern" and "traditional," in juxtaposition; urban growth is accelerated because of the greater access to medical services but without a concomitant decrease in birth rates; regional differentiation is accentuated; and a severe shortage of skills needed for the modern sector develops, while there is a surplus of traditional skills.

Migration

Nomadism, historically, has been the way of life of a small portion of the Arab peoples. A mutually beneficial relationship has evolved between pastoral nomads, agriculturalists and urbanites. Over time the nomadic segment has decreased as a result of sedentarization and migration to urban areas, a process which became quite rapid during the second half of the twentieth century. Whereas in the 1950s about ten percent of the population of the Arab World was nomadic, by the late 1970s the figure was down to one or two percent. Sedentarization is encouraged by most governments for then such social services as education and health can reach more citizens on a continuing basis.

Nomadism

ECONOMIC ACTIVITIES

Agriculture continues to be the mainstay of most of the Arab peoples. Paramount among the food crops are wheat (especially along the eastern Mediterranean and in northwest Africa), barley (especially in Iraq, Libya and Morocco), rice in a few well-watered areas (such as the Nile delta, southern Iraq, and parts of coastal Morocco), maize (mostly in Egypt), and millet (Arabia and Sudan). Of great dietary importance, though occupying very small areas, are vegetables and legumes (tomatoes, potatoes, cucumbers, onions, melons, lentils, chickpeas, beans). Important tree crops are olives, vines, figs, bananas, citrus fruits, apples, pears, cherries and dates.

Crops

Increasingly there is a commercial component to these crops, especially vegetables and fruits. Markets are mostly domestic urban areas, though limited exporting does occur. More traditional cash crops are cotton (especially in Egypt, Sudan and Syria), sugarcane, sugar beets, sesame and groundnuts.

To many people the Arab World is overwhelmingly associated with oil. This association, while partially correct, can also be misleading. The distribution of oil is highly localized, so that more Arab areas are nonproducers than are producers.

Oil

Oil is found in sedimentary rocks. A major geologic basin containing a series of sedimentary layers is found in southwest Asia, underlying Mesopotamia and the Arabian Gulf. The chances for finding oil exist throughout this geologic basin whether the surface is land or water. Several countries share the basin and thus have a good chance of possessing significant resources: Saudi Arabia, Kuwait, Iraq, United Arab Emirates, Qatar, Bahrain, Oman and Syria. Non-Arab Iran also

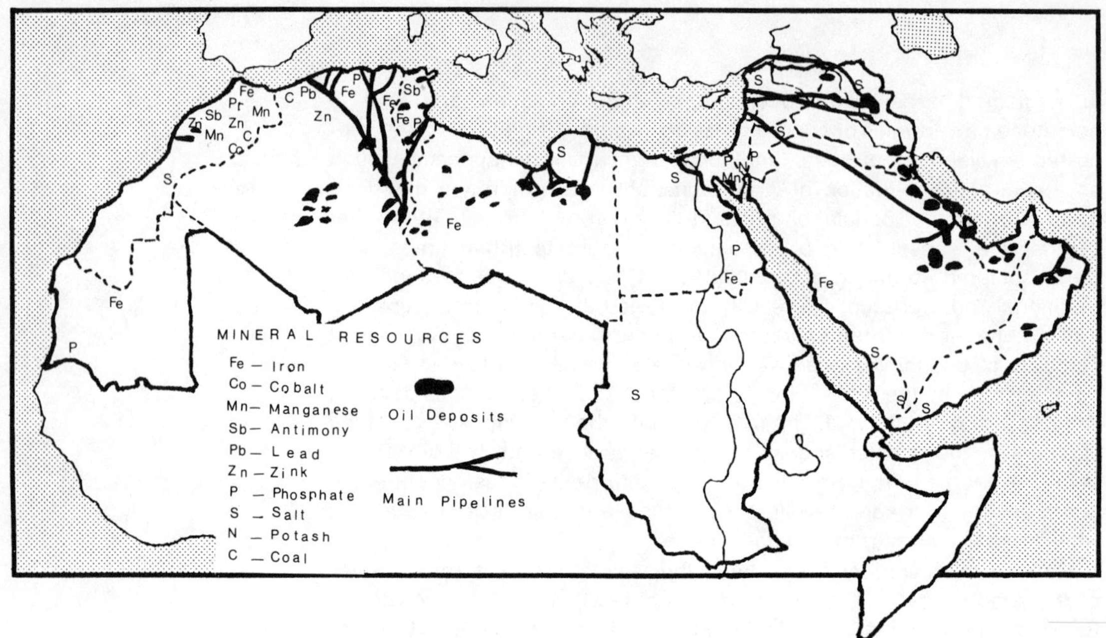

shares part of the basin, as does, to a smaller extent, non-Arab Turkey. In terms of actual production Syria and Oman (and Turkey) are of relatively lesser importance than the others. In North Africa, major deposits are found in the Sahara in Libya and in Algeria. Egypt is a minor producer, and there have been finds in Morocco.

Some nonproducing countries have benefited because of their location relative to producers by means of royalty income accruing from permitting pipelines to cross their territories. For example, much of Algeria's oil reaches the Mediterranean Sea by way of Tunisia. The Trans-Arabian Pipeline (Tapline) extends from eastern Saudi Arabia to the Mediterranean Sea by way of Jordan, Syria and Lebanon. From Kirkuk in Iraq a pipeline reaches the Mediterranean by way of Syria and Lebanon. Royalty can be in cash or in kind. The latter is illustrated by Jordan. A nonproducer, Jordan takes a prescribed quantity of oil from Tapline for processing in its own refinery, specially built for this purpose in Zarqa, 12 miles northeast of Amman.

Other Minerals

Other than oil, the Arab World is generally not well endowed with mineral resources. New discoveries are being made in Saudi Arabia, and indications favor substantial deposits of iron, copper, lead, zinc, chromite and gold. There is a fair amount of iron in Egypt, and phosphates are mined in Syria, Jordan, Egypt, Tunisia, and especially in Morocco, the world's largest exporter of this fertilizer source. Morocco also has significant deposits of cobalt and manganese, and some iron and zinc. Building materials, such as stone and clay, are generally abundant. There is a notable lack of coal so that hydroelectric power, where feasible, has become an important source of energy other than oil. An outstanding example is Egypt, where water power has been developed at both the Aswan Dam and the High Dam. The use of animal and human power is still widespread, especially in rural areas.

Industry

Traditional industries include textiles, pottery, leather goods, silver and other metal work. During the twentieth century there has been an upsurge in building, food processing, and consumer product industries. Heavy industry is still limited, and assembly plants for imported machinery and vehicles exist or are planned in several countries. Important strides have been taken in petrochemicals in Egypt, Saudi Arabia and Kuwait.

GEOPOLITICAL CONSIDERATIONS

Every location is relative to other locations. The relationship and interactions between locations can be analyzed at different levels, from the most local to the most global.

Over the centuries and millennia the Arab World has faced as much outward as inward, and more often than not in different directions. To the Romans the Mediterranean was the sea in the middle of the land, so that North Africa was close, both perceptually and in terms of accessibility. The Greeks and the Phoenicians had also found the Mediterranean to be an effective link to lands on opposite shores. Thus, peoples inhabiting today's Morocco, Algeria, Tunisia and Libya faced northwards more than in other directions—and not very often southwards, where the great Sahara stretched for a couple of thousand desolate and forbidding miles. The inhabitants of Mauritania, by contrast, had continuing involvement with inland kingdoms and empires, such as Mali and Ghana. Egypt has always been unique in that, in addition to its Mediterranean frontage, it is located at the point of contact between Africa and Asia. Also unique has been Egypt's location at the lowermost part of the Nile valley. Thus, Egyptians have always been concerned about those living upstream, that is to their south, and about the continued flow of the river water. Egypt's location, at the same time, has involved it in power politics beyond its control, such as the British intent to control the Suez Canal and to forestall the control of the upper Nile by other European powers. Sudan has been more of an inland state than a maritime one, despite approximately three hundred miles of Red Sea coast. Its southern regions have had more contact with central Africa than with the country's own central and northern regions. Somalia, too, has experienced the vicissitudes of European power politics, and its orientation has been clearly seaward rather than landward.

Arab Africa

Moving from the African to the Asian part of the Arab World, the land of Palestine has witnessed as much political and military turmoil as perhaps any other land on earth. Most recently, the Zionist invasion and colonization is reminiscent of the Crusader period. To the north is Lebanon, home of the ancient Phoenicians and a land of maritime and commercial peoples. Syria has been at the crossroads between the sea and the land, between the desert and the farm, and between the two ends of the Fertile Crescent. Jordan, too, shares in the Fertile Crescent and strides the desert and the farm. Iraq has housed Sumerians, Assyrians, Babylonians and Seleucids, and it has been conquered by, among others, Persians, Romans, Turks and British. It has also been actively involved in the geopolitics of the Arabian Gulf and of the Tigris-Euphrates river system. The Gulf states, Kuwait, Bahrain, Qatar, and United Arab Emirates, have been in the path of a succession of European explorers, especially after the Cape of Good Hope was rounded in 1497. At the same time they have been within spheres of interest presumed by Iran, Saudi Arabia and Turkey. Oman and the People's Democratic Republic of Yemen (Aden) have also become involved with the expanding European commercial exploration and the attendant political and military involvements. At the same time their contacts reached to India and to Africa's eastern coastlands. The Yemen Arab Republic (San'a) has been more of an inland than a coastal country, its people living mostly in the rugged highlands at the southwestern corner of the Arabian plateau. Saudi Arabia has generally been inward-looking and, save for its borderlands, little affected by what happened beyond. One spectacular exception was the burst of energy produced by the rise of Islam and its

Arab Asia

swift and far-reaching expansion. Another exception, also spectacular, has been the manner whereby oil discoveries have thrust Saudi Arabia onto center stage relative to regional and international economic and political matters.

It is possible to identify regions which over time have acquired a greater internal interaction than a sustained relation with other regions of the Arab World. Notable are the Nile valley on the one hand and the Tigris-Euphrates valley (Mesopotamia) on the other. These two valleys have been linked by a third regional construct, the Fertile Crescent. A fourth region is the Arabian peninsula. A fifth is the Maghrib (the "west"), consisting of today's Morocco, Algeria and Tunisia. At a more detailed level of analysis smaller and smaller regions can be identified, and some of these are noted in the individual country chapters.

Waterways

The Arab World contains or shares a large number of strategic waterways. Everyday millions of gallons of oil pass out of the Arabian Gulf through the Strait of Hormuz, the Gulf's only and narrow outlet to the high seas. Some ninety percent of Japan's oil and two-thirds of Europe's must pass through this strait. The Strait of Bab el Mandeb is a similarly narrow entrance at the southern end of the Red Sea. The Strait of Tiran is the entrance to the Gulf of Aqaba, and thus to Jordan's only port, Aqaba. The Strait of Jubal is the southern access to the Gulf of Suez, which in turn leads to the Suez Canal. The Sicilian Channel, between the eastern and western basins of the Mediterranean Sea, is flanked by Tunisia and Sicily; this channel gave prominence to the island of Malta which Britain considered a link along the lifeline of the British Empire. Finally, the Strait of Gibraltar, between Spain and Morocco, is the only outlet to the high seas from the Mediterranean other than the Suez Canal; conversely, it is the only access from the high seas to the Mediterranean without having to go through the Strait of Bab el Mandeb, the Strait of Jubal, the Gulf of Suez, and the Suez Canal.

It is useful to think of location as a resource, and not only as a characteristic of a place. Like any resource, its significance remains dormant until activated by human decisions. Like a resource it can be both an asset and a liability, an asset because it gives advantageous access to important places and because it affords command over certain events, and a liability because a prized location, like a prized resource, can be coveted by outsiders whose covetousness will not always be passive. Unlike many resources, location is not "exhaustible." It will always be there: sometimes a blessing, and sometimes a curse.

One of the most strategic waterways, the Suez Canal, is shown here, in an artist's rendering, on its opening day, November 17, 1869.

THE ARAB WORLD: AN HISTORICAL SURVEY

INTRODUCTION

In the making of the Arab World, three fundamental common denominators stand out: a historical process, a religious-cultural tradition and a language.

Historical Process

The outstanding landmark in the historical process was the beginnings of the Arab Empire in the seventh century A.D. Under the Caliphs ("successors" to the Prophet), residing first in Medina and later in Damascus, Baghdad and Cairo, the Arabs moved out of Arabia and established an empire, which, only a century after the Prophet Muhammad, reached an extent greater than that achieved by the Roman Empire during the latter's maximum expansion. From France and Spain in the west, across north Africa and southwest Asia, and extending all the way to within the borders of China and India, the armies of Arabia, under the banner of Islam, established a new political system, a new society and a new civilization. The area covered by this empire comprise most of the Arab World as defined in this work. Only today's Sudan, Somalia and parts of Mauritania remained outside the reach of the early empire builders.

Religious and Cultural Tradition

The emergence of today's Arab World was brought about not only by the factor of expansion, but by cultural factors as well. The founders of the Arab Empire were inspired by a faith, a system of ethics and a legal code. These elements, which made that venture successful, were integrated by Islam, the religion which Muhammad preached in Mecca and Medina. While the present-day Arab World has its historical roots in the Arab Empire of the seventh and eighth centuries, that Empire could not have been built independently of Islam. Yet the territorial extent of Islam transcends that of the Arab World. For while it is true that the birth and growth of early Islam coincides with the birth and growth of the Arab Empire, the courses of the two were not identical. When the Empire waned, Islam was still on the ascent. In fact the majority of the world's Muslims are outside of the Arab World, and at the same time the Arab World contains non-Islamic communities, as it always has. The cultural traditions that bind the Arab World are deeply rooted in Islam, just as Western civilization owes so much of its content to Christianity. But in both cases the distinction between faith and culture has to be maintained.

Language

The Arabic language was a most important factor in the consolidation of the Arab Empire and in the development of an Arab-Islamic civilization. As the language of revelation and devotion in Islam and as the cultural vehicle of the Arabs, it played an important role in providing continuity for an Arab identity through history. Soon after the conquest, Arabic became the lingua franca of millions of people living between the Atlantic coast and the Chinese borderlands and the most important vehicle of culture in the Middle Ages. More works in various fields of knowledge—science, humanities, literature—were written in Arabic between the ninth and twelfth centuries than in any other language. Arabic words found their way into most European, Asian and African languages. Many of the scientists, philosophers and linguists, and even poets who expressed themselves in Arabic, were not ethnically Arabs. Yet their products and their achievements cannot be separated from the cultural vehicle in which they were expressed, or the religious and cultural background in Islam, or the institutions of the Caliphate.

The Arabic language remains the most important determinant of the terms Arab and Arab World. While the Caliphate has run its course in history, and Islam as a universal religion belongs to a multitude of peoples, the Arabic language and its literary, scientific and philosophic treasures remain the binding force among peoples from Morocco to Iraq and the basic heritage of the Arab World.

PRE-ISLAMIC HISTORY

The Arab World stretches from the Indian Ocean to the Atlantic and extends along the eastern and southern shores of the Mediterranean Sea. This area has an incomparably rich and long history.

Early Civilization

The earliest civilizations of Mesopotamia and Egypt arose on the banks of their great rivers, the Tigris, the Euphrates and the Nile. Great empires rose and fell on the region's plains and deserts. The Egyptians developed the first organized state; they built great pyramids and impressive temples. Their armies and traders penetrated deep into Africa and Asia. The Babylonians carried their great achievements in mathematics, astronomy and law far beyond their borders. The Assyrians created a large empire and a powerful military society. The Phoenicians carried on a brisk trade from the cities on the Lebanese coast all over the Mediterranean and beyond into Britain, and possibly across the Atlantic into the New World. Their colonies spread along the coast of North Africa, and Carthage became a mistress of trade and a challenge to Rome. The Aramaeans dominated the trade routes to the East all the way into the heart of Asia, and Aramaic became the lingua franca of the Near East until Arabic displaced it.

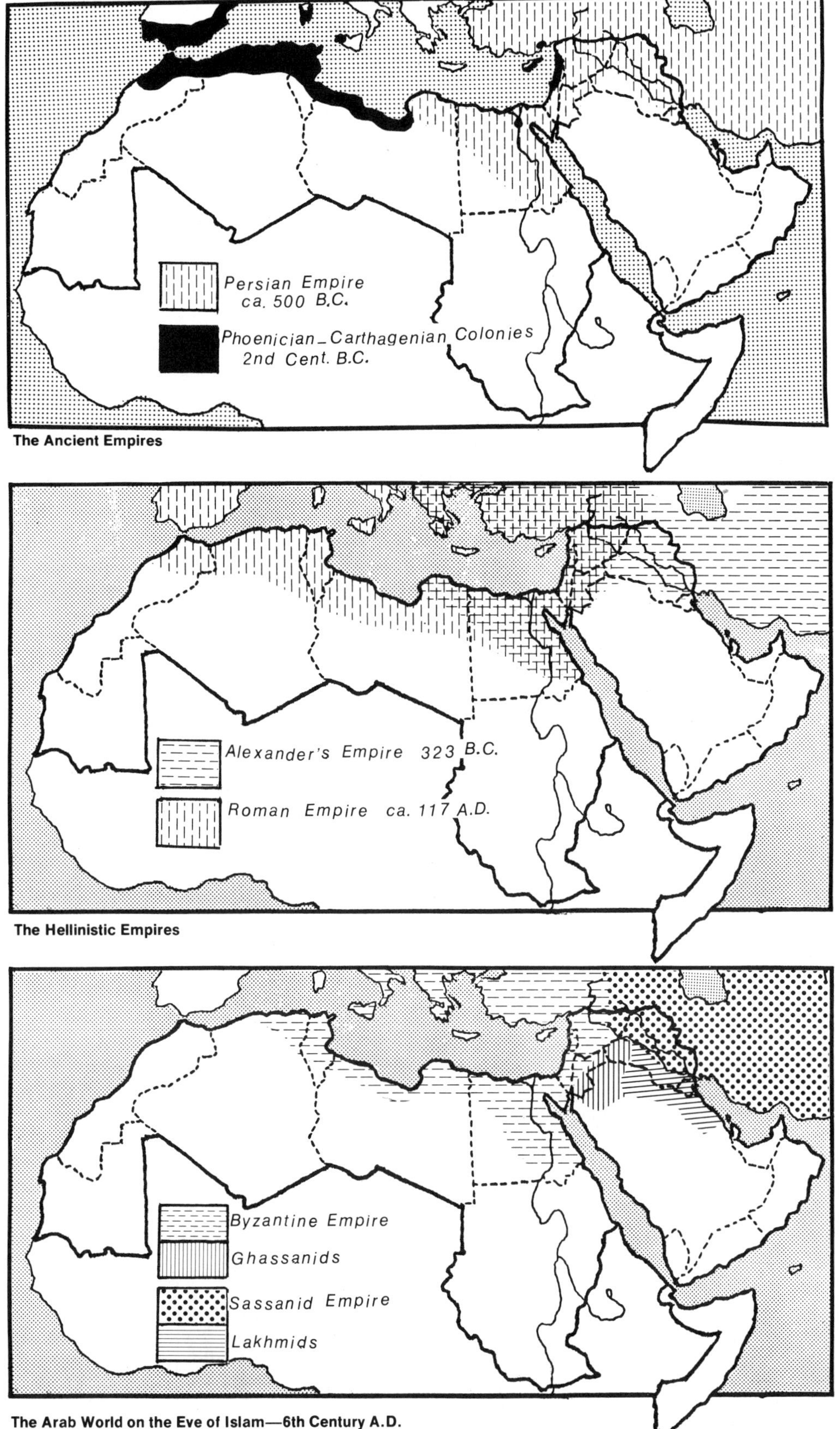

The Ancient Empires

The Hellinistic Empires

The Arab World on the Eve of Islam—6th Century A.D.

Ideas, institutions, trends and goods were profusely produced in this area, and their distribution covered the whole world. Writing and the alphabet, mathematical concepts and notations, trade, justice, education, and especially religions were born here; they grew to maturity and made profound contributions to civilization.

Persians and Greeks

All of the Fertile Crescent and Egypt came under the authority of the Persian Empire with the Fall of Babylon to Cyrus in 538 B.C. This ushered in a period of history in which parts of the Arab World were dominated by powers alien to it. Alexander the Great of Macedonia seized all the lands that were under Persian rule in 332 B.C. and opened a period of Hellenization. From the third century B.C. to the establishment of the Arab-Islamic Empire in the seventh century A.D.—a period of almost a thousand years—most of the Arab World was under European rule. Hellenistic empires were followed by the Romans and by the Byzantines. The Hellenistic states dominated the Fertile Crescent (Seleucids) and Egypt (Ptolemies). The Romans at first penetrated the North African area after conquering and destroying Carthage, then they expanded their rule to include Syria and Egypt.

Arabia before Islam

The great empire builders, with all their desires for more territory, left the Arabian peninsula unconquered and undominated. Poverty of resources and an expansive desert kept them away. The Arabs refer to their peninsula as the Island of the Arabs. However, its isolation from the rest of the Near Eastern political systems did not mean that it was not exposed to some cultural and religious contacts. Yemen, referred to by the Romans as Arabia Felix in contrast with the rest of Arabia (Arabia Deserta), was in close contact with Africa, especially Ethiopia. Flourishing states were established in this mountainous part of Arabia as early as the second millennium B.C.

Arabian Trade

South Arabic developed as a separate language with a separate script derived from Aramaic. The trade routes from Africa, India and China led through Yemen. It was a starting point for caravans to Syria and Egypt and their Mediterranean ports. This caravan route passed by two towns in Arabia, namely Mecca and Yathrib (later named Medina), which served as trade stations on the long journey. Mecca was also a religious center for the Arabian tribes, and a center for a poetry festival.

To the north, two great empires, the Byzantine and the Persian Sassanid, were as close as Syria and Iraq. To the south the Ethiopians were attempting to spread their rule to Yemen and had approached once as far as Mecca itself. The Arabian tribes were divided, poor, weak, and hemmed in from all sides by mighty states with long traditions and large armies. All the odds were against what was about to happen: an Arabian union, a new religion and a successful conquest. That this did happen was nothing short of a miracle.

ISLAM AND THE ARAB EMPIRE

Islam

The religion of Islam burst into world history at the same time that the Arabian population, united under its banners, acquired an extensive empire. This commonality of origin and, to a certain extent, of purpose caused the confusion between the two institutions: the religion and the empire. While there is good reason for this confusion, the historical progress of Islam and of the Empire makes clear a divergence which should not be ignored.

As a religion, Islam shows a tremendous adaptive power and a universal appeal. People of different races, color, language, and geographic location are its adherents: Indonesians, Philippinos, Indians, Mongols, Persians, Kurds, Arabs, Berbers, Nigerians, and others. On the other hand the empire, despite its variety of races and languages, kept its Arab character in many ways, especially in its ruling elite and language. The decline and fall of the Arab Empire did not mean the decline of Islam nor the cessation of its appeal. On the contrary, Islam spread far beyond its reaches at the time of the Empire's decay and after its collapse.

Arab Nation

While the modern Arab World is defined historically in terms of the Arab Empire of the seventh century and its subsequent spread, it is not a continuation of that empire. The enduring role of Islam and of the Arabic language and culture is an important factor in the rise of the modern concept of the Arab World, and of the striving for the realization of the concept of the Arab Nation. The roots of this concept reach into Arabia and to the beginnings of the message of Muhammad. Muhammad, born in Mecca about the year 570 A.D., gave his message of the worship of one God, of community solidarity, and of simple and strict morality. It was a faith simple enough to be accepted by the culturally unsophisticated Arabian, but a religion sophisticated enough to become one of the universal religions of the civilized world.

Arabia in the Sixth Century

The sixth century A.D. was a time when two old but well-established empires ruled the Mediterranean and the Near East area: the East Roman Byzantine Empire and the Persian Sassanid Empire. The former extended eastwards into Syria and Egypt and the latter westwards into Iraq, thus dividing and orienting the Fertile Crescent in opposite directions. Christianity had become the religion of the Byzantine State. But Christianity had developed multiple schisms. The Syrians and the Egyptians were restless under the dogmatic religious despotism of Constantinople; the Empire was losing its hold and religious and political persecutions were rampant. This situation reflected badly on the State as well as on the Church. The time was ripe for a movement which would correct this condition of chaos. Such a movement could only come from an area outside the sphere of cultural and political influence of both Byzantium and Persia. It was at this time that Muhammad established Islam and the first State in the Arabian peninsula. The state was to be established for the glory of Allah, the one God, and to be guided by His Law. Christians, Jews and others were accepted in Islamic society as People of the Book. Islam recognizes the prophets of the Old Testament, and assigns a special place to Jesus.

Basic Concepts of Islam

The basic concepts of Islam are that there is one God who is just and compassionate, and who will judge men who should submit to his will. The will of God is expressed very eloquently in the Qur'an, Islam's sacred book. The Qur'an, written in rhymed Arabic prose, has had a very great impact on the religious and cultural history of Islam and the Arabs. It standardized and canonized the language. It propagated Arabic throughout the Empire and helped make it the vehicle of the most brilliant cultural achievements of the Middle Ages.

Muhammad's message has three basic concepts: (1) Strict, uncompromising monotheism. The oneness of God cannot be compromised, diluted, or complicated; (2) Islam is the identity and bond among the believers. The brotherhood of Muslims should prevail over the distinctions of tribe, nation, color or race. Belief is more important than blood; (3) The message of truth is to be told to the world, and the realm of Islam is to be expanded. This is the basis on which the empire of the Caliphs was built.

The Caliphate

The Arab Empire, established on lands to the north, east and west of Arabia, had as its political instrument the Caliphate. This office, although primarily political, also had religious overtones. The first four Caliphs ruled from Medina. Under the second Caliph, Omar, the armies of Islam in a series of brilliant campaigns extended the Arab domain into Syria and Iraq, and ventured into Persia and Africa as well. By the time of the fourth Caliph, Ali, son-in-law and cousin of the Prophet, the Arab Empire reached to India in the East and Tunisia in the West. But Ali's rule was contested by the governor of Syria, Mu'awiyah, who succeeded in asserting his claim. He moved the seat of government to Damascus in Syria and intitated the dynastic line of the Umayyads. The religious character of the Caliphate was certainly relegated to the background. And this underemphasis, in the long run, proved salutary for the spread of Islam, which occurred independently of the Caliphate's vicissitudes and which later was outside the reach of its authority.

Umayyads

Arabization

The expansion which marked the first century of the Empire (under the first four Caliphs and the Umayyad Dynasty) led to the development of the administrative apparatus for governing such a large territory. At first the Arabs formed a special military class, separate and distinct from the subject population. But soon Arabization began to occur in Syria, Egypt, Iraq, and the North African littoral. When instead of war there was peace, the distinction between the Arabians and the people of the annexed lands began to disappear. Both the spread of Islam and the use of Arabic made this process a quick one. The aristocratic system began to crumble when the Empire reached its greatest extent, and war was no more the noblest of pursuits.

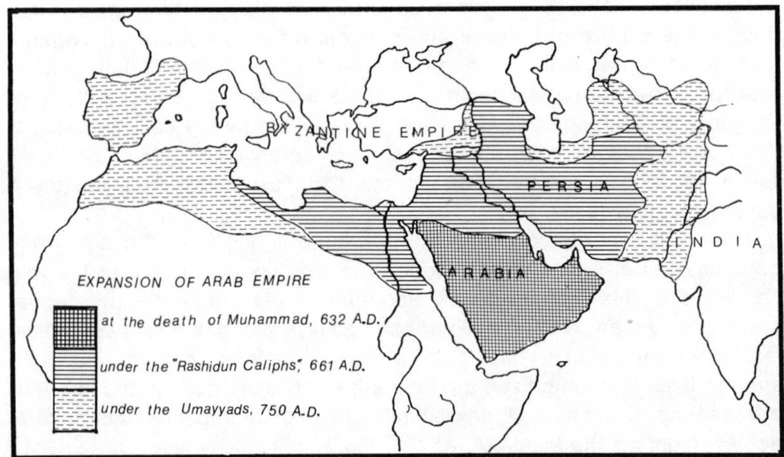

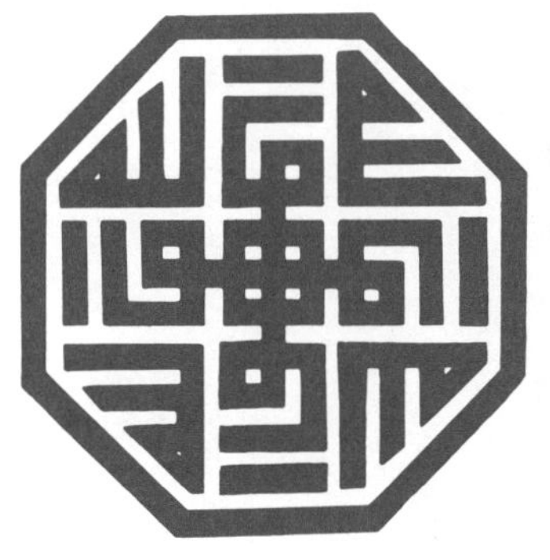

The partisans of Ali (the Shi'a) who had been driven underground by the strong arm of the Umayyads began to agitate in Iraq and Persia toward the end of the seventh century. The Umayyad Dynasty was swept aside by a coalition of forces working for the Abbasids (descendents of Abbas, uncle of the Prophet). Although the Shi'a had a great hand in bringing about the success of the Abbasids in 750, the Dynasty was firmly Sunni (Orthodox Islam). The center of power moved from Syria to Iraq, and Baghdad was built as the new seat of the Caliphate. This move resulted in an eastern orientation, and the westernmost end of the Empire, Spain, was detached from the Caliphate and ruled by the only survivor of the Umayyad line.

Abbasids

The first of the Abbasid Caliphs maintained the strength of the Empire, in spite of the loss of Spain. The early Abbasid Caliphs even showed occasional military strength in dealing with the Byzantines to the north and the Chinese to the east. But increasingly the Caliphate encouraged arts, letters, sciences and philosophy. The Golden Age of Arab learning falls in this era.

Decline of the Caliphate

Partly because of the decline of the power of the Arab elite within the framework of the Empire, the political structure of the Abbasid Caliphate began to weaken. By the end of the eighth century signs of fragmentation began to appear. Local rulers became powerful enough to maintain their autonomy, although they continued to pay the Caliphate lip service. Other claimants to the Caliphate appeared. The Spanish Umayyads first claimed the title. In the tenth century, the Fatimids in North Africa—a Shi'a dynasty—ruled as Caliphs, extending their control to Egypt and Syria, in defiance of the Baghdad ruler. Buwayhids, Tulunids, Hamdanids, Ayyubids, to name but a few, were all dynasties of emirs and sultans that controlled parts of the Arab World between the eighth and twelfth centuries. While learning and poetry flourished, the political structure was shaky. Into this disunity and competitive political systems came the first attempt by Europeans to control the Arab World. As Crusaders, Europe's armies came in the name of God to conquer in His name the Holy Land.

Crusades

The first wave of Crusaders succeeded in establishing the Kingdom of Jerusalem, as well as other Christian realms along the Syrian Coast in 1099. More than a century passed before Saladin, ruling Egypt and Syria, could reconquer Jerusalem and destroy the Crusaders' kingdom. Almost another century passed before the last remnants of the Crusaders were driven completely from Syria.

End of the Empire

For all practical purposes the Arab Empire ceased to exist as a viable political entity by the end of the tenth century. By the beginning of the eleventh century the Seljuk Turks ruled a vast territory from Baghdad, the seat of the Caliphate, thus further weakening the authority of the Caliph. The Abbasid Caliphs, however, remained the titular heads of a number of virtually independent states, within and without the Arab World. In the middle of the thirteenth century, the Mongols, who had been advancing throughout the Islamic world, finally reached Baghdad and destroyed it.

In the sixteenth century the Ottoman Turks, now masters of a great Islamic Empire and rulers of a large segment of the Arab World, claimed the Caliphate and moved the center of Islamic power for the first time out of the Arab World, to Constantinople, the capital of their emerging empire.

THE ARAB EMPIRE—ITS PLACE IN HISTORY

Cultural Interaction

For more than half a millennium (roughly 700-1300 A.D.), the Arab Empire under the Arab Caliphs (Umayyad and Abbasid) dominated world history—geographically, economically, politically and culturally. One of the most important historical effects of the Arab Empire—certainly one of the most apparent—is that, by creating a political entity extending from Western Europe to Eastern Asia, it caused a link among the great civilization centers of the known world. The components of the *ecumene,* consisting of the civilized centers of China, India, the Near East, the Mediterranean area and Europe, were in actual cultural, social and economic contact. Islam was the last—but not the least—link between the great world religions: Buddhism, Hinduism and Christianity. The Arabs were instrumental in bringing the outlying areas of the world closer together, spiritually and materially. They not only moved goods between the far East and the far West, but enabled the diffusion of useful scientific ideas to take place, ideas such as Indian numerals and the concept of zero (Arabic numerals), medicinal products, navigational skills, and entertaining tales and games (such as chess). The scholars of Islam held dialogues with both Christians in the West and Buddhists and Hindus in the East.

Cultural Radiation

Arab traders, teachers, counselors, and soldiers were active beyond the boundaries of the Empire. Their language was the richest and the most influential, reflecting the cultural energy of the Empire. Arabic words in all fields of knowledge, but especially in science, left a rich deposit in the vocabularies of the European, Indian, Persian and Turkish languages. Arabic and Islamic radiation also reached areas beyond the well-known cultural centers of Europe, India and China. In the East this penetration reached the Spice Islands, and today Islamic communities prosper in Indonesia, Malaysia and the Philippines. In Africa, in some cases without the help of political and military power, this influence crossed the great Sahara and produced an era of great African renaissance in the Niger Valley. Timbuktu became a great center of Islamic learning with a famous library.

Intricate calligraphy from the Alhambra in Spain.

Cultural Preservation

In addition to bridging the spatial chasm that existed between the East and the West, the Arabs also preserved traditions and philosophical and scientific systems by bridging the ancient world to the modern. The great accomplishments of the ancient Near East, including the Greek and Hellenistic cultures, would probably have been lost without the Arab link in the chain of civilization. In the Middle Ages for instance, Europe was almost totally ignorant, not only of the achievements of Egyptians, Babylonians, Persians, Indians and Chinese, but even of Greek culture, now considered the cultural parent of Western civilization. Neither Aristotle nor Plato were known to Christendom during the early Middle Ages. While the Church was content to stay in a shell of self-sufficiency, Muslim scholars and philosophers were asking the important questions and assimilating the learning of the Greeks, the Persians and the Indians. Europe actually first rediscovered the Greek philosophers through Arabic translations.

Arab Contributions

Arab culture, however, was not only a bridge. It was also a well of inventive genius in most of the fields of knowledge, thought and enterprise. Scholars and philosophers in the Empire, especially from the ninth to the thirteenth centuries, were active in investigating the depth of human thought and in delving into the mysteries of the physical world. They experimented in chemistry, optics, geography and other earth sciences. They made great strides in developing mathematics, geometry and trigonometry. They made great discoveries in medicine and pharmacology. Their political power was most supreme among all the nations between the seventh and ninth centuries. But their supremacy in cultural and scientific accomplishments remained unchallenged for at least three more centuries.

Many ethnic and religious groups participated in this cultural fluorescence, but their vehicle of expression was Arabic and the institutional home of that culture was the Arab Caliphal State. These two elements were crucial to their achievements. Arabic was the language of cultured men, not only in the Arabic-speaking countries, but also in Europe—especially Spain—in Persia, and even in India and China. It was carried to such a vast expanse by traders, scholars, physicians, travelers and diplomats.

Learning

More than a century in advance of the West, the Arab World established formal centers of learning. Schools of higher education were founded in Basra, Kufa, Baghdad, Cairo and other cities. Arab universities in Spain (Cordoba in particular) trained many Christian Europeans. The influence of Arab philosophy and science, coming by way of Spain and Sicily, upon the universities of Paris, Oxford, and Northern Italy, and upon Western European thought generally, was very considerable. This growth of learning led to some of the most important developments in mathematics. The introduction of the new system of numerals (Arabic numerals) facilitated computations much as the invention of the alphabet had facilitated writing. Arab mathematicians developed algebra and improved trigonometry. They conducted experiments in earth measurements and computed the degrees of earth curvature.

Great strides were made in astronomy. Observatories with complex measuring devices were constructed, and the angles of the ecliptic and the procession of the equinoxes were measured. The impact of Arab astronomy on the West is evident by the large number of Arabic names for stars and constellations still in use in the English language, and the use of Arabic words related to astronomy such as zenith, nadir and azimuth.

A 13th century illustration of a lady lecturing in a Baghdad mosque.

Medicine

Europe's debt to Arabic medical works is sizeable. The works of Avicenna (Ibn-Sina) and Rhazes (Al-Razi) were standard texts in European medical schools until the end of the Middle Ages. Arabic innovations in medicine included the discovery of contagious disease, development of pharmacological lists of remedies and herbs, and the production of chemicals. Chemical compounds were synthesized and many new products were introduced as a result of an earnest investigation into the nature of matter. Hospitals for physical and mental illnesses were established in a number of cities. Manuals on diseases, cures and herbs abounded.

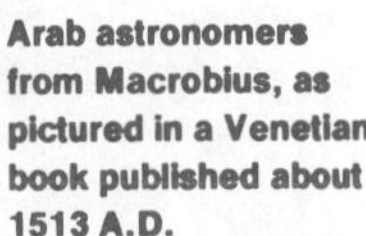

Arab astronomers from Macrobius, as pictured in a Venetian book published about 1513 A.D.

Geography

By the end of the tenth century geography and history reached a high degree of sophistication. Travelers crossed Islamic and non-Islamic lands describing, recounting and analyzing. Geographers developed maps and charts, and some of them cultivated the notion of the earth as a sphere.

Arab philosophy developed as early as the eighth century. The works of the Greek philosophers, especially Aristotle, were translated into Arabic early in the Abbasid period. Arab philosophers, such as Al-Kindi, Al-Farabi, Avicenna, Ghazali and Averroes, left their impact on speculative thought, particularly during the formative period of Western philosophy. This influence extended to the Renaissance. Averroes, who wrote on medicine in addition to his influential commentaries on Aristotle, inspired a group of European philosophers who were called Averroists. Averroism had a great impact on the work of Thomas Aquinas, among others.

Averroes (1126-1196)
Ink drawing by Raphael

The importance of Arab culture throughout the Middle Ages is paralleled by the dominance of Arab trade in that period. Arab commerce was active in the movement of goods of all kinds, especially from the East to the West. Silk, paper, perfumes, spices, and other luxuries, as well as new products such as soap, sugar and a number of fruits and vegetables, were distributed throughout the Arab and Islamic World and introduced into Europe. The movement of goods from south to north brought gold, ivory and other African commodities (as well as slaves) to the major world markets. The Arabs dominated maritime trade in the Indian Ocean (and its extensions, the Red Sea and the Arabian Gulf) as well as the Mediterranean. The overland caravan trade linked the outlying cities of China with Baghdad, Damascus, Cairo and the cities of North Africa. Arab trade in the Indian Ocean flourished until the advent of the Portuguese ocean-sailing ships in the fifteenth and sixteenth centuries. In the Mediterranean, by the twelfth century the Italians, the Venetians in particular, started to control trade routes between Europe and Arab ports. The overland caravans declined around the fourteenth century. The dismemberment of the Empire, decline of central authority, and the disrupting influence of Mongol raids contributed to that decline.

Decline

The political and administrative structure of the Caliphate was virtually in ruin by the time of the Mongol invasion. The destruction of Baghdad by Hulago in 1258 A.D. may be considered the end of the great era of Arab hegemony. But, although they were very much weakened, the basic components of the Arab achievements survived the destruction of the political structure. Islam as a culture and religion, in fact, continued its expansion. Arabic and Arabic letters and sciences flourished for a time beyond the thirteenth century. Subsequently they declined and remained in a dormant state, especially during the Ottoman period.

A library in Baghdad in the 13th century A.D., as illustrated by al-Wasiti (1237 A.D.)

OTTOMAN PERIOD

Ottomans Conquer Arab Lands

Early in the sixteenth century the Ottoman Turks, by then in control of Anatolia and a large area of Eastern Europe, started their expansion into the Arab World. The Ottomans, who were Muslims, had succeeded in destroying the Byzantine Empire, a task which could not be achieved by either the Umayyad or the Abbasid Caliphs. The political power of Islam was expanding into Europe from the east at the same time it was being driven out of Spain. The Ottomans were strong enough to attempt restoring the great power lost to the Arab Caliphate a few centuries earlier. In 1516, their armies began the conquest of Syria. They quickly added Egypt, Iraq, Libya, Tunisia and Algeria, as well as the coastal parts of Arabia, to their domain. This success gave them control over most of the Arabic-speaking peoples as well as the three holiest cities of Islam: Mecca, Medina and Jerusalem. Soon, the Ottoman Sultan in Constantinople assumed the title of Caliph.

European Colonialism

At about the same time European commercial and colonial activities in the area were beginning to be felt. The Portuguese, the Dutch and the English were at first interested in securing routes of trade to India and the Spice Islands. But by doing so, they competed with, and eventually suppressed, Arab trade in the Indian Ocean. Since the ocean lanes directly connected the Far East and Europe, the commercial advantage of the geographical position of the Arab World was greatly weakened. It was not until the opening of the Suez Canal late in the nineteenth century and the rerouting of trade lines of communication between the West and the Far East through the Mediterranean and the Red Sea that the strategic importance of Arab land was again felt. By that time, and because of that strategic importance, Britain and the other colonialists had established bridgeheads of control and/or influence in the most sensitive areas along the "Route to India," especially in Egypt and South Yemen.

In the seventeenth and eighteenth centuries the Arabs were left without political or economic power. In science, the arts, and even the letters, this was a period of decline. The Ottoman Empire, although officially heir to the Caliphate (historically an Arab institution) was a European power. While the Ottoman Turks were rooted in Asia, and their state was born in Anatolia, their empire was geographically and geopolitically more an heir of the Byzantine than of the Arab Empire. The Arabs were isolated from the mainstream of world power now centered in Europe. During the Ottoman centuries, the Arabs, in their cocoon-like existence, held on to Islamic tradition, old customs and their spoken language. Without these their identity as Arabs would have disappeared with the loss of a central political role and the transfer of power to Europeans.

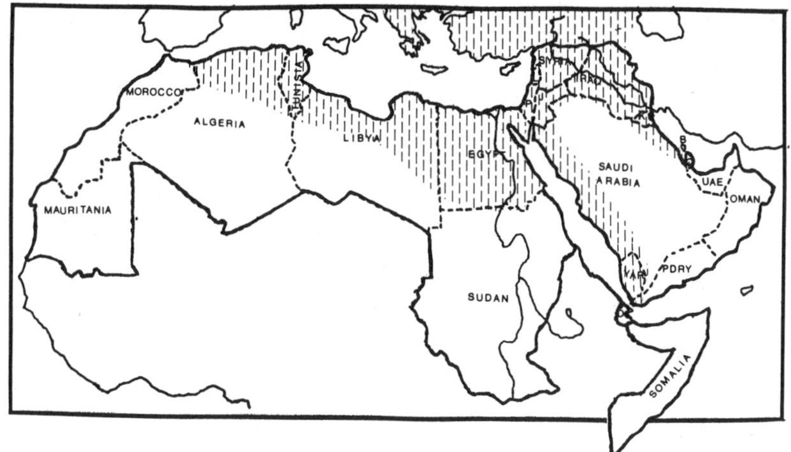

Ottoman rule over Arab lands in the 18th and 19th centuries

Arab Awakening

The awakening of Arab identity occurred in the nineteenth century with the weakening of Ottoman control and the introduction of challenging new ideas from the West. The assertion of Arab identity vis-a-vis the overwhelming Turkish political control was expressed by a revival of Arabic literature and poetry. Islam alone could not have been the vehicle of this reawakening, because Islam was shared with the Turks and all ethnic groups. But Arabic, as an identifying and unifying factor, conformed with the concepts of nationalism then current in Europe.

Egyptian Revival

By the end of the nineteenth century most Arab provinces of the Ottoman Empire reached very depressing conditions in terms of economics, technology, education and cultural achievement. Even population dwindled because of poverty and bad sanitary conditions. The irrigation system in Mesopotamia choked in silt and sand. The rich land of Syria lay fallow. The heavy hand of the tax collector left the peasants barely on a subsistence level. Only Egypt showed signs of revival. This was due to the work of Muhammad Ali who was sent to Egypt by the Ottoman Sultan to establish order after the withdrawal of Napoleon's troops. Muhammad Ali followed an enlightened policy of modernization; he introduced education, the press, and health services. As ruler of Egypt, he built up the army and the navy with the help of European advisers.

In 1830, Muhammad Ali was not only virtually independent, but felt strong enough to challenge the authority of Constantinople. The Egyptian army invaded Syria and marched into Anatolia. The European powers (mainly England and France) stopped the Egyptians from destroying the Ottoman Empire. Ten years later, these same powers helped force the Egyptians out of Syria. The opening of the Suez Canal in 1869, which was supposed to be a boon for Egypt, instead became one of the reasons for British occupation.

European Control

The British, French, Italians and Germans throughout the second half of the nineteenth and first quarter of the twentieth centuries were scrambling for control of parts of the Arab World as well as Africa. The Ottoman Empire was by then the "Sick Man of Europe" and the European powers were still hungry for more colonial real estate. The French had moved into Algeria in 1830, and their subsequent expansion into Tunisia led to conflict with Italy. Later the French move into Morocco almost led to war between France and Germany. The British expanded their control of Egypt into the Sudan, which had been under Egyptian suzerainty. They also extended their rule to South Arabia and the lands on the Arabian (Persian) Gulf. In the Horn of Africa the British (1884) and the Italians (1889) established colonial domains. In 1911 Libya fell to the Italians.

The Ottomans, on the eve of World War I, were only in control of Syria, Mesopotamia, and parts of Arabia.

Meanwhile the Arabs had formed movements of independence against the Ottoman yoke. In the early years of World War I many nationalists, especially in Syria (which included today's Lebanon and Palestine) were hanged for treason. The Arab revolt started in the Hijaz in Arabia in 1915 and moved steadily during the war years to Damascus. This revolt is romanticized in the West because of the controversial role played by Lawrence of Arabia. The Arab revolt was a help to the British army's invasion of the Ottoman domain from Egypt. Through talks with the British government (the famous Hussein-McMahon correspondence of 1915-1916), the Arabs were working for an independent Arab state comprising all the Arab provinces of the Ottoman Empire at that time. But the British government was simultaneously engaged in talks with the allies to divide the spoils of the Ottoman Empire. To complicate matters further, the British in 1917 also issued the Balfour Declaration which stated that the British government viewed with favor "the establishment in Palestine of a national home for the Jewish people."

Arab Revolt

The years following World War I witnessed the destruction of the Ottoman Empire, but not the emergence of the hoped-for Arab Kingdom. As a matter of fact, this period was one of intensification of European colonial control. The French remained entrenched in Morocco, Algeria, Tunisia and Mauritania, and added to that list Syria and Lebanon as mandated territories, an arrangement the European powers made in 1916 (the Sykes-Picot treaty) and legitimated in the League of Nations following the war. The Italians remained in Somalia and Eritrea. The British took over Iraq, Palestine and Transjordan as mandated territories. They also consolidated their control over the southern coast of the Arabian Peninsula: Aden, Hadramawt, Oman, Qatar, Bahrain and Kuwait. In the interior of the Peninsula, Ibn Saud established his rule over the eastern coast, Najd, and the Hijaz, with the Holy Cities of Mecca and Medina. Yemen remained independent. Of all the Arab World only Saudi Arabia and Yemen were not under direct or indirect control of the European powers.

Post WW I

The Arab people at this stage, while well aware of their identity, were frustrated in their attempts to express it in the form of independence and progress. They felt deceived because the promises of the Allies during World War I to help oppressed people achieve independence through self-determination, such as President Woodrow Wilson's Fourteen Points, did not apply to them. Agitation and revolts against foreign rule sprang up in North Africa, Egypt, Syria and Iraq. In Palestine the action was directed not only against British rule, but also against the settler-colonialism of European Zionists, who sought to displace the Arab population and to establish a Jewish State with Jewish migrants, mainly from Eastern Europe.

But this period was also one of continued awakening, education and development. Culturally and economically, the area had already started on the road to recovery late in the nineteenth century. The opening of the area to the East and the West, after the isolation of the Ottoman regime, brought new ideas, technologies, goods, and expectations to the Arab World, even an awareness of the existence of such a world. It would be a long time before this awareness took an institutional form in the League of Arab States (organized in 1945), but a common feeling of sharing one language and one historical experience was already developing among educated Arabs before the nineteenth century was over.

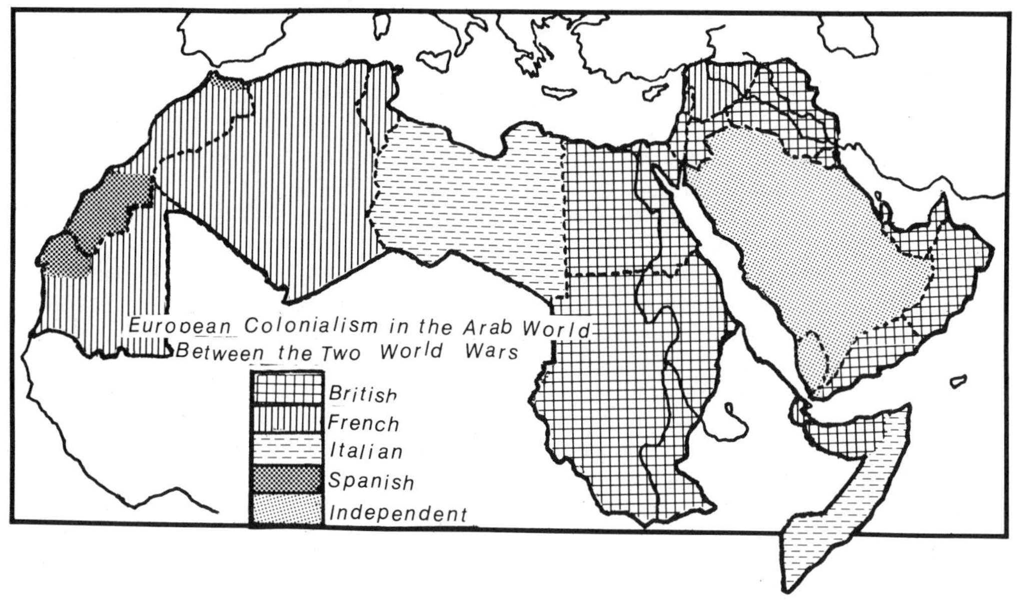

THE MODERN PERIOD

Decline of Colonialism

The decline of European power after World War II hastened the demise of colonialism in the Arab World. Italy, defeated in the war, relinquished its hold on Libya and Somalia. France's mandate over Syria and Lebanon and its control over Morocco, Tunisia and Mauritania came to an end after short periods of struggle. British control was relinquished gradually over Egypt, Sudan, Jordan, Iraq, Kuwait and the southern parts of the Arabian Peninsula. Spanish enclaves in Arab Africa were eliminated later, and the last territory to gain independence was that of the French Afars and Issas which became independent Djibouti in 1976.

Settler Colonialism

But in Algeria and Palestine, settler colonialism blocked the road to complete freedom. The Algerian Arabs finally rose in open and organized revolution against French direct rule. A war of liberation was declared in 1955 and, after seven years of bloody struggle and sacrifice, ended in independence for Algeria in 1962.

Palestine Question

In Palestine, however, the Zionist settlers succeeded with the consent and support of the emerging world powers, the United States and the Soviet Union, in legitimizing the takeover of the land for the establishment of an exclusive Jewish state. The colonizing of Palestine by the Zionists did not place the country under the direct control of a foreign power as was the case in Algeria. But Zionist influence in Western Europe and in the United States provided Israel with a strong foreign base of support. With this support, and bent on expansion, Israel attacked Egypt in 1956 in collusion with Britain and France. The aim of the attackers was to occupy Sinai and the Suez Canal and to discredit President Nasser of Egypt. The United States and the Soviet Union put a stop to this campaign. Again in 1967, Israel attacked Egypt, Syria and Jordan in a lightning war that lasted only six days. All Palestine came under direct Israeli control as a result of this war, and many more Palestinians became refugees. By this time the United States had become the main supporter and arms supplier of Israel. Relations between the United States and the Arab states became strained, and some countries severed diplomatic relations with the United States and turned to the Soviet Union for support and for the supply of armaments.

June War

October War

In 1973 Egypt and Syria attacked Israel and scored initial success, such as the crossing of the Suez Canal by the Egyptian army. But the war was limited in scope and total American support of Israel turned the tide against the Arabs. The Arab Oil Exporting Countries retaliated with an embargo on oil shipment to the United States, using, for the first time, their powerful economic power.

The Palestine question remains to this day the pivotal crisis of the Arab World. It is not only a threat to the security of the area and a travesty against the human and political rights of an Arab people, but it has international ramifications and threatens to become a wider world conflict.

Oil and Development

During this period the Arab World developed into a powerful bloc of nations within the international community. Its power was enhanced greatly by the discovery of huge oil deposits especially in its desert areas. The countries of the Arabian Peninsula and Libya were propelled in a few years from a stage of economic poverty and underdevelopment to one of wealth and rapid development. The Arab Oil Exporting Countries, OAPEC (Saudi Arabia, Kuwait, Bahrain, Qatar, UAE, Iraq, Libya and Algeria), dominate the powerful OPEC (Organization of Petroleum Exporting Countries) acquiring thus a tremendous influence on oil production, distribution and pricing. The oil embargo these countries imposed on the United States during the October War in 1973 was a serious threat to American industry, as well as danger to the economic status of industrialized Europe and Japan.

The Arab countries gradually wrested control of their own oil resources from foreign companies. With more funds, especially after the rise in price after 1973, development projects in these countries increased rapidly, and some of the revenues were earmarked for development in other Arab countries. The Arab Fund for Economic and Social Development has extended loans to Arab countries exceeding one billion dollars since 1973. The Gulf Organization for the Development of Egypt spent almost two billion dollars since 1977. More cooperation among Arab states is projected to procure more development funds especially for industrial and agricultural projects in countries which are not oil exporters but which posses undeveloped agricultural potential and adequate labor force.

Political Integration

Movements of political integration in the Arab World have not, so far, produced any appreciable results. Plans for regional unions within the Arab World have existed, such as the union of the North African countries (Morocco, Algeria, Tunisia), the union of the Nile Valley (Egypt and the Sudan) which has been contemplated for a long time, and the Greater Syria and the Fertile Crescent plan involving Syria, Iraq, Lebanon, Palestine and Jordan. But all of these plans remain in the theoretical stage. A merger of Egypt and Syria (the United Arab Republic) in 1958 was executed hastily, primarily for political considerations. It was dissolved in 1961 when Syria pulled out after a military coup. Other projects of union include the now existing, but unfunctioning, Union of Arab Republics which includes Egypt, Libya and Syria.

Cultural Integration

However, the trend toward integration in the Arab World can be seen at work in other fields such as education and communications. A network of roads and airlines makes movement between Arab countries easier than it has ever been. Intellectual communication between Arabs is even a stronger agent for integration. Newspapers, magazines, books, radio broadcasts and films are shared, enjoyed and understood by all Arabs regardless of the difference in dialects. Classical Arabic, and a developing language of simplified Classical Arabic, have brought all educated

Arabs closer together. Common textbooks, exchange of students and teachers and the mobility of skilled and unskilled labor are contributing to an integration in speech, manners, customs and outlook. Human, cultural and economic interaction in the Arab World promises to increase in the future. The dream of union can be realized only after this interaction reaches a higher level of awareness and involves a larger number of Arabs. Development projects, universal education and a more active intellectual elite may, over a period of a decade or two, promote the integration of the Arab World to its logical conclusion.

The Arab League

Cooperation among the Arab states in the political sphere and in the fields of communication, education and economics is the reason for the existence of the League of the Arab States. On March 22, 1945 seven Arab countries, Egypt, Iraq, Jordan, Lebanon, Saudi Arabia, Syria and Yemen, established the League as a regional organization to coordinate their efforts to achieve two common objectives: first, complete independence, and, second, unity. The founding members set forth the aim of the League as follows: 1) to strengthen the ties between Arab States and coordinate their political activities in such a way as to effect real collaboration between them, to protect their integrity and safeguard their independence, and to consider, in general, the affairs and interests of Arab countries; 2) to ensure that closer cooperation and greater collaboration exist in political, cultural, health, economic, legal and social fields. By 1974 the number of Arab states in the League reached twenty, and in the 1976 it rose to its present membership of twenty-two, including Palestine as a full voting member. (Text of the League's charter is on p. 235-239.)

As a regional organization of twenty-two states with a combined population of over one hundred million and a territory extending from the Atlantic to the Indian Oceans and commanding an important strategic position, the Arab League represents a tremendous potential power. But the political as well as the cultural and economic potential of this group is often crippled by vested interests, rivalries, ideological differences and international arrangements. Many conflicts between neighboring Arab states motivated by territorial claims or ideological differences do exist. Such conflicts have occurred between Morocco and Algeria, between North and South Yemen, Syria and Iraq, Egypt and Libya. Although the League members are in unanimous agreement in their support of the rights of the Palestinian people and their opposition to Israel, their disagreement on the means of achieving the goal of liberation often stands in the way of unified action.

But the Arab League, and its agencies, is the only practical expression of the desire and hope for Arab integration. The League does not now have enough authority to control actions of its members, to regulate relations among them, or even to represent the general will of the Arabs in the international arena. But the League, as long as it exists, has the potential of becoming more active in coordinating the cultural, social and economic activities of its member states and of disseminating information about the Arabs throughout the World.

Arab Unity

The road to Arab integration and Arab Unity remains long and difficult. The Arab World still teems with conflicting ideologies, religious parties, sectarian loyalties, and regional nationalistic movements. The civil war in Lebanon which started in 1975, and has not yet abated, is an example of strife among religious sects, ideologies, and economic and social classes. Unrest in the Kurdish areas of Iraq or in the southern Sudan reflects typical conflicts based on local national, ethnic and religious identities. The Arab World remains in great need for political, social, and economic reform. Independence brought with it political and social turmoil to most, if not all, Arab countries. Change, at times, was violent. Military takeover of governments occurred, or was attempted, in almost all of the states. In some, such as Syria, Iraq and Sudan, a series of coups occurred. Egypt, Iraq and Libya changed from monarchies to republics as a result of coups d'etat.

The goal of a single Arab Nation may still be a faraway dream. But there is a concensus on the desirability for cooperation and ultimate union among these people who speak the same language and share in a common historical experience.

(For more detail on historical events, refer to individual chapters and to the Chronological Tables on p. 225-234.)

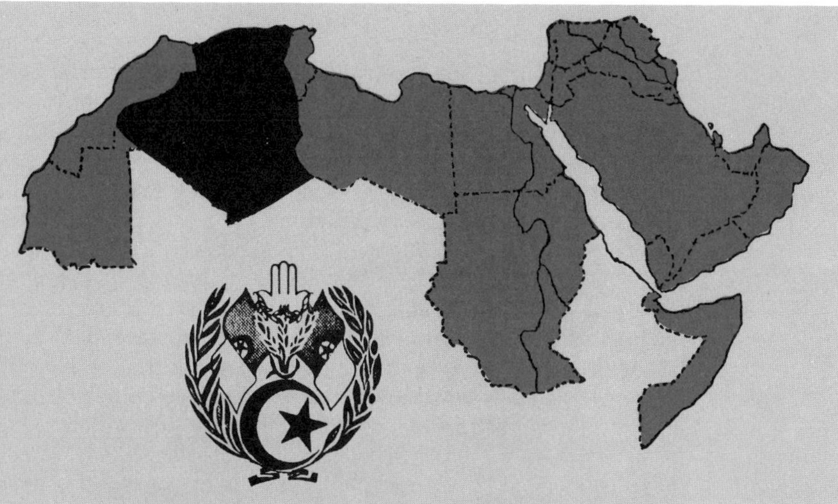

ALGERIA

الجمهورية الجزائرية الديمقراطية الشعبية

PROFILE

Official Name: Algerian Democratic Popular Republic (Al-Jumhuriyyah al-Jaza'iriyyah al-Dimuqratiyyah al-Sha'biyyah

Head of State: Houari Boumedienne

Government: Republic

Area: 919,951 sq. mi. (=3.5 × Texas)

Population: 17,800,000

Population Density: 19/sq. mi.

Capital: Algiers

Other Urban Centers: Oran, Constantine, Annaba, Setif, Tlemcen, Blida

National Holiday: November 1

Currency: Algerian Dinar ($1.00 = 4 AD)

Press: Dailies: Al Chaab, El Moudjahid, An Nasr

Radio and Television: Radio and Television stations in main cities.

Sites of Interest: Famous gardens in Blida (Hespides), Phoenecian Carthagenian and Roman ruins

Main Airports: Algiers (Dar el Baida), Oran, Constantine

Main Seaports: Oran, Algiers

Date of Joining the United Nations: October 9, 1962

Date of Joining the Arab League: August 16, 1962

ALGERIA

INTRODUCTION

The Democratic and Popular Republic of Algeria covers an area of 919,951 square miles, making it the second largest country in Africa and the tenth largest in the world. By way of comparison, Texas has an area of 267,339 and Alaska 586,412 square miles.

Throughout its long history, Algeria has interacted with cultures and civilizations of three continents: Africa, Asia and Europe. Thus, it is an amalgam of various influences and experiences from which its own character and individuality have evolved. It became independent after an eight-year (1954-1962) liberation war waged against France, and Algeria proclaimed itself a neutralist, socialist, anti-colonialist and anti-imperialist republic. It has engaged in a continuous effort of economic, cultural and technological construction designed to overcome the problems of underdevelopment, socioeconomic inequality and widespread poverty, following in the wake of 132 years of French colonialism. To accomplish these tasks Algeria has launched a series of consecutive development plans.

PHYSICAL GEOGRAPHY

Tell Atlas

Moving southwards from the Mediterranean there is a series of well-defined east-west physical zones. Along the coast are the ranges of the Tell Atlas, about 50 miles wide and varying in height from 1500 to 7500 feet. Deep valleys and gorges, especially in the west, divide them into distinct regions. The Tell Atlas mountains are separated from the sea to the north by a narrow and discontinuous coastal plain which is largely the lower valleys of mountain streams. These lowlands comprise only two or three percent of the area of Algeria, but they contain over half of the country's population and most of the irrigated lands.

Shotts Plateau

The Shotts Plateau is south of the Tell Atlas. It is a hundred miles across along the Moroccan border and narrows eastwards, ending near the Tunisian border. Occasional rain here can lead to the formation of extensive shallow lakes which, following evaporation and percolation, leave salt and mud flats and swamps. These swampy and salty basins are known as shotts; hence the name of the region. South of the plateau are the Saharan Atlas mountains. They are less continuous and thus less of a barrier to movement than the Tell Atlas, but their scenery can also be rugged and spectacular. Mount Chelia at 7638 feet is the highest point in all of northern Algeria. Eastwards the Saharan Atlas merge with the Tell Atlas.

Sahara

To the south is the immense desert, part of the great Sahara. For the most part there is little variation in elevation. There are enormous expanses of gravel surfaces and occasional plateaus. Three particularly large sandy areas (Grand Erg Oriental, Grand Erg Occidental and Erg Chech) cover thousands of square miles each. In the far south the high Ahaggar massif with its lunar landscape of rugged volcanic and crystalline forms has the nation's highest peak (9850 feet).

Climate

Climatic belts also run in an approximate east-west direction. Rainfall generally increases from west to east and decreases from north to south. From the Tunisian border to about fifty miles west of Algiers rainfall exceeds 30 inches and reaches over 60 inches in the highlands. The Shotts Plateau receives less than 20 inches in the north and 10 inches in the south. The Saharan Atlas receive only 5-10 inches, despite their height, for the rainbearing winds lose most of their moisture well before

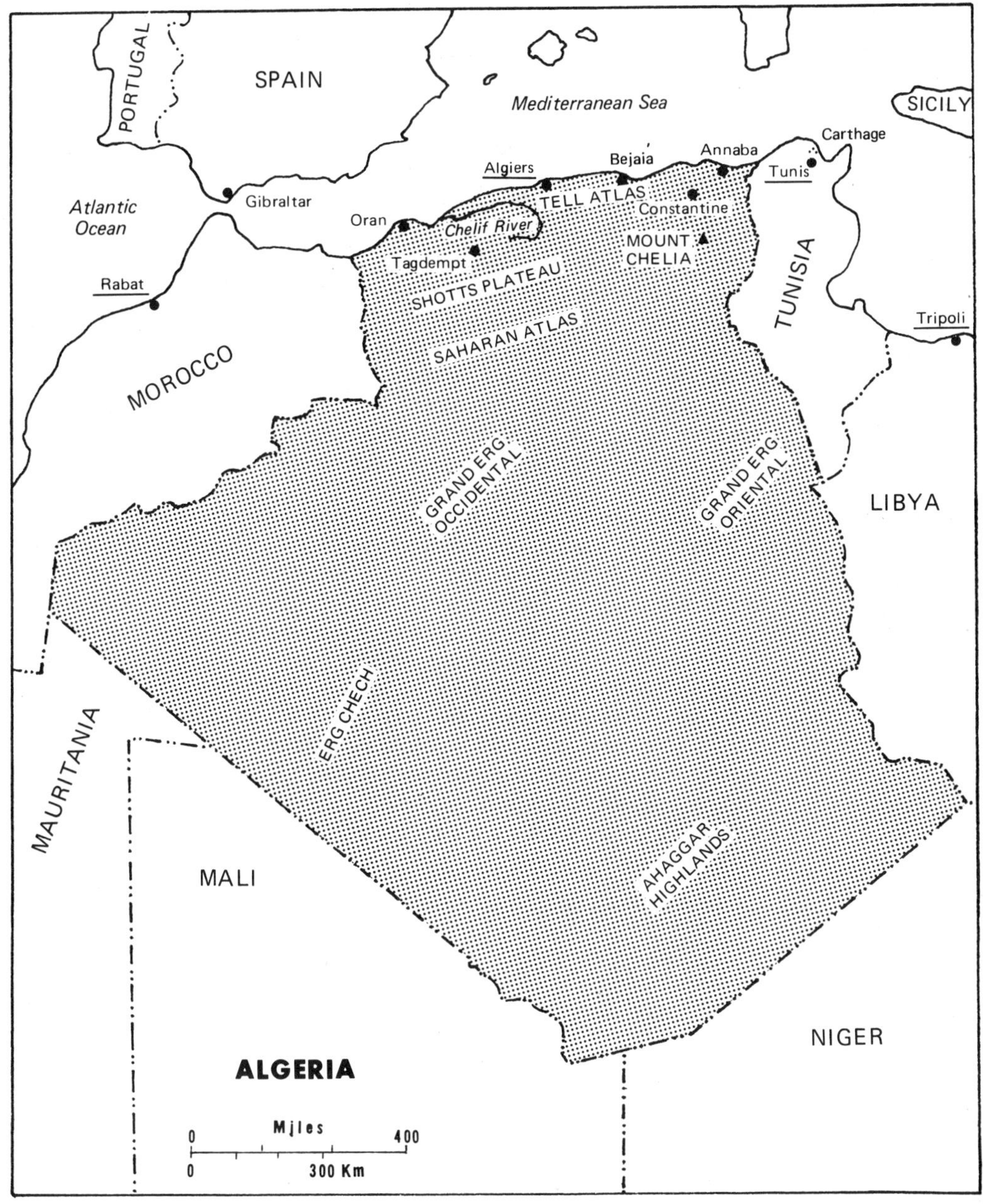

reaching them. In the Algerian Sahara rain is sparse and averages no more than two or three inches a year, if that much. Throughout the country there is a considerable year to year variation in both the amount and timing of rain. At the same time, there is a distinct mediterranean regime of wet winters and dry summers. July temperatures average 76°F along the coast, 90°F in the Shotts Plateau and in the mid-90s°F in the Sahara. In January, the coldest month, temperatures average in the mid-50s°F, but can drop below freezing.

ALGERIA

HUMAN GEOGRAPHY

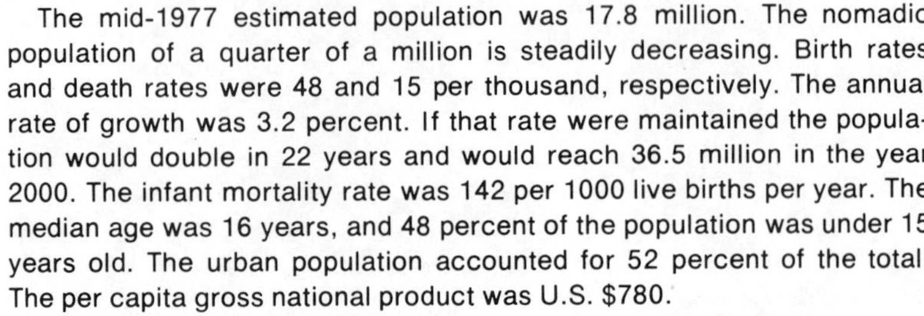

Vital Statistics

The mid-1977 estimated population was 17.8 million. The nomadic population of a quarter of a million is steadily decreasing. Birth rates and death rates were 48 and 15 per thousand, respectively. The annual rate of growth was 3.2 percent. If that rate were maintained the population would double in 22 years and would reach 36.5 million in the year 2000. The infant mortality rate was 142 per 1000 live births per year. The median age was 16 years, and 48 percent of the population was under 15 years old. The urban population accounted for 52 percent of the total. The per capita gross national product was U.S. $780.

Most Algerians live in the small coastal lowlands where most of the country's irrigated lands are located. Major crops are the vine, citrus fruits, vegetables and some deciduous fruits. Cotton and tobacco are also grown. The lowlands are the site of Algeria's major cities: Algiers, Oran, Constantine and Annaba. French colonists were attracted to the fertile plain, and the indigenous people they displaced moved to the adjacent mountains. Consequently, despite the inhospitable character of the Atlas mountains, portions of them have become densely populated. Major highland crops are barley, wheat, chick peas and lima beans. Important tree crops are figs, olives and cork. Orange groves, cereals and vegetables are also common. Erosion is often severe, land use is one of subsistence agriculture, and poverty is widespread. In the drier western part of the Tell Atlas pastoralism and transhumance are practiced.

On the Shotts Plateau there is seminomadic and nomadic herding and some grain production. In some valley oases of the Saharan Atlas high quality dates are raised. Extensive grazing is also practiced in the region. The enormous Algerian Sahara has a sparse population totaling less than three-quarters of a million. The majority live in oases and engage in intense cultivation, particularly date production. Algeria is a leading exporter of dates.

Algerians working in a reforestation and rural development project.

The population of Algeria is almost totally Muslim. The majority speak Arabic. Berber, the language of the pre-Arab Maghrib, is still spoken by a minority of Algerians. Most educated Algerians, however, speak French. Nearly all the European settlers (almost one million in 1960) have left the country since it attained independence in 1962.

ECONOMY

The problems faced by independent Algeria were mammoth. The war of liberation had a devastating effect on the economy. Industry, finance and communication were almost completely paralyzed. Over two million people were unemployed in the cities. There were innumerable orphans, widows, and others disabled by the war. In 1965 the government nationalized all mineral resources, foreign banks, insurance companies, and property vacated by settlers who returned to France. Between 1968 and 1972 there was a 55 percent increase in the financing of public developmental assistance programs, such as education, public health, welfare, cultural affairs, public administration and regional economic planning, and investments in agriculture increased threefold.

Development Plans

After 1967 Algeria relied on central planning to achieve an integrated multi-sectored economic development. A three-year plan (1967-1969) raised productivity in many sectors, for instance, energy output was increased by 75 percent and mining production was doubled. Two four-year plans followed (1970-1973 and 1974-1977). In the first of these 45 percent of the investment went to heavy industry, 15 percent to agriculture, 16 percent to housing and transportation, 11 percent to education, and 8.5 percent to regional development and civil engineering. All major objectives were achieved. The second four-year plan was far more ambitious, fueled to a considerable extent by the rapid increase in Algeria's oil income. An annual growth rate of 10 percent was projected. Industry again received primary attention. Emphasis was also given to light and diversified industry. A major objective was to raise the level of consumption, thus creating a domestic market wide enough to absorb industrial output. One hundred thousand housing units were to be built in the cities with severe housing crises. Constantine alone had a surrounding slum-belt of 50,000 inhabitants.

View of the modern city of Algiers, capital of Algeria

Oil

Oil was first discovered in Algeria in 1956. Production rose steadily reaching 36 million metric tons by 1971, and about 50 million in 1977. Pipelines connect the fields in the south to Mediterranean ports. The national oil and gas company, SONATRACH, now controls production and distribution of oil and gas.

Huge reserves of natural gas exist in Algeria. Gas from Hassi R'Mal, one of the largest gas fields in the world, is piped to Arzew where most of it is processed at a modern gas liquefaction plant.

Industry

Petrochemical industry is growing at a fast rate. The Annaba Steel Complex, completed in 1969, is one of the largest and most modern in Africa; it consists of a smelting plant, a steel works, rolling and pipe mills. In addition to the oil and mining related industries, a number of plants produce processed food, beverages, textiles, leather goods, engineering products, radios and assembled automobiles.

Algeria has over 22,000 miles of paved roads. A railway system connects the principal cities. Air Algeria provides air transportation between the country's major cities and Arab, African and European terminals.

Despite the fact that Algeria has nationalized the basic sectors of its economy and achieved an impressive rapid industrialization, basic problems remain. One of the most important is the persistence of socio-economic disparity between the peasantry and the urban population and the further polarization between the rich and the poor within these two sectors. Although over eight million Algerians lived in the countryside, land reform was delayed until 1971. Before that time 3 percent of the national landlords controlled 25 percent of all cultivated lands; three quarters of the peasants owned less than 25 acres, and about 500,000 peasant households were completely landless. A rural exodus to the cities resulted in one of the most rapid paces of urbanization in Africa. The land reform plan of 1971 aimed to limit the size of landed property. In 1973 the government began registering the large landholdings to be redistributed to cooperatives set up for the benefit of the poor peasants.

Ruins of the Roman town of Timgad in eastern Algeria, sometimes called the African Pompeii.

HISTORY

Early History

By the neolithic period Algeria was already inhabited by tribal peoples who came to be called Berbers. They identified themselves primarily along tribal lines but collectively referred to themselves as Imazighan, "free men." They were known in various historical periods as Libyans, Moors and Numidians. The Berbers speak several dialects of a language related to the ancient Hamitic and Egyptian languages. Most scholars agree that the Hamitic peoples—which include the ancient Egyptians and their descendants the Copts, the Berbers (Libyans and Numidians) of North Africa, certain tribes of Abyssinia and Somalia—are related ethnically to the Semites. They migrated into Africa from the Red Sea area in two different directions, one to Egypt and North Africa and the other to East Africa.

When the Phoenicians established trading relations with North Africa in about 850 B.C. the aboriginal inhabitants of Algeria were already cultivating wheat, barley, legumes and fruits, and were herding pigs, sheep, goats and cattle. Phoenician culture penetrated the most remote tribes of Numidia. Berber coins dating back to 200 B.C. reveal that the Numidians had already adopted the Punic Phoenician alphabet to transcribe their language. When threatened by Carthage (the Phoenician city in Tunisia) the Algerian Berbers proceeded to unify the tribes in order to create a state strong enough to resist the encroachment of both Carthage and Rome.

Roman Conquest

Numidia, which extended along the Mediterranean from the confines of Mauretania to Tunisia, was organized locally along tribal lines. Before the Third Punic war between Carthage and Rome (149-146 B.C.) all the tribes had been united and led by the great king, Massinissa. Under his reign Numidia achieved economic prosperity and political unity. He managed not only to liberate extensive areas from Carthage but also to attack its capital city in 150 B.C. But Rome, realizing his aims and fearing the rise of a strong power in the western Mediterranean, intervened quickly in the conflict under the pretext of militarily supporting its Numidian ally. Carthage was finally destroyed in 146 B.C. and northern Tunisia was occupied by the Roman legions. In 106 B.C. Rome defeated Numidia. The majority of Numidian cultivators lost their fertile lands and orchards to Italian settlers, and they withdrew to the Atlas mountains or to the Sahara. From there they harassed the Roman soldiery for five centuries. The lines of fortification, known as the "limes," still bear witness to their steadfast resistance to Roman imperialism. They lived poor but free in their desert and mountain havens, thereby earning the Roman name "barbars" and their own, Imazighan. Even those that remained in

Desert gate at Timimoun on the edge of the Sahara.

the occupied zone resorted to armed struggle and insurrection to free themselves from Roman domination. By the second century A.D., Christianity had spread among North Africa's oppressed classes who utilized this new religion as an ideological and organizational means for opposing the Roman rulers. Eventually the Byzantine army of occupation was forced to withdraw behind fortified walls which were easily overrun after 647 A.D. by the Muslim cavalry.

Arab Period

From 647 to 1830 Algerian history became closely associated with that of the Arab countries. The initial conquest of the cities and plains by the Arab army was immediately followed by the Islamization and later the Arabization of the indigenous population. The Arab conquest of the Maghrib (North Africa) introduced a numerically small military and civil corps of personnel that ruled through Islamized Berbers. Evenutally, the Berbers became dissatisfied with the differential treatment of different Muslims, and they embraced the Kharijite reformist doctrine. Several small Berber states arose in Algeria starting in the eighth century. Of these, the most important was the Kharijite theocratic republic whose capital was established at Tiaret, today's Tagdempt, 170 miles southwest of Algiers, and which extended its authority throughout Algeria, from the eighth to the tenth century. It was during this period that a large number of Algerian people became linguistically and culturally Arabized.

Ottoman Period

After the thirteenth century the general decadence of Muslim classical civilization coincided with the rise to prominence of a Turkish military caste which eventually succeeded, in Algeria as well as in the rest of the Arab world, in making the Turkish elements the ruling classes of the Islamic lands, unified and integrated into the Ottoman Empire. The cities of Algeria and their immediate hinterlands came under the control of the Ottomans after 1518, but by the seventeenth century the country had become independent from Turkish rule.

A commercial treaty signed in 1674 granted trading privileges to France. By the turn of the nineteenth century the French Africa Company had already monopolized not only Algerian international commerce but also the exploitations of certain raw materials such as coral. It owned various commercial establishments in Algiers and other cities. As a result of trading monopolies granted by the ruling caste to the European merchants the Algerian traders were gradually driven out of business. In time, the source of income of a large segment of urban dwellers was eroded. As a consequence, certain coastal cities lost close to half or more of their inhabitants. For example, Algiers had a population of 100,000 during the eighteenth century; by 1830 the population was about 60,000.

French Conquest

From the outset France proceeded to colonize Algeria. In the cities, which were occupied first, the French confiscated property and distributed it to French settlers. Between 1830 and 1940, 8,509,150 acres of land were transferred to French settlers. Those who were spared were eventually ruined by an inflation aggravated by the introduction of French currency. A large number of urban dwellers fled to other North African and Middle Eastern countries in the 1830s and 1840s. At the same time, the 19th century was marked by a series of rebellions, the most successful of which was in the west and was led by the able Berber leader Abdel Kadir between 1839 and 1847.

By 1954 the 45 million acres of the Algerian Tell were apportioned as follows: 24,900 French settlers owned privately 7,479,160 acres of arable land, the colonial state domain was 17,784,000 acres, and the eight million Algerians still in control of only 17,611,100 acres, of which two-thirds were on unproductive mountain slopes and in semi-arid steppe. Over 92 percent of the urban industrial sector was controlled by the French settlers who comprised only about 8 percent of the population.

War of National Liberation

The roots of the freedom movement go back to 1923, when the first Algerian nationalist mass party, the North African Star, was established in Paris by deracinated Algerian workers. The Star was banned by the French government in 1929, but it reappeared in 1936 in Algiers as the Algerian People's Party. Three years later, it was dissolved again but reappeared in 1946 as the Movement for the Triumph of Democratic Liberties. The war of liberation began on November 1, 1954, led by the National Liberation Front and supported by a wide cross section of Algerians. France eventually recognized Algeria's independence by signing the Evian Agreement on March 19, 1962. Over a million Algerians had been killed out of a population of 9 million, 800 villages were destroyed, and over three million peasants were dislocated. Formal independence came on July 5, 1962, and 132 years of French occupation came to an end.

Instructor and students in the workshop of the Telecommunications Center in Algiers.

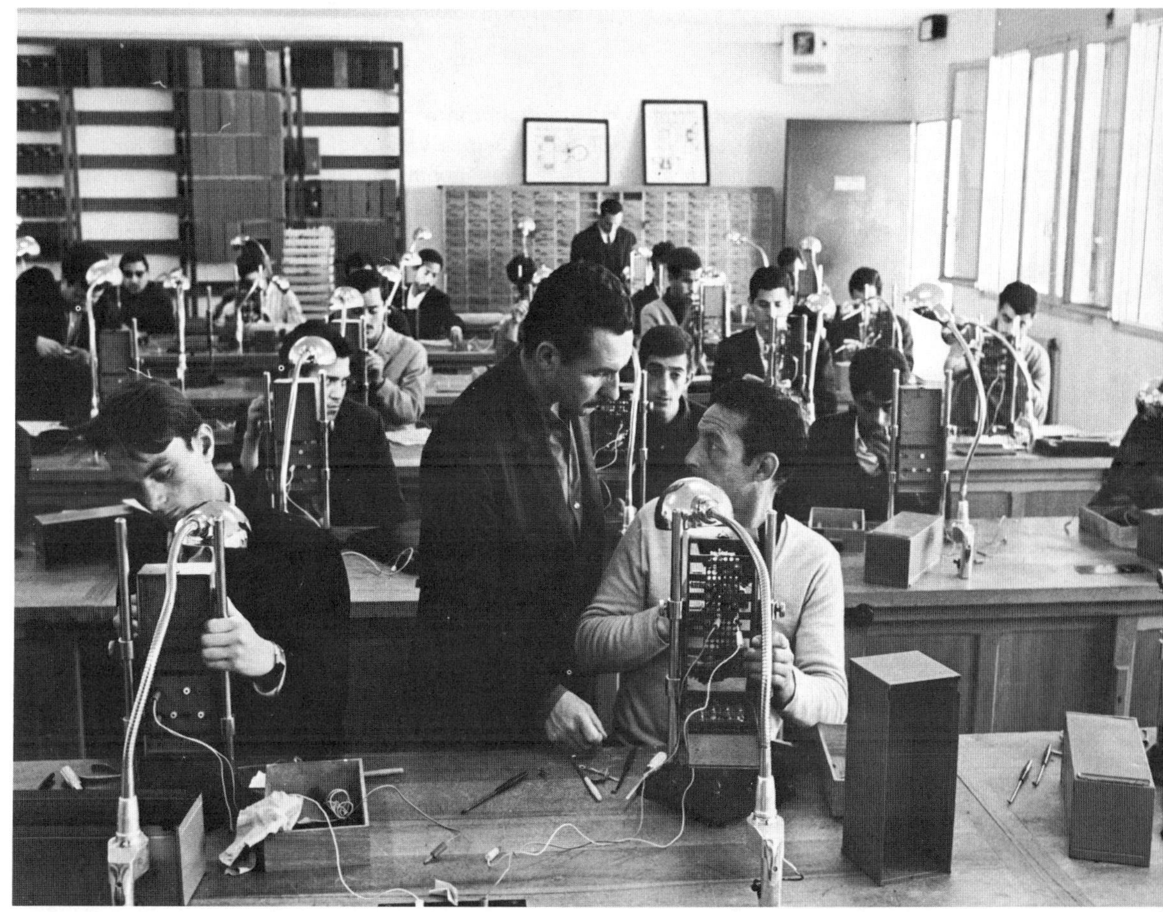

GOVERNMENT AND SOCIETY

Administration

According to the 1963 constitution Algeria is a republic with a president, elected for a five year term, and a unicameral National Assembly. But this constitution was suspended in 1965; the National Revolutionary Council and the Council of Ministers are, for an interim period, the supreme policy making organs of the state.

Administratively, the country is divided into fifteen departments. The commune is the basic collective unit, administered by an elected assembly.

Health

Algeria has 148 general and 13 specialized hospitals. The number of doctors increased steadily from one for 8,550 inhabitants in 1966 to one for 7000 by 1973. A network of health centers has been established in previously neglected areas.

Education

About 60 percent of the school age children were attending school in 1974, contrasted with 10 percent in 1954. The second four-year plan (1974-1977) aimed at making universal education a reality by providing at least nine years of schooling to all children. Twenty-two thousand additional classrooms were planned; secondary and higher education would also be promoted by establishing 100 high schools, 32 technical institutes, and four regional universities by 1977. The goal was to achieve universal literacy by 1985. In 1962 there was only one university, at Algiers. Since then four others have opened in Oran, Constantine, Tlemcen and a University of Science and Technology in Algiers.

PROSPECTS

Algeria made substantial progress during the 1960s and 1970s. At the same time it is still faced with a variety of developmental tasks. These include an expansion of educational opportunities and social services, a substantial reduction in the widespread rural and urban poverty, an improvement in the efficiency and quality of agricultural productivity, and a greater integration of both society and economy. Given the record of success of the development plans, and given a substantial wealth in the form of oil resources, the prospect of making a steady headway in these directions is encouraging.

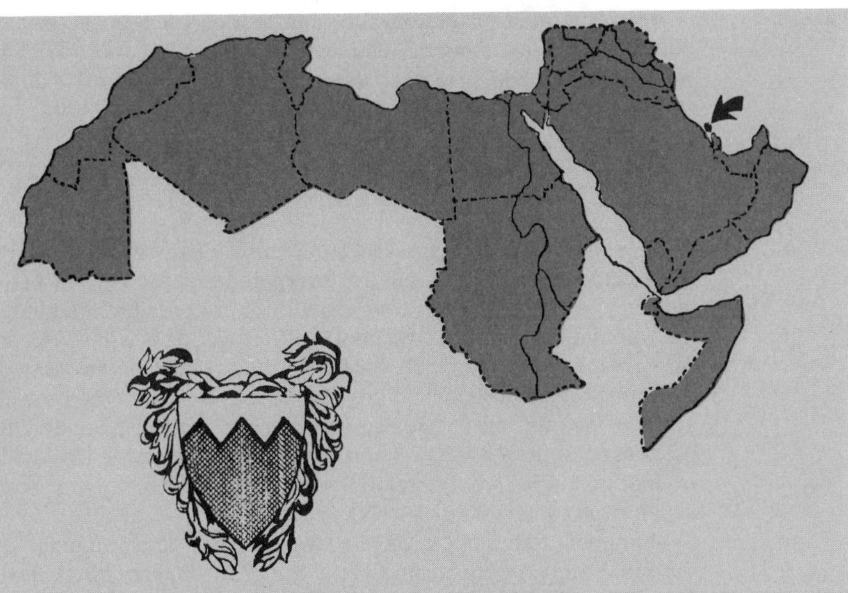

BAHRAIN

دولة البحرين

PROFILE

Official Name: State of Bahrain (Dawlat al-Bahrain)

Head of State: Sheikh Isa bin Sulman Al Khalifa

Government: Emirate

Area: 258 sq. mi.

Population: 250,000 (est. 1977)

Population Density: about 1000/sq. mi.

Capital: Manama (90,000)

Other Urban Centers: Muharraq, Awali, Rafa'a

Currency: Bahraini dinar (1 BD=$2.55)

Press: Awali Evening News, other periodicals

Radio & Television: Color television

Sites of Interest: Archeological sites, burial mounds.

Main Airport: Muharraq

Main Seaports: Manama, Muharraq

Date of Joining the United Nations: September 21, 1971

Date of Joining the Arab League: September 11, 1971

Most Bahrainis of employable age work in the public sector (over 10,000). The oil industry employs around 4,000. The construction, wholesale and retail trade, manufacturing and transport industries are also important employers. Approximately 3,000 Bahrainis are involved in agriculture and fishing.

ECONOMY

Oil is the mainstay of Bahrain's economy. Commercial quantities of oil were discovered in 1932, but it is estimated that the known reserves will last only about another twenty years. The concession has been held by the Bahrain Petroleum Company (BAPCO), which is a joint venture of the Standard Oil Company of California and Texaco, Inc. Bahrain's oil revenues rose to $80 million in 1974, based on a 12 percent royalty, a 55 percent income tax on local crude oil, and a fee on Saudi Arabian oil processed at the BAPCO refinery, the second largest in the Middle East. In March, 1975 the Bahraini government announced its intention to assume full ownership of BAPCO.

Industry

Aluminum Bahrain (ALBA) is owned by a consortium of Bahraini, European and American interests. The $150 million aluminum smelter has a capacity of 120,000 tons per year. The Bahraini government has a 27½ percent share in the consortium, and the natural gas fuel required for smelting is supplied by BAPCO. Bahrain Atomizers produces aluminum powder and an extrusion plant is planned.

Bahrain is a bustling commercial hub. Bahrain International Airport can service the most modern aircraft. One of the two simultaneous 1976 inaugural flights of the Concorde was from London to Bahrain. In addition to inter-Gulf travel, it is a major port of call for flights between Europe, the Far East and Australia. There are plans to expand the large port at Mina Sulman. Construction of a $100 million dry dock has begun. The dry dock, Arabian Gulf Repair Yards, is sponsored by the Organization of Arab Petroleum Exporting Countries and will handle tankers up to 375,000 tons. A four-lane causeway links Bahrain and Muharraq. International commerce is actively encouraged through tax relief and freedom to repatriate profits. Most of the new industrial activities have been established in the Free Zone.

The building of the secretariat of the Government of Bahrain is a blend of modern and traditional architecture

Agriculture

The agricultural sector produces some dates, vegetables and fodder crops. Date palms, figs, bananas, citrus fruits, mangoes, and pomegranates are grown under spring irrigation in the northern part of Bahrain Island. Also found here are vegetables, alfalfa, and cattle. Camels and horses are bred for racing. There are several soft drink factories, brick making plants and a plastics plant on the island. The Bahrain Fishing Company (60 percent Bahraini, 40 percent British) exports frozen prawns to the United States and Japan.

Traditional occupations like fishing and dhow building continue a limited existence. From ancient times Bahrain has been famous for the quality and luster of its natural pearls. The pearl oyster still thrives in Gulf waters, but the ancient craft of pearl diving has almost vanished.

HISTORY

Bahrain has been continuously inhabited by man since the Stone Age. Thousands of flint chippings left by Stone Age man lie directly on the surface of the island, particularly in the region of Awali, the Bahrain Petroleum Company town. From approximately 3000 B.C. to 700 B.C. a flourishing civilization grew up on the island built around maritime trade between city-states in Mesopotamia, the Indus Valley, and the land of Makan (probably Oman). Bahrain has been almost certainly identified as the land of Dilmun, well-known in Sumerian religion as the home of Ziusudra, the survivor of the Deluge in the Gilgamesh epic. Two temples and a city-site from this period are still being excavated by archaeologists.

About 600 B.C. Dilmun was reduced to a Babylonian province. In 323 B.C. the admirals of Alexander the Great reported that the island was ruled by an independent king. In the fourth century A.D. Bahrain was annexed by Persia. It appears that Bahrain was also the site of a Nestorian bishopric, although Christianity was not the dominant religion.

Al-Khalifa Family

From 1521 to 1602 the Portuguese were the dominant influence and they were succeeded intermittently from 1602 to 1782 by the Iranians. In 1776 members of the al-Khalifa family left Kuwait and settled in the coastal town of Zubara in Qatar. The al-Khalifas were pearl merchants. Bahrain was famed for its pearls, and in 1782 Sheikh Ahmad al-Khalifa conquered Bahrain. The al-Khalifas have ruled ever since, save for a brief period prior to 1811.

Through a series of nineteenth-century agreements (1820, 1861, 1880 and 1892) Great Britain gained almost complete control over Bahrain's external affairs. This enabled the al-Khalifas to consolidate their rule internally. By the mid-twentieth century, however, Bahrain began to move toward independence. On August 14, 1971 full independence was officially proclaimed, and in December, 1972, elections were held for a Constitutional Assembly. In 1973 the new Constitution were adopted, and elections for a National Assembly were held on December 7, 1973.

Women in the police force of Bahrain

INTRODUCTION

Bahrain is a small sheikhdom consisting of a group of islands in the Arabian Gulf off the shores of Saudi Arabia and Qatar. For thousands of years the islanders have been engaged in fishing, pearling, and trading. Bahrain was known to, and influenced by, the succeeding ancient civilizations of Mesopotamia and Persia, and the more recent European maritime powers, especially the Portuguese and the British. As a result of the discovery of oil, Bahrain has been transformed and modernized rapidly.

PHYSICAL GEOGRAPHY

The State of Bahrain is an archipelago of some thirty-three low-lying islands and islets. Only six of the islands are inhabited. Bahrain (Two Seas), the main island, has an area of only 217 square miles and supports over two-thirds of the archipelago's population of 300,000. The country's total area is only 258 square miles compared to Rhode Island's 1214 square miles. Bahrain has a fairly high population density of close to a thousand per square mile.

Bahrain Island

The nation's second largest island, Hawar (Young Camel), is uninhabited. The third largest island and the second most populated is Muharraq, which is connected to Bahrain by a 1.5-mile causeway. Most of the remaining population live on Sitra Island. About three hundred people live on Nabi Salih and Um al-Na'san islands. The penal colony is located on Jidda Island.

Although Bahrain is small in area, it displays marked contrasts in landscape, vegetation and climate. The northern end of the island contains a number of underground springs which allow some cultivation. South of this area, however, the land is barren and rocky. The terrain is composed mostly of low rolling hills and dry wadis.

Bahrain is surfaced with hard limestone rock, often covered with sand dunes. From the shoreline the terrain gradually rises toward the center of the island, where it drops down sharply into a basin surrounded by steep cliffs. Near the center of the basin a rocky hill juts up 250 feet above the plain and 450 feet above sea level. This hill is known as the Jabal al-Dukhan (Mountain of Smoke), because a haze often surrounds it.

The soil is extremely salty. Rainfall averages a scant 2.5 inches annually and falls mostly in the winter months from December to March. Winter temperatures average 68°F. The hottest months are June to September when temperatures average 91°F. The relative humidity remains fairly constant with a maximum of 85 percent and a mean minimum of 48 percent.

Plant and Animal Life

Vegetation and animal life are limited to those types native to desert regions. In spite of these handicaps, desert plants number some 200 species. A few gazelle are found in the southern desert, as are the jerboa and the hare. The mongoose is sometimes found in date gardens. There are several species of lizards, ranging from the 21-inch dhab of the desert to the tiny household gecko. Domestic animals include the camel, donkey, saluqi hound and horse. There are many species of migrant birds, of which the Macqueen's bustard is hunted by the sheikhs with peregrine falcons.

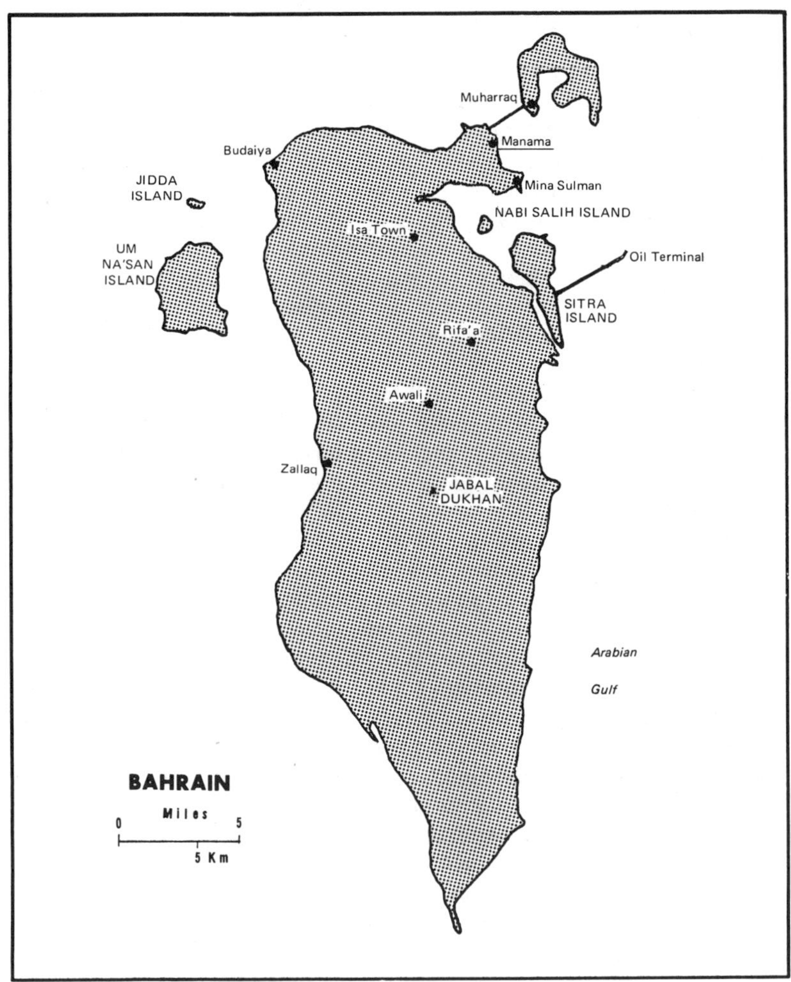

HUMAN GEOGRAPHY

The indigenous population is Arab, composed almost equally of the Shi'ite and Sunni sects of Islam. The ruling family belongs to the Sunni sect. Islam is the official religion and Arabic is the official language.

Vital Statistics

The mid-1977 estimated population is more than a quarter of a million. The birth rate is 43 per thousand, and the death rate is 8 per thousand, giving an annual growth rate of 3.5 percent. If this growth rate continues, the population will double in 20 years and will surpass half a million in the year 2000. The infant mortality rate is 78 per 1000 live births. Forty-four percent of the population is under 15 years old, and the median age is a very young 17.8 years.

Urban Centers

About 80 percent of the population is urban. Manama, a busy port on Bahrain Island and the seat of government, has a population of 90,000. Muharraq town's population of 40,000 is mainly Arab. About 38,000 foreigners reside in Bahrain and their occupations range from representatives of business concerns to domestic workers. Most of them are Omanis, followed by Indians, Pakistanis, Iranians, and British. Omanis and Iranians are largely in the construction industry, while Indians and Pakistanis are important in trade.

GOVERNMENT AND SOCIETY

National Assembly

Bahrain is ruled by an amir, Sheikh 'Isa bin Sulman al-Khalifa, who exercises his authority through a Council of Ministers. The Council of Ministers is headed by the ruler's brother who is also the Prime Minister, Sheikh Khalifa bin Sulman al-Khalifa. The heir apparent, Sheikh Hamad bin 'Isa al-Khalifa, is also the Minister of Defense. The country has a Constitution, promulgated in 1973, and a 44-member National Assembly. The National Assembly contains 30 elected members and 14 members of the Council of Ministers. Political parties are not allowed in Bahrain, so all elected members of the Assembly ran as independents. In practice the Assembly is about equally divided between conservative, moderate and more radical members.

The Constitution states that Islamic law is to be considered a primary source of legislation and that the judiciary is independent and autonomous. However, the three branches of government are not separated as in Western democracies; all of them are to some degree controlled by the ruler.

Education

Education is free but not compulsory. From six to twelve years of age children attend primary school; this is followed by two years of intermediate and three years of secondary school. Advanced educational facilities include the Men's Teacher Training College, Women's Teacher Training College and the Gulf Technical College. In 1972, 426 Bahrainis, of which 375 were men, received college degrees in universities abroad; this total is rapidly increasing.

Medical care is free, and housing is subsidized by the state.

Bahrain maintains an army of approximately 1,100 men. The armed forces are divided into 1 infantry battalion and 1 armored car squad; in addition there are some police patrol launches and police helicopters.

All Islamic religious customs are strictly observed. During the month of Ramadan eating, drinking, and smoking during the day are forbidden. Most of the towns fire a cannon at sunrise and sunset to announce the times of fasting and eating. The end of Ramadan is marked by the *'Id al Fitr,* a three-day holiday, a time for wearing new clothes, feasting and visiting friends and family. A similar celebration, the *'Id al-Adha* in the month of *Thu al-Hijja,* marks the end of the annual pilgrimages to Mecca. During the first nine days of the month of *Muharram* members of the Shi'ite sect mourn the martyrdom of their religious leaders, Hasan and Husayn. Mullas recite the tale of the martyrdom night and day. On the ninth day a public procession takes place in Manama in which mourners beat their breasts and flagellate themselves in sorrow. Photographs are strictly forbidden, but outsiders are permitted to watch.

Cultural Life

Bahrain boasts several talented native painters, and a major show of their works is held at least once a year. Bahrainis are eager to preserve their folklore; each year on Education Day school children don traditional clothing and perform native dances and songs. The amir sponsors horse and camel races south of the royal town of Rifa'a every Friday afternoon from November to May.

PROSPECTS

Despite the projected depletion of its oil resources, Bahrain's future remains reasonably bright. Auxiliary industries are being developed, and Bahrain is making every effort to insure that it is the home base of operations for every major company in the Gulf. The country is also actively considering ways to promote tourism, in addition to remaining the major trade center of the region. Intensive manpower planning is needed because of the increasing modernization of Bahraini society and its high population density.

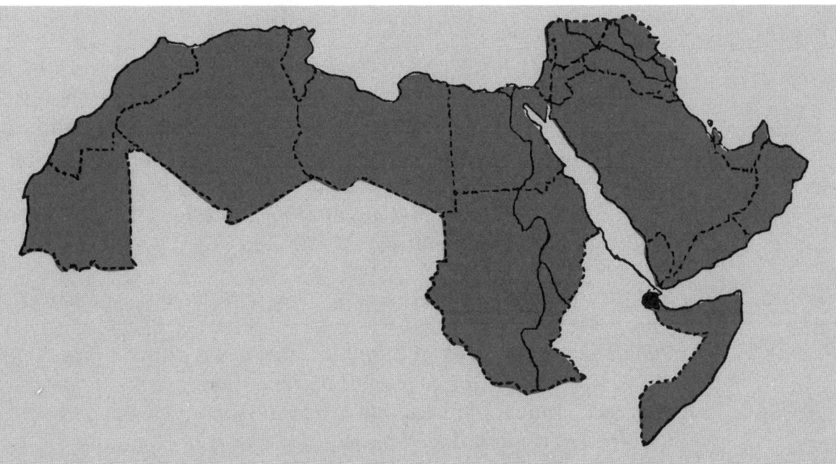

DJIBOUTI

جمهورية جيبوتي

PROFILE

Official Name: Republic of Djibouti (Jumhuriyyat Jibouti)

Head of State: Hassan Gouled Aptidon

Government: Republic

Area: 8,880 (smaller than New Hampshire)

Population: 220,000

Population Density: 25/sq. mi.

Capital: Djibouti

Other Urban Centers: Tadjoura

National Holiday: June 27

Main Airport: Djibouti

Main Seaport: Djibouti

Date of Joining the United Nations: September 20, 1977

Date of Joining the Arab League: September 3, 1977

DJIBOUTI

INTRODUCTION

The Republic of Djibouti, formerly the French Territory of Afars and Issas, became independent on June 27, 1977. On September 3, 1977 it became the twenty-second member of the League of Arab States, and on September 20, 1977 it became a member of the United Nations. Djibouti's natural resources are limited, and its importance on the international scene is related to its strategic location at the strait of Bab el-Mandeb, the southern entrance to the Red Sea.

PHYSICAL GEOGRAPHY

Climate

Djibouti has an area of 8,880 square miles, and it shares land borders with Ethiopia and Somalia. Its 200-mile coastline includes the deep indentation of the Gulf of Tadjoura, a feature which was an important factor in the selection and development of the port of Djibouti. The topography consists mostly of low-lying plateau surfaces strewn with volcanic rocks. It is broken by depressions that are related to the extensive rift valley system in east Africa which continues through the Red Sea to the Jordan valley. Some of the depressions are below sea level, such as that occupied by Lake Assal. Along the northern coast of the Gulf of Tadjoura are the Mabla and Gouda mountains, where elevations exceed 6,000 feet. Climatically, Djibouti is a hot desert. The annual average temperature is a very high 86°F. An average of 92°F prevails during the summer months of May through October. Humidity is high all year, especially during the summer and in coastal areas.

HUMAN GEOGRAPHY

The population is estimated at over 200,000, half of whom live in and near the capital port city of Djibouti. The rest are mostly pastoral nomads. The two largest segments of the population are the Issas (about 80,000), who are in the south and are related to peoples in Somalia, and the Afars (about 70,000) who are in the north and are related to peoples in Ethiopia. Both groups are Hamitic. They are Muslim and speak related Cushitic languages. There are perhaps 12,000 Arabs, and other groups include Greeks, Indians, Sudanese and Somalis. The annual rate of population growth is between 2.5 and 3 percent. French is an important language of business and commerce. Other important towns include Ali-Sabieh and Dikkil in the south, and Tadjoura and Obok on the northern side of the Gulf of Tadjoura.

A panoramic view of the city of Djibouti, capital of the newly independent country.

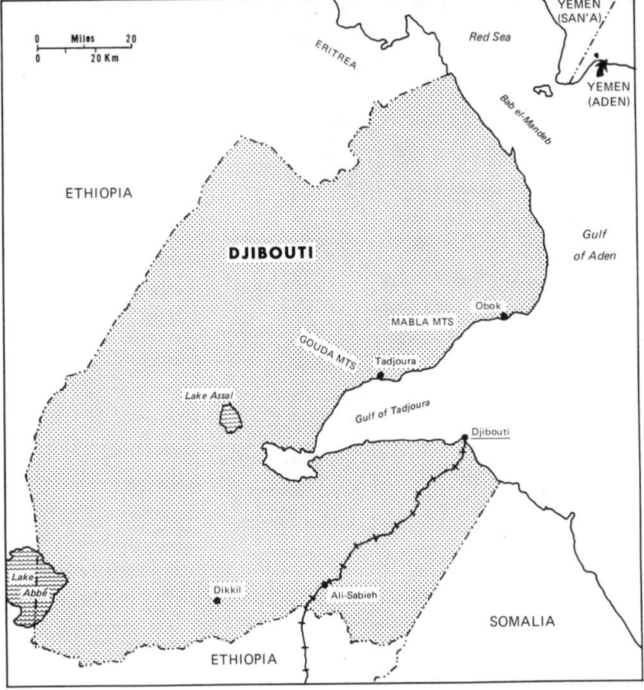

DJIBOUTI

ECONOMY

Port Activities

Djibouti's greatest asset has long been its location. For many years it served as an important port of call and as a bunkering port. However, it experienced a considerable reduction of activity because of the closure of the Suez Canal between June, 1967 and June, 1975. For instance, the number of ships calling on Djibouti dropped from 3074 in 1965 to 983 in 1968, and cargo dropped from 360,000 tons to 290,000 during the same period. While there has been an increase in port activity, the re-opening of the canal has not resulted in a return to the earlier level of traffic because Djibouti's oil prices have not been competitive with those elsewhere.

Internal trade consists almost entirely of Ethiopian transit business utilizing the railroad between Djibouti and Addis Ababa. It is possible that this business will decrease because of realignments in political relationships between Djibouti and its neighbors, and because Ethiopia has been developing its own Red Sea ports. On the other hand, Ethiopia's difficulties in Eritrea underline the importance to Ethiopia of the Djibouti outlet.

Agriculture

There is little cultivated land. About 10 percent consists of meadows and pastures, less than 0.5 percent is classified as wooded, and the remaining 90 percent is wasteland. There are about 19,000 cattle, 96,000 sheep, 567,000 goats, 3,000 donkeys, and 24,000 camels. Thus livestock products, such as meats and skins, are the main domestic economic activity. Dates, other fruits, and vegetables are grown on a small scale, and there is some fishing. There are about 50 miles of bitumen-surfaced roads and about 600 miles of graded earth roads.

HISTORY AND GOVERNMENT

Djibouti was part of the overall African stage on which the European scramble for Africa was played in the latter half of the nineteenth century. The French consular agent in Aden, Henri Lambert, was instrumental in bringing about the signing of a treaty of friendship and assistance between France and three sultans, and in the purchase by France of the

The port of Djibouti is linked to Addis Ababa, Ethiopia, by rail.

anchorage at Obok. In 1884-85, at the time of the Berlin Conference at which most of modern Africa's political boundaries were established, France designated this territory as French Somaliland and defined it to include the hinterland of the Gulf of Tadjoura. The boundary with Somalia was established in 1888 by an Anglo-French agreement, and the boundary with Ethiopia was delimited in 1897 with Emperor Menelik II and reaffirmed in 1945 and 1954 with Emperor Haile Selassie. The administrative capital was moved in 1896 from Obok to Djibouti, and the railroad between Djibouti and Addis Ababa was built between 1897 and 1917.

During World War II the territory was involved in the French and Italian activity in Somaliland and Ethiopia. In July, 1957 an administrative reorganization permitted a degree of self-government. Following a September, 1958 constitutional referendum French Somaliland became a French Overseas Territory and thus acquired representation by one deputy and one senator in the French Parliament. In July, 1967 the name was changed from French Somaliland to the French Territory of Afars and Issas. The 1970s were marked by an increasingly asserted preference for independence, and the 115-year French rule formally ended on June 27, 1977 when the Republic of Djibouti was proclaimed, with Hassan Gouled as president.

Administration

The president is advised by a Council of Government consisting of nine ministers: Plan and Development, Interior, Public Works, Rural Economy, National Education, Civil Service, Public Health, Labor and Professional Training, and Finance. The country's first Chamber of Deputies had 65 seats, distributed as follows: 33 Issas, 30 Afars, and 2 Arabs.

PROSPECTS

The initial delimitation of Djibouti's borders was a product of European colonial compromises. With the departure of colonial rule from Djibouti and neighboring areas, the country's welfare, and even the safeguarding of its territorial integrity, will be importantly related to the dynamics of relationships among its neighbors and the activities of other parties with an interest in this region. The importance of the country's strategic location persists, and this importance will continue as both a possible liability and as an asset—a possible liability because of the country's military weakness relative to the potential designs of others, and an asset because of the needs of water and land transit traffic to use Djibouti's services.

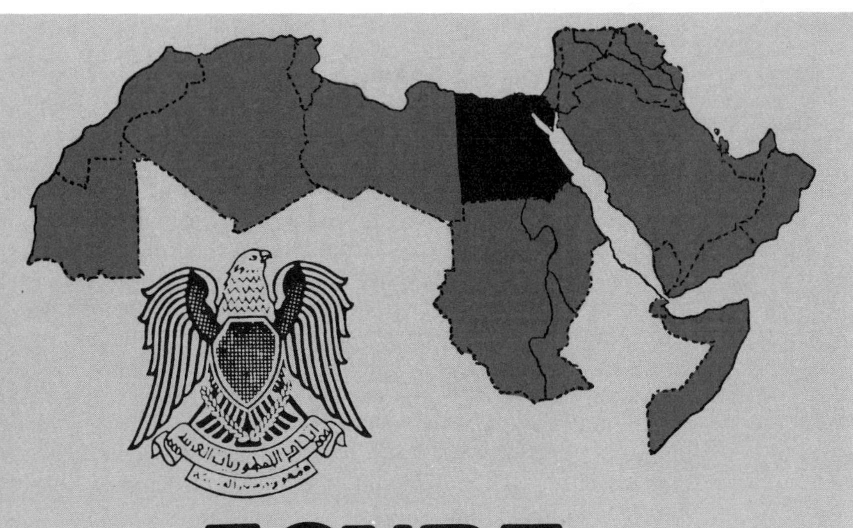

EGYPT

جمهورية مصر العربية

PROFILE

Official Name: The Arab Republic of Egypt (Jumhuriyyat Misr al-Arabiyyah)

Head of State: M. Anwar al-Sadat

Government: Republic

Area: 386,661 sq. mi. (= Texas and New Mexico)

Population: 40 million (1978)

Population Density: 100/sq. mi. (2700 in cultivated areas)

Capital: Cairo (over 6 million)

Other Urban Centers: Alexandria, Port Said, Suez, Asyout, Luxor, Aswan.

National Holiday: July 23

Currency: Egyptian Pound (1 E.P. = $2.25)

Press: Al-Ahram, Al-Gumhuriyyah, Al-Akhbar, and many other.

Radio & Television: Two radio and one television stations.

Sites of Interest: Pyramids of Giza, Cairo, Valley of the Kings, Abu-Simbel, Aswan.

Main Airports: Cairo, Alexandria, Aswan.

Main Seaports: Alexandria, Port Said, Suez.

Date of Joining the United Nations: October 24, 1945.

Date of Joining the Arab League: March 22, 1945.

EGYPT

INTRODUCTION

No country name in the Arab World is likely to be more recognizable to Americans and other Westerners than Egypt. The term brings forth vivid images of the Nile across the desert, of the pyramids and the sphinx, of a crowded and noisy Cairo, and of a constant involvement in international affairs. All of these associations are true. Egypt is a desert land and the Nile carries through it life sustaining waters. It is a textbook example of a land with an enormously long known history and with evidences of human accomplishment spanning millennia. Egypt's population is one-fourth of that of the Arab World, and perhaps one-fourth of Egypt's people live in the sprawling and densely settled Cairo metropolitan area. Egypt's interests in other areas and the interests of others in Egypt have constantly involved it in international affairs, whether five thousand years ago or today, an involvement related to a considerable extent to the unique nature of the Nile River system and to the country's location at the junction of Africa and Asia and its proximity to Europe across the link of the Mediterranean Sea.

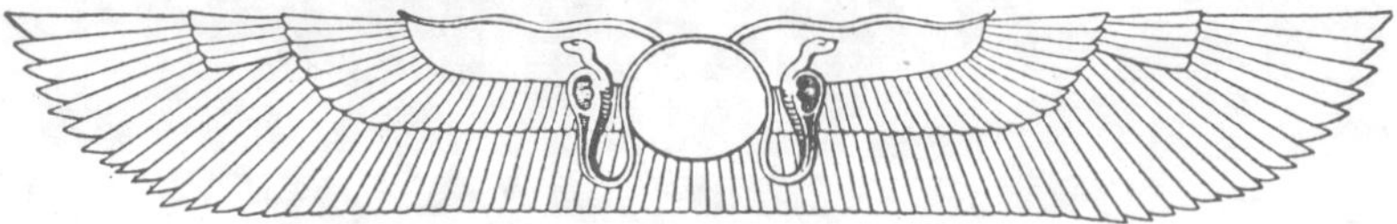

PHYSICAL GEOGRAPHY

Topography

Egypt's area of 386,661 square miles is about equal to the combined areas of Texas and New Mexico. The land is a desert plateau which is cut across from south to north by the verdant valley of the Nile. The larger western section contains numerous oases, and sand accumulations become dominant as the western border with Libya is neared. In the north, about 300 miles west of Cairo, is the Qattara Depression, where the surface is 436 feet below sea level. The Eastern Desert, between the Nile and the Red Sea, is characterized by rugged uplands and numerous wadis. The uplands reach elevations of 7000 feet in places, and the descent to the narrow Red Sea coast is precipitous and deeply dissected. Across the Suez Canal, the Sinai Peninsula has a low-lying sand covered surface in the north. Southwards, elevation increases and rugged mountains prevail, culminating in the 8668 foot Mount Sinai, Egypt's highest peak.

The Nile River traverses over 800 miles of Egyptian soil. Its trough-like valley is narrowest in the south (less than half a mile in places), and it gradually widens downstream (northwards) to ten or twelve miles at Cairo. Beyond, the Nile bifurcates into two main channels across the flat delta.

Climate

The climate is hot and dry in summer (May to September), and warm and dry in winter (November to March). Alexandria, the wettest part, has an annual precipitation of only about 9 inches (falling in winter), which is not enough to classify it as non-arid. In the south rainfall is less than 2 inches a year, and some years may pass with no rain. Summer temperatures exceed 100°F and may reach 120°F in the southern and western deserts, while they reach about 90°F along the coast. The average minimum January temperatures are in the 50s in Alexandria and about 60°F in Aswan. Winter nights are quite cool, and frost may be experienced. Hot dry sandy winds (khamsin) often blow, particularly in spring, and can be damaging to crops.

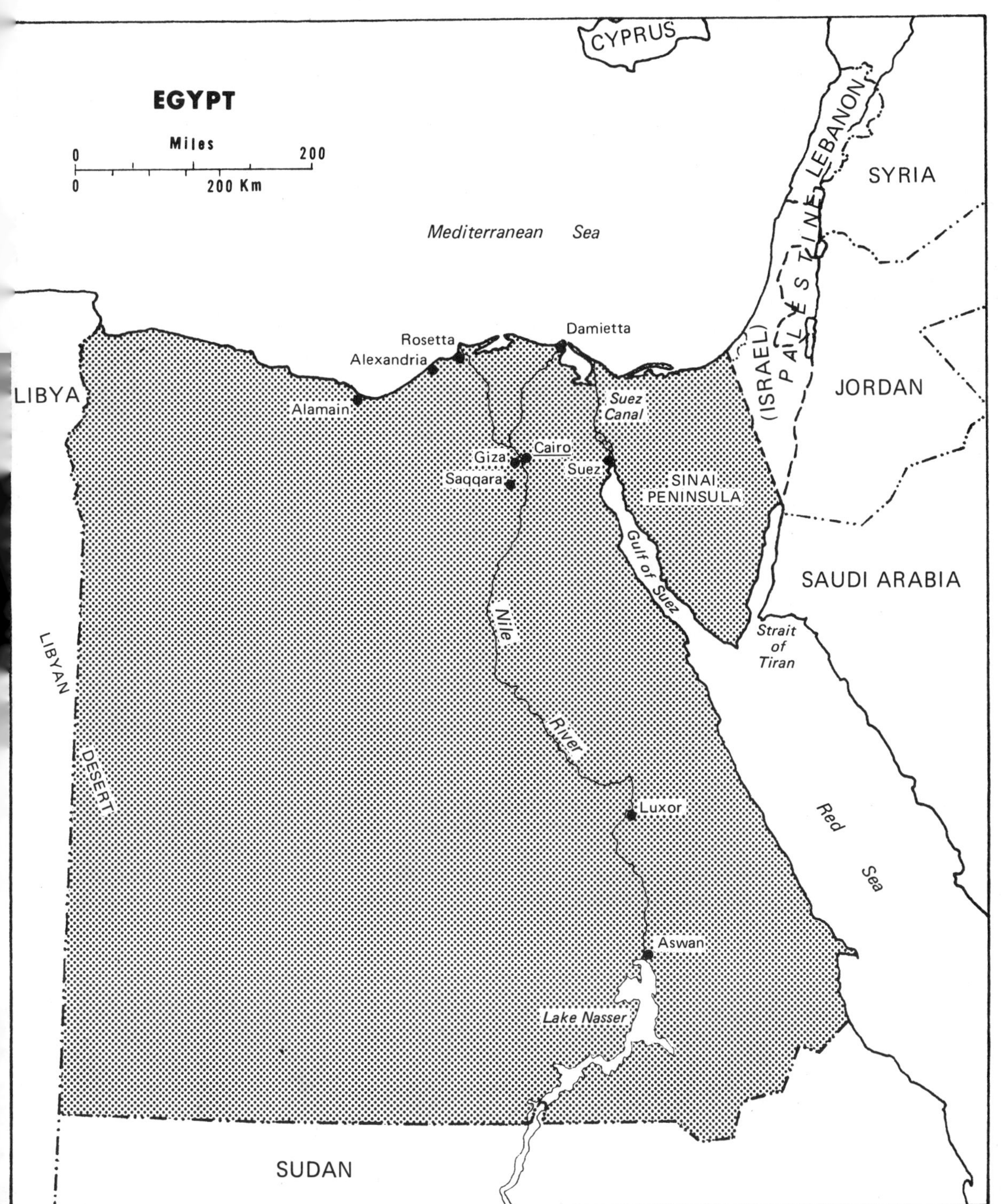
EGYPT
Miles
0
200
0
200 Km
CYPRUS
LEBANON
SYRIA
Mediterranean Sea
PALESTINE
(ISRAEL)
JORDAN
Damietta
Rosetta
Alexandria
Alamain
LIBYA
Suez Canal
Cairo
Giza
Suez
Saqqara
SINAI PENINSULA
Gulf of Suez
SAUDI ARABIA
Nile
Strait of Tiran
LIBYAN
River
DESERT
Red
Luxor
Sea
Aswan
Lake Nasser
SUDAN

HUMAN GEOGRAPHY

Egyptians are a relatively homogeneous group, though over the centuries there has been an admixture of various peoples. Predynastic Egyptians apparently came from Nubian and Hamitic origins. Over time European and Asian stocks were added as the result of such invaders as the Romans, Greeks, Persians, Crusaders and Turks. These influences are more apparent in the cities and in central and northern Egypt. Southwards, Nubian influences are more evident. The peoples of the Sinai and the Eastern and Western deserts comprise only about one percent of the population, and they include slightly different racial mixes.

Religion

All monotheistic religions, and a few others, have found a home in Egypt. Akhenaton of the 18th Dynasty, who reigned from 1379 to 1362 B.C., may well have been the first monotheist in recorded history. Moses, who some archeologists believe to have been an Egyptian prince, introduced many Egyptian ideas and practices, such as circumcision, to his new religion. St. Mark (first century A.D.) proselytized in Egypt, which became the first country to accept Christianity; since the fourth century the see of Alexandria has been called "the chair of Mark" (cathedra Marci). Islam was introduced in the seventh century, and Egypt eventually became a predominantly Muslim country with a Christian minority mostly belonging to a Monophysite faith, the Coptic Church.

Vital Statistics

The population distribution is rather simple to describe: perhaps 98 percent of the people live in the Nile valley and delta, giving a density of 2700 people per square mile of cultivated land and a ratio of about 6 persons per cultivated acre. Because population growth is more rapid than the rate of land reclamation, these two figures will continue to increase. About two-thirds of Egyptians live in Lower Egypt, that is Cairo and the delta. Urbanization in the delta is higher than in Upper Egypt (southern Egypt). Cairo, the capital, has more than 6 million people, and some estimates of the Cairo urban area are 10 million.

The mid-1977 estimated national population was 39 million, of whom 45 percent were classified as urban. Birth and death rates were 36 and 12 per thousand respectively, giving an annual rate of increase of 2.4 percent. If these rates are maintained the population will double in 30 years and will be 63.9 million in the year 2000. About 41 percent of the people are under 15 years of age. Alexandria is the second largest city with a population of about 3 million. About 15 other cities have populations of over 100,000.

An Egyptian tourist guide. Some of these guides are proficient speakers of many languages.

THE ECONOMY

Agriculture

Agriculture accounts for 30 percent of the gross national product, and industry accounts for about 20 percent. About 40 percent of the labor force is in agriculture, which provides 60 percent of export earnings. Three-fourths of the agricultural income is from field crops and one-fourth from fruits, vegetables, dairy products and livestock. The primary crop is cotton, and Egypt is the world's primary producing country, accounting for from 33 to 40 percent of the world production of long-staple cotton (1 1/8 inches or longer). Cotton is grown on about one fourth of Egypt's arable land, it accounts for 40 percent of the value of field crops, and it constitutes more than 50 percent of exports by value. Rice is another important export crop. Other crops, mostly for domestic consumption, include wheat, maize, millet, barley, sugar cane, beans, potatoes, onions and garlic. Egypt is a net importer of meat.

Land Reform

The Egyptian revolution which in 1952 overthrew the monarchy of King Farouk initiated a sweeping land reform program, the main aim of which was to eliminate the feudal system whereby 5.8 percent of the land-owners held 64.5 percent of the land. Also implemented were the regulation of tenure, consolidation of fragmented holdings, and the formation of cooperatives. But scarcity of land is a persistent problem, and the national average landholding is about two acres. Another continuing problem is ownership distribution, for half of the land is still owned by only 5 or 6 percent of the owners and their average landholding is only about 19 acres.

Irrigation

The quest for more land and more efficient uses of land is as old as agricultural history in Egypt. Production can be doubled by cultivating the same plot twice a year. Because of the year round growing season and the reliability of water supply, this practice has been common, and today three and even four crops a year are raised on some plots. But there is a limit to increasing production in this way, an alternative is to increase the area under production. To do so has meant a judicious use of the Nile waters. Initially, irrigation was dependent on the river's flooding, a predictable annual event which spread water and fertile silt over adjacent lands. Canals made it possible to irrigate on a continuing basis and to irrigate lands father from the river. Both of these benefits were increased by the construction of weirs which slightly raised the level of the water at the head of the canals. The maximum discharge of the Nile, occurring early in September, averages 715 million cubic meters/day, and the minimum, occurring during the second week of May, averages 45 million cubic meters/day.

Aswan Dam

The construction of reservoir dams allowed the storage of the fall surplus for use in the spring. The first such project, the Aswan Dam, was built in 1902 and subsequently raised twice, in 1912 and 1934, to increase the reservoir's capacity. One problem still remained. Whereas the timing of the Nile flood has been remarkably reliable, the volume of the discharge has not been consistent. There have been variations of as much as 80 percent above and 50 percent below the annual average of 84 billion cubic meters. To permit overyear storage, that is from years of high flow to years of low flow, thus bringing more land under cultivation and minimizing Egypt's dependence on other countries for the reliability of its water supply, the idea of a massive dam came into being. Such a dam would also provide cheap hydroelectric energy, thus facilitating industrialization, which in turn would decrease the country's dependence on agricultural products. This project was started in January, 1960 and

Egyptian farmers. A modern Egyptian interpretation of ancient pharaonic art.

completed in July, 1970. Its generating capacity of 10 billion kilowatt hours was two and one-half times Egypt's 1967 electric production. Its official name is simply the High Dam, though commonly it is called the Aswan High Dam to associate it with Aswan. The Aswan Dam is located about 4 miles downstream (north) of the High Dam. With the completion of the High Dam the Nile flood ceased because of the capacity of the enormous reservoir created behind the dam, the 300-mile-long Lake Nasser. One result was the loss of the fertile silt which had annually covered the fields. Power from the High Dam is used in the production of chemical fertilizers to substitute for the lost silt.

Industry

The industrial sector is dominated by food processing and textiles, which together account for 55 to 60 percent of the total industrial output. The iron and steel complex at Helwan is planned to have an annual capacity of 2 million tons by 1982. An aluminum plant with a planned capacity of 100,000 tons opened in 1975. The bauxite comes from Australia and Guinea. In addition to the availability of hydroelectric energy there seem to be promising deposits of oil and gas. There are producing wells in the Gulf of Suez and in Sinai, and there is optimism about substantial discoveries in the Western Desert.

The River Nile at Aswan in Upper Egypt.

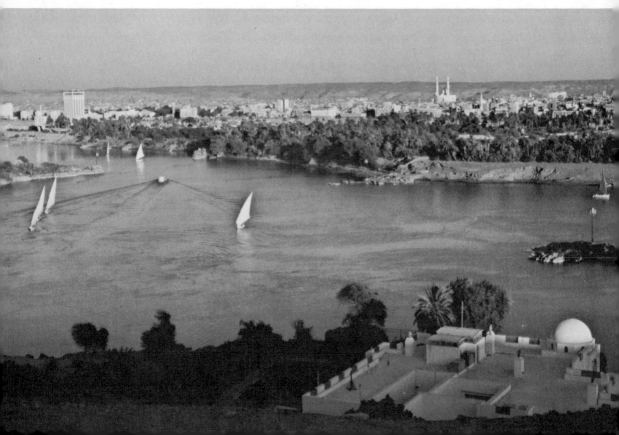

EGYPT

HISTORY

Ancient

Neolithic settlements date back to before 4000 B.C. Separate kingdoms developed in Upper (southern) and Lower (northern) Egypt during the 4th millennium B.C. and were united by the semilegendary King Menes around 3188 B.C. The First and Second Dynasties are dated at about 3100-2686 B.C. The Third through the Sixth Dynasties (2686-2181 B.C.) are known as the Old Kingdom, a time of creative achievement that included the pyramids. Its capital was Memphis, near the apex of the Nile delta on the west bank, across from and southwest of Cairo. An intermediate period of relative decline preceded the Middle Kingdom (2133-1786 B.C.), the golden age of art and craftsmanship. About 1674 B.C. the Hyksos (the "Shepherd Kings") crossed the Sinai and invaded Egypt. They introduced the horse and chariot. In 1570 B.C. they were expelled by the founders of the New Kingdom who extended their empire to the Orontes (in the northwest part of modern Syria), the Euphrates, and to 250 miles south of the present Egyptian border. Eventually the empire collapsed and was overrun by Libyans, Nubians and Assyrians. In 525 B.C. it was conquered by the Persian Cambyses II, son of King Cyrus the Great.

Alexander

Nearly two centuries later Alexander conquered Egypt and gave his name to a city he founded on the Mediterranean Sea. The Alexandrian period (333-323 B.C.) ushered in Macedonian and Ptolemic rule and marked the beginning of the Hellenic age in Egypt. Alexander's successors were the Ptolemies. Their dynasty (303-30 B.C.) ended with Queen Cleopatra when Augustus Ceasar, the first Roman Emperor, made Egypt a Roman province (30 B.C.-284 A.D.). Nonetheless, by the second century A.D. Alexandria was an important intellectual center for Hellenic Christianity; it contributed monasticism to Christian practices when St. Anthony (approximately 250-355 A.D.) established the first monastery. When the Council of Chalcedon in 451 A.D. propounded the doctrine of the dual nature of Christ, the Egyptian church rejected that doctrine and clung to its Monophysitic faith. The Byzantines, whose rule in Egypt lasted from 284-640 A.D., therefore persecuted the Egyptians for what they regarded to be schismatic beliefs.

Arab armies under Amr ibn al'As entered Egypt in 639 A.D. They met no resistance from the native Egyptians who were glad to see an end to the rule of Byzantium. Eventually the mass of the population became Muslim, and Arabic gradually replaced Coptic as the main language. Coptic was then relegated to religious usage and later became only a liturgical language. The sequence of Arab dynasties and dates of their rule in Egypt are: Umayyad and Abbasid Caliphate, 640-969; Fatimid, 969-1171; Ayyubid, 117-11250; Mamluks, 1250-1517. The Mamluks were Turco-Circassian slaves who had become a military elite under the last Ayyubid. Although their official rule ended with the Turkish Ottoman conquest in 1517, the Mamluks continued to wield political power in Egypt until they were destroyed in 1811 by the Egyptian ruler Muhammad Ali.

Minarets of Al-Azhar mosque and university. Al-Azhar is the oldest continuously functioning university in the world. It was founded in 970 A.D.

EGYPT

Modern

In 1798 Napoleon Bonaparte invaded Egypt in his attempt to cut Britain off from its colonial possessions. The French stay was ended by the British in 1801. However, the French invasion marked the first Egyptian encounter with a "modern" European power, an encounter which continued for a century and a half. The British evacuated in 1803. An Albanian contingent of the Ottoman army (for Egypt was still ostensibly part of the Ottoman Empire) asserted independence from Turkey, and one of its leaders, Muhammad Ali (1769-1849), gradually strengthened his own position. After becoming viceroy in 1805, Muhammad Ali established his rule over Egypt and created a dynasty. He attempted to modernize the administration and to industrialize the land using French advisors and technocrats. He created a modern army and navy, and embarked on his own program of territorial expansion. Southwards his control reached well beyond Khartoum, though largely limited to the Nile. Northwards he conquered Syria in 1831 and thus came into conflict with his suzerain, the Ottoman Sultan. The Egyptian armies were eventually stopped in south central Turkey. In 1841 the Treaty of London imposed Egyptian withdrawal from Syria, but Muhammad Ali's governorship was made hereditary.

British Protectorate

Muhammad Ali's successors had neither his vision nor his political acumen. Sa'id, the third successor (1854-63), signed the Suez Canal concession, the terms of which were highly disadvantageous to Egypt, and incurred the first foreign debt. Work on the canal began in 1859, and it was opened in 1869. Isma'il (1863-79) continued to borrow money to pay for a massive program of public works, irrigation canals, dams, bridges and lighthouses, a program which, while improving the infrastructure of the country, led to bankruptcy and consequently to foreign control. In 1879 Isma'il was deposed and his son Tawfiq (1879-92), a puppet maintained by Britain and France, found himself in the throes of an army revolt (1881-82) led by the nationalist leader Urabi. Tawfiq appealed for British help. British forces arrived in Alexandria in 1882 and began a military presence which persisited till 1955.

A nationalist movement arose at the turn of the century under Mustafa Kamil, and in 1907, the first political parties were created. World War I roused a great deal of discontent among most clases of Egyptians. Martial law was imposed and an official British protectorate was declared, thus severing Egypt's legal links with the Ottoman Empire. The peasants were conscripted, and their animals were confiscated for the war effort. Wilson's Fourteen Points encouraged the Egyptians to believe that self-determination was imminent. When none of the promises seemed forthcoming, a nationalist movement under the leadership of a former pro-British leader, Saad Zaghlul, arose. Zaghlul was deported by the British. In 1919 a massive revolt protested such actions and expressed solidarity with Zaghlul and his party, the Wafd.

Independent Kingdom

The British government eventually recognized the need for a change of policy. In 1922 the protectorate was ended and Egypt was declared an independent kingdom, though with reservations which included continued British military presence, the defence of Egypt against all foreign aggression or interference, direct or indirect, and the protection of foreign interests in Egypt. A constitution was promulgated in 1923, and the first parliament was elected with a Wafd majority of 188 seats out of 206. The next decade was dominated by a political struggle between King Fuad (a son of Isma'il and grandson of Muhammad Ali) who owed his throne to the British, the Wafd which sought complete independence from Britain, and Britain whose interests were safeguarded by the King. A

Cairo and the Nile at dusk. The capital of Egypt is the largest city in the Arab world.

major and emotional issue was the safeguarding of the Nile waters, and in 1929 an Anglo-Egyptian Nile Waters Agreement was signed. Related was the status of Sudan, which in 1899 had become an Anglo-Egyptian condominium, with Egypt as very much the junior partner in the arrangement. Egyptian nationalists sought a union with Sudan. The rise of Italian power, which was present in Italian Somaliland (the southern part of modern Somalia) and had designs on Ethiopia, was seen by both Egypt and Britain as posing a threat, and a new arrangement was reached in the 1936 Anglo-Egyptian treaty which was to have a twenty-year duration. The British occupation was formally terminated and protection of foreign interests became an Egyptian sovereign prerogative, but Britain continued to maintain troops in the Suez Canal Zone. In 1937 Egypt joined the League of Nations. The internal political struggle in Egypt continued from 1936 to 1952. Fuad's son, Faruq, was the king during this whole period, and he continued the palace's opposition to the Wafd. The defeat of the Egyptian army in the Palestine campaign of 1948-49 made the King's principal support, the army, turn against him and his blatant corruption.

Republic

In 1952 a group of Free Officers carried out a bloodless coup d'etat and deposed King Faruq. The following year Egypt was declared a republic under the presidency of General Muhammad Najib, who in 1954 was replaced by the real leader of the Free Officers movement, Colonel Jamal Abd al-Nasser. In October, 1954 an Anglo-Egyptian agreement was signed, whereby British troops would be withdrawn from the Suez Canal Zone within twenty months, and the Canal was recognized as "an integral part of Egypt." On July 26, 1956 President Nasser announced the nationalization of the Suez Canal Company, whose Board of Directors represented France, Britain, the Netherlands, the United States and Egypt. The nationalization was a means of financing the High Dam, and it followed by one week a withdrawal of a U.S. expressed intent to invest in the financing. In October, 1956 Egypt was invaded by Israel, Britain and France, with the intent of toppling Nasser and establishing an Anglo-French military presence in the Canal Zone. Their efforts failed, and under American and Soviet pressure the three aggressors withdrew from Egyptian territory. Nasser emerged as a greater hero in Egypt and throughout the Arab World. In 1959 a Nile Waters Agreement was concluded between Egypt and Sudan, the latter having become independent in 1956, which superseded the 1929 Agreement between Egypt and Britain.

UAR

In February, 1958 a union between Egypt and Syria formed the United Arab Republic. But the union was ill-planned and hasty, and Syria withdrew in September, 1961. For the next decade the name "United Arab Republic" meant only Egypt, and it was dropped in September, 1971 when the official name became the Arab Republic of Egypt. Nasser died in September, 1970 and was succeeded by Anwar Sadat. In September 1976, Sadat was reelected for a second six-year term.

In June, 1967 Israel launched an attack on Egypt and quickly occupied all of the Sinai Peninsula to the eastern bank of the Suez Canal, as well as the West Bank of Jordan and the Golan Heights of Syria. In October, 1973 Egypt and Syria attacked Israeli troops in occupation of their respective territories. Agreements reached in January, 1974 and September, 1975 reestablished Egyptian presence in a narrow zone east of the Suez Canal. The Canal, which had not been navigable since the 1967 Israeli attack, was cleared with U.S. assistance and reopened on June 5, 1975, the eighth anniversary of that attack. In November, 1977 President Sadat made a dramatic visit to Jerusalem in his search for a peaceful resolution of the conflict with Israel. As of January, 1978 no territorial rearrangements had been made.

Alexandria, second largest city of Egypt and a crowded summer resort.

GOVERNMENT AND SOCIETY

Administration

A Permanent Constitution of the Arab Republic of Egypt was approved by public referendum on September 11, 1971, replacing a provisional constitution promulgated after the 1952 coup and successive constitutions and amendments. Next to the president there are a vice president, a prime minister, 5 deputy prime ministers, and 26 ministers. The People's Asembly has 360 seats, of which 10 are appointed and 350 elected. There are three political parties: the Arab Socialist Party, the largest and a supporter of President Sadat; the Liberal Socialist Party, which favors a greater freedom for private enterprise; and the small National Progressive Unionist Party.

An Egyptian dancer in a modern interpretation of the ancient Egyptian "stick dance."

Education

Education in Egypt has a long and illustrious tradition. The world's oldest continuously functioning university is Al-Azhar University in Cairo, founded in 970 A.D., the only university in the world which has already celebrated its one-thousand-year anniversary. Egyptian teachers and professors are found throughout the Arab World. There are numerous learned societies and research institutes.

Education is compulsory through primary school. Upon successful completion of the final examination the student may enter preparatory school (grades 7 through 9). After that the choice is between a general secondary school (grades 10 through 12), a technical school (industrial, commercial or agricultural), or a special training institution administered by a ministry. There are eight universities with about 270,000 students.

Social Conditions

Very few attempts to deal with social problems were made by the governments before 1952. In the 1940s illiteracy was 75 percent, while today it is expected that every child will get some measure of education. Inroads have been made against disease. Bilharzia, which afflicted 60 percent of the population in 1952, fell to 30 percent a decade later, while trachoma which once struck 87 percent of the population fell to 25 percent. Potable water, once limited to the major cities, is now spreading to rural areas. However, because population growth keeps up with and sometimes surpasses economic growth, the general standard of living continues to be low. Despite the considerable and commendable health measures taken since 1952, a low standard of health continues as a major social problem. The emancipation of women which started with the 1919 revolution is now a palpable reality. Women are found in all professions and at all administrative levels.

Cultural Life

The cultural life clearly mirrors a historical continuity that goes back to the time of the pharoahs. Whether it be in folklore, art, music, or literature, the themes of ancient Egypt, Christian Egypt, and Muslim Egypt are overlain and interwoven to form a distinctive mosaic. Folk art has come into its own, and, while in the past only copies of Western art were admired, artists have become conscious of their own roots and have delved for inspiration into their own history. Festivals of art and of folk music and dancing abound. The government regularly sponsors tours of rural groups who demonstrate their talents to urban audiences, and vice versa, so that local talent receives exposure on the national scene.

The spread of television has given a boost to playwrights and to the theater in general, and the 1960s and 1970s have seen a flowering of cultural life. Egypt is by far the leading film maker in the Arab World. This tradition predates World War I but became more pronounced after the founding of Misr Studios in 1934. There are close to 20 film production companies.

Tourism

Whether the tourist is interested in archeology, early Christian churches, or Islamic art and architecture, these attractions are present in an enormous variety. The pyramids of Giza and of Saqqara and the tombs and temples of Luxor are complemented by the mosques and madrasas and mausolea of Cairo. The Mediterranean coast has sunny sandy beaches, while the Red Sea littoral provides a variety of aquatic sports from deep sea fishing to scuba diving among fabulous coral reefs. For the desert buff there are five major oases and numerous Coptic monasteries tucked away in remote places.

PROSPECTS

A perennial concern for Egyptian planners has been the inexorable increase in population without an equivalent increase in cultivated land. A reduction in the rate of population growth and the prospect of more efficient and cheaper desalination methods for urban inhabitants would be of considerable help toward improving the well-being of the individual Egyptian. A significant drain on the national economy are the military expenditures necessitated by the "no peace" situation in the Middle East. If the promise of discovering additional and substantial oil deposits is realized, it will be possible to divert precious funds from the purchase of energy to social needs. The burgeoning tourist business is of considerable help, as are the increasing revenues from the Suez Canal. Still, the population is large and impoverished. A decrease in the dependence on agricultural products with a concomitant increase in industrial diversification and a streamlining of services will help toward achieving a higher level of production and consumption, and, therefore, a higher standard of living.

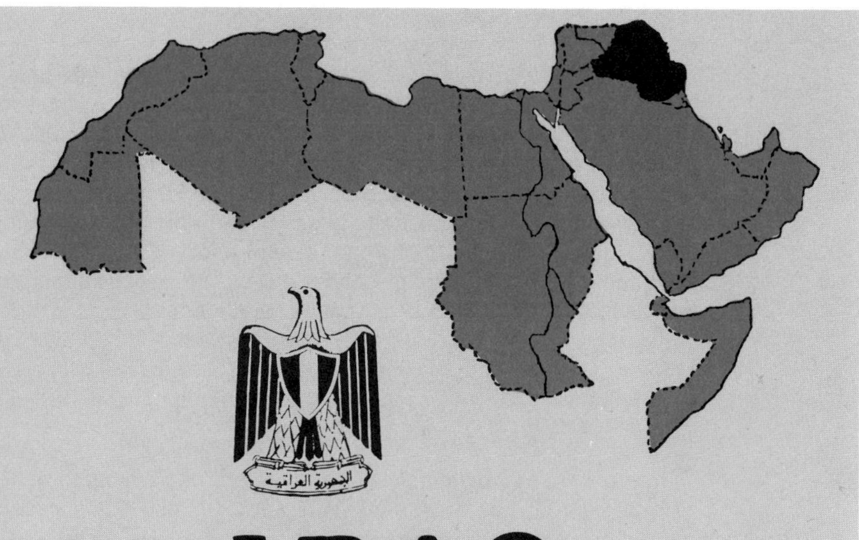

IRAQ

الجمهورية العراقية

PROFILE

Official Name: The Iraqi Republic (Al-Jumhuriyyah al-Iraqiyyah)

Head of State: Ahmad Hassan al-Bakr

Government: Republic

Area: 175,000 sq. mi. (= California)

Population: 12,000,000

Population Density: 68/sq. mi.

Capital: Baghdad (2,000,000)

Other Urban Centers: Basra, Mosul, Kirkuk, Sulaimaniya

National Holiday: July 14

Currency: Iraqi Dinar (1 ID = $3.40)

Press: Dailies: Al-Thawra, Al-Jumhuriyya; Baghdad Observer (English)

Radio and Television: Transmissions in Arabic and English, short wave; six television channels

Sites of Interest: Archeological sites of Babylon, Nineveh, Ur and many sites of Islamic and Persian origins

Main Airports: Baghdad, Basra

Main Seaport: Basra

Date of Joining the United Nations: December 21, 1945

Date of Joining the Arab League: December 22, 1945

IRAQ

INTRODUCTION

The Republic of Iraq lies at the northeastern extremity of the Arab world. Modern Iraq corresponds to the area known as Mesopotamia (from the Greek: the Land between the Two Rivers). The oldest civilizations known to man grew on the shores of these two rivers—the Tigris and the Euphrates. Iraq's heritage includes the Sumerians, Babylonians, and Assyrians. The greatest city of antiquity, Babylon, and its successor, Baghdad, were centers of power and culture for most of history's course. Baghdad was the center of the Abbasid Caliphate, whose culture radiated into Asia, Africa and Europe during the Middle Ages.

PHYSICAL GEOGRAPHY

Iraq covers approximately 175,000 square miles in southwestern Asia (roughly the size of California). It is approximately 620 miles long and 450 miles wide. Its neighbors are Turkey (north), Iran (east), the Arabian Gulf, Saudi Arabia and Kuwait (south), and Syria, Jordan and northeastern Saudi Arabia (west).

Topography

Iraq extends over four major geographic regions, differing in climate, social composition and the availability of water: the Southern Plains, the Upper Plain, the mountainous region of Kurdistan and the western desert.

The Southern Plains cover the area between the Tigris and Euphrates Rivers; it extends from the Arabian Gulf to a point just north of Baghdad. Because of limited rainfall, cultivation is almost entirely dependent on irrigation.

The upper plains, north of Baghdad to the northwest of the Zagros Mountains, tend to be rolling and grassy. The potentially rich farmland is solely dependent on rainfall.

The mountain region occupies the northeastern part of the country and contains peaks which rise up to 12,000 feet. Gorges of several rivers flow into the Tigris, among them the Great and Little Zab and the Diyala. The mountains are barren and scantily wooded while the low and middle slopes and valleys are fertile and provide good pasture.

The desert region lies on the west of the Euphrates River. It joins the great Syrian Desert (*Badiyat ash-sham*).

Climate

Summer is overwhelmingly hot and dry. Temperatures of over 100°F from June to September cause many inhabitants to retire to underground rooms during the day. Winter may be surprisingly cold; frost, though very rare at Basra, can be severe in the north. Spring and autumn are moderate, especially in the north. December to February are the wettest months. The average yearly rainfall in Baghdad is 5.5 inches, in Basra 7.3 inches, in Mosul (in the north) 15.1 inches.

Drainage

The Tigris, 1,156 miles in length, rises in Turkey and is joined by large tributaries in both Turkey and Iraq. Over the years its course has been altered by frequent flooding. The Tigris is navigable all year round as far as Baghdad by shallow draft streams; in high water season smaller craft can get as far north as Mosul. The Euphrates, 1,420 miles in length, also rises in Turkey but flows first through Syria. Wider than the Tigris, it carries less water and is a slower flowing, more meandering river. The two rivers join at Qurna, 140 miles northwest of Basra, to form the stream known as Shat al-Arab which travels for 115 miles before emptying into the Arabian Gulf.

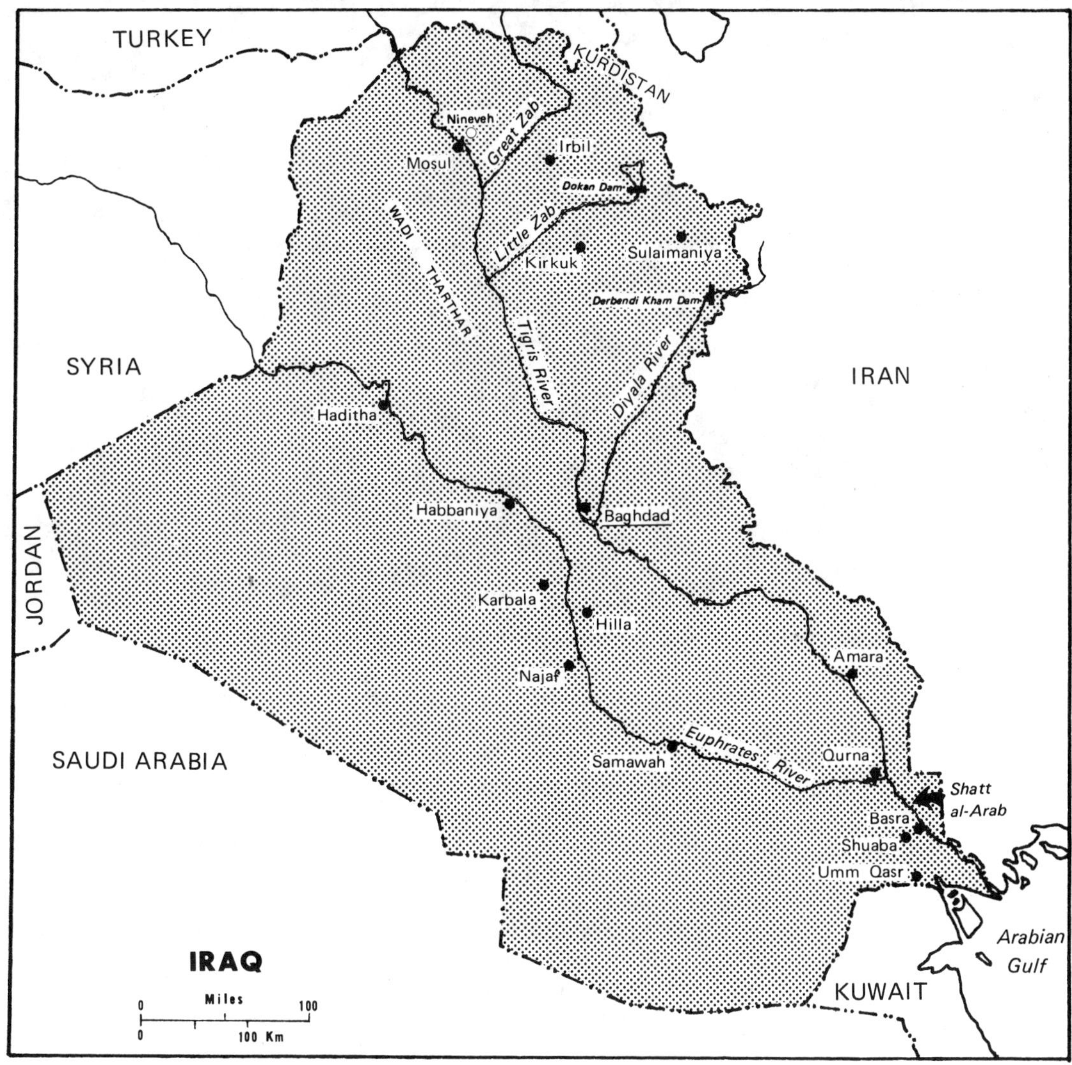

Much of Iraqi life revolves around these two rivers and their tributaries. The river basins are home for most of the population. Iraqis rarely refer to the Tigris and the Euphrates separately but speak of al-Rafidayn, a collective noun meaning two rivers. The extreme annual variations in flow result in years of drought and years of flood. The Tigris reaches its maximum in April, the Euphrates in May, too late for the winter crops and too early for the maturing summer crops. Since 1956 the government has built numerous barrages—dams such as Wadi Tharar, Dokan, Derbendi Kham and Halsaniya—to control the flood waters and regulate irrigation.

HUMAN GEOGRAPHY

People

The population is about 12 million with an annual growth rate of approximately 3 percent. Density averages 55 persons per square mile. About 60 percent live under essentially rural conditions and 35 percent are classified as urban dwellers. Three-fourths of the people think of themselves as Arabs. Between 15 and 20 percent are Kurds, the largest ethnic minority residing mainly in the northern part of the country. Smaller minorities include Turkomans, Persians and Lurs. Emigration is relatively low and principally to neighboring Kuwait, where work is available in the oil industry.

Baghdad on the Tigris has grown to a sprawling metropolis of more than 2 million inhabitants

Arabic is the official language, used by nearly 80 percent of the population. Kurdish and dialects of Turkism are spoken in the north, while variants of Persian are spoken by tribesmen in the east.

Religion

Islam is the predominant religion encompassing 96 percent of the population. The Muslims in Iraq are divided into two sects, the Sunni and the Shi'a. The Sunni are found mainly in the north and central portions; the Shi'a are mainly in the south central and southern parts of the country. Approximately 400,000 persons (4 percent) are non-Muslim, of whom some 300,000 are Christians; the remainder are Yezidis, Jews and Sabeans, plus a small group of Bahais.

Urban Centers

Baghdad is the capital and the largest town. It is a modern cosmopolitan center with over 2 million inhabitants. Over 60 percent of the industrial establishments are located there. Other towns are Basra (350,000), Kirkuk (200,000) and Mosul (250,000).

ECONOMY

Agriculture

Over two thirds of the population derive their income from agriculture and animal husbandry (sheep, goats and cattle). While about one third of Iraq is fit for cultivation, less than 50 percent of this area is utilized.

Before July 14, 1958, absentee landlords controlled most of the cultivable land. In September, 1958, a land reform law limited landholding to a maximum of 600 acres of well-irrigated land or 1,200 acres of rain-dependent land. The excess land was distributed to landless peasants. In 1970 landholding was limited to 500 acres irrespective of the type of land. The present government has enacted laws 66 and 67 to provide the machinery and structure for cooperative societies and collective farms. By the end of 1974 there were 1,400 cooperatives with 197,000 members.

Dates are the main crop. Iraq has an 80 percent share of total world production; its 18,000,000 palm trees produce about 140,000 tons annually. Date exports bring in $16-20 million annually.

Barley and wheat are grown both in rainfed and irrigated zones. Rice and cotton are grown in the irrigated zones. Other crops include tobacco, fruit and nuts.

Excluding the oil industry, the industrial sector still is underdeveloped and contributes 10-15 percent of the gross national product. Most industries are small. Out of 148,008 industrial establishments in 1968, only 1,318 employed ten persons or more.

Industry

Until recently government policy emphasized light industry based upon existing raw materials such as food processing, textiles, cigarettes and shoes. The new development plan for 1976-1980, however, includes provisions for steel, iron and petrochemicals. The petrochemical industry will receive $1.875 billion more than 25 percent of the total industrial quota. The processing of fertilizers, plastics, synthetic fibers and dyestuffs are to be developed. Two large complexes are planned for the Basra region at a cost of $400 million.

Oil

Oil is Iraq's largest industry, the mainstay of the economy and principal source of capital for state and municipal programs. In 1974 it provided over 80 percent of foreign earnings and represented over 40 percent of the gross national product.

Iraq ranks eighth in world production and fourth in Middle East production. In 1974 Iraq produced 93 million tons. The proven reserve is estimated at 31,500 billion barrels—the fourth largest proven reserve in the Middle East. The total refining capacity is 9.39 million tons a year and is expected to double over the next few years.

Until 1972 the oil industry was exclusively in foreign hands: the Iraq Petroleum Company (IPC) and its associated companies controlled the industry through concessions given to them in the 1920s and 30s, a time when Iraq was under British influence. In June, 1972, the government nationalized Iraq Petroleum Company and in October, 1973, it nationalized the American, Dutch and Gulbenkian shares in Basra Petroleum Co., an IPC associate. Iraq now controls about 80 percent of its oil resources and the government is in the process of taking over the rest.

Transportation

The two raillines, totalling 1,700 miles, are government owned. A standard gauge runs from the Arabian Gulf at Umm Qasr to the northwestern border and links the nation to Europe via the Syrian and Turkish systems. A narrow gauge line from Irbil in the northeast runs through Baghdad and ends at Basra near the Arabian Gulf Coast.

Iraq's two international airports are located in Baghdad and Basra; other airfields are at Mosul and Kirkuk. Basra is also the main seaport. Umm Qasr, near Kuwait, is being developed as a second port for ocean-going traffic.

Artist's conception of Iraq's social revolution dominates a Baghdad square.

IRAQ

HISTORY

Iraq was probably the earliest center of civilization. With Egypt, Mesopotamia shares the distinction of being the parent of succeeding civilizations. The Sumerians flourished in the Land between the Two Rivers around 3,000 BC. They are credited with the earliest judicial system and schools, as well as the invention of writing and the wheel. Their literature and art forms, which were inherited and modified by the Babylonians, Assyrians and Hittites, have had an important influence on the course of world civilizations.

The Akkadians, a Semitic people, dominated Mesopotamia and the area beyond the two rivers early in the Third Millenium. The Old Babylonian Dynasty in the Second Millenium is most famous for Hammurabi whose code of laws is considered one of the earliest in history.

Assyrians

The vast empire of the Assyrians of northern Iraq extended into Egypt. From their capital at Nineveh their armies roamed over the Near East for more than two centuries. They were succeeded by the Neo-Babylonian (or Chaldean) Dynasty based in the great city of Babylon renowned for its hanging gardens. But soon it was overrun by the Persians, who established an empire in 538 BC that extended from Egypt to India.

Alexander the Great destroyed the Persian Empire in the fourth century. Upon his death, Mesopotamia became a part of the Hellenistic Seleucid Kingdom based in Syria and then fell, first to the Parthians and later to the Sassanids. Both dynasties ruled from Persia until the Arab conquest of the seventh century.

Abbasid Empire

Iraq then became the center of the Abbasid Empire (750-1258 AD). By the time of Harun al-Rashid and Mamun, Baghdad had grown into an international center of knowledge and trade. Invading Mongolian armies in 1258 destroyed Baghdad and ruined the country's irrigation system, libraries and works of art.

Between 1535 and World War I, Iraq was part of the Ottoman Empire and development came to a standstill. After British wartime occupation, Iraq became a British mandated territory. Independence in 1932 merely altered the form of British influence; the 1930 treaty provided full consultation in foreign affairs and the maintenance of air bases at Habbaniya and Shuaba.

On July 14, 1958 a military coup ended the monarchy and marked the start of the republican regime. The next decade brought several coups and countercoups.

Baath Party

This period ended on July 17, 1968, when the Baath Party came to power. Several attempts to oust the Baath Party failed. In July, 1973, a National Front was formed by the Baath and the Iraq Communist Party. In March, 1975, Iraq and Iran settled their long border dispute and the agreement also brought an end to Iranian support of the Kurdish rebellion in Iraq.

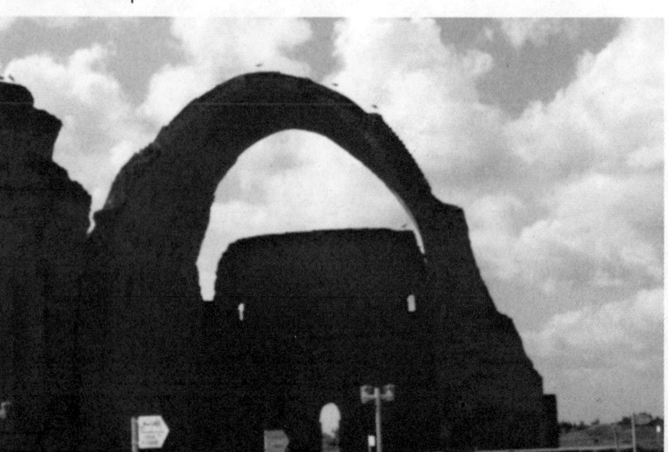

The arch of Ctesiphon, built in the fourth century A.D., is the longest self-sustaining brick arch in the world.

GOVERNMENT AND SOCIETY

Administration

The present Provisional Constitution (adopted in July, 1970) affirms the 14 man Revolutionary Command Council (RCC) as the Supreme legislative and decision making body. Through it the Baath Party has ruled Iraq since 1968. The president is chief of state and supreme commander of the armed forces and is elected by a two-thirds majority of the RCC. The prime minister presides over the Council of Ministers which is appointed by RCC and has administrative and legislative responsibilities. Legislation is also enacted by decree by the RCC. The Provisional Constitution calls for the establishment of a national assembly, but to date no such body has been formed.

Health

The Ministry of Health is faced with shortage of medical personnel and facilities. Certain steps are being taken to correct the situation. In 1958, Iraq had only one college of medicine; it graduated about 30 doctors a year. Today there are three colleges of medicine located in Baghdad, Mosul and Basra, graduating over 300 doctors a year. Two more colleges are planned, one at al-Mustinsiyrah University in Baghdad and the other in Sulaimaniya. The remote and rural areas suffer from severe shortages of doctors and medical facilities. In the last decade the government has enacted several laws requiring new doctors to serve a number of years outside the capital before they are permitted to practice in Baghdad.

Education

With the establishment of the republican regime in 1958 the development and expansion in educational facilities was rapid. The educational budget rose from $43.2 million in 1958 to $89.7 million in 1962. Succeeding years brought even greater increases and in 1974 the figure jumped to $400 million. The five-year plan ending in 1980 allocated $3 billion for educational development.

There are six universities: Baghdad (1956), Basra (1967), Mosul (1967), Sulaimaniyh (1971), Mustansiyrah (1963), and the technological university (1974). Total enrollment was over 49,194 in 1972-73. About 7,000 Iraqi students study abroad. More than half of them have government scholarships.

The twin golden domes of the Kadhimain mosque in Baghdad.

Vocational education on both primary and secondary levels is regarded as of much importance. Various types of technical vocational schools have been opened to provide the urgent need for developing skilled labor and technicians. The enrollment in vocational schools in 1974-75 was 21,021, eight times that of 1958. However, female education is proceeding at a much slower rate than the male. Only one-fourth of the total enrollment in secondary schools was female in 1970-71.

Mass Communication

Broadcasting is controlled by the government. In 1973 the country had 17 transmitters of which four were medium wave and the rest were shortwave. In 1957 Iraq became the first country in the Middle East to have television. At the present time there are six operating stations (Mosul, Kirkuk, Baghdad, Amara, Samawa and Basra). Stations at Hilla and Haditha are planned.

Tourism

Iraq's many past civilizations—Sumerian, Akkadian, Babylonian, Persian, and Muslim—have each left its traces. Artifacts representing different aspects of these civilizations are contained in twelve museums scattered throughout the country. The Baghdad museum, one of the best museums in the Middle East, holds antiquities from the early Stone Age to the beginning of the seventeenth century AD including Islamic objects in almost uninterrupted sequence. Historical and archeological sites are abundant. The site of Babylon displays some of the features of one of the largest cities of antiquity. The site of Nineveh in the northern city of Mosul and of nearby Khorsabad testifies to the greatness of the ancient Assyrian Empire. Baghdad, Karbala and Najaf contain shrines of great importance and beauty.

PROSPECTS

Iraq has a great potential for growth with its agricultural wealth, water supplies and mineral resources. The government is committed to economic development and the modernization of the social, cultural, and administrative institutions. Given a period of stability and freedom from internal and international turmoil, the standard of living in Iraq, in spite of the fast growth of population, will be much higher in the foreseeable future.

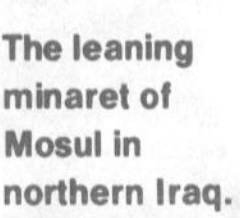

The leaning minaret of Mosul in northern Iraq.

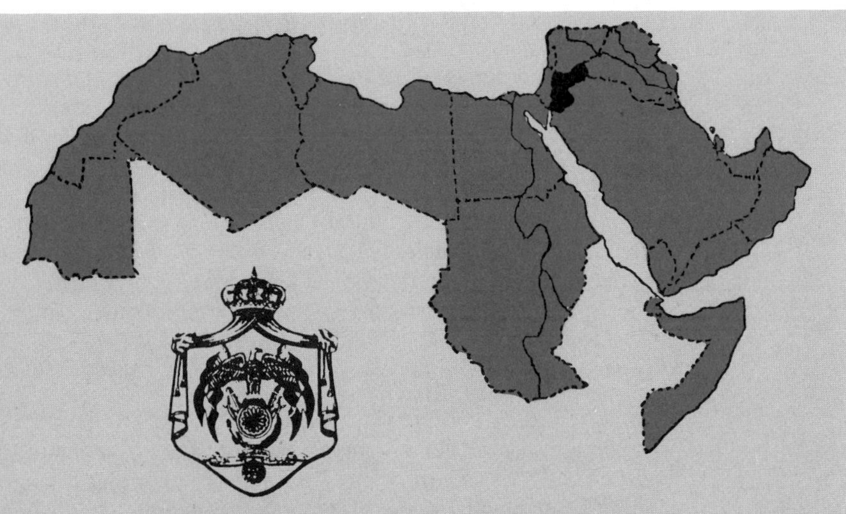

JORDAN

المملكة الاردنية الهاشمية

PROFILE

Official Name: The Hashemite Kingdom of Jordan (Al-Mamlakah al-Urduniyyah al-Hashimiyyah)

Head of State: H. M. King Hussein bin Talal

Government: Constitutional Monarchy

Area: 36,715 sq. mi. (=Indiana)

Population: 1.7 million (est. 1971, not including West Bank)

Population Density: about 50/sq. mi.

Capital: Amman (750,000)

Other Urban Centers: Irbid, Salt, Zarqa, Maan, Aqaba

National Holiday: May 25

Currency: Jordanian Dinar (1 JD=$3.02)

Press: Al-Dustur, Al-Rai (daily) and many other periodicals

Radio & Television: Radio broadcasts in Arabic and English

Sites of Interest: Petra, Jarash, the Dead Sea, Karak, Wadi Rum, Aqaba

Main Airports: Amman, Aqaba

Main Seaports: Aqaba

Date of Joining the United Nations: December 14, 1945

Date of Joining the Arab League: March 22, 1945

JORDAN

INTRODUCTION

The land of Jordan is replete with relics of past rules and memorials of great empires. Historical sites from the days of Hellenic, Roman, Islamic, Ottoman, and Arabic influences confirm its crucial role throughout civilization. Jordan is not a young state whose precarious political and economic existence makes it insignificant to international affairs. Because of its historical and cultural value and its strategic position in the Arab world (most Middle East capitals are within a 1,000-mile radius from Amman), events in Jordan can have worldwide repercussions. In recent history, Jordan has been in the limelight of international politics, closely watched by neighboring countries and superpowers alike.

PHYSICAL GEOGRAPHY

Topography

The topography provides many contrasting features within a relatively small area (36,715 square miles). There are three major distinguishable regions. The highlands region of the north and northeast is mountainous and rocky. The terrain is often green and cultivable. With a climate influenced by the Mediterranean Sea, the area enjoys Jordan's highest level of rainfall—an average of 16 inches per year. The temperature is moderate in the summer and cool in the winter.

The eastern and southeastern steppes and desert lands comprise about 80 percent of the total land area. Rainfall averages five inches in the steppes and declines to less than one inch at the eastern fringe. Except for a few rainy days between November and February, the region is sunny and dry. Summer, especially the month of August, brings the hottest days.

Dead Sea

The western region encompasses the deepest spot on earth. The Dead Sea occupies the central portion of the rift that forms the Jordan-Dead Sea-Wadi Araba valley between two blocks of highlands. Its surface is 1,290 feet below sea level; its bottom, in the larger northern basin, is 2,598 feet below sea level. This area, often referred to as the Ghor, has a temperature pattern unique in the country. The average summer high is more than 96°F. In January, the coldest month, the temperature seldom falls below 45°F.

Camels and riders in Wadi Rum in the south of Jordan

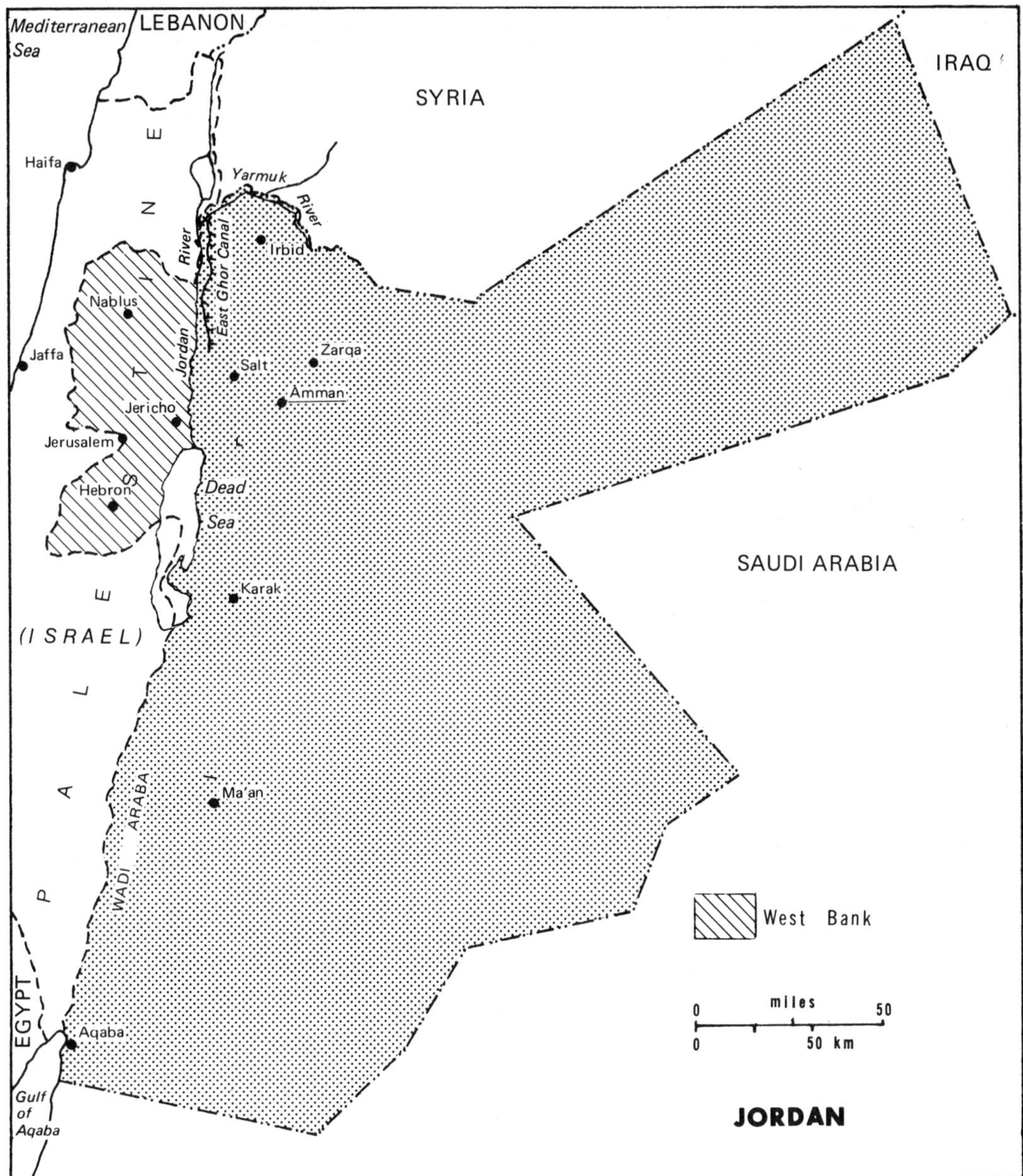

HUMAN GEOGRAPHY

Archaeological investigations indicate that Jordan has been populated from the earliest prehistoric times and subjected to numerous influences, the most lasting of which began in the seventh century with the Arab-Islamic integration.

Population

The population is concentrated in the north and west. Because of economics and climate, more than 96 percent of the population lives on about 24 percent of the land. Population figures have tripled in recent times because of the unification of the East and West Banks in 1950 and the influx of Palestinian refugees. In one year alone 1.5 million refugees entered Jordan. A 1971 estimate placed 1.7 million in the East Bank and 700,000 in the West Bank.

Urbanization

The urban segment (settlements of 10,000 or more, excluding Palestine refugee camps) has increased dramatically. The Amman-Zarqa urban area grew from 30,000 in 1947 to nearly 744,000 in 1971. About

Amman, capital of Jordan, with the Roman amphitheater in the foreground.

60 percent of the people were classified as urban dwellers in 1971. Much of the increase is due to migrations from rural areas in search of jobs and better economic prospects. Amman is the seat of economic, trade, educational and industrial institutions as well as the center of administration, politics and finance.

Villages and small towns are spread throughout the highlands where rainfall supports cultivation. The East and West Banks contain more than a thousand villages, but less than one hundred of them have 2,000 or more inhabitants. The largest concentration of villages is in the northern province around Irbid. The rural population was estimated at 37 percent in 1971.

Bedouin

The smallest population group (3 percent) are the nomadic Bedouins, who live in goat-hair tents and move in the steppes with their livestock in search of water and pasture. Their number is steadily declining as they become semi-sedentary in response to government programs—schools, roads, water supplies, etc.

Religion and Language

More than 85 percent of Jordanians are Sunni Muslims. Arabic is the official language and is spoken by nearly the entire population. The Christian minority is estimated at 12 to 15 percent. About half of these follow the Greek Orthodox church while the rest are divided among Roman Catholic, Greek Catholic (Melkites), and a small number of Protestant denominations.

Minorities

There is a high degree of physical and ethnic homogeneity. Ethnic and linguistic minorities are numerically insignificant. One exception is the Circassians who number about 12,000. The Circassians are Sunni Muslims who came to the Transjordan in the 1870's after the Russian conquest of the Caucasus.

Minorities are usually represented in the political leadership. A proportionate number of Christians and Circassians are elected to the House of Deputies, and one Circassian and two Christian Arabs are usually appointed to the Cabinet. Members of the Circassians have occupied the position of prime minister as well as chief of staff of the armed services.

ECONOMY

Direct aid from Arab and other foreign countries is the largest cash input into the Jordanian economy. The services sector, including commerce and tourism, is the most important domestic source of income. Remittances by Jordanian citizens working abroad, especially in oil-producing countries, provide another major source.

Agriculture

Agriculture, mining, and industry contribute modestly, but their impact and significance are growing. Jordan traditionally has been considered an agricultural society. This description is no longer valid, because the services sector constitutes about 66 percent of the gross national product (GNP). Agricultural workers make up no more than 35 percent of the total work force, and agricultural output in relation to GNP ranges between 15 and 18 percent.

Agricultural production is highly influenced by variations in rainfall. Less than 6 percent of the land is irrigated. Most of the farmlands are concentrated in the north and northwestern highlands and some parts of the Ghor area. Extreme fluctuations in rainfall particularly affect the cereal and olive crops. For example, in 1969 the cereals crop yielded about 300,000 tons. It dropped to 60,000 the next year, increased to 200,000 the following two years and then returned to 60,000 in 1973.

Vegetable crops are less susceptible to rainfall variations because about half of the crop is grown on irrigated land. Vegetables, fruits and citrus products are exported to neighboring Arab countries. Vegetables and fruits constitute the largest portion of Jordanian exports, ranging between 31 and 47 percent of the total export in the last decade.

Irrigation

Most agricultural production depends upon dry farming. Irrigation methods and soil and water conservation programs have been given high priority. The East Ghor Canal diverted waters from the Yarmouk River to irrigate 30,000 acres in the Jordan Valley by gravity flow. The Canal is the first stage of a massive scheme to irrigate 200,000 acres by harnessing the Yarmouk. Jordan has high hopes in the project, which will cost an estimated $180 million. Some parts of the construction were destroyed by Israeli air raids, but after each raid Jordanian workers quickly restored the damaged portions.

There is also a search for underground water and ways to bring it to the surface with artesian wells. Minor dams gather water during the rainy season. Nine such reservoirs were constructed between 1962 and 1970 with a total capacity of 238 million cubic feet.

The government has employed various means to increase agricultural production. By 1972 about 3,500 tractors were used in the fields. Legislative acts provide marketing services to farmers and agricultural loans. Cooperatives are encouraged. Agricultural vocational schools have been established and expanded.

Industry is still in the infant stage. Most businesses are small-scale, family-owned, and rely on simple technology and manual labor. About 90 percent employ nine workers or less. Industrial progress is beset with the same problems that confront most developing nations. Raw materials, capital, and technical expertise are scarce. The domestic consumer market is small. Local industries must compete with imports that often have higher quality and lower prices.

Phosphate

Phosphate mining, petroleum refining, tanning, and the manufacture of cement and cigarettes are the major industries. Despite extensive exploration, no oil has been discovered in Jordan.

Phosphate was discovered in the thirties, but serious production and marketing did not begin until 20 years later. The port of Aqaba was expanded and modernized with the help of foreign loans. As the world demand for phosphate increased, phosphate exports more than tripled in the sixties and seventies to exceed a million tons. Phosphate exports netted about $50 million in 1974. Jordan has about 300 million tons of reserves. An agreement has been signed with U. S. corporations to build a multimillion-dollar chemical fertilizer plant with a capability of producing $100 million worth of exports annually. This would make Jordan competitive in the international market and reduce its dependence on foreign aid.

HISTORY

Nabateans

As an independent state, Jordan is a recent development. In biblical time, this area was referred to as Moab and Edom. In the sixth century B.C., the Nabateans, an Arabian tribe, established a state centered on the city of Petra, south of the Dead Sea. Under the rule of the Syrian Seleucids (third and second centuries B.C.) the northern part of the country was thriving with urban centers such as Philadelphia (modern Amman) and Gerasa (modern Jarash). In the first century B.C., the Nabateans extended their influence over most of present-day Jordan and Syria until Roman rule gradually took hold of the whole area of the Eastern Mediterranean. In Byzantine times, the Ghassanids ruled the area from the fifth century A.D. until the coming of Islam.

Arab period

Ottoman period

The Arab-Islamic integration of the territory in the seventh century gave Jordan its prevailing cultural and religious life (Arabism and Islam). In 1516, Jordan fell under Ottoman rule with the rest of geographic Syria (Syria, Lebanon, Palestine, and Jordan). For four hundred years the Ottoman Empire dominated and oppressed most of the Arab world, leaving an indelible mark on Arab society. The Arab revolution for independence from Ottoman rule during World War I and the Arab alliance with the West against the German-Turkish forces brought Jordan with the other parts of geographic Syria under British and French colonial rule. Consequently, the boundaries of Transjordan were delineated in the 1920's and the Jordanian political entity emerged.

Modern period

The Palestine conflict in 1947 and the establishment of Israel had a profound effect on the territory, population, economy, and politics of Jordan. In 1950, about 2,165 square miles of the eastern part of Palestine united with Transjordan. This merger, in addition to the influx of Palestinian refugees from areas conquered by the Israelis, tripled the population of Jordan in less than one year. Traditional patterns of trade and transport were shattered when access to Mediterranean seaports in Palestine, especially Haifa and Jaffa, was lost. Most trade was diverted through Aqaba, a fast-expanding port on the northeastern tip of the Gulf of Aqaba; some was channeled through Beirut, Lebanon, and Latakia, Syria.

In spite of increased defense costs after 1948, Jordan achieved a high rate of economic development and was recognized as one of the fastest-growing economies in the Third World. The 1967 war and the Israeli occupation of the West Bank were severe political and economic blows. Loss of tourism, shrinkage of markets, more Palestinian refugees, and greater defense needs resulted.

West Bank

The future of Jordan on the West Bank is questionable after the recognition of the Palestine Liberation Organization (PLO) as the representative of the Palestinian people. The Rabat Summit Conference of Arab states (October, 1974) further legitimized the position of the PLO within the Palestinian communities under Israeli occupation or in the Arab world. Jordan is trying to adjust her political and economic situation to recognize the possible permanent loss of the West Bank.

GOVERNMENT AND SOCIETY

Administration

Jordan is a constitutional monarchy with extensive powers in the king's hands. The 1952 constitution established the principle of executive responsibility to Parliament. Legislation, which can be vetoed by the king, is the function of Parliament, which can overrule a veto with a two-thirds majority. An independent judiciary interprets the constitution and other legislation.

Although political forms often do not reflect the dynamics of political life in a developing country, in Jordan the evolution of political, military and bureaucratic structures has been constrained by tribal, religious and historical traditions. These constraints have lent stability and resilience in an area of the world identified with political upheaval and dramatic change.

Education

Educational opportunities in Jordan have increased phenomenally since 1951. Today one person in four is a student. Free education is universal at the elementary and preparatory levels and offered to qualified students at the secondary stage. Schools have been established in many communities for the first time, and university education is available to more people through the University of Jordan and a governmental program of grants and scholarships. About 27,000 Jordanians study abroad, excluding those in the United States; most of them are at universities in Syria, Lebanon or Egypt. Those in the U. S. number 1500.

Petra, the rose-red city of the ancient Nabateans who flourished in the 1st century B.C.

The increase in education resulted in far-reaching changes in society. The Ministry of Education had an eight percent share of the entire national budget from 1963-73. According to a 1972 survey by the Department of Statistics, illiteracy was reduced to 41 percent against 67.5 percent in 1961. Especially noteworthy are the extension of educational opportunities to women and the ensuing changes in attitudes and societal values that opened the way for women to compete in the job market and in the political arena.

Transportation

Transportation in Jordan depends on a network of roads linking the capital, Amman, with the port of Aqaba on the Red Sea, and with Syria and Lebanon. Transit trade is carried on the Beirut-Amman and Amman-Baghdad highways.

The railway traversing the country from north to south was originally built to transport pilgrims from Damascus to Medina. Only the segment within Jordan is now in operation.

The state airline has grown rapidly in recent years, operating routes to Arab capitals and beyond. A New York-Amman service was initiated in 1977.

Health

Jordan has a national health insurance program covering medical, dental, and eye care at a modest cost. Hospitals in Amman, Irbid, Karak, and As-Salt provide free services to the indigent. The Ministry of Social Affairs supervises more than 350 social and charitable organizations and administers a welfare program.

Cultural life

Private and government efforts have been made to encourage and foster the arts. Folk art survives in tapestry work, leather, ceramics, and other handcrafts. A national troupe has been formed to perform folk dances. There are several newspapers and magazines in Jordan. The government runs radio and television stations.

PROSPECTS

The prospects for Jordan are closely linked with the Arab-Israeli conflict. The danger of war is a constant threat. The government, however, is introducing improvements in social services and undertaking many urban and rural projects of development, in spite of the scarcity of resources.

Further expansion and restoration of the once thriving tourist trade depend on the prospects for peace in the area.

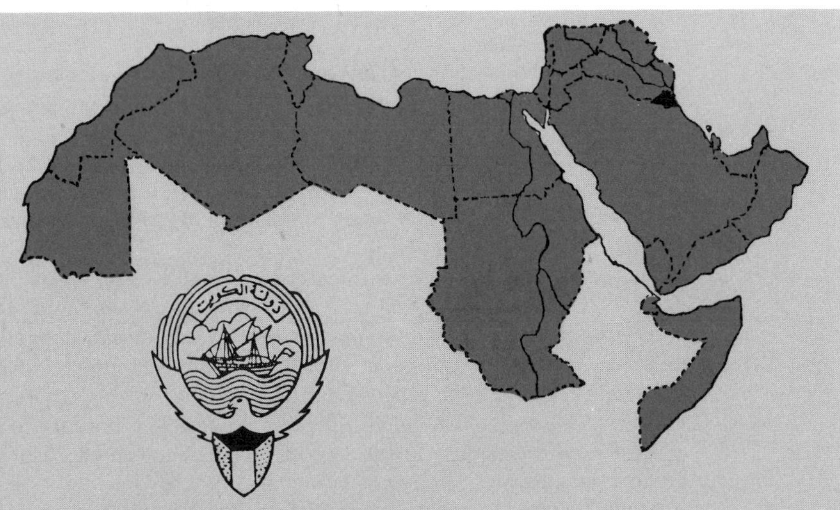

KUWAIT

دولة الكويت

PROFILE

Official Name: State of Kuwait (Dawlat al-Kuwait)

Head of State: Emir Sabah al-Salem al-Sabah

Government: Emirate

Area: 7780 sq. mi. (smaller than New Jersey)

Population: 1,100,000

Population Density: 140/sq. mi.

Capital: Kuwait City (78,000)

Other Urban Centers: Hawalli, Salimiyah

National Holiday: February 25

Currency: Kuwaiti Dinar (1 KD = $3.45)

Press: Important dailies: Al-Qabas, Al-Rai al-'Am, Al-Siyasah

Radio and Television: Radio programs in Arabic, English and Urdu. Color television.

Sites of Interest: Archeological remains of ancient civilization on Failakah Island; Kuwait Museum.

Main Airport: Kuwait

Main Seaport: Kuwait

Date of Joining the United Nations: May 14, 1963

Date of Joining the Arab League: July 20, 1961

INTRODUCTION

Kuwait is something of an anomaly in the developing world: its revenues are much larger than its expenditures. The population of 1.1 million (1976) is not large enough to absorb the colossal amount of money that Kuwait receives for its oil exports. Despite a cradle-to-grave welfare system, guaranteed employment, and free education and health services, the country still ends up with a multi-billion dollar annual surplus.

The petroleum cornucopia does not solve all Kuwait's problems. It is still faced with a shortage of trained personnel, a need which has been filled primarily by an influx of foreigners. While the employment of outsiders solves the immediate problem, it poses the more complex question of how to keep Kuwaiti identity in a state in which more than half the members are non-Kuwaiti. Kuwait also needs to prepare for the day when the oil runs out. Apart from oil, Kuwait is extremely resource poor and must diversify the economy to insure a secure future.

Kuwait is more fortunate than most developing countries in possessing vast oil reserves and a small population, but Kuwaitis, too, are having to cope with the problems and changes that an accelerated rate of growth inevitably brings.

PHYSICAL GEOGRAPHY

Climate

Kuwait is a small state with an area of 7780 square miles (smaller than New Jersey) and occupies a strategic position on the northwest corner of the Arabian Gulf. It has a rather compact shape and shares borders with Iraq and Saudi Arabia. It lies on a gently sloping coastal plain between 28° and 30° north of the equator. Kuwaiti sovereignity also encompasses several offshore islands with a total area of some 300 square miles. An important geographic asset is the Bay of Kuwait, one of the Gulf's finest natural harbors.

Kuwait is a tropical desert; hot, dusty and arid. Annual precipitation amounts to no more than 5-10 inches anywhere in the country. The plain rises gradually from the coast, reaching an elevation of 900 feet along the ridges of the western border. There is little vegetation, except for marsh plants along the shore and some grasses inland.

HUMAN GEOGRAPHY

Immigrant Population

The indigenous people are of predominantly Arab stock with some mixture of African and Persian elements. The oil boom has, however, affected the demographics of Kuwait to a considerable extent. By 1962, foreign-born immigrants accounted for more than half of the population, reaching 54.8 percent in 1974. In 1975 the figure was 52.6 percent. Between 1965 and 1975, the total population increased by 100 percent, jumping from 467,000 to one million. This phenomenal growth rate is attributable about equally to natural increase and to further foreign immigration. Although these immigrants are primarily easily integrated Muslim Arabs, others such as Pakistanis, Iranians, and Westerners are not uncommon.

Vital Statistics

The mid-1976 population was estimated at 1.1 million. The birth rate is 45 per thousand, and the death rate is a low 8 per thousand. The annual rate of growth is 5.9 percent, which means that the estimated in-migration rate is 22 per thousand, or about half the birth rate. If this combination is maintained, the population will double in 12 years and will

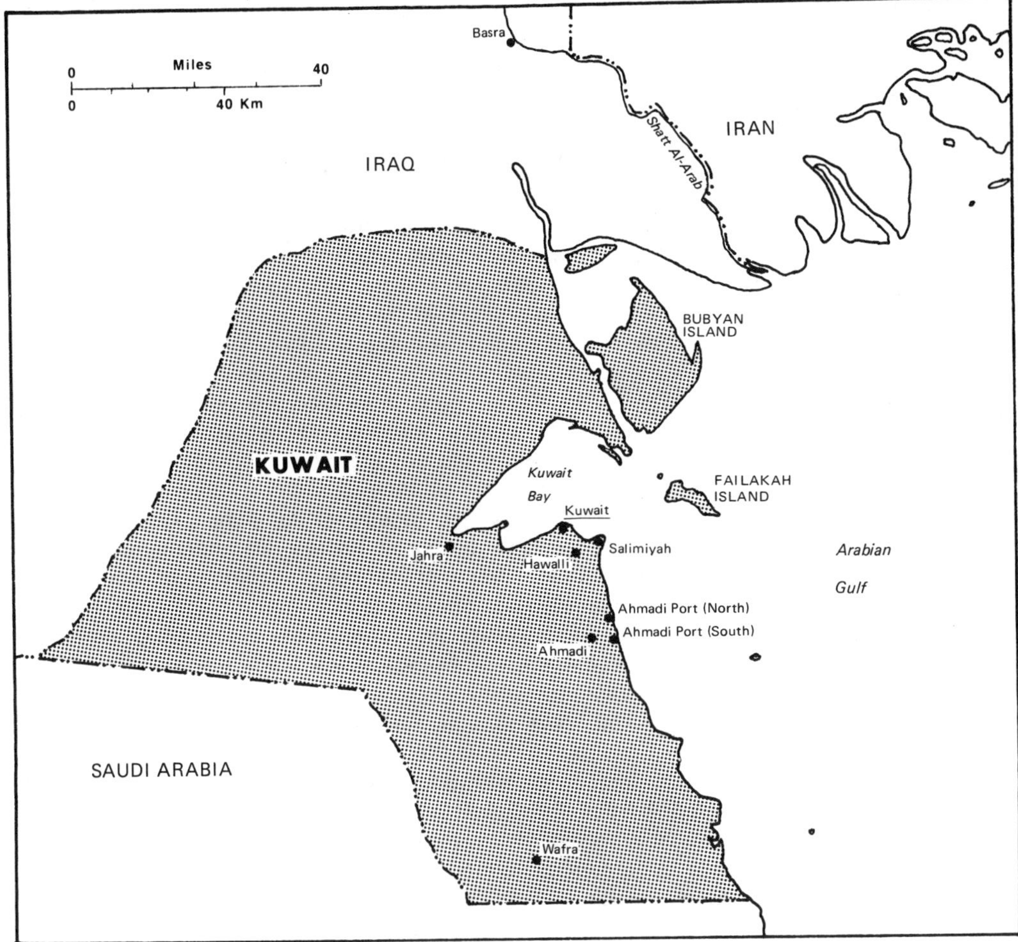

reach 3 million in the year 2000. The infant mortality rate is 44 per 1000 live births per year. Forty-three percent of the population is under 15 years old, and the median age is 19.1 years.

Religion

The state religion is Islam and a majority of the people are of the Sunni or orthodox sect. Religious freedom is guaranteed for the Shi'ite minority and for non-Muslims, mainly Hindus and Christians. Catholic, Protestant, and Greek Orthodox churches have been established.

Urban Centers

At least three-fourths of the population live in urban areas, and the proportion continues to increase as nomads are attracted by government welfare and opportunity programs and as outsiders come seeking employment. The largest cities and their 1975 estimated populations are Hawalli (130,000), Salimiyah (114,000), and Kuwait City (78,000).

Employment

Most native Kuwaitis are employed in the government and services sectors of the economy, and a sizeable proportion are engaged in trade and commerce. Over one-third of non-Kuwaitis also find positions in the government and services sectors. The construction trades are almost exclusively the province of non-Kuwaiti nationals. The oil industry employs less than 5 percent of the population.

Statistics on the Kuwaiti work force are enlightening, as they indicate the extent of Kuwaiti dependence on foreign personnel. Non-Kuwaitis make up 77 percent of the country's total labor force and 97 percent of workers in the private sector. Kuwaitis account for only 5 percent of the country's medical doctors, engineers, and teachers. Most of the nationals who do work have high-level governmental positions. The first five-year development plan calls for encouraging women to join the labor force.

ECONOMY

Dominance of Oil

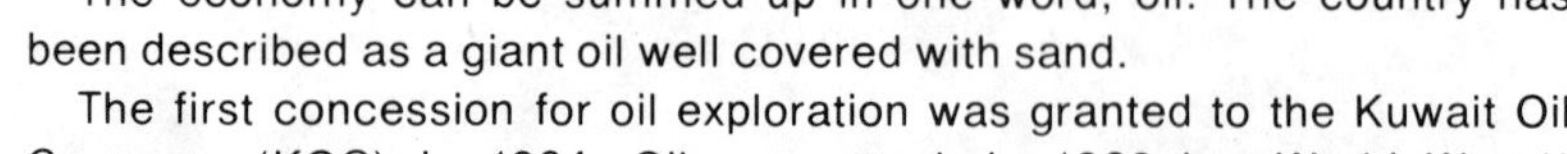

The economy can be summed up in one word, oil. The country has been described as a giant oil well covered with sand.

The first concession for oil exploration was granted to the Kuwait Oil Company (KOC) in 1934. Oil was struck in 1938 but World War II prevented rapid development. Production began in 1946 and escalated rapidly thereafter. In 1950 126 million barrels were produced; in 1960, 623 million; in 1970, 1.1 billion; in 1972, 1.2 billion. Production was cut down drastically in connection with the October, 1973 Arab-Israeli war; that year's production totaled only 102 million. Production was up to 929 million barrels in 1974. Revenues increased sharply after the fourfold increase of the oil price in 1973-74, reaching $3.2 billion in 1974-75.

KOC was jointly owned by the British Petroleum Company and Gulf Oil Corporation in the distribution, production and marketing of Kuwait's oil. On January 29, 1974, however, these two companies entered into an agreement giving the Government of Kuwait 60 percent ownership of KOC. Paralleling this development was the inauguration of a program to train Kuwaitis to take over oil operations.

The Kuwait Fund for Economic Development is the prototype for the planners in oil-rich, high-reserve nations who lack the population or size to profitably invest their surplus revenues. Established on December 31, 1961 as an Arab development fund with an original capital of $600 million, the Fund has increased to $3.5 billion in 1974-75 and its scope extended to include non-Arab developing countries. This share-the-wealth scheme benefits Kuwait in several ways. It contributes to Kuwait's international standing, and returns small but steady dividends. It also counteracts propaganda aimed against members of the Organization of Petroleum Exporting Countries.

Shipping

The traditional interest in shipping and maritime trade has been enhanced by the oil boom. The Kuwait Oil Tanker Co. maintains a 1.5 million ton fleet. The Kuwait Shipping Co. owns 25 ships with a combined capacity of 375,000 tons. Efforts in this direction represent one of the more viable avenues for diversification.

The vast oil revenues have had an enormous impact on the present national scene and will continue to exert a formidable influence in the future. The first five-year development plan was enacted in 1967. The overall objectives were: to raise the level of per capita income; to ensure a more equitable distribution of income; to achieve a greater degree of diversification in the sources of national income; to train the human resources of the country so as to fulfill the development requirements of the economy; and, lastly, to coordinate the economic development of Kuwait with that of the surrounding Arab countries. Kuwait is making notable progress in these directions.

The Chamber of Commerce and Industry building in Kuwait City.

HISTORY

The area now known as Kuwait appears to have been a flourishing port as early as the Sumerians (3000 B.C.). Archaeological excavations have unearthed Bronze-Age dwellings similar to those of Sumer. Greek colonists arrived at Failakah Island in the wake of Alexander's conquests, about 324 B.C., but in these pre-Islamic times there were few large settlements on the coast, and the people led a simple and severe life.

One of the closing battles of the Islamic Conquest, the Battle of Chain, was fought in the vicinity in 636 A.D. Kuwait shared, to some extent, in the prosperity of the Gulf in the Orient trade, though this trade was secondary to such traditional economies of the region as pearl fishing and the building of dhows. Kuwait was also left relatively untouched by later Portuguese ventures in the area, although a Portuguese base was established on Failakah Island in the sixteenth century.

Sabah Dynasty

The migration of the Utbi segment of the Aniza tribe from Central Arabia around 1716 marked the foundation of Al-Kut (the Fortress), what is now Kuwait City. In 1756 the settlers of what had become an autonomous sheikhdom elected as ruler a member of the Sabah family, thus starting the dynasty which rules Kuwait today. Pearling, fishing, boat building and seaborne and caravan trade sustained Kuwait through most of the eighteenth and nineteenth centuries. The ambiguous relationship with the Ottoman Empire enabled the Sabahs to maintain a considerable degree of autonomy in an area which the Ottomans considered a part of the vilayet (administrative unit) of Basra.

Kuwait's strategic position at the head of the Arabian Gulf first attracted the attention of the European powers at the end of the nineteenth century. Germany, Russia, and Britain all realized its potential as a railway terminus. Britain won the battle for influence when Sheikh Mubarak al-Sabah sought British protection against Ottoman attempts to exercise control. An 1899 treaty prohibited Kuwait from entering into relations with any other power "without the previous sanction of the British Government." Britain also took charge of Kuwait's foreign affairs. In return, Britain undertook responsibility for the "defense" of Kuwait. In October, 1913 another agreement with the British Empire obliged it not to grant oil concessions without British consent.

Independence

The 1922 Treaty al-Uqair defined the boundary with Saudi Arabia and resulted in the creation of a 2200 square mile neutral zone on Kuwait's southern border. This zone was divided among the two countries in 1969. The northern frontier with Iraq was affirmed in 1923. In June, 1961 Kuwait became independent and the 1899 treaty with Britain was revoked by mutual agreement. That same month Iraq asserted a presumed historic claim to Kuwait as "an integral part of Iraq." Responding to a Kuwaiti appeal for aid, British troops were dispatched to deter Iraqi action. These were later in that year replaced by a joint Arab defense force which eventually completed its withdrawal in February, 1963. Iraq recognized Kuwait in October, 1963; in May of that year Kuwait had been admitted to the United Nations.

Internal developments since 1963 have been largely concerned with endeavors in the direction of parliamentarianism and paternalism. There are no political parties. Members of the National Assembly represent shades of opinion rather than specific ideologies. In 1972 the government expressed its concern over the second-class status of the non-Kuwaitis by extending free medical treatment to all residents. The alien population thus acquired greater access to the nation's comprehensive welfare system.

GOVERNMENT AND SOCIETY

Kuwait is a hereditary amirate ruled by the Sabah family. A Constitution was published in 1962, drafted by the Constituent Assembly. In addition to appointed ministers, this Assembly contained 20 members elected the previous year in the first elections held in the country. Executive power is vested in the Amir, and an Heir Apparent must be appointed within one year of accession of an amir. The Amir appoints the prime minister and, at the prime minister's recommendation, he also appoints and dismisses ministers. Laws can be promulgated by the Amir, but they must be approved by the National Assembly, and they become effective upon publication in the *Official Gazette.* The National Assembly has 50 members and is elected every four years by literate natural-born Kuwaiti males over 21 years old. A majority must approve the Heir Apparent designated by the Amir. If the Amir requests reconsideration of a bill passed by the Assembly, the latter can still make it into law by a two-thirds majority, or by simple majority at a later sitting. A minister must resign if the Assembly passes a no confidence vote in him, but such a vote cannot be made about the prime minister. Instead, the Assembly would approach the Amir who might then either dismiss the prime minister or dissolve the Assembly. The country is divided into three governorates, Ahmadi, Hawalli, and Kuwait City (or Capital City).

National Assembly

Elements of British and French law have been incorporated in the judicial system, although Islamic law is still the basis for the Domestic Court which deals with marriage, divorce and inheritances. The eclectic mixture of judicial systems dates from November, 1960 when the medieval legal system was overhauled. The judiciary system is supervised by the minister of justice, who is appointed by the Amir.

Kuwait grew rapidly from a small fishing town to a modern city with wide boulevards.

Education

Education is encouraged on a wide scale. Although not compulsory, the incentives are strong enough to attract most potential students. Higher education is especially relevant to fulfilling the needs of a developing society. Kuwait is especially sensitive to this problem, given the fact that foreigners staff so many administrative and technical positions. Secondary school graduates have traditionally been sent abroad by the government for university level studies, but in 1964 the University of Kuwait was opened. This institution, together with the technical college inaugurated in 1954, will play an important role in the efforts to Kuwaitize the operations of the government and the economy.

Defense

The abrogation of the 1899 defense treaty with Britain necessitated the establishment of the armed forces. Iraqi annexation threats underlined the need for a strong defensive posture. The Ministry of Defense was formed in January, 1969, and a share of oil revenues was promptly put to use in the purchase of the latest military equipment. The Kuwaiti Army is manned largely by volunteers, although the possibility of conscription is being considered. High pay and benefits provide the necessary incentive. The military services also perform an important educational function.

Cultural Life

The thin veneer of Westernism that overlays Kuwaiti society barely conceals the traditional heritage of Arabism and Islam. Muslim practices and customs are maintained in the modern city of Kuwait. Chief among these and most noticeable to Westerners is the fasting and abstinence during the Holy Month of Ramadhan. During this period, from sunrise to sunset, smoking, eating or drinking in public is strongly discouraged. Working hours are reduced to ease the strain on employees. After sundown friends and relations meet to celebrate the Iftar (breakfast) with an enormous meal.

The second most important period on the Islamic calendar is the 12th lunar month. Thu al-Hijjah, the month of the pilgrimage to Mecca. All Muslims are expected to make this journey once in their life. As with Ramadhan, the government provides for employee leave with pay to enable all to make the pilgrimage.

Several other prevalent customs can be traced to traditional desert living. Emphasis on kinship, generous hospitality, stylized greetings and mandatory sharing of coffee and tea on visits to government offices, all reflect the survival of tribal customs in a modern society. For Westerners, perhaps the most painful religious restriction is the prohibition of the sale of alcohol.

Kuwaiti sailors fixing a boat. Before oil, Kuwait was a center of fishing and pearling.

Mass Communications

The most evident manifestations of Kuwait's modern culture are found in the growing media and information services. The Voice of Kuwait, the national broadcasting service, reaches listeners throughout the Middle East. The Ministry of Guidance and Information's monthly magazine *al-Arabi* claims the largest regular circulation in the Arab world. The Kuwait television station offers a variety of news, religious and entertainment programming.

Tourism

Kuwait's potential as a tourist magnet is not high. Summer temperatures would be high enough to discourage visitors and winter weather is cold and unpredictable. Only for brief transitional seasons is the weather suitable for prolonged outdoor activity. Archaeological excavations dating back to 2500 B.C. are nearby, but these are primarily of academic interest. The nomadic Badu would certainly provoke some tourist curiosity, but they are vanishing, most being absorbed into the urban areas. Religious festivals are primarily of interest to Muslims, and there are similar and more elaborate festivals in other countries. Similarly, Kuwait's desert has no unusual features not found elsewhere. Bathing in the Gulf is limited by the high temperatures and salinity of the water. Kuwait's premiere attraction is probably its status as a social and political test tube, an attribute of interest only to a specialized audience. Most visits are for business reasons generated by the immense oil income.

PROSPECTS

Kuwait's economic prospects are outstanding. Oil reserves should last well into the next century and oil revenues will help finance ambitious development plans. The government is committed to the maintenance of both the public and private sectors of the economy. Cooperation between these two spheres is vital for economic expansion and prosperity. The private sector is not always easily reconciled with the needs of planned economic development. Private capital tends to seek profit to the exclusion of economically necessary investment. The government does not lack capital, however, and the state should be able to underwrite necessary but unprofitable ventures. The private sector will, under these conditions, nicely compliment the public sector.

Kuwait has taken measures to insure that the oil wealth filters down to the mass of citizens. The country has already gone a long way in this direction, and more can be done. A more equitable distribution of income will only strengthen the already strong support for the government.

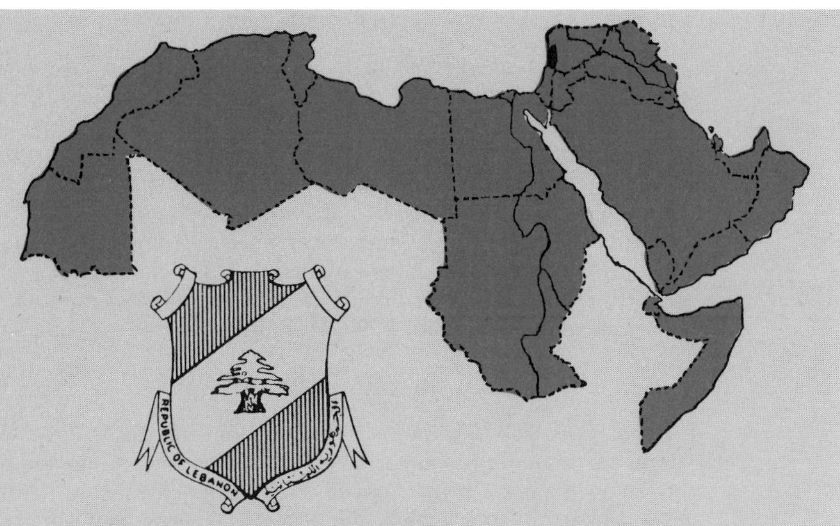

LEBANON

الجمهورية اللبنانية

PROFILE

Official Name: Republic of Lebanon (Al-Jumhuriyyah al-Lubnaniyyah)

Head of State: Elias Sarkis

Government: Republic

Area: 4,015 sq. mi. (=½ Massachusetts)

Population: about 3 million

Population Density: 750/sq. mi.

Capital: Beirut (750,000)

Other Urban Centers: Tripoli, Sidon, Tyre, Zahlah, Baalbak

National Holiday: November 22

Currency: Lebanese Lira ($1.00 = 3 LL)

Press: Numerous dailies and other periodicals

Radio and Television: Official Radio and color television

Sites of Interest: Baalbak, Byblos, Sidon, Tyre as historical sites. Many scenic sites, entertainment and sports activities

Main Airport: Beirut International

Main Seaports: Beirut, Tripoli

Date of Joining the United Nations: October 24, 1945

Date of Joining the Arab League: March 22, 1945

LEBANON

INTRODUCTION

Lebanon is a small republic at the eastern end of the Mediterranean Sea. It has an area of 4,015 square miles, and by comparison Connecticut's area is 5,009 square miles. Its beautiful mountains, gorgeous beaches, and well-preserved remnants of past civilizations are a magnetic combination which has attracted as many as two million visitors a year. An almost equal number of business people has been attracted by the government's economic policy of laissez-faire and by the availability of such services as well managed financial institutions and good and effective systems of communication and transportation. As a result, a high standard of living has been attained by much of the population.

PHYSICAL GEOGRAPHY

Lebanon is approximately 130 miles long and 20 to 35 miles wide. There are four north-south physiographic regions. Along the Mediterranean is a very narrow coastal plain, sometimes only a few yards wide, while in a few places there is an expanse that supports such cities as the capital Beirut, Tripoli and Sidon. Eastwards, the next physical region is the Lebanon Mountains, the central portion of which is known as Jabal Lubnan (Mount Lebanon). The highest peak of 10,131 feet is in the north, and in the south the landscape becomes more hilly than mountainous. The proximity of the often snow-capped peaks to the sea provides a striking contrast. Steep and composed largely of porous limestone, the mountains are not well suited for agriculture, but there are innumerable springs which are used for irrigation at lower levels. Many restaurants have been built on the sides of the mountains near these springs, and the icy waters serve as a natural air conditioner.

Eastwards is the Beqa' Valley, lying between the Lebanon Mountains and the Anti-Lebanon Mountains. The valley is approximately 100 miles long and 6 to 16 miles wide. It has a fertile topsoil deposited by runoff from the mountains, and its level surface makes it well suited for agriculture. The Anti-Lebanon are not quite as high as the Lebanon Mountains, and their highest peak is Mount Hermon (Jabal Shaykh) in the south, reaching 9,232 feet.

The Mediterranean type of climate prevails: mild wet winters and hot dry summers. Annual rainfall totals are 30-40 inches along the coast, upwards of 50 inches on the mountains (much of it in heavy snow), and only about 15 inches in the Beqa'. In summer the coast is hot and oppressively humid, and the mountain roads are clogged for hours with cars carrying Lebanese and tourists fleeing the sweltering heat of Beirut. Daytime summer temperatures reach highs of 90°F along the coast and in the Beqa', and in January the highs are 60°F and 50°F respectively.

There are two main rivers, both of which rise in the Beqa' but flow in opposite directions. The Litani is entirely within Lebanon from source to mouth, reaching the sea 45 miles south of Beirut. It has been developed for irrigation and power generation. The Orontes River flows northwards to Syria and eventually to the Mediterranean.

In ancient times Lebanon was almost completely covered by forests. The cedars were used to build the funerary rooms of the pyramids, the Temple of Jerusalem, boats and other structures. But centuries of overcutting have drastically reduced the natural vegetation cover, though several famous cedar groves remain in the north. An active reforestation program is being pursued.

The ruins of Baalbek in Lebanon are the most spectacular remains of Roman architecture.

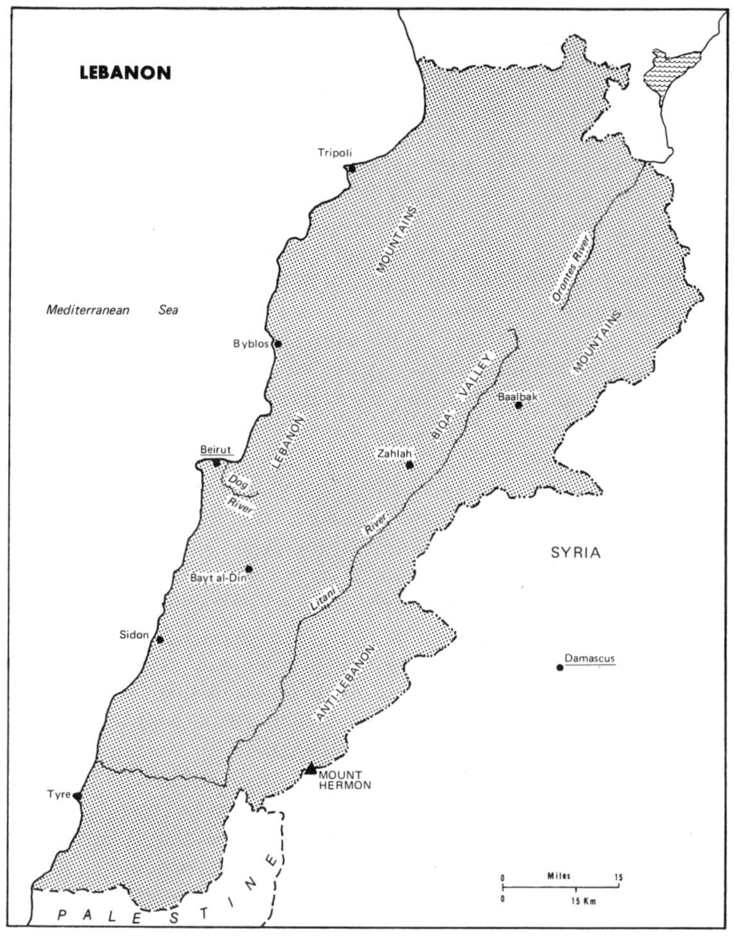

HUMAN GEOGRAPHY

Vital Statistics

Lebanon's population is about 3 million. The mid-1977 estimated birth and death rates were respectively 40 per thousand and 10 per thousand, giving an annual growth rate of 3.0 percent. If this rate were maintained, the population would double in 23 years and would reach almost 6 million in the year 2000. About 41 percent of the people were under 15 years old, and 60 percent lived in urban communities. The Beirut metropolitan area has a population of about 750,000, and Tripoli has over 150,000 people. Other cities are Sidon and Tyre in the south and Zahlah in the Beqa'.

Religion

In terms of composition Lebanon is a mixture of Phoenician, Greek, Byzantine, Crusader, Arab, Armenian and other ethnic groups. The population is about half Muslim and half Christian, with a slight Muslim majority, and there are 17 recognized religious communities. The Muslim groups, in descending order of size, are Sunni, Shi'a, Druze, Alawi, and Ismaili. The Christians are Maronite, Greek Orthodox, Greek Catholic, Armenian Catholic, Syriac Catholic, Eastern Nestorian, Chaldean, Evangelical, and Latin. The largest Muslim sect, the Sunni, comprises perhaps 25 percent of the total population, the Shi'a 22 percent, and the Druze 9 percent. Approximate percentages of the national population of some of the Christian sects are: Maronite 25, Greek Orthodox 8, Greek Catholic 5, Armenian Orthodox 3.

Language

The official language is Arabic. A majority of the people are bilingual or trilingual. English and French are widely known because of close financial, tourist, religious and educational ties with the West.

ECONOMY

Services

Historically, the Lebanese economy has been dominantly of a mercantile character. The country has functioned as an information, services and financial hub of the Arab Middle East. In June 1975 there were in Beirut 72 offices of foreign banks. Whereas exports were only 62 percent of imports, the deficit was more than made up by the invisible income of services, transit trade, tourism and remittances from Lebanese in North and South America. This income includes royalties from the oil pipelines terminating at Tripoli (from Kirkuk, Iraq) and Sidon (the Trans-Arabian Pipeline from eastern Saudi Arabia). It also includes transit traffic to and from Syria, Jordan, Iraq, Saudi Arabia, and Kuwait.

Industry

Manufacturing industry is on a small scale and consists of such production as food processing, textiles, furniture, cement, ceramics, pharmaceuticals and plastics. Commercially viable oil deposits were announced in April 1975, located in the Beqa' and along the coast, but development was not actively pursued because of the civil war and its aftermath.

Agriculture

Agriculture employs close to half the labor force but generates not much more than 10 percent of the national income. Given the mountainous nature of the country, only about 23 percent of the land area is cultivated, mostly in the Beqa' valley. The narrow coastal zone is extremely productive, and main crops are olives, citrus fruits, bananas, cotton, and onions. The steep slopes are under extensive terracing, and such fruits as apples are grown at higher elevations. A variety of crops are grown in the Beqa', and the main cereals are wheat and barley. Vegetables include potatoes, onions, tomatoes, cucumbers and melons. Dairy produce is of good quality, and poultry is also important.

Lebanon's transportation system is of good quality, though congested. The same is true of the harbor facilities. The airport, before the onset of the 1975 civil war, was one of the busiest in the Middle East, with upwards of 100 takeoffs or landings a day from more than 30 international airlines.

The town of Bsharri near the famous Cedars of Lebanon perches on the edge of Qadisha gorge.

The civil war of 1975-76 affected all aspects of Lebanon's economy. Financial institutions closed for several months, as did the Beirut international airport. Reconstruction began in 1977, and the prospect that foreign businesses and banks would return to Beirut was strengthened by the fact that no other Middle Eastern capital seemed a satisfactory alternative. It is likely that the emerging economic scene will evolve under a greater governmental guidance than has been true of Lebanon's laissez-faire practice.

Ancient bridge on the Dog River where conquerors from the ancient Egyptians and Assyrians to modern ones have left records of their exploits on the rocks.

HISTORY

Phoenicians

The first identifiable inhabitants were the Canaanites, a Semitic people who came to be known as Phoenicians. The Phoenicians were seafarers and traders who flourished in the second and early first millennia B.C. from city-states at Tyre, Sidon and Byblos. They founded colonies in North Africa (Carthage), Europe (Marseille, Palermo), and in the Mediterranean (Malta, Sardinia). The Phoenicians invented the alphabet and were the first to sail by the stars. Recent discoveries suggest that they discovered the land of tin (Britain), the Atlantic Ocean, the Baltic Sea, and the Western Hemisphere. Herodotus states that the Phoenicians were the first to sail around Africa. Other ancient writers credit them with inventing music.

Eventually the power of the Phoenicians was challenged by Persians, Greeks and Romans. Under the East Roman Empire and, since the 8th century, the Islamic Caliphate, the mountains of Lebanon became a haven for a number of Christian and Muslim sects. The area took on the multi-religious character which it still maintains. The population slowly became culturally Arabized.

Ottomans

Turkish Ottomans came to power in geographic Syria in the sixteenth century, but local Lebanese feudal lords maintained control. The weakening Ottomans agreed to the French presence beginning in 1860. The period from 1860 until World War I brought a revival of Arabic literature, the birth, perhaps, of Arab nationalism, an influx of European and American missionaries, the establishment of Western-style schools and universities, and the gradual process of Westernization. Westernization was hastened by the Ottoman defeat in World War I.

French Mandate

As a result of the secret Sykes-Picot Agreement of May 1916 between Britain and France, the French occupied Lebanon and controlled it under a League of Nations Mandate. In 1920 the French announced the State of Greater Lebanon, the first time that Lebanon's present borders were delimited. According to the terms of the League mandates, the colonial powers were to aid in the eventual independence of those placed in their care. In 1926 Lebanon became a republic, a constitution was promulgated, and its first president was elected. In 1941 it was proclaimed independent by the Free French government, and French troops were finally withdrawn in 1946.

Civil war in Lebanon left ugly scars on Beirut. The capital of Lebanon was one of the most prosperous cities of the Arab world.

The National Pact

An unwritten agreement reached in 1943 by Bishara al-Khuri, the Maronite leader, and Riyad al-Sulh, the Sunni spokesman, has since played the dominant role in Lebanese politics. This agreement came to be known as the National Pact. It asserted that Lebanon was an Arab state and that it would seek no Western protection. Lebanon's borders were declared permanent. The balance of power established was based on the census of 1932. Accordingly, Christians assumed the dominant position. Because of a higher Muslim birth rate and a higher proportion of Christians among emigrants from Lebanon, the population composition changed. The population ratio was probably reversed by the 1960's, so that the proportion became six Muslims to five Christians. However, no census has been taken since 1932, so as not to destabilize the political system. The sectarian differences become accentuated by economic inequalities, and Christians benefited more than Muslims. Understandably, the former became more comfortable with the status quo and the latter became increasingly dissatisfied. Muslims demanded more political participation, commensurate with their numbers. However, disagreement over how political power would be reallocated forestalled a reformation of the system. The potential for communal strife fluctuated in intensity. A severe crisis occurred in 1958 and was related to opposing attitudes towards inter-Arab policies. The crisis also involved the landing during the summer of United States marines in Beirut in support of the pro-Western government of Lebanese President Camille Chamoun. A much more serious civil war erupted between March 1975 and October 1976, with casualties estimated at 60,000 dead and 100,000 injured. Complicating the conflict was the presence of a large number of displaced and disadvantaged Palestinians and a historic Zionist covetousness of southern Lebanon. The latter was expressed in massive Israeli bombings and in the involvement of Israeli troops in pursuit of a policy of eliminating Palestinians as a political factor.

Lebanon was a founding member of the League of Arab States (March 1945) and of the United Nations (October 1945). Although technically at war with Israel since the establishment in 1949 of armistice demarcation lines, Lebanon has not been militarily involved.

GOVERNMENT AND SOCIETY

Administration

The political system is based on a constitution promulgated in 1926 and on the 1943 National Pact. The unicameral parliament, the Chamber of Deputies, is elected by universal suffrage, and in turn it elects the president by a two-thirds majority. He appoints the prime minister, who then forms his cabinet. The cabinet is responsible both to the president and to the parliament. The number of Deputies must be a multiple of 11, reflecting the ratio of six Christians to five Muslims determined by the 1932 census. According to the National Pact, the president would always be a Maronite, the prime minister a Sunni, and the president of the Chamber of Deputies a Shi'ite. Other governmental positions, even minor ones, are distributed on a sectarian basis. The system was rigidly fixed, and it could not accommodate change; hence the disastrous nineteen-month civil war of 1975-1976. In September 1976 Elias Sarkis assumed the office of president, succeeding Suleiman Franjiyya.

There are two separate court systems. The religious court system handles matters of marriage, inheritance, and property according to the laws of the religious communities, Christian, Muslim, and Jewish. The civil courts use a Western system, although some older Ottoman laws are still in force.

Education

The religious and secular duality of the political system is also present in the educational system. There are more children in private schools, often religiously based, than in the public system. The literacy rate is a high 86 percent. Perhaps Lebanon's greatest pride has been an extensive university system. The oldest is the American University of Beirut, founded in 1866. It has served the peoples of the Middle East and Africa for well over 100 years and has one of the best medical facilities on either continent. Second in importance is St. Joseph's University, founded in 1875 by French Jesuits. There are also the large Beirut Arab University and the Lebanese University, plus four other schools of higher education. Lebanon has had a traditional appeal as a center for higher learning. In the late 1970s more than 50,000 students, over half of them foreign, attended Lebanese universities.

Social conditions

The standard of living is generally high, and medical and social services are well developed. Modern appliances are in common use. Good quality housing is widespread, and the latest in clothing fashions is worn. However, there is a large disparity between the wealthy and the poor, a condition which was one of the primary causes of the 1975-76 civil war.

The scenic beauty of Lebanon made of it the resort and playground of the Arab World, in Summer as well as in Winter.

Press

Until the 1975 civil war, Beirut was one of the largest printing and publishing centers in the Arab world. A large variety of books, magazines and journals in many languages was published. The city boasted about 35 daily newspapers in Arabic, French and English

Cultural life

The presence of numerous communal groups and the cosmopolitan character of the country have fostered and nurtured a wide range of cultural expression, such as poetry, fiction, literary criticism, art, music, and theater. The Baalbek International Festival has become a major annual musical event of worldwide appeal. Films of various national origins are a very popular pastime. There are two Lebanese television companies. These factors, combined with rich archeological remains, magnificent scenery, varied winter and summer recreational opportunities, and an attractive climate have made Lebanon especially appealing to tourists.

PROSPECTS

Lebanon's prospects must be viewed in the context of the causes, impact, and resolution of the devastating 1975-1976 civil war. The origins of the war are varied and complex, but two primary causes are a political-economic system unresponsive to Lebanon's poor and events related to the Arab-Israeli conflict. Both of these are further complicated by having religious sectarianism at the basis of the social and political system in Lebanon. The solution of Lebanon's social problems awaits the emergence of a new sense of national unity and a just solution to the Palestinian problem.

Certainly Lebanon's reputation as the chief commercial center of the Arab world has been damaged. But those elements which made her important—an intelligent population and a fortuitous geographic location—have not changed. Thus a program of economic and political reform, national reconciliation, and continued support for the Palestinian people presents the best prospects for stability and prosperity in Lebanon. Important positive indicators will be the return of foreign business activity and financial institutions, and the resurrection of the tourist trade.

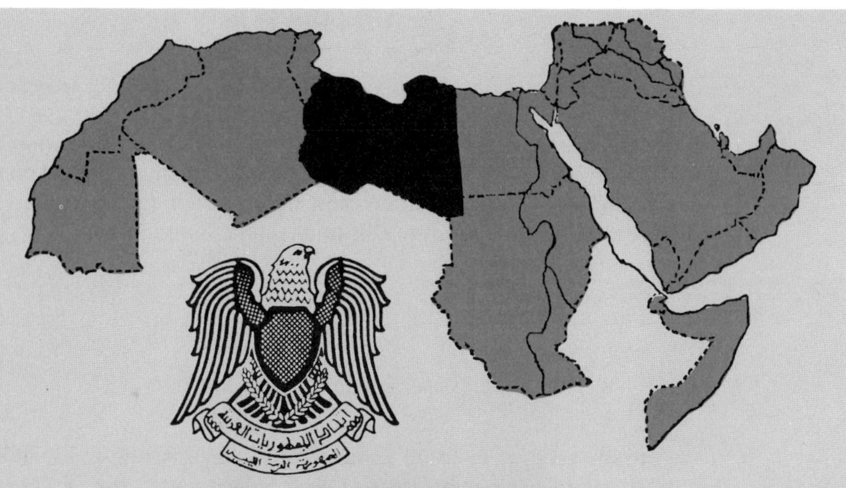

LIBYA

الجماهيرية العربية الليبية الشعبية الاشتراكية

PROFILE

Official Name: The Popular Socialist Libyan Arab Jamahiriyyah (Al-Jamahiriyyah al-Arabiyyah al-Libiyyah Al-Sha'biyyah al-Ishtirakiyyah)

Head of State: Mu'ammar al-Qadhdhafi

Government: Jamahiriyyah

Area: 675,200 sq. mi (=2.5 x Texas)

Population: 2,300,000

Population Density: less than 4/sq. mi.

Capital: Tripoli (555,000)

Other Urban Centers: Benghazi, Zawiyah, Misratah, Darnah, Sabhah

National Holiday: September 1

Currency: Libyan Dinar (1 LD = $3.40)

Press: Three important dailies: Al-Fajr al-Jadid, Al-Fateh, Al-Jihad

Radio and Television: Radio transmissions from Tripoli and Benghazi.

Sites of Interest: Phoenician and Carthagenian ruins. Roman cities of Sabratha, Leptis Magna, and other ancient and medieval sites.

Main Airports: Tripoli, Benghazi

Main Seaports: Tripoli

Date of Joining the United Nations: December 14, 1955

Date of Joining the Arab League: March 28, 1953

LIBYA

INTRODUCTION

Libya was, for many years, one of the world's least endowed countries. The discovery of oil in 1958 and the start of oil exporting in 1961 resulted in a rapid transformation of the economy. Libya was catapulted into the forefront of international events involving oil economics and oil politics. At the same time, after decades and centuries of foreign rule, Libya is affirming its ties to its own Arabic and Islamic heritage.

PHYSICAL GEOGRAPHY

Topography

With an area of 675,200 square miles Libya is one-fourth the continental United States, or more than 2.5 times as large as Texas. The central part is dominated by a hilly plateau, which covers 15,400 square miles and contains hundreds of inactive small volcanic peaks. Along the Mediterranean the coast is broad and low lying in the center, rising gradually from the Gulf of Surt southwards to the interior. By contrast, in the east and west the plateau rises abruptly from the sea to heights of 2000-2500 feet within a distance of 24 miles. Around Tripoli in the west there is a small but important coastal plain, the Jefara, which extends westwards to the Tunisian border. In the east the coastal plain is narrow and discontinuous, reaching its widest extent of ten or so miles near and south of Benghazi and gradually blending with the central coastal lowlands.

Climate

Libya is almost entirely a desert, and most of it is part of the Sahara. There is not one permanent river in the country. Instead, water courses are of the wadi (dry valley) type; they are usually dry and contain water only after infrequent and brief rains. Such rain tends to be heavy, producing sudden floods of short duration.

There are two exceptions to the prevailing aridity. In the northeast, along the northernmost bend in the coastline east of Benghazi, a 150-mile strip has a Mediterranean climate—hot dry summers and mild wet winters. Benghazi itself receives only 10 inches a year. Rain occurs elsewhere along the coast and on the adjacent high terrain. Almost all of the rain falls from September through April. The relative abundance of rainfall and the resultant heavy vegetation growth has led to the region's descriptive name of Jabal al-Akhdar, the Green Mountain. The second exception to the prevailing aridity is along the northwest coast, from the western coast of the Gulf of Surt to about 50 miles west of Tripoli. Largely because of the orientation of the coast relative to the prevailing winter rainbearing winds, total amounts are not enough to result in a Mediterranean climate. Rather, conditions of semiaridity, or steppe, are attained. Tripoli's annual rainfall is about 13 inches. For both Tripoli and Benghazi the warmest months are July and August, averaging about

Temperature

80°F. The coolest months are December through February, averaging upwards of 55°F. Days are hot, exceeding 100°F, and an extreme reading of 136°F was recorded at Al-Aziziyah on the Jefara plain southwest of Tripoli. Nights can be quite cool, even in the desert, and freezing conditions are common in winter. A notable climactic feature is a strong and disastrous sand wind (ghibli) off the Sahara which ten or more times a year reduces visibility to less than 20 yards.

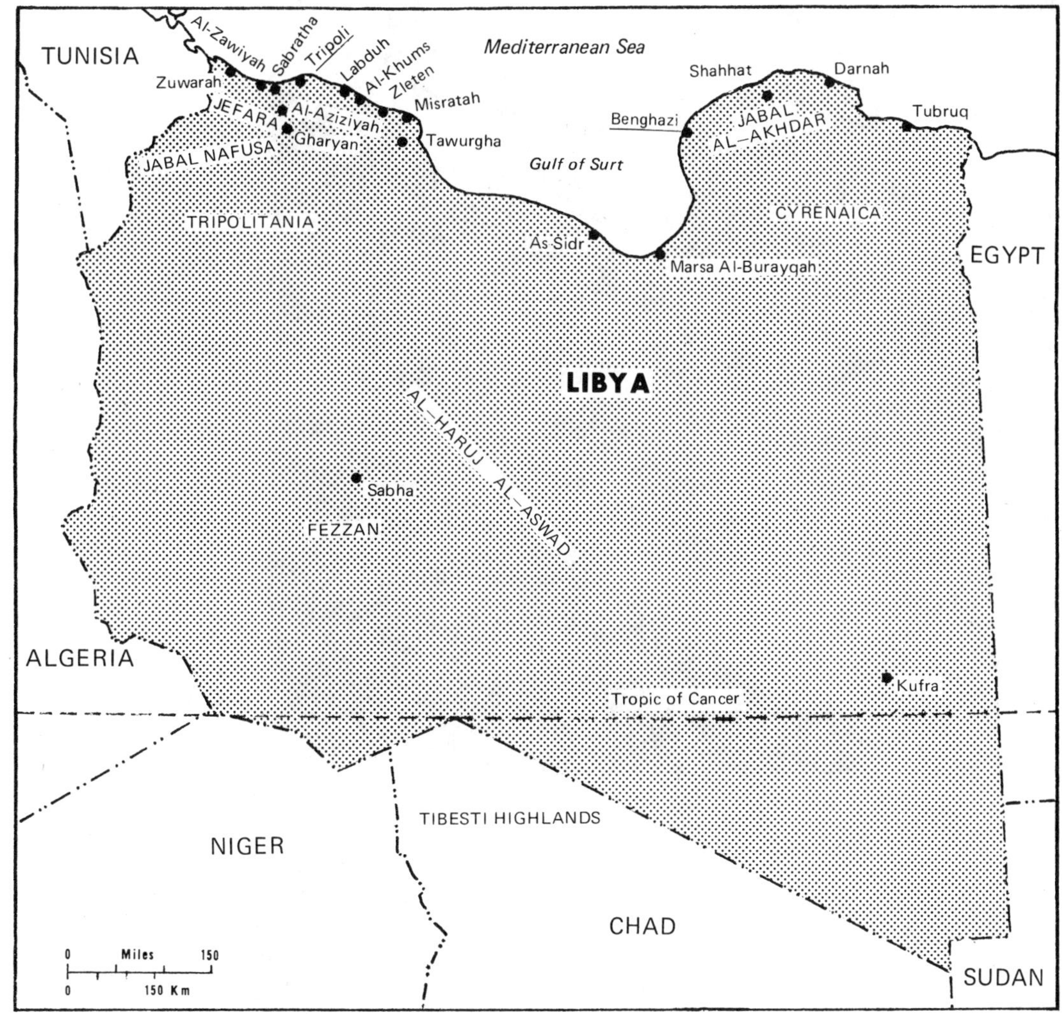

HUMAN GEOGRAPHY

Arab and Muslim

Libyans are overwhelmingly (98 percent) Arab and Muslim. Arabic is the official language. The original element in the population are the Berbers, who were sedentary agriculturalists and lived in coastal oases. Today they are largely assimilated, except for about 50,000 who speak their own Hamitic language and live in the Jabal Nafusa region, the highland area south of Tripoli. There are other, smaller, groups, such as the Tuareg in the southwest and the Tebu (Teda) in the southeast.

Vital Statistics

During the first two decades of independence, Libya's population more than doubled, increasing by 107.3 percent between 1954 and 1973 (or from 1.1 million to almost 2.3 million). During the first decade the increase was 43.7 percent. The mid-1977 population is estimated to be 2.7 million. The birth rate is 48 per thousand, and the death rate is 9 per thousand, giving a high annual growth rate of 3.9 percent. If this growth rate is maintained, the population will double in 18 years and will reach 5.2 million in the year 2000. The infant mortality rate is 130 per 1000 live births per year. Forty-nine percent of the population is under 15 years old, and the median age is a very young 17.8 years.

A general view of Benghazi, Libya's second largest city and capital of Cyrenaica

Population Distribution

Relative to its enormous area, Libya's population is quite small. Given the fact that almost the whole country is a desert, it is not surprising that most of the people are found in the two small non-arid areas in the northeast and northwest, and in fact about three-quarters of the people live within 20 miles of the Mediterranean Sea. More striking, perhaps, is that some 37 percent of the total population is found in the growing municipalities of Tripoli, the capital (555,000), and Benghazi (300,000).

Agriculture

Land Use

Sedentary agriculture has been the traditional occupation. Given the paucity of rain and of surface running water, irrigation based on underground and spring water has been a common practice. More extensive forms of land use, such as pastoralism and shifting cultivation, are found in the subhumid-semiarid regions, notably on the southern flanks of Jabal al-Akhdar and the plateau south of Tripoli. Over the centuries, villages developed as service sites for nomadic tribes, trans-Saharan caravan routes and shifting cultivators. They also evolved around military posts and administrative centers of occupying powers. Today, with the dominant movement toward the coastal urban areas, the nomadic population may be as low as 5 percent.

ECONOMY

When Libya became independent in 1951 it was regarded as one of the world's poorest and least endowed countries. Livelihood, both sedentary and nomadic, was of the subsistence type. A considerable portion of its income came from the United States and the United Kingdom for the use of military bases. Intensive exploration for oil began in 1955, and the first big strike was made in 1959 at Zelten, 250 miles south of Benghazi.

Exports started in 1961, and since then production has increased rapidly. Libya's proximity to the huge European market was an advantage over the Arabian Gulf producers. This advantage was heightened during the closure of the Suez Canal between 1967 and 1975. The first favorable balance of payments was achieved in 1963 and subsequently the surplus increased spectacularly. Exports of crude oil and petroleum products now account for 99.9 percent of the value of all exports. In September, 1973 the government took control of all oil companies.

Trade

The oil income is being used for a large number of projects: agricultural schemes, inexpensive urban housing, new social, educational and medical amenities, roads, improved telephone service, rapid expansion of the saturated harbor facilities, desalination, and foreign aid. Investment in non-oil activities is given special attention so as to diversify the economy and to prepare for the day when the oil reserves will be depleted. Examples are bottling, salt, tobacco, food processing, leather goods, metal work, textiles, rugs, furniture, ceramics, cement, asbestos, tires, bicycles and pre-fabricated housing. A major handicap is the lack of enough skilled labor.

Oil

The considerable rural-to-urban migration has affected the economy in various ways. One is the overpopulation of urban centers with sprawling bidonvilles (shanty towns). These have been largely replaced by low-rent government housing and the "surplus" labor is gradually being trained and absorbed by the growing trades and services sector.

A second consequence is the disruption of agricultural productivity. The decline started in 1956 at the height of oil exploration, and by 1963 Libya had already imported over $20 million worth of foodstuffs, including olive oil, a traditionally domestic product. The task of reviving agricultural production was given a high priority after the 1969 revolution. In the Tawurgha project, 125 miles southeast of Tripoli, 300 farms are being established on 7500 irrigated acres and 75,000 newly planted trees will provide windbreaks. In the Jabal al-Akhadar region, 20,000 acres are being reclaimed and irrigated in an integrated project which includes reservoir construction, electrification, transportation, forestry, and fruit and nut trees. The objective is to settle semi-nomadic pastoralists and to integrate them in the sedentary agricultural population, with cereals and orchards as primary crops. A third project uses 6 million gallons of

Reviving Agriculture

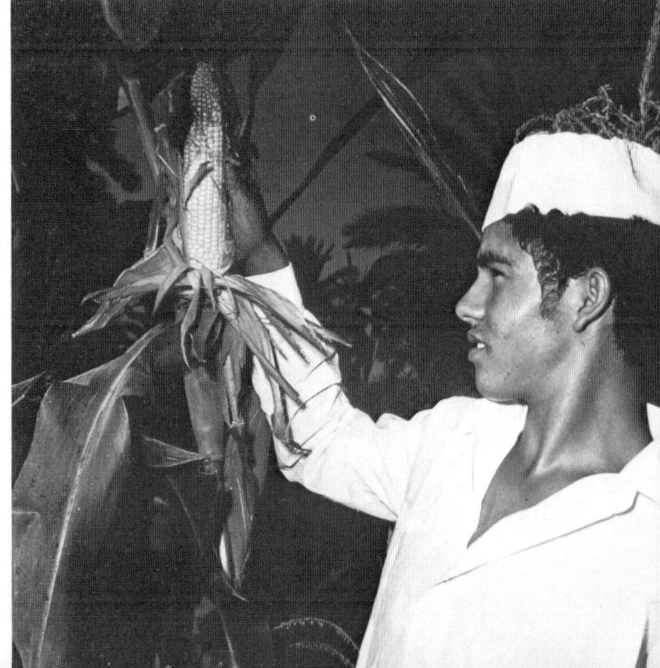

A young Libyan farmer inspects his corn crop.

purified sewage water a day from Tripoli to irrigate 1500 acres and 100 farms; its primary function is to provide the nearby urban market with fruits and vegetables. A similar project is in effect near Benghazi.

Kufra Project

The large Kufra project is in the Sahara 550 miles southeast of Benghazi, barely 60 miles north of the Tropic of Cancer, where large quantities of ground water have been discovered. Using wells and sprinkler irrigation, 25,000 acres are being reclaimed. A hundred wells, equipped with rotating sprinkler pipes, each irrigate 250 acres of fodder for sheep. The end product is mutton, thus reducing the country's considerable imports of meat. Eventually 250,000 sheep are to be raised, and wool has become an important side product. Coupled with this livestock scheme is an agricultural program with a projected resettlement, largely from nearby oases, of 4500 people.

Ruins of the Arch of Trajan in Leptis Magna of the Mediterranean coast, east of Tripoli.

HISTORY

The three major areas of Tripolitania (northwest), Cyrenaica (east) and Fezzan (southwest) have been an integral part of the history of the Mediterranean region rather than that of the desert interior.

Tripolitania

The northwest was colonized in the seventh century B.C. by Phoenicians, whose cities of Labqi, Oea and Sabratha formed a region later referred to by the Romans as Tripolitania (Three Cities). The three cities later formed the eastern province of the Carthaginian state (based in what today is Tunisia). Carthage fell in 146 B.C., and Tripolitania came under the successive rule of Numidians, Romans (46 B.C.), Vandals (435 A.D.), and Byzantine Greeks (534 A.D.). It was taken by the Arabs in 645 A.D., though effective Arabization of the Berber population occurred only after the 1049 invasion of the Banu Hilal and the eleventh century attacks by the Banu Sulaym. In 1551 it was conquered by the Ottoman Turks, who made Tripoli a colonial capital.

Cyrenaica

The northeast was settled by Greek colonists as early as 639 B.C. One of the five major cities, Cyrene (whose site is partly occupied by present-day Shahhat), was the source of the regional name. Another city, Barce (al-Marj), evolved to become Barqah, the Arabic name of the region. The Egyptian Ptolemaic kings ruled Cyrenaica from 322 until 96 B.C. when it came under Roman rule. In 67 B.C. it was united with Crete as one senatorial province with Cyrene as the capital, and from 400 A.D. to 642 A.D. it was under Byzantine rule. The Arab conquest, led by Amr ibn al-As, started in 642 A.D. Nominal Turkish control was extended from Tripolitania in 1635, and more effective control was asserted between 1835 and 1858.

Fezzan

Fezzan's earliest contacts were southwards into Africa. With the Roman conquest in 19 B.C., it was given the name Phazania (hence the name Fezzan). After a period of local autonomy in the fifth century A.D., it was conquered by the Arabs in 666. Following a succession of local dynasties, Fezzan was incorporated into the Ottoman Empire in 1842.

Italian Rule

In the wake of the late nineteenth century European scramble for Africa, Italy asserted its colonial ambitions in Libya in 1911. Italy's ultimatum to Turkey claimed a historical connectivity with the days of the Roman occupation almost two thousand years earlier. Following the Italo-Turkish war of 1911-12, all three areas came under Italian rule. In 1939 Cyrenaica and Tripolitania were incorporated into the metropolitan Kingdom of Italy. Much fighting took place here during World War II, mainly between the German and British armies. In 1951 the three provinces became administrative units in the independent Kingdom of Libya.

Sanusiyyah

The Sanusi movement (Sanusiyyah) produced an important political and military challenge to Italian rule. This Muslim Sufi (mystic) brotherhood was established in 1837 by Algerian-born Sidi Muhammad ibn Ali as-Sanusi. The reformist movement aimed to reassert and reestablish the basic faith of early Islam. It was strongest in Cyrenaica and spread to most of interior Libya, western Egypt, and the Hijaz in western Arabia. When the United Kingdom of Libya came into being on December 24, 1951, Idris, head of the Sanusiyyah, was proclaimed king. The king was overthrown on September 1, 1969 by a military junta led by Colonel Muammar al-Qadhdhafi, and a socialist Arab republic was proclaimed. In March 1977, the official name became The Popular Socialist Libyan Arab Jamahiriyah.

Republic Proclaimed

GOVERNMENT AND SOCIETY

Administration

Libya's only political party is the Arab Socialist Union, formed in 1971. A General People's Congress of the Union was held in March 1977, at which the new name of the country was adopted. A five-member General Secretariat was established, with Colonel Muammar al-Quadhdhafi as General Secretary. A 26-member General Popular Committee was formed, succeeding a Council of Ministers. It consists of 25 Secretaries of Departments plus the Head of the Committee. Power is vested in the people through People's Congresses, Popular Committees, Trade Unions, Vocational Syndicates, and the General People's Congress. In 1963 Libya's three administrative provinces (Tripolitania, Cyrenaica, Fezzan) were replaced by ten governorates (muhafathas), which in turn were abolished in 1975 in order to improve administrative efficiency by removing one bureaucratic layer.

There is a considerable business traffic, both by contractors and employees, as Libya lacks an adequate pool of skilled labor. There is an excellent potential for a thriving tourist trade: the numerous and sometimes spectacular remains of previous cultures and civilizations, the expansive and varied desert scenery, the unusual Kufra agricultural project, the many hundreds of miles of unspoiled beaches, and the cultural diversity of the population. However, Libya is giving tourism low priority. It wants to avoid the negative consequences associated with tourism and, given the oil wealth, there is no pressing financial reason to change this policy.

Projects

Special attention has been paid to the construction of roads, port facilities, and a new, modern airport in Tripoli. Projects of railway lines connecting Libya with neighbouring Arab countries are under study.

The Libyan Arab Airlines has scheduled service between Libyan, Arab, and European cities. A fleet of tankers and other merchant ships is in the formation stage.

Education

Libya has a policy of "education for all and free of charge." Education is compulsory in the preparatory stage. Special attention has been given to university education. The number of students at Tripoli and Benghazi Universities increased from 9905 in 1967 to 13,000 in 1977. Libyan students are sent abroad for higher studies and specialization. The Libyan government has adopted a plan to eradicate illiteracy by 1980.

A Libyan beauty displaying traditional dress and jewelry.

PROSPECTS

The rapid transformation following the sudden acquisition of wealth will continue for the coming two or three decades. Libya will still need to depend on non-Libyan labor, though probably at a decreasing rate once the considerable investment in education starts to bear fruit. Pastoral and nomadic activity, already being practiced by less than a tenth of the population, will virtually disappear and will be replaced by sedentary commercial activity. Urban expansion can only continue, despite the large agricultural projects and the considerable incentives to attract settlers there. Oil wealth has helped catapult the country into a position of international importance, and this prominence is likely to continue for the balance of this century.

Perhaps more important than Libya's international role and its galloping economy is the growing integration of its population. The country's three main regions faced away from each other for most of their histories. A sense of national cohesion is being forged, inexorably, and this historic development can only enhance the national good.

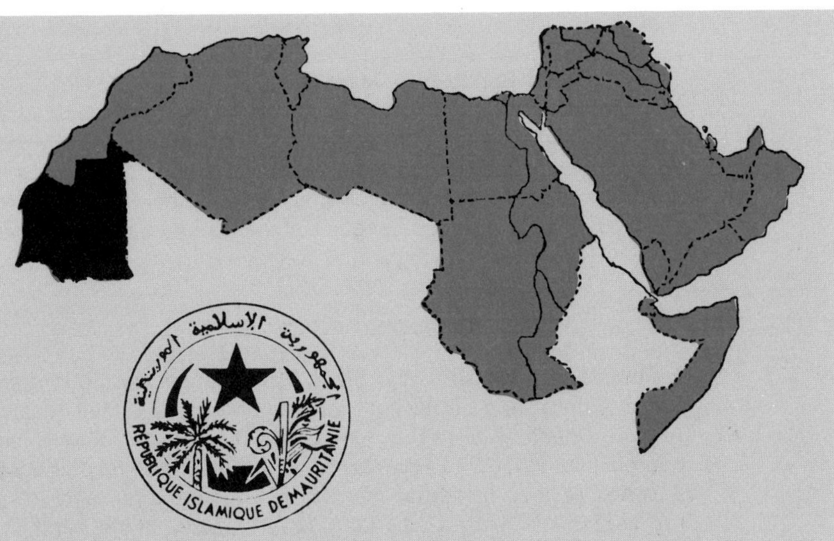

MAURITANIA

الجمهورية الإسلامية الموريتانية

PROFILE

Official Name: Islamic Republic of Mauritania (Al-Jumhuriyyah al-Islamiyyah al-Mauritaniyyah)

Government: Republic

Area: 400,000 sq. mi. (about twice the size of Texas)

Population: 1,300,000

Population Density: 3/sq. mi.

Capital: Nouakchott (80,000)

Other Urban Centers: Nouadhibou, Aioun-el-Atrouss, Atar, Kiffa.

National Holiday: November 28

Currency: Ouguiya ($1.00 = 45 ouguiyas)

Press: The daily Ach-Chaab in Arabic and French

Radio and Television: Radio transmissions in Arabic, French and local dialects.

Main Airports: Nouakchott and Nouadhibou

Date of Joining the United Nations: October 27, 1971

Date of Joining the Arab League: November 26, 1973

MAURITANIA

INTRODUCTION

The Islamic Republic of Mauritania is, in the words of its President Moukhtar Ould Daddah, a hyphen and a link between black sub-Saharan Africa and Arab North Africa. Its northern portion has an Arab-Islamic past, and its southern part, especially the Senegal River region, is deeply steeped in the life of the Sahel. Mauritania is the African spokesman in the Arab League, and the League's ambassador to its African partners of the Third World.

PHYSICAL GEOGRAPHY

Topography

Mauritania is a vast west African plain bounded by the former Spanish Sahara (north and northwest), Algeria (northeast), Mali (east) and the Atlantic Ocean (west). The Senegal River forms its southern border. Its approximately 450,000 square miles in the western end of the Sahara are a series of four plateaus: the Adrar, Tagant, Affole and Assaba. The highest peak is Kedia d'Idjil (2,900 feet) located in the Adrar at F'Derik; iron ore is mined at nearby Jabal al-Hadid. Copper is mined near Akjoujt at Guelb el-Moghrein.

Climate

There are four climatic and geographic zones. The Saharan zone which receives 2-5 inches of rainfall annually includes the northern two-thirds of the territory. The Sahel region ends about 20 miles north of the Senegal River; rainfall reaches the 10-inch mark. Sahel vegetation supports cattle, goats, and sheep. Wells and springs permit the cultivation of extensive date palm groves in the Adrar and Tagant oases, and the herding of camels. The Chemama, or Senegal River Valley, is Mauritania's millet basket and represents the greatest concentration of sedentary life. Lastly, the Coastal, or sub-Canarian zone, stretches along the 400-mile Atlantic coast from the Senegal River to Nouadhibou in the north.

HUMAN GEOGRAPHY

Population

Population estimates can vary greatly and have ranged from 1.2 to 1.5 million inhabitants. This is due to the difficulty of surveying the nomads who account for about 75 percent of the entire population. Rural and sedentary inhabitants account for 15 percent; urban residents total 10 percent.

Islam is the religion of all Mauritanians. Two religious fraternities prevail, the Qadiriyah and the Tijaniyah. Arabic is the official language. Nouakchott, the capital, is on the Atlantic coast. It is the largest city in the country, with a population of about 80,000. Other towns are Nouadhibou, the economic center (30,000), Aioun-el-Atrouss, Atar and Kiffa (15,000 each).

Maures

The great majority of the population is Maure. Defining a Maure does not rest on skin color, but rather depends on paternal descent. White-skinned Maures account for 54 percent, and black-skinned Maures for 27 percent. The remaining 28 percent consists of Fulbe, Tukulor, Soninke, Wolof and Bambara who are mainly sedentary cultivators clustered in the Senegal River Valley.

The development of the mining industry and its ancillary services, as well as the terrible drought in the 1970s that crippled the whole Sahel from Dakar to Djibouti, have greatly contributed to a sedentarization trend that may ultimately upset the very structure and fabric of Mauritanian society.

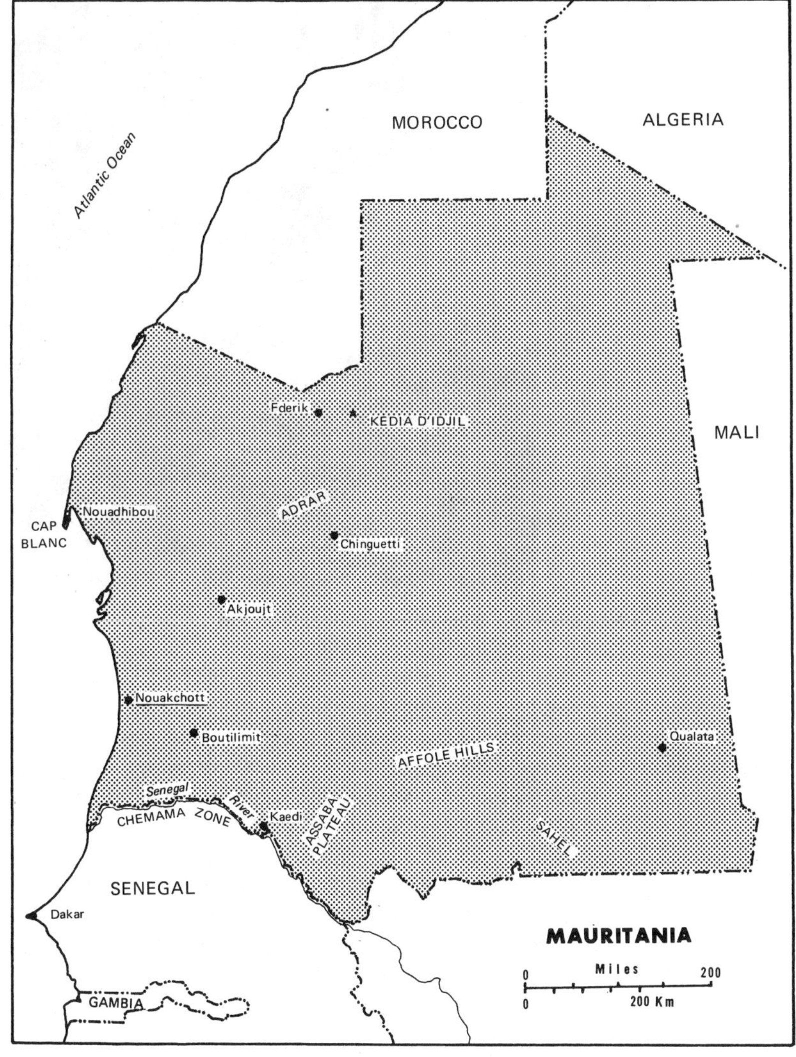

ECONOMY

Agriculture and animal husbandry constitute the traditional sector of the economy, while mining and fishery represent the modern sector. Agriculture, declared a priority sector at the 1968 Congress, is centered along the Senegal River and some northern oases. The primary crops are dates, gum arabic, millet and rice. The animal wealth, measured in camels, sheep and cattle, was partly decimated after the six-year Sahelian drought. The fishing industry is now being fully developed. A number of organizations have been created to tap the rich fish resources. International agreements regulate fishing rights within the new 30-mile territorial water limit.

Mining

Iron and copper are the major mining interests. Iron ore reserves at F'Derik are estimated at 100 million tons of 66 percent pure hematite iron. Copper reserves at Akjoujt are estimated at 32 million tons.

A number of industrial projects evidence stronger ties with the Arab world. A steel mill is projected for Nouadhibou as is the creation of an Arab Society of Metallurgical Industries with a $20 million capital, half of which provided by Kuwait. The copper foundry planned for Nouakchott will have an annual capacity of 30,000 tons.

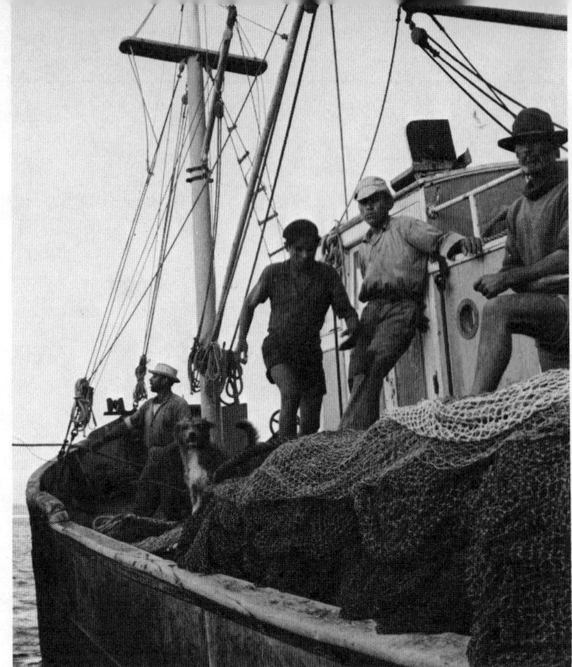

Fishing boats at Nouadhibou on the north coast of Mauritania.

Transportation

Growing industrialization has led to the expansion of ancillary industries such as housing, electrical power stations, modernization of the iron ore port of Nouadhibou and a railway linking F'Derik and Nouadhibou and extending to Akjoujt and Nouakchott. However, despite the rail link, transportation is inadequate with only about 3,875 miles of roads. Investments have also been made to modernize the traditional economy. These include an agricultural research center and a land reclamation scheme which was initiated in the Gorgol Valley near Kaedi in March, 1975.

The most direct result of the mining industry has been an increase of foreign trade and national income which made it possible for Mauritania to abandon the Franc zone and establish its own currency (the ouguiya) in 1973. Until independence, foreign aid was provided by France. At present there is a diversification of sources of aid including the United States, the People's Republic of China, and Arab states.

HISTORY

Sanhajah Confederation

Forming a bridge and a terminus to numerous migrations and invasions, Mauritania is intimately linked to the economic and political life of both its northern and southern neighbors. The Sanhajah Confederation (Lamtunah, Masufah and Juddalah) played an essential role from the eighth to the tenth century in the trans-Saharan trade from its capital at Awdaghust. This role of intermediary was curtailed during the Almoravid interlude in the tenth century. It was resumed again during the Golden Age of the Sudanic Empires of Ghana, Mali and Songhay until the defeat of the Songhay in 1590 by Juder, the Spanish renegade. Juder had been sent by Muhammad al-Dhahabi, the Moroccan monarch who coveted the gold coming from the forest regions.

French Rule

European contacts began when the Portuguese established a trading post at Arguin in 1448. They were determined to reach the source of gold in the hinterland. In the growing commercial relations, the Maures often played one European power against another. The Congress of Vienna (1815) recognized France as sovereign over the coast of West Africa from Cape Blanc in the north to the Senegal in the south. With Louis Faidherbes as governor of Senegal (1854-1861, 1863-1865) the policy of influence was replaced by a French presence. Until 1934, ruthless military actions were used to effectively control the mercurial Maures.

Independence

France governed Mauritania as part of French West Africa and relied heavily on some traditional Maure chiefs in a policy not unlike that of Indirect Rule as practiced by Lugard in Northern Nigeria. The Brazzaville Conference (1944) resulted in a series of reforms that culminated in the Constitution of 1946 in which Mauritania was separated politically from Senegal.

Political life developed with the 1946 legislative elections, and a succession of parties appeared. Independence came on November 28, 1960. The Parti du Peuple Mauritanien (PPM) eventually became the sole national party.

After a period of close collaboration with France, Mauritania has opted for a policy of nonalignment and good relations with both the Western and Communist blocs.

GOVERNMENT AND SOCIETY

Administration

After experimenting with Western parliamentary government and the 1961 Constitution, Mauritania adopted a "Presidential system" to reflect the need for a strong centralized leadership. The legislative branch is represented by an elected 50-member National Assembly. The legal system is a compromise between French law and the Shari'ah, both at the level of First Instance courts and the six-man Supreme Court. The Mauritanian People's Party (PPM) includes all interest groups (women, traditional chiefs and traditional unions) and offers a forum and an instrument for nation building.

A class in a school at Nouakchott.

Education

Because of the impact of the Arabic language, education was a delicate problem. Arabic is the national and official language while French is a working language. Troubles occurred in 1966 when an attempt was made to impose Arabic as the medium of instruction. Strong objections of students caused the government to change its position. Arabic is now gradually introduced at the elementary level.

Traditional Islamic education is still provided in Koranic schools and at the Institute of Islamic Studies (1955) at Boutilimitt. Modern secondary education is provided in the urban centers. A vocational school was established in Nouadhibou in 1965. There is presently no university in Mauritania and most students study abroad, in Africa, Europe, or the United States.

Social Divisions

Mauritanian society has two major divisions: the Maures and the Negroid minorities. The Maures are a mixture of Arabs, Sanhajah Berbers and the inhabitants of the Senegal River Valley. The Bani Hasan Arabs of the Bani Ma'qil reached Mauritania in the sixteenth century. Since then Maure society has consisted of four major classes: the Bidah (whites) who form the nobility ('Azmah) and are divided into two groups, warriors and monastic people (Zwayah); the client (Lahmah) or tributary (Zanagah) tribes; the servile class ('Abid) and liberated serfs (Harratin); and a network of castes that includes craftsmen, bards, saltminers, hunters and fishermen. In addition, there are other ethnic groups who have their own social systems.

Cultural Life

The rich cultural life mirrors the dichotomy of its ethnic makeup. The Maures, proud of their Arab heritage, express their art in Arabic poetry and music, while the ethnic groups of the Senegal River Valley reflect the influence of the Sahel and forest regions in their music and dances. Traditional handicrafts, such as silverwork, leatherwork and carpet weaving, are promoted by the government's Bureau de l'artisanat (handicraft bureau). One almost untapped resource of Mauritania's cultural heritage is the Arabic manuscript collections held by the great families.

Tourism

Mauritania offers much to the unconventional tourist: the River region, the oases of the North during the date harvest, the intriguing city of Oualata, and Chinguetti and its "Beau Geste" fort and venerable mosque. Accommodations in the interior have not yet reached the level of their urban counterparts.

PROSPECTS

Mauritania has firmly established the authority of the PPM in spite of some opposition groups and is seriously involved in forging a nation out of a state. The development of the mining industry is providing the government with the means to implement its social and economic program. A delicate balance between East and West is the mainstay of Mauritania's foreign policy while membership in the Organization of African Unity and the Arab League shows its determination to strengthen and affirm its Arab-African personality.

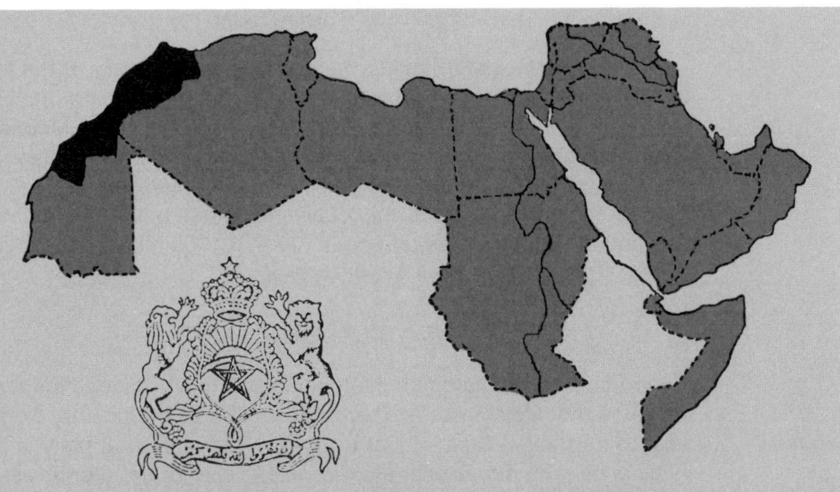

MOROCCO

المملكة المغربية

PROFILE

Official Name: Kingdom of Morocco (al-Mamlaka al-Maghribiyya)

Head of State: H. M. Hassan II

Government: Constitutional Monarchy

Area: 172,415 sq. miles (=California)

Population: 18.3 million (est., 1977)

Population Density: 106 per sq. Mi.

Capital: Rabat (370,000)

Other Urban Centers: Casablanca, Marrakesh, Fez, Meknes, Tangier, Tetouan, Agadir

National Holiday: March 3

Currency: Dirham ($1.00 = 4.00 dirhams)

Daily Press: 10, circulation 197,000

Radio and Television: Programs in Arabic, English and Spanish

Sites of Interest: Remains of Phoenecian civilization; the "red city" of Marrakesh; Kutubiyya Mosque; Fez and Mulay Idriss

Main Airports: Casablanca, Rabat, Tangier

Main Seaports: Tangier, Casablanca

Date of Joining the United Nations: November 12, 1956

Date of Joining the Arab League: September 1, 1958

MOROCCO

INTRODUCTION

The Kingdom of Morocco is the westernmost country of the Maghrib, or the West, the Arabic designation for the region now occupied by Morocco, Algeria and Tunisia. In Arabic Morocco is al-Mamlakah al-Maghribiyyah, the Western Kingdom. Its area of 172,415 square miles is a little larger than California's 158,693 square miles, and its 1977 population was over 18 million. It has coastlines along both the Mediterranean Sea and the Atlantic Ocean, about 300 and 1000 miles respectively. The largest cities are along the Atlantic coast.

PHYSICAL GEOGRAPHY

Topography

Morocco is dominated by the highest and most rugged components of the Atlas mountain system. The ranges traverse the country from southwest to northeast. From Rabat to Essaouira the coastal plain is 20 to 30 miles wide with occasional alluvial extensions to the interior associated with river valleys. The alluvial plain of the Sebou River north of Rabat covers 47,000 acres and produces 38 percent of Morocco's citrus fruits. Other river valleys are those of the Oum er-Rhbia and Tensift (south of Casablanca), the Sous (at Agadir) and the Moulouya (between Melilla and the Algerian border).

To the interior of the coastal plain is the meseta, a 700-foot high plateau which is about 80 miles wide and extends approximately from Meknes to Marrakesh. The meseta's soil is less fertile than that of the plains, but it contains the world's largest deposits of phosphates. These are mined at Khouribga and Youssoufia. Between the plateau and the Atlas mountain ranges are two inland alluvial plains, the Tadla plain of the upper Oum er-Rhbia River and its tributaries, and the Haouz plain of the upper Tensift River and its tributaries. As in the coastal areas, the main crops are cereals, especially wheat and barley.

Fez, one of the "Imperial Cities" of Morocco and a favorite spot for tourists.

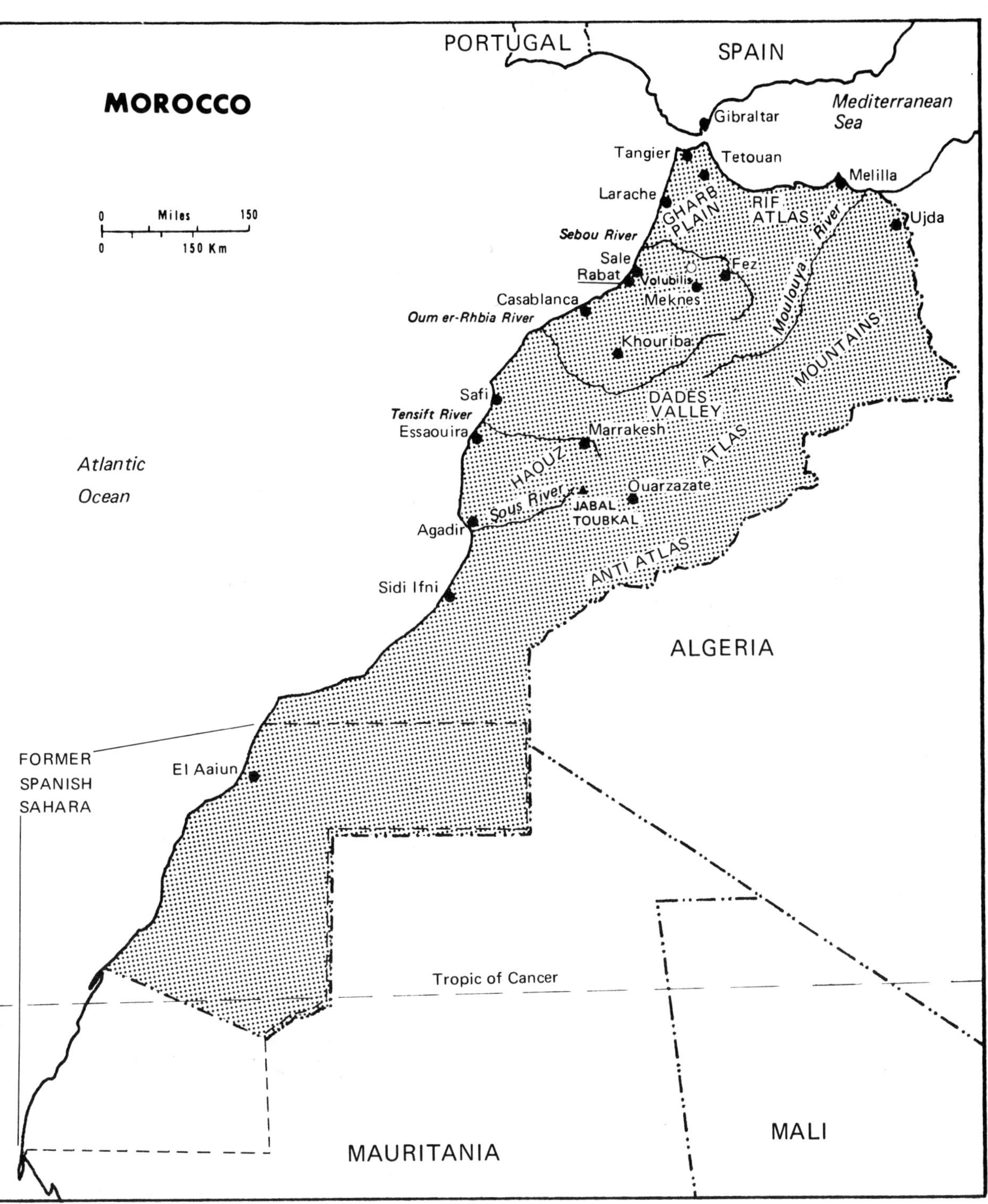

The High Atlas Mountains, the highest of Northwest Africa's Atlas system, extend for 500 miles from the Atlantic coast between Essaouira and Agadir eastwards to the Algerian border. They are about 70 miles wide. In the west all peaks are higher than 10,000 feet and they include North Africa's highest mountain, Jabal Toubkal, at 13,665 feet. North of the

High Atlas and east of the meseta are the Middle Atlas, a lower range though also containing many peaks over 10,000 feet. South of the High Atlas and east of the Sous River are the Anti Atlas, the lowest of the Atlas ranges. The northernmost range is the Rif Atlas, along the Mediterranean between Tangier and Melilla.

Rainfall

The Atlas ranges effectively block the Atlantic rainbearing winds from reaching the south and east, and protect the north and west from the desiccating Saharan winds. The Rif and the Middle Atlas receive upwards of 47 inches a year, and northwestern Morocco as a whole receives over 16 inches. Amounts decrease southwards as well as with a decrease in altitude. Tangier receives 35 inches, Fez 21, Casablanca 15, Marrakesh 9.4, and Agadir 8.8. It is important to note the seasonality of precipitation, one of wet winters and dry summers. Southeastern Morocco fringes on the Sahara, and annual rainfall is less than 4 inches.

HUMAN GEOGRAPHY

Vital Statistics

The mid-1977 estimated population was 18.3 million. Birth rates and death rates were 48 and 16 per thousand, respectively, giving an annual growth rate of 3.2 percent. If that rate were maintained the population would double in 22 years and would exceed 35 million in the year 2000. The infant mortality rate was 130 per 1000 live births per year. The median age was 18.2 years, and 46 percent of the population was under 15 years old. The urban population accounted for 38 percent of the total. The per capita gross national product was U.S. $470.

Settlement

Most Moroccans live in the northwest in such areas as the coastal plain, the lower river valleys and the meseta, and most are engaged in agriculture, pastoralism and fishing. Nomads and seminomads live in the Middle Atlas and adjacent plateaus, though nomadism is declining rapidly. Villages are also losing population because of the migration to urban centers.

Arab and Berber

In terms of composition, Morocco's population is Arab with a strong Berber component. The difference today is mainly linguistic. The Berber language is found in the mountains, historically areas of refuge and isolation, and it is spoken by perhaps a third of the people. Most Berbers speak Arabic as well. Islam is the religion of 98 percent of the people.

A woman from southern Morocco displaying her wealth in jewelry.

ECONOMY

The economy is based primarily on the export of raw materials and the import of manufactured goods. This pattern is a legacy of colonial rule and the main task facing Morocco is to change it.

Agriculture

Forty million acres of land in Morocco are cultivated, primarily in the, western plains. Principal crops are cereals, legumes and citrus fruits. Cork is an important forest commercial product, and Rabat has one of the world's largest cork factories. But much of the land is engaged in subsistence cultivation using traditional methods of low productivity. Modern farms produce and export citrus fruit, tomatoes, green vegetables and grapes. Income from livestock constitutes one-third of all agricultural income.

Mineral Wealth

Morocco contains 40 percent of the world's known phosphate deposits, and since 1921 phosphates have been among Morocco's major exports. Almost all phosphate is exported as unrefined ore. Morocco also has less important deposits of iron, lead, manganese, zinc, cobalt and copper. The limited oil reserves in the Gharb plain have been exhausted and most of the crude oil processed by Morocco's two refineries is imported. Domestic coal is a major source of energy, and about 50 percent of the hydroelectric potential of Morocco's rivers is presently utilized.

Transportation

Cities and towns are well connected by paved roads. A railroad connects Casablanca with Algiers and Tunis. Another railroad connects the meseta phosphate mines, Rabat, Casablanca, Marrakesh, and Safi. There are thirty commercial airfields, nine of which serve international traffic. The busiest are at Tangier, Casablanca and Rabat. Tangier and Casablanca also handle the greatest passenger maritime traffic. Tangier is the busier of the two because of active ferry traffic from Gibraltar, and in fact consideration is being given to building a bridge across the strait.

Fishing

Agadir is the main fishing port. Also important are Safi, Casablanca and Essaouira. Catches include sardines, mackerel, tuna, and anchovies. An important factor in the presence of rich fishing waters is the Canary Current, a cool ocean current which flows from northeast to southwest. It also causes cooler and drier conditions along the coast than would otherwise be the case.

Modern industry is limited. Among the more modern industrial processes are automobile assembly, textile spinning and weaving, and food processing, especially the processing and canning of fish. Some textiles are exported, as are fish.

The government's economic policy favors private enterprise, although the government itself has been forced to become the country's main investor because of the lack of sufficient Moroccan private investment. Foreign investment is actively encouraged, and the private sector of the economy is still dominated by the French minority that remained after independence. The two exceptions are the textile and hotel trades which are largely owned by Moroccans. Most of Morocco's trade—50 percent of imports and 60 percent of exports—is with the European Economic Community, or Common Market.

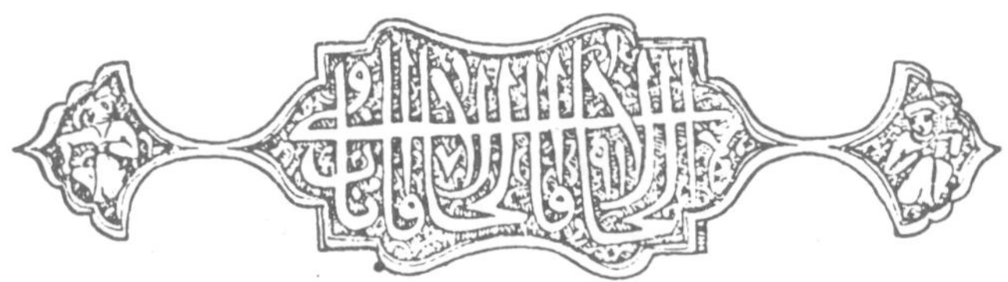

MOROCCO

HISTORY

Roman Period

After the fall of Carthage (in what is today Tunisia) in 146 B.C., the Berber kingdoms of northern Morocco came under Roman influence. In 46 A.D. northern Morocco was annexed by Rome and became the Roman province of Mauretania Tingitania, with its capital at Tangiers. During the following centuries, most of Morocco consisted of independent tribes and small kingdoms, although some coastal cities came under Byzantine control. In 710 A.D., the Arab expedition led by Musa ibn Nusair resulted in the conversion of the Berber people of Morocco to Islam, and in the same year Morocco came under the rule of the Umayyad Caliphate in Damascus. However, in 740 the Berbers revolted against Umayyad rule in connection with the Muslim Kharijite doctrine that the caliphate was not an inheritable position. In 757 a Kharijite kingdom was founded at Sijilmassah on the Sahara border 250 miles east of today's Marrakesh, and Sijilmassah was the most important kingdom in Morocco until the eleventh century because of its domination of the trans-Saharan gold trade.

Arab Period

Idrissid Dynasty

At the end of the eighth century, a kingdom was established in northern Morocco by Idris I, a descendant of the Prophet Muhammad's son-in-law and cousin Ali. Idris I and his son Idris II built the city of Fez as their capital. The Idrissid state was the first non-tribal Islamic state in Morocco. After the death of Idris II in 828, it split into several Idrissid principalities. The next great Moroccan dynasty was that of the Almoravids in the eleventh century. A puritanical religious movement that consisted only of the Sanhaja nomads of the Sahara, this dynasty brought all of Morocco and Muslim Spain under its control by the end of the eleventh century. The famous Almoravid Sultan Youssef ben Tashfin established the Almoravid capital at Marrakesh in 1070. The Almoravids were in turn replaced by another puritanical religious movement, that of the Almohads of the Atlas mountains. The Almohads reigned from 1147 to 1269 and eventually controlled most of the Maghrib as well as Muslim Spain. The Almohad Sultan Abd el-Mu'min brought a number of nomadic Arab tribes

Almohad Dynasty

Minaret of the Koutoubiyyah Mosque in Marrakesh

to Morocco to help fight the Christian kingdoms of Spain. Most historians agree that the arrival of these tribes and their settlement in the plains near the cities resulted in the Arabization of the plains, whereas Berber dialects continued to be spoken in the mountains.

After the death of Sultan Yaqoub el Mansour in 1199, the Almohad empire was weakened by defeats in 1212 and 1248 in Spain, by the revolt of the Abd el-Ouadids in what is now western Algeria, and by the revolt of the Hafsids in what is now Tunisia. In 1269 the Marinid dynasty from the steppes of eastern Morocco conquered Marrakesh and destroyed the last remnants of Almohad power, and by the middle of the fourteenth century the Marinids had reunited all of the Maghrib under their rule. But this unity was short-lived, and the Hafsids of Tunis, the kingdom of Tlemcen in what is now western Algeria, and the Maqil tribes of southern Morocco came to control the most important trans-Saharan trade routes, thus weakening the economic basis of Marinid power. These factors along with the Portuguese occupation of many Moroccan coastal towns during the fifteenth century led to the downfall of the Marinids and their replacement by the related dynasty of the Wattassids in 1471.

The capital of Morocco, Rabat is its third largest city. This is a view of the Modern Avenue Mohammad V.

Qasbah on the road to Ksar er-Souq

Alawite Dynasty

Portuguese conquests on the coast continued and religious brotherhoods developed all over the country in response to the general state of insecurity. A group of such brotherhoods brought the Saadian dynasty to power in 1554. In 1666 the Saadians were replaced by the Alawites, who continue to rule up to the present day. The Alawite Sultan Moulay Ismail, who reigned from 1672 to 1727, succeeded in suppressing the tribes and brotherhoods that had become very powerful during the Wattassid and Saadian dynasties. He also succeeded in driving out the English from Tangiers and the Spanish from coastal Larache and Mamora. But after the reign of Moulay Ismail, the "Shareefian," or Moroccan, empire was once again weakened by European domination of trade and consequent internal conflicts.

Independence

During the nineteenth century, the European powers imposed a series of treaties upon the Alawite Sultans. These treaties, "opening" Morocco to European imports, culminated in the 1912 Treaty of Fez which divided Morocco into a French "Protectorate" over most of the country, a Spanish "Protectorate" over the north and an "International Zone" in and around Tangier. The French and the Spanish did not completely defeat Moroccan resistance until 1934. The policy of the French and the Spanish was to preserve the pre-colonial Moroccan government and the Alawite dynasty, but real power was held by the colonial bureaucracy. Moroccan resistance to colonial rule was renewed after World War II, and after many years of bitter political conflict and guerilla warfare Morocco regained its independence in 1956. It remains a monarchy under the Alawite Sultan Hassan II.

GOVERNMENT AND SOCIETY

Morocco is a monarchy and the king is the center of political power. There is a parliament which had considerable power from 1963 to 1965 but which is now largely controlled by the king. The main political parties are the Istiqlal and the Union Nationale des Forces Populaires. The Istiqlal, or Independence, Party led the struggle for independence in the 1950s and has continued to dominate Moroccan politics ever since. Dissatisfied with the conservatism of the Istiqlal leadership, many of its younger and more radical members formed the Union Nationale des Forces Populaires in 1959. There have also been several more temporary parties formed by very conservative tribal leaders in alliance with the king. The members of parliament are elected by municipal councils and committees and by various professional and labor organizations.

Administration

Administration is highly centralized. The *qa'ids,* chiefs of rural administrative units, and the *pashas,* chiefs of urban administrative units, are appointed by the Ministry of the Interior. The governors of the nineteen provinces and of the prefectures of Casablanca and Rabat-Sale' are appointed by the king. These officials are aided by consultative councils.

Law

Moroccan law is basically of French origin, although law pertaining to personal status is based on Islamic law. French magistrates are employed under a special arrangement with France. The Ministry of Justice officially conducts its affairs in Arabic, but the process of Arabization of the legal system has been slow.

Cultural Life

French influence is evident in various aspects of Moroccan life. Education is still largely in French, and most Moroccan intellectuals write in French more often than in Arabic. The continued presence of a substantial French minority in Rabat and Casablanca and the growing number of Moroccan workers in France and Belgium contribute to a continuation of this influence throughout much of Moroccan society. The conflict between French and Arab culture is the basic theme running through most contemporary Moroccan art. The government is trying to preserve and foster Morocco's artistic traditions by supporting art schools and musical conservatories in Rabat, Casablanca, Tetouan, and elsewhere. Folk culture, especially traditional dance, is greatly encouraged by the government.

Education

Morocco spends more than 20 percent of the annual budget on education. The number of students attending elementary and secondary schools is increasing yearly (1,544,422 in 1972). There are four universities and a number of independent colleges. Al-Qarawiyin University in Fez was founded in 859 A.D. The other three universities are in Rabat, Marrakesh and Tangier.

Tourism

Morocco's famous cities, mountains, beaches and festivals have always attracted tourists from all over the world. However, since the late 1960s, tourism has increased phenomenally. The government has placed great stress on tourism and has encouraged the construction of hotels. Those tourists seeking beaches and surf tend to go to Agadir in the south and Tangier in the north. Those who seek to spend their vacations near mountain springs and lakes usually go to the Middle Atlas, especially in the region of Ifrane, 30 miles southeast of Meknes, where there is also skiing. Those interested in the traditional culture of Morocco usually visit the "Imperial Cities" of Rabat, Meknes, Fez and Marrakesh, all of which contain many beautiful mosques, palaces, gardens and museums. The madinas, or old cities, of Fez and Marrakesh are also famous for their markets and handicrafts.

A beach scene at the resort of Restinga on the Mediterranean in Morocco's Rif.

Most visitors to Morocco try to see a "moussem," a festival for a local "saint" involving displays of horsemanship and marksmanship. The most famous moussem is that of Moulay Idris, the founder of the Idrissid Dynasty, whose sanctuary is eighteen miles north of Meknes. Nearby are the Roman ruins of the city of Volubilis, covering 100 acres. Other attractions include the castles of Telouet and Ouarzazate in the High Atlas mountains, the Dades and the Todgha valleys near Ouarzazate (80 miles southeast of Marrakesh), and the desert in the far south.

PROSPECTS

During its long recorded history Morocco's external contacts have been northwards with Europe and eastwards with Arab influences. Contacts have certainly existed, and endured, southwards with the Sahara and places beyond, but these have been less sustained and less intense. This pattern of relationships is evident today. Western Europe, especially France, is the primary economic partner. French linguistic and cultural influence is still strong. At the same time, Morocco is an active member of the League of Arab States and is involved with the Arab world's varied political and economic concerns.

Domestically, the process of modernization is progressing steadily. There continues to be a maldistribution of national income. For instance, half of the national income comes from the modern sector which involves only ten percent of the population. Significant steps still need to be made to combat illiteracy and thus actively to incorporate more of the population in production and especially in its rewards. More advantage can also be taken of the country's varied mineral resources and agricultural opportunities, of its unusual geographical location along both the Mediterranean and the Atlantic, and of the great tourist potential of its physical, historical and cultural attributes. The quality of life of the individual Moroccan is improving, and the rate of improvement can be increased to the advantage of both the individual and the nation.

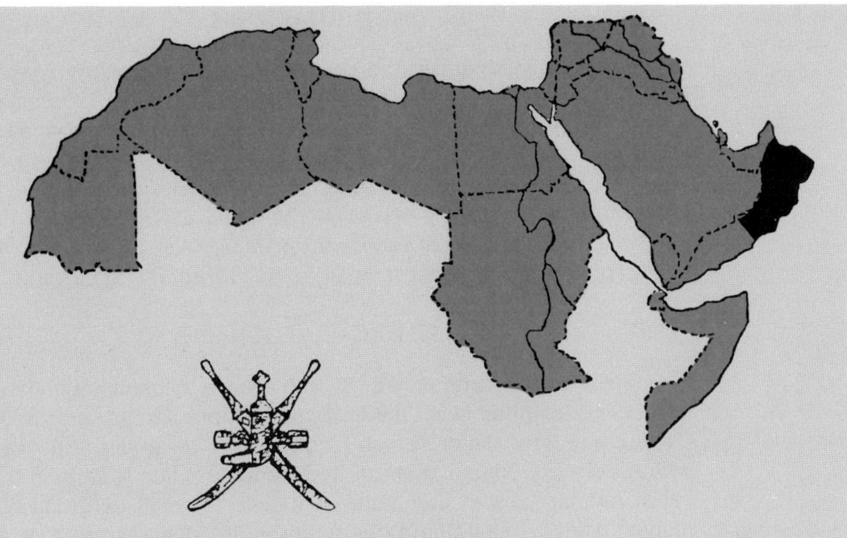

OMAN

سلطنة عمان

PROFILE

Official Name: Sultanate of Oman (Saltanat Oman)

Head of State: Qabus ibn Said

Government: Sultanate

Area: 82,000 (estimated)

Population: 800,000

Population Density: 10 per sq. mi.

Capital: Muscat

Other Urban Centers: Matrah, Nizwa, Sohar

Currency: Indian Rupees

Press: Weekly Arabic (Al-Akida) and English (Gulf Mirror)

Principal Products: Crude Oil

Date of Joining the United Nations: October 7, 1971

Date of Joining the Arab League: September 29, 1971

OMAN

INTRODUCTION

Oman is a sultanate in the southeastern corner of the Arabian Peninsula. For many decades Oman was one of the most isolationist countries in the Arab world, and its affairs were conducted with the advice of the United Kingdom. Until 1970 it was known as Muscat and Oman, a nomenclature which reflects a historic internal differentiation. Oil was discovered in the desert interior in 1964, and export began in 1967. Reserves and production are modest, however, and oil has had very little impact on the population, especially if compared with the Gulf States.

PHYSICAL GEOGRAPHY

Oman's area is estimated at 82,000 square miles; its boundaries have not been delimited with either Saudi Arabia (west) or the People's Democratic Republic of Yemen (southwest). The land is largely a plateau with hardly any coastal plain. A dominant mountain system in the north, Jabal Akhdar (Green Mountain), parallels the Gulf of Oman coast. Its highest point is Jabal Sham (9900 feet). The southeastern division of the ridge, Hajar Sharqi, rises quite precipitously from the coast and stretches to Ras al Hadd, the easternmost point in the Arabian peninsula. In the northwestern portion of the highlands, Hajar Gharbi, there is a narrow coastal plain, 10 to 25 miles wide, called the Batinah. Towards the interior the highlands decrease in altitude in a rugged and rough manner to about 4000 feet; there the now gentler slope blends into the Rub'al-Khali (great sandy desert) along the undefined border with Saudi Arabia.

Topography

Rub 'al Khali

In the south near the coastal city of Salalah the plateau edge also rises abruptly from the sea to about 4500 feet and then slopes gradually toward the great desert. The escarpment itself becomes lower northeastwards, and at about Masirah Bay (near Masirah Island) it is virtually lost in an extensive sandy region which is almost continuous with Rub'al-Khali. Dhofar's coastal plain is 10 miles wide and 40 miles long.

Oman possesses a small but important exclave on the Musandam Peninsula which separates the Gulf of Oman from the Arabian Gulf. The northern part of this peninsula belongs to Oman and is known as Ru'us al-Jibal (the Mountaintops). The topography is a continuation of the Omani mountain system and there is no coastal plain.

A typical Omani town, mountain and oasis.

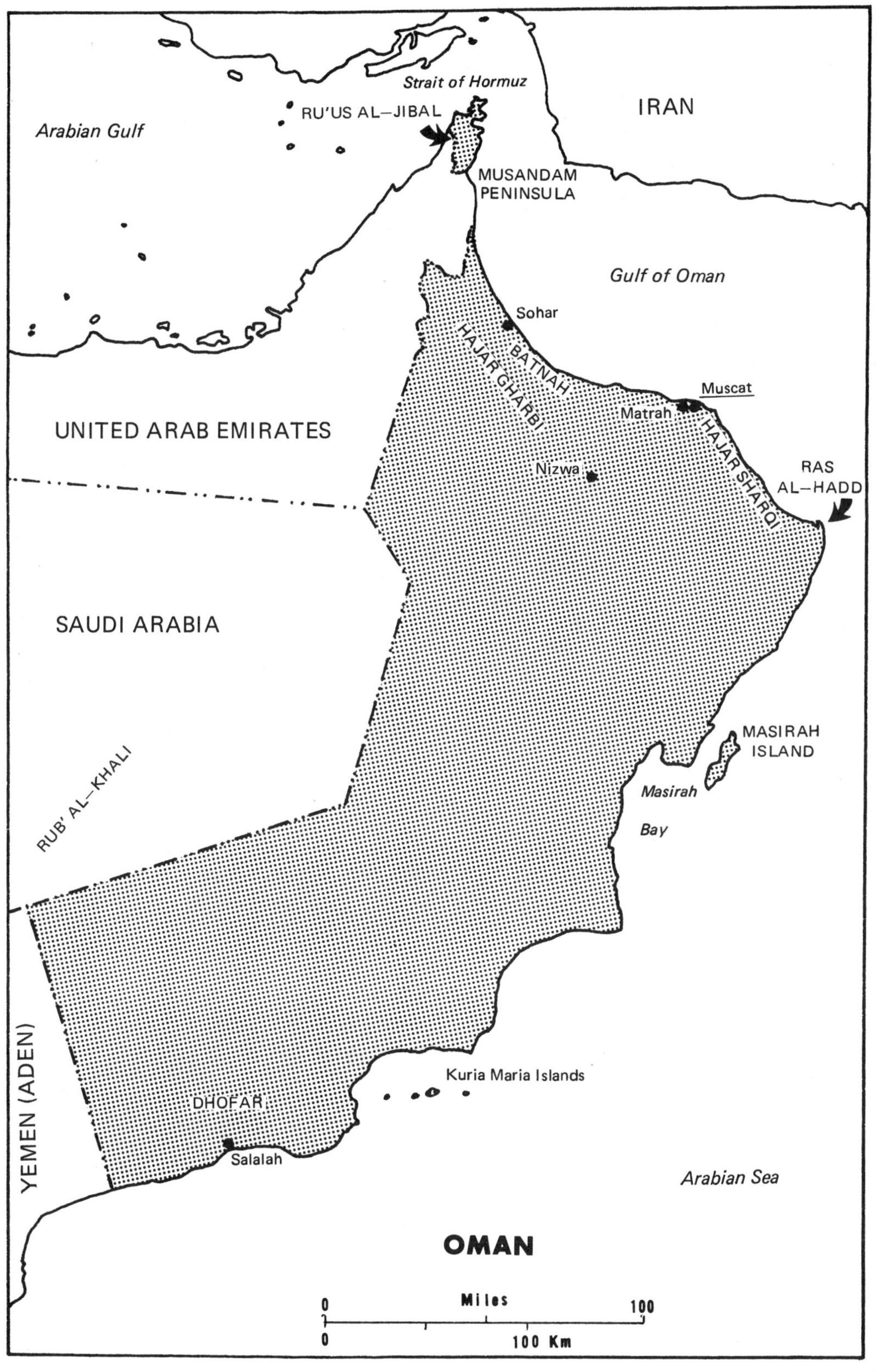
Strait of Hormuz
RU'US AL–JIBAL
IRAN
Arabian Gulf
MUSANDAM
PENINSULA
Gulf of Oman
Sohar
BATNAH
HAJAR GHARBI
Muscat
Matrah
UNITED ARAB EMIRATES
HAJAR SHARQI
Nizwa
RAS
AL–HADD
SAUDI ARABIA
MASIRAH
ISLAND
Masirah
Bay
RUB' AL–KHALI
Kuria Maria Islands
DHOFAR
YEMEN (ADEN)
Salalah
Arabian Sea
OMAN
0
Miles
100
0
100 Km

OMAN

Governor's house and courts in Rustaq, a small mountain town in the interior

There are three general regions. Muscat, the coastal part of the north, is the site of the capital and historic port city of Muscat. South of Jabal Akhdar is Oman and the regional center of Nizwa. Oman has been one of the world's most isolated regions, bounded as it is by rugged mountains and the vast expanse of Rub 'al Khali. The southern region is Dhofar, with Salalah as its capital, and it is separated from the north by 500 miles of a virtually empty desert.

Climate

Parts of Oman are reasonably well-watered if compared with most of the Arabian Peninsula. Jabal Akhdar receives between 15 and 20 inches of annual rainfall. In the Batinah lowlands amounts vary between 3 and 6 inches. Winter is the rainy season in the north. By contrast, Dhofar receives most of its 10 inches of rain between May and September. A relatively heavy growth of shrubs extends up to 40 miles inland, an extension of the wetter and greener conditions in Yemen. But rainfall and vegetation growth rapidly taper off further east along the coast. Temperatures are hot almost everywhere, except in the Jabal Akhdar uplands where winter nights will occasionally bring freezing conditions. Summer months average 100°F or even 110°F along the coast, and high humidities leave a stifling mist which hovers over the embayments and narrow Batinah plain. In the interior, away from the highlands, similarly high temperatures occur, though here the air is dry and shimmering from the intense heat.

OMAN

Leila, a woman from Oman

HUMAN GEOGRAPHY

Population

The population is estimated at 800,000. No census has ever been taken. Ninety to 95 percent are non-urban. Of this majority perhaps 75 percent are engaged in subsistence agriculture, some as pastoralists.

ECONOMY

Batinah

Muscat

The economy is overwhelmingly agricultural and varies between Oman's three main regions. The distinction between the hadhar (settled) and the badu (nomad) is most evident on opposite sides of Jabal Akhdar and the attendant lifestyles of Muscat and Oman. Along the 200-mile Batinah coast a series of small villages raise dates, coconut palms, oranges, sweet limes, tomatoes, beet roots, carrots, cauliflowers, peppers, cabbages, radishes, melons, papaya, mangoes, bananas, alfalfa and chickpeas. The villages are 15 to 20 miles apart. Fresh water is from springs fed by subterranean flow from the mountains. The sea is also important to the economy and the catch includes sardines, whitebait, crayfish and sharks. Further inland, a level gravel plain supports scattered shrubs and extends to the foothills. On the slopes there is more cultivation, both in wadis and on terraces. Muscat, just beyond the southern end of Batinah, is an administrative town of about 7,000. On each point of its tiny crescent-shaped bay stands a fort of ancient vintage, Merani Fort and Jalali Fort, built by the Portuguese respectively in 1587 and 1588. The forts have guarded the harbor and occasionally they became the refuge of opposing factions. A mile to the northwest is Matrah, a coastal city with a physical setting similar to Muscat's. But Matrah is two or three times larger. It is the commercial center of Batinah, and its hinterland includes Sumayl Gap, the main link through Jabal Akhdar with Oman.

Like the coastal population, Omanis receive their water supply from Jabal Akhdar's runoff and underground reservoirs. Man-made underground water channels (falajs) are dug at regular intervals. These channels likely were introduced by the Persians. Towns are oases, and there are palm groves wherever there is water. Alfalfa is always present, for it is the local animal fodder, and vegetable gardens are common. Whereas along the Batinah coast cultivation is almost continuous, in Oman settlement is discontinuous. Small towns are akin to city-states, each dominated by a fort or castle and associated with a tribal faction. They are located about a dozen miles apart and, unless there is a wadi or a falaj to carry water occasionally, they are within a dozen miles of Jabal Akhdar's slopes. Some thirty-five miles from these slopes sedentary living ends, and pastoral nomadism becomes the norm. The nomadic Omanis are famed for the quality of their camels, allegedly the best in the Arab world. Their contacts have been with Arabs to the north and west, around Rub'al-Khali, along the Gulf coast of Arabia, and from there either to interior Arabia or, more remotely, across the Gulf to Iran.

Dhofar

There are four or five small villages to the east and west of Salalah, Dhofar's regional capital located on the coast. Along the coast fishing, trading and agriculture are the means of livelihood. The mountain residents are pastoral farmers, mostly with cows, an unusual economic activity in the Arabian peninsula, though there are also goats and camels. They trade ghee, cattle and frankincense with coastal settlers for such foodstuffs as rice, tea, sugar and vegetables, and for cloth and utensils. Dried fish is used as cattle fodder. Figs, pomegranates and tamarinds are grown on the mountains.

Oil

Oman's oil was discovered in the hinterland of Jabal Akhdar. The fields are in the vicinity of Fahud, 200 miles southwest of Muscat. The pipeline ascends the landward crest to Nizwa, where it descends through the Sumayl Gap to a terminal just north of Matrah. Export began in 1967.

The Ministry of Development, which houses the Department of Agriculture, has initiated, with the help of foreign consultants, water re-

Omani ships sail past Fort Jalali in Muscat

source surveys and experimental and demonstration farms, as well as a program to develop fishing for domestic and commercial purposes. A modest experimental farm is located in Sohar, about 175 coastal miles northwest of Muscat.

HISTORY

Early Contacts

Oman's isolation and isolationism during most of the twentieth century belie a history of extensive and far-reaching contacts. Records indicate an ongoing trade with Sumer in the lower Euphrates River Valley about 3000 B.C., and a similarly ancient trade with Syria, Egypt, and Persia. Classical Romans and Greeks made references to Oman, and contacts have been more or less continuous with interior Arabia. In the other direction, across the sea, Omanis maintained contact with East Africa and South Asia.

Islam came to Oman even before the death of the prophet Muhammad in 632 A.D. During the eighth century Omanis adopted the Ibadi doctrine which maintained that the caliphate should not be hereditary and need not be kept in the same family, and they established their own separate Imamate. Today Ibadis are mostly on the landward side of Jabal Akhdar, with the city of Nizwa as the center of the Imamate. The last imam was exiled in 1948 by the British.

Portuguese

Involvement in modern international affairs started a decade after the 1497 rounding of Cape of Good Hope. In 1507, the Portuguese Alfonso de Albuquerque captured, sacked and destroyed one coastal town after another on his way to establishing Portuguese hegemony in the Indian Ocean and beyond. Portuguese control was limited to the coast. In the early seventeenth century the Yaariba dynasty became strong in the interior, and in 1650 it captured Muscat and evicted the Portuguese. Muscat became the capital of the Yaariba, starting with Sultan bin Seif I (1649-1668), and for two centuries it was the commercial center of a flourishing Indian Ocean empire. By 1730 the Muscat sultanate had captured the east African ports of Mogadishu (in today's Somalia), Mombasa (Kenya) and the islands of Zanzibar and Pemba (Tanzania).

Al bu Said Dynasty

The Yaariba's greatest challenge came from the interior. In 1749 Ahmad bin Said was elected imam and became the founder of the Al bu Said dynasty which still rules Oman. At first the dynasty was centered in Rustaq, a city at the landward foothills of Jabal Akhdar, but in the 1780's the capital was moved to Muscat. For the first time religious and political power was separated; the office of imam remained with interior tribes while the Sultan of Muscat ruled over the Omani Empire. In the nineteenth century Muscat's economic importance gave it stature with the Western powers, and treaties for the exchange of consular relations were concluded with the United States (1833, the first treaty ever to be signed by the United States with an Arab state), Britain (1839), France (1844), and the Netherlands (1877). The only one of enduring significance was that with Britain, and in the years before Oman joined the United Nations in 1971 its interests were expressed to the United Nations through the British delegation.

Empire Weakens

At the same time, Oman's commercial empire was weakening, in part because of competition from the European maritime powers, and in part because of internal difficulties and incursions into the interior by the Persians (finally evicted about 1744). The age-old competition between the coast and the interior occasionally erupted, and eventually an armed rebellion (1957-1959) sought to establish a separate political independence for the interior, with Nizwa as the capital. The rebellion was suppressed with the aid of British aircraft and soldiers. Guerrilla activity continued intermittently. In Dhofar, the sense of local patriotism has been even stronger. Even the language spoken by the mountain people, the Qara, is distinct from Arabic, though related. In 1964 an active rebellion began. In subduing the Dhofar revolt, the Oman government received military aid from Iran starting in 1973. Assistance also came from Saudi Arabia, United Arab Emirates, Jordan and Britain.

Sultan Qabus

Said bin Taimur, the thirteenth member of the Al bu Said to rule Oman, had become sultan in 1932. He was deposed on July 24, 1970 by his 28-year-old son, Qabus. Sultan Qabus, trained at Sandhurst, was a contrast to his father's isolationist and reactionary predisposition. He embarked upon domestic development projects and on an active participation in international organizations. The name of the country was changed in 1970 from Muscat and Oman to Oman to symbolize the need for internal integration. The following year Oman joined the Arab League and the United Nations.

GOVERNMENT AND SOCIETY

Administration

The administration of Oman is in the process of changing from a traditional direct rule by the Sultan to a modern apparatus of government with ministries and departments. Foreign advisors are used to run many government offices until enough Omanis are trained to take their place.

Health

Oman faces many health problems. Infant mortality is still high. But the government has started an ambitious program to establish hospitals and clinics and to get enough doctors and nurses to improve the health conditions.

Education

Primary education was a recent introduction to Oman. It is now available for boys and girls. For secondary and higher education Omanis have to go abroad.

PROSPECTS

Oman's internal diversity will not be eradicated. The sultanate's effective viability will depend foremost on the extent to which the differences will be harmonized. Secondly, and relatedly, it will depend on the extent to which enlightened development projects are effected, whether material improvements in communications and utility services, or social investments in educational and medical programs. Thirdly, it will need to be supported by Oman's oil income, modest but for Oman quite substantial. So far more than half of this revenue has been consumed by military expenditures. A greater diversification of expenditure allocation is needed.

Fort Mirani in Muscat, one of two dominating the trading town.

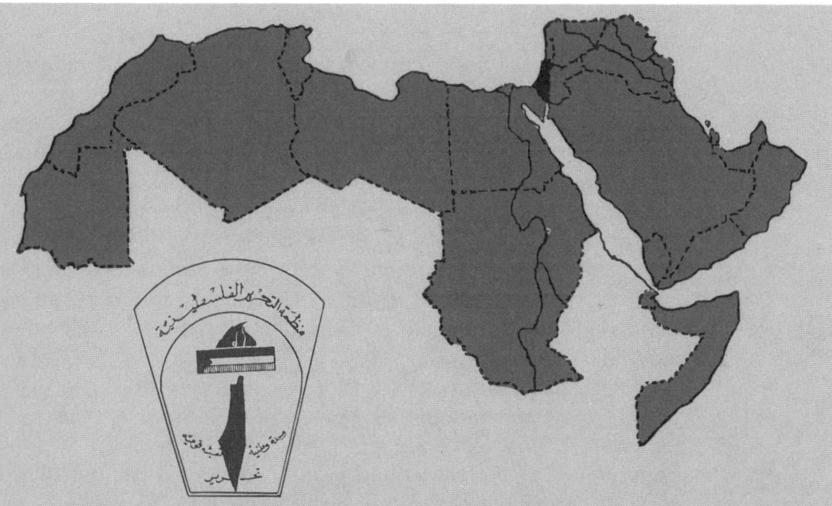

PALESTINE

فلسطين

Area: 10,159 sq. mi. (= Maryland)

Population: about 7 million (including Palestinians in forced exile and 3.1 million Israeli Jews)

Government: Projected secular democratic republic

- Palestine joined the League of Arab States as a non-voting member (special annex to the Alexandria Protocol) in 1945

- Palestine, represented by the Palestine Liberation Organization (PLO), became a voting member of the League, September 9, 1976

- Palestinian independence and sovereignty affirmed by the United Nations, November 22, 1974

- Palestine Liberation Organization, as representative of Palestine, joined the United Nations as observer, November 22, 1974

PALESTINE

INTRODUCTION

Palestine today does not exist as a political unit; as a geographic unit, the majority of its inhabitants today are non-Arab. Nevertheless, the representative of the Palestinian Arab people, the Palestine Liberation Organization (PLO), is a voting member of the League of Arab States, which confers full membership only on sovereign Arab States. The PLO is also recognized as the representative of the Palestinian people by more than one hundred and thirty States as well as the United Nations. The implication of all this is quite clear. The Palestinian people have been classified as a "colonized people" entitled to liberation. With the attainment of liberation, then a Palestinian State in Palestine would become a reality.

This peculiar situation is the consequence of the historical development of the Palestine Question under the British Mandate of Palestine. Though Palestine was conquered by the British in 1917 and controlled by them until 1948, Palestine had always been an organic part of the Arab world. Its severance from the Arab world by the establishment of Israel has not been accepted by either the Palestinians or the Arab people at large. In view of the checkered history of this country in modern times, this discussion will deal alternately with the Palestine of the Mandate period and with the Palestinian Arabs subsequent to their dispersion in 1948.

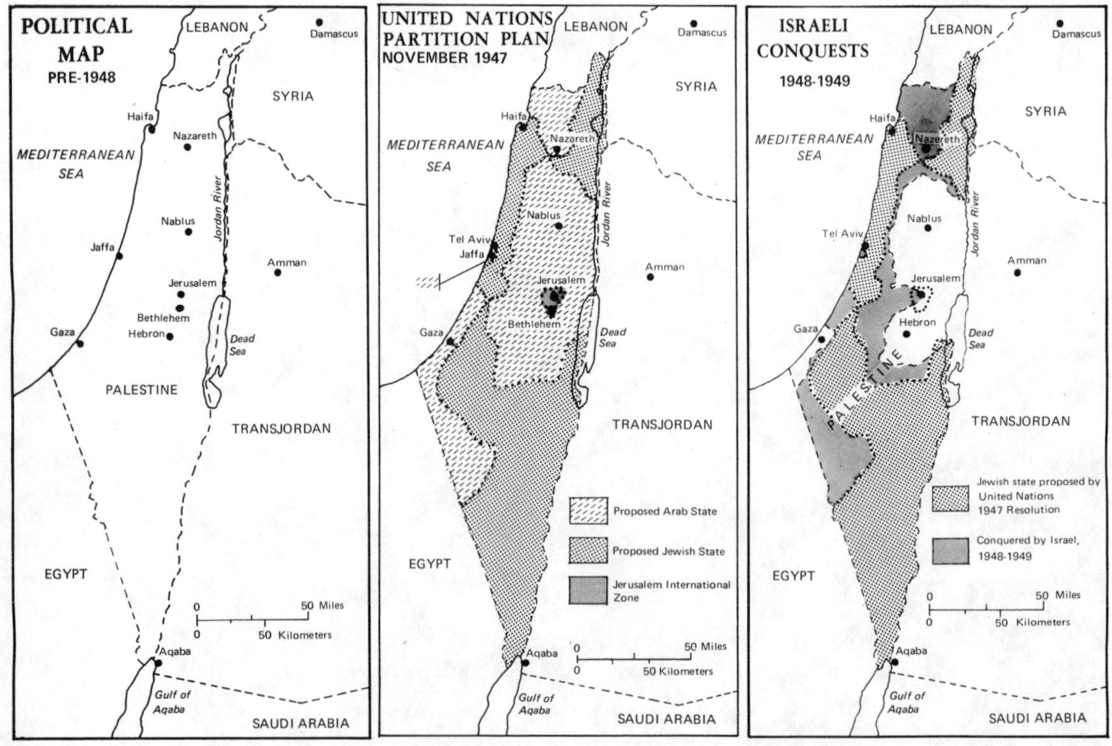

The three maps show, from left to right, the transformation of Palestine from a British mandated territory, to a Zionist state in 1948-1949.

Shepherds in Galilee tend their sheep as they did in the time of Jesus.

PHYSICAL GEOGRAPHY

As a term and concept "Palestine" may be familiar to students of history and geography, but its exact territorial connotation has varied from time to time. In ancient times, Palestine may have referred to only the sea coast, or it may have referred to the hill areas, or it may have referred to areas both west and east of the Jordan River. The Palestine of the twentieth century is much more precise and fixed. It is the land area carved up by European Imperialism in the wake of World War I. That land was occupied by Britain, and that occupation, in turn, was legitimated by the League of Nations when it entrusted Britain to govern it as a Class A Mandate. As such, the territory of Mandated Palestine (1923-1948) refers quite specifically to the approximately 10,159 square miles which was recognized by the League of Nations and subsequently by the United Nations as having been comprehended by British Mandate control. The specific delimitation of the area was a result of the Sykes-Picot Agreement of 1916 between Britain and France to partition the Arab world between them; within its area, Britain undertook to honor its promise to facilitate "the establishment in Palestine of a national home for the Jewish people" in accordance with the Balfour Declaration of 1917. To do so, Britain, with the concurrence of the League of Nations, denied the Palestinian people their right to self-determination and crushed their constant endeavors to attain national independence.

Location

The Palestine of the Mandate period lies at the western edge of Asia. It is bounded by Lebanon (north), Egypt's Sinai and the Gulf of Aqaba (south and southwest), the Mediterranean (west) and the Jordan River (east). It was made up of severed portions of the Ottoman province of Beirut and the Sanjak of Jerusalem; the former included the sea coast area from South Lebanon to north of the Arab city of Jaffa whereas the latter included southern and eastern Palestine. The entire territorial arrangement was agreed upon by the two European imperialist powers that were in military control of the entire region.

PALESTINE

Boundaries of British and French Mandates (in green) and Ottoman administrative boundaries (in black).

Topography

While Palestine exhibits varied physical and climatic features, four principal divisions are easily identified: a coastal plain, hilly interior, the Jordan Valley, and a desert region. The maritime plain stretches from South Lebanon to Egypt's Sinai. Historically and for obvious reasons, this area has been a region of agricultural settlements and of crop production; here the ancient Palestinians settled and thus gave the country its name. The hill region of the interior comprises the Galilee, the mountains of Samira (Samaria), Jerusalem and Hebron. Population density is lower than along the coast. This region historically has supported fruit production, olives and other mountainous products. The Jordan Valley stretches south from Lake Huleh (which was drained and eventually dried out in 1958) to the Dead Sea. Finally, the Naqab (Negev), Palestine's principal desert, is located in the south. It is an extension of the Sinai and Jordan deserts and constitutes slightly more than forty percent of Palestine's total land area.

Economy and Trade

Throughout history, geographers, pilgrims and other visitors noted the land's fertility and diverse agricultural production. Wheat, barley, corn, maize, sesame, kersenneh, tobacco, cotton, olives, figs and other fruits and vegetables are the traditional agricultural products. Food production met local needs and often Palestine was able to export its surplus to neighboring areas and, eventually, to European markets. Oranges were produced beginning in the tenth century, and the fruit became internationally known particularly after its commercial export to Europe in the nineteenth century. The second economic base of the country, its religious significance to Muslims, Jews and Christians, and its strategic location led to the rise of the historic Palestinian cities of Jerusalem, Gaza, Haifa, Akka, Nazareth, Nablus, Jaffa, and Safad.

HISTORY

Palestine's history is inextricably linked with the history of the entire region. At no point in the past or present has it been possible to isolate Palestinian development from political, cultural, military, religious or linguistic movements in the surrounding countries. Similarly, developments in Palestine, whether in terms of religion or politics, had their repercussions on the surrounding region. The movements of people and ideas has been a constant feature of Palestine's history. At different points in history, one can speak of a Palestine predominantly Palestinian Canaanite, Aramaic or Jewish; at different points, one can speak of a Jewish, Christian or Muslim Palestine. Normally, when people or ideas came to Palestine, irrespective of their form of entry, fusion of the old and the new was the outcome. This fusion accounts for the richness and variety of the land's culture. Only rarely was there an uprooting of Palestinian people: when the ancient Hebrews assumed political control and defeated the ancient Philistines and Canaanites, they endeavored, ultimately without success, to subdue and expel them from the land; when the Crusaders of the Middle Ages gained control, they expelled its Jewish inhabitants as well as many of its Muslim people. This kind of transformation was later to be tried by the modern Jewish settlers who, influenced by the doctrine of Zionism, have been attempting to displace the Palestinian Arab People.

Culture and Language

Historically, Palestine experienced three major cultural and language transformations. With the defeat of the ancient Palestinians, Palestine acquired a Jewish identity and Hebrew became the official language of the ancient Jewish States. With the appearance of Christianity, Palestine became largely a Christian country whose language had already become Aramaic, another Semitic language. And in the seventh century, Palestine, like the rest of the region, was transformed into an Islamic and eventually Arabic-speaking country. Just as some of Palestine's Jewish population successfully resisted the Christian transformation, some of the Jewish and Christian population resisted the Islamic transformation. Thus modern Palestine, through the Mandate period, contained an indigenous Palestinian population that had lived on the land since time immemorial, whose language was Arabic and whose religious commitment was split between Islam, Christianity and Judaism. However, the overwhelming majority was Muslim.

Arabic

As a result of its major transformation of the seventh century, Palestine became an important component of the Arab-Islamic world. Whereas political sovereignty was exercised by various groups within the Islamic State of which Palestine was an important part, Palestine retained its identity as an Arab-Islamic country, and the Palestinian people participated in the cultural life of the Arab people and region. This was true until Palestine was dismembered in 1948 and Israel emerged in part of it.

Ottoman Era

When Britain colonized Palestine, it had been part of the Islamic-Ottoman State for over four centuries. Palestinians had contributed to the intellectual and political life of the Empire. In the nineteenth century Palestinian representatives sat in the Ottoman Parliament. The Ottoman Empire was subjected to the challenge of secular nationalism in the latter part of the nineteenth century, and Palestinians actively participated in the Arab nationalist movement which sought the dismemberment of the Ottoman State in favor of an independent Arab State in its Arab portions. Palestinian leaders were severely punished by the Ottoman government; many were hanged by the Turkish military authorities for their struggle for

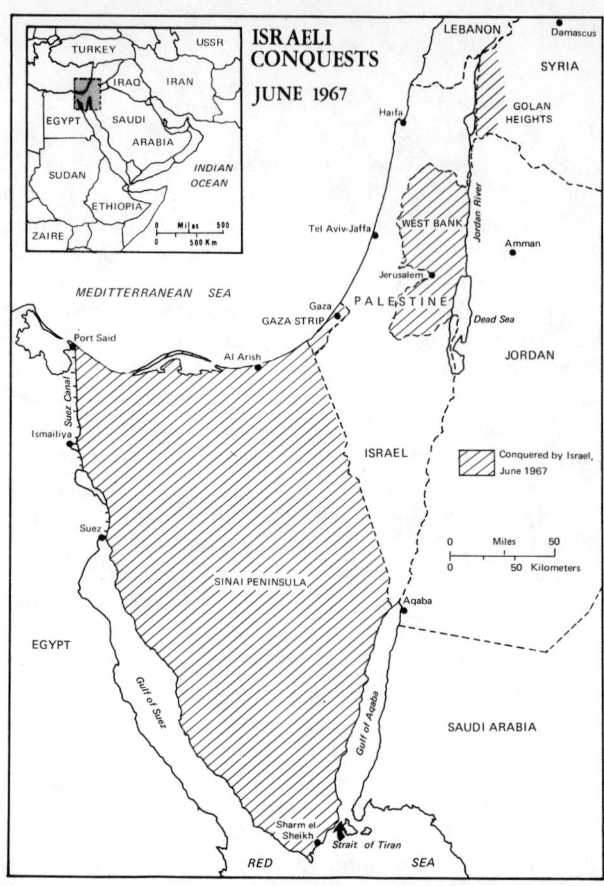

independence. When the Empire was finally broken in World War I, the Arab nationalist hope for an independent Arab State which would have included Palestine was again crushed—this time by Britain and France.

British Mandate

The history of modern Palestine is essentially the history of a triangular struggle for control and sovereignty. Officially, Palestine, once severed from the rest of the region, was placed under the British Mandate. The Palestinian Arabs rejected the Mandate and continued their struggle for independence, first against the British and later against the Zionists who were working to transform Palestine into the site of the Jewish State. The British thus denied the Palestinians the right to self-determination; they carried out policies that would promote the establishment of the "Jewish National Home" to honor their unilateral commitment to the Zionists expressed in the Balfour Declaration. Two particular aspects of British policy posed serious threats to the Palestinian Arabs; they were the British commitments to (1) facilitate the migration and settlement of European Jews in Palestine, thereby seriously altering the demographic balance, and (2) to facilitate the acquisition of land by Jewish-Zionist groups. The Palestinians reacted, frequently by waging armed revolutions, against both British colonial control and the impending Zionist threat to change the national character of the land.

U.N. Partition

The struggle of the Palestinians was ultimately crushed by the combined British-Zionist forces. Up to the forties, it was the Palestinians who were contesting British control, but by that time the Zionists had built up sufficient strength and organization in Palestine to contest both the British and the Arabs. The weakening of Britian during World War II and the intensification of the conflict in Palestine persuaded Britain to abandon the Mandate. Thus it brought the question before the United Nations in 1947 which on November 29, 1947 recommended the partition

A general view of the city of Haifa and its port

of Palestine into two States—one Jewish and the other Arab. Ironically, the slight majority of the proposed Jewish State would have been Arab and the land of the Jewish State was approximately ninety percent Arab-owned. Palestinian Jews naturally welcomed the partition resolution, whereas Palestinian Arabs rejected it since it was in violation of the right of self-determination. Immediately thereafter, Palestine experienced its worst bicommunal war. The Zionists, by a combined policy of force and terror, managed to expel the Palestinians first from the area proposed for the Jewish State and, after May, 1948, from other areas. More than 700,000 Palestinian Arabs were driven from Palestine and came to be known as the Palestine Refugees. While Israel declared itself a State on May 14, 1948, portions of the proposed Palestine Arab State were either crushed and taken by Israel or taken under protective control by adjacent States.

POPULATION AND LAND OWNERSHIP

Population

Palestine's population at the onset of the Mandate was approximately 760,000. The following table illustrates the type and number of population by religion and ethnicity.

Palestine's Population, 1922*

	Number	Percent
Muslim	590,890	78
Jewish	83,794	11
Christian	73,024	9.6
Other	9,474	1.2
Total	757,182	

*The figures are taken from the *Census of Palestine, 1922.* The enumeration is believed to have erred significantly in the direction of undercount.

Note: In those days Palestine's population was Arab of various faiths. The Arab-Jew distinction, as a national identification, was subsequent to the coming of Zionism.

The natural population growth among Arabs and Jews was strongly augmented by induced Jewish migration (principally from Europe), so that Palestine's population at the end of the Mandate was approximately two million, of whom 68.5 percent were Arab and 31.5 percent were Jewish.

By 1978, Palestine's population, including the Palestinian Arabs who continue to live in forced exile in the Arab world and elsewhere, approximated 7 million, of whom about 3.8 are Palestinian Arabs of different citizenship and 3.1 million are Israeli Jews. The population increase among Palestinian Arabs is entirely accounted for by natural increase whereas the increase in Israel's population is a combination of natural increase and continued migration.

Land Transfer

Just as Britain facilitated European Jewish migration to Palestine so that the would-be Jewish State would have an adequate population base, it was committed to facilitate land transfer. At the onset of the Mandate indigenous and European Jewish migrants and companies owned no more than 1 percent of the total land area of Palestine. The rest was either owned by Arabs or was part of the public domain. Britain enabled European Jewish immigrants and their holding companies, principally the Jewish National Fund, to acquire land from the public domain, and adopted an onerous taxation system of the Arabs with an absence of support for the agricultural population. Still by the end of the Mandate the Jewish sector owned only about 6.5 percent of the total land area. After the establishment of Israel, its government, empowered by a series of laws, confiscated Arab lands. By now the remaining Palestinian population within Israel is almost landless.

The dismemberment of Palestine became an accomplished fact when Israel concluded armistice agreements with the adjacent states of Egypt, Syria, Lebanon and Jordan. Israel exercised de facto control over eighty percent of the total land area of Palestine although its international frontiers were never stated nor recognized by any State. Portions of eastern and central Palestine that eventually became known as the West Bank were incorporated by Jordan in 1950 while the Gaza Strip came under Egyptian administration pending a final settlement of the Palestine Question. The entire area was conquered by Israel in June, 1967. Thus the Palestine of the Mandate period is now totally controlled by Israel. Throughout this period, the Palestinian people and their representatives refused to acknowledge the finality of this conquest and instead asserted their claim to their lands and homes and pressed for their independence.

Arab Jerusalem is an occupied city. An Israeli military patrol in the streets of the old city.

The city of Jerusalem with the Dome of the Rock in the foreground.

THE PALESTINIAN RESPONSE

PLO

For more than a decade after 1948, the Palestinians were quiescent politically but were able differentially to achieve a certain degree of economic and social recovery particularly in the adjacent states of Jordan, Syria, Lebanon and eventually in the developing Gulf region. With that social and economic recovery, the Palestinians began to reassert their initiative to regain their national sovereignty in Palestine. They convened the First Palestine National Council, held in Jerusalem in 1964. Among other decisions the Council resolved to establish the Palestine Liberation Organization (PLO) to press the struggle of the Palestinian people to return to Palestine and to national liberation. It adopted the Palestine National Charter which affirmed the unity and indivisibility of the Palestinian people, who constitute a national unit, and reaffirmed that Palestine is part and parcel of the Arab National Homeland. The Charter declares that Israel is an illegitimate entity, established against the will of the Palestinian people and serving the interest of world imperialism. It states that the task of the Palestinians is to work for national liberation. The PLO then began to assert itself as the only representative of the Palestinian people, thereby reasserting the Palestinian role in dealing with the Palestine Question, but it obtained that status only after the June War of 1967. By 1974, the PLO succeeded in the struggle for international recognition as the sole, legitimate representative of the Palestinian people and obtained a resolution from the U.N. General Assembly endorsing the Palestinian right to independence and sovereignty in Palestine. International endorsement of Palestinian independence came in the wake of the Palestinian war of national liberation.

PROSPECTS

The fate of Palestine and the Palestinians will be determined by the confluence of several factors: the capacity of Israel to maintain an exclusive Jewish State which denies equality to the Palestinian on grounds of ethnicity and religion; the capacity of the Palestinians to successfully wage a war of national liberation; and finally the degree of support which both parties receive from the international and regional communities. Two things are certain: on the one hand the Question of Palestine will continue to disturb international peace until Israeli Jews and Palestinian Arabs arrive at a mutually acceptable solution which assures them all a dignified and productive life on a footing of complete equality, and, on the other hand, until Palestine is reintegrated into its natural region and resumes its history and place in the Arab world at large.

The serene silhouettes of a church and a mosque in Bethlehem symbolize hope for peace and brotherhood in a troubled land.

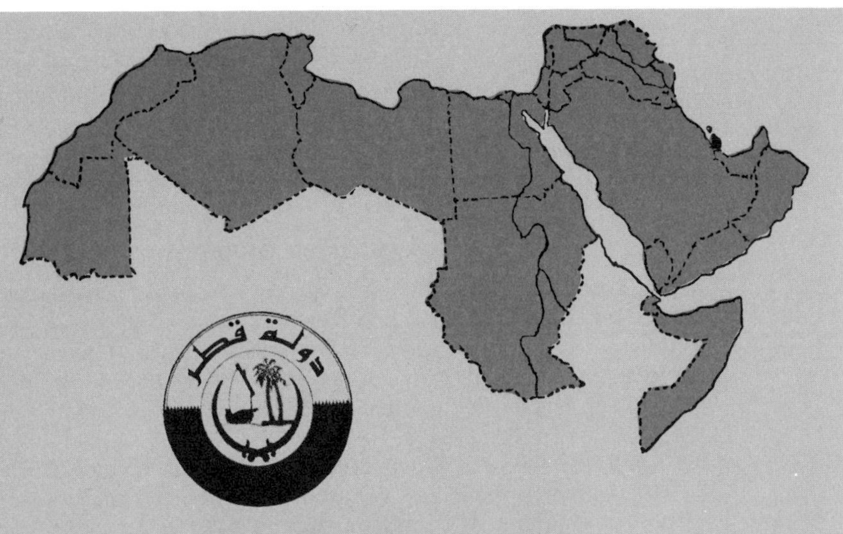

QATAR

دولة قطر

PROFILE

Official Name: State of Qatar (Dawlat Qatar)
Head of State: Sheikh Khalifah bin Hamad Al Thani
Government: Emirate
Area: 4500 sq. mi. (smaller than Connecticut)
Population: about 200,000
Population Density: 45/sq. mi.
Capital: Doha (al-Dawah)
Other Urban Centers: Khor, Warkah, Umm Said
Currency: Riyal ($1.00 = 4 QR)
Press: One daily: Dar al-Uruba. Al Doha Magazine.
Radio & Television: One radio and one Television station.
Main Airports: Doha
Main Seaports: Umm Said
Date of Joining the United Nations: September 21, 1971
Date of Joining the Arab League: September 11, 1971

QATAR

INTRODUCTION

Like everyone of its Arabian Gulf neighbors, Qatar has been rapidly transformed by oil revenues from a relatively simple life of fishing, pearling and nomadic herding to bustling urban living with a planned earth satellite station. It is an important factor in matters related to the international oil economy, and already it has become a contributor to international aid programs.

PHYSICAL GEOGRAPHY

The State of Qatar occupies a low-lying peninsula, roughly 100 by 40 miles, which extends north into the Arabian Gulf from Saudi Arabia. Its area is close to 4500 square miles (smaller than Connecticut). The exact area is indeterminate because the land boundary has not been delimited. Qatar shares a land border with Saudi Arabia and the United Arab Emirates.

Climate

Qatar is a desert country. Summer temperatures regularly exceed 100°F with high humidities. Winter months are warm and pleasant. About half the water supply comes from some 300 artesian wells in the north, but more and more of the water needs are supplied by desalination.

HUMAN GEOGRAPHY

Migrants

The population is slightly under 200,000. Most Qataris are Sunni Muslims of the Wahhabi sect, a conservative branch which originated in Arabia during the eighteenth century. At the same time, more than 60 percent of the residents are not citizens but recent migrants attracted by the boom generated by the oil industry. Omanis and Iranians are especially associated with the construction industry and agriculture;

A Qatari student.

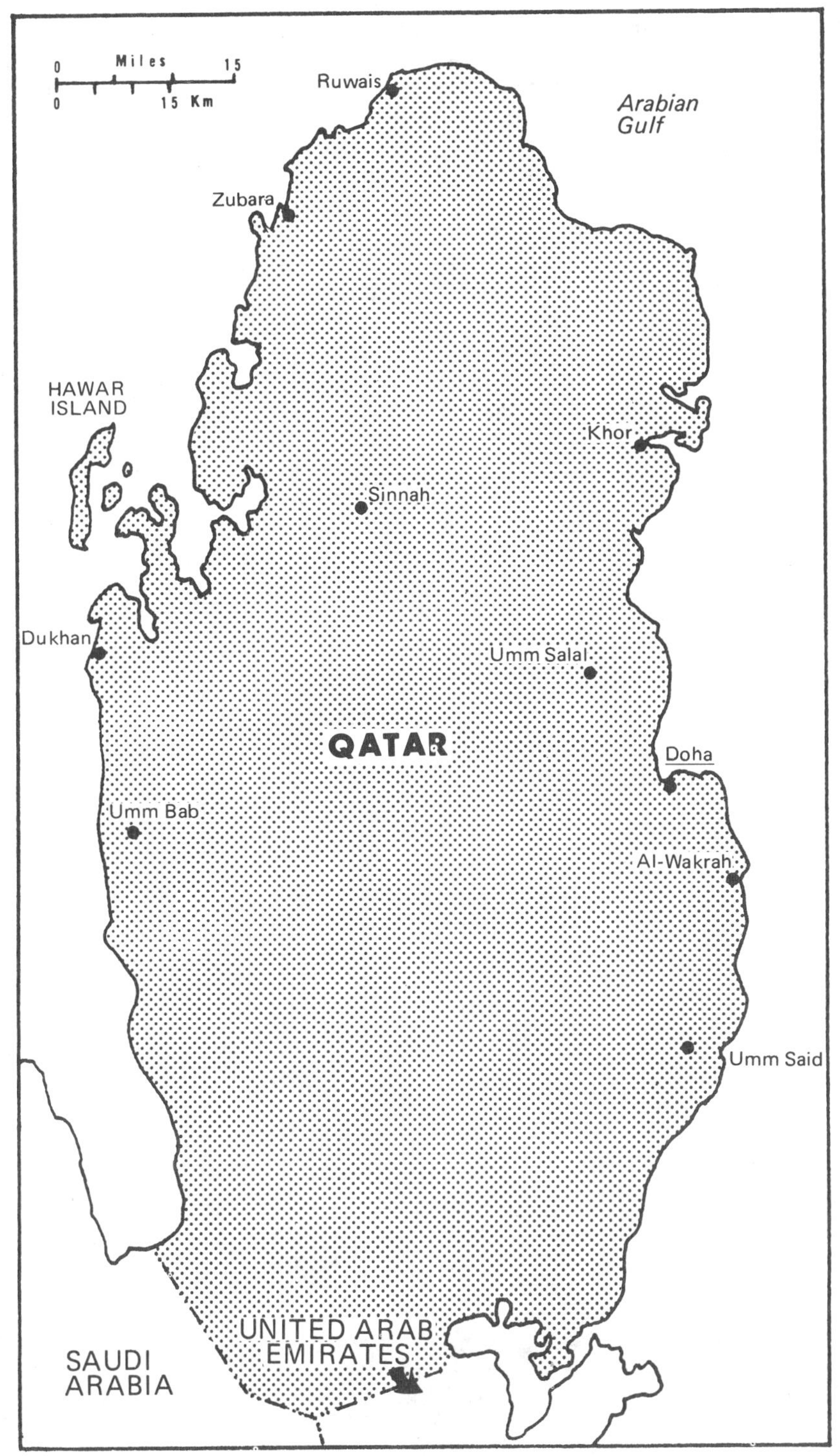
0 Miles 15
0 15 Km
Ruwais
Arabian Gulf
Zubara
HAWAR ISLAND
Khor
Sinnah
Dukhan
Umm Salal
QATAR
Doha
Umm Bab
Al-Wakrah
Umm Said
UNITED ARAB EMIRATES
SAUDI ARABIA

Indians and Iranians are in the commercial life; Jordanians and Egyptians are especially prominent among the school teachers; other northern Arabs (such as Palestinians) are active in clerical and mid-level administrative posts; and Europeans and Americans perform specialized and technical tasks. Such an employment structure is similar to that found elsewhere in the Gulf Arab states, as is the rapidity of population increase. For instance, the late 1970s population figure of 200,000 shows a dramatic increase over the 1969 figure of 80,000, and that, in turn, was a 300 percent increase over the preceding two decades. Part of this increase, it should be noted, has resulted from a reduced death rate, especially infant mortality, because of improved health and medical facilities.

Population Growth

The economic and demographic transformation is visibly evident in Qatar's urban growth. Doha (Al Dawhah) is the capital city. Its urban area contains some 80 percent of the country's population, a phenomenal proportion. Such a concentration reflects a consequence characteristic of rapid oil development: the oil industry itself employs very few people. The income it produces generates a tremendous increase in labor demand elsewhere, notably in construction and governmental services. Other cities are Khor (on the east coast 30 miles north of Doha), Wakrah (10 miles southeast of Doha), Ruwais (at the northern end of the peninsula), Umm Said (the deepwater port for oil shipment, 25 miles south of Doha), and Dukhan (where oil is produced, in the central part of the western coast).

Urban Centers

Doha, capital of Qatar with the Clock Tower, the Grand Mosque and the Palace in the foreground.

ECONOMY

Oil

Exploration for oil started in 1937, and discovery was made two years later. Eventually, following an interruption because of World War II, the first shipment was made at the end of 1949. Production increased rapidly starting in 1971. The oil deposits are along the west coast, southwards from Dukhan, and crude reserves are estimated at 400 million tons. The waters here are shallow, however, and a deep sea harbor has been constructed at Umm Said. Oil crosses the peninsula by means of a fifty-mile pipeline, originating at Umm Bab, 15 miles south of Dukhan. All oil companies operating in the country were nationalized in December, 1974. In January, 1969 Qatar became a member of the Organization of Petroleum Exporting Countries (OPEC), and in May, 1970 it became a member of the Organization of Arab Petroleum Exporting Countries (OAPEC).

Industry

Development projects are varied: an ammonia and urea fertilizer plant at Umm Said (1973); flour milling at Umm Said (1972); a fish refrigeration and processing plant near Doha harbor (1966); and cement manufacturing at Umm Bab (1969). Further development plans include natural gas liquefaction, iron and steel, an electric furnace steel mill, a detergent factory, an aluminum smelter, a glass plant, a petrochemical plant, a national electrification system and an earth station satellite communication system.

Agriculture

Of special significance are developments in agriculture. In the mid-1950s no crops were grown on the peninsula. Except for a few private gardens, vegetables and fruits had to be imported. Today, Qatar is not only self-supporting in vegetables, but it also has a surplus which is exported to neighboring countries. Similar progress is being made in fruit production. These projects are a major development and rather spectacular for a desert area once dismissed as agriculturally sterile. Heretofore the limiting factor has been the availability of water. With the advent and continuing improvement of desalination technology, the whole global ocean becomes the reservoir.

Transportation

There are some 600 miles of surfaced roads in Qatar. Through Saudi Arabia, the country is linked to the Arab countries on the Mediterranean. Oil pipelines link the oilfield of Dukhan with the loading terminal of Umm Said. Natural Gas is pumped to Doha where it is used as fuel for a power station and water distillation plant.

HISTORY

Utub Settlement

Qatar's past, like its present, has much in common with the record of other Gulf States. There is evidence of Stone Age and Iron Age habitation going back to 4000 B.C. Over the ages it has been involved with and affected by political and economic competition within the Gulf as well as far beyond it. One of the more enduring developments, in terms of contemporary conditions, was the settlement of Qatar during the eighteenth century by the Utub tribe, from Arabia by way of Kuwait and Bahrain. Their orientation was toward the sea rather than the interior, and they established a stronghold at Zubara on the northwest coast, 20 miles southwest of Ruwais and hardly 25 miles across the waters from Bahrain. Late in the eighteenth century this town withstood a joint assault by the Qawasim of the Sharjah and Ras al-Khaimah area (in the present day United Arab Emirates) and Arab settlers from southern Persia.

Like much of the Arabian peninsula, Qatar was at least nominally part of the Turkish Ottoman Empire until World War I. At the same time, British influence in the Gulf was being firmly established to preserve

The National Museum of Qatar (History, Geography, Culture).

British imperial interests and lines of communication; Britain competed with Portugual, Holland and France in the Indian Ocean and points beyond. Treaties concluded with Bahrain (1880 and 1892), Trucial States (1892) and Kuwait (1899) gave Britain control of these territories' defense and foreign affairs. A similar treaty was concluded in 1916 with Qatar, at which time Qatar was already ruled by the present ruling family, the Al Thani.

Independence

Britain eventually curtailed its global political and military involvement, and by the 1960s she was rapidly withdrawing from the Gulf. In this context there was talk of establishing a federation of the smaller states, eventually proclaimed in December, 1971 as the United Arab Emirates. Qatar and Bahrain had participated in the preliminary talks in 1968, 1969 and 1970. Both elected not to join, and Qatar became an independent country on September 1, 1971. The same year Qatar became a member of the League of Arab States and of the United Nations.

GOVERNMENT AND SOCIETY

Administration

Qatar declared its independence in 1971 when the special treaty arrangements with Britain came to an end. Prior to independence, a Basic Law which called for a government by prime minister, cabinet and advisory council was promulgated. The cabinet is appointed by the emir. In 1972, the prime minister, Sheikh Khalifa Bin Hamad al-Thani, took over control of the administration as emir and chief of state.

Justice

Justice is administered by five courts on the basis of codified laws in addition to the traditional shari'a courts applying Islamic laws in certain specified cases. The constitution guarantees the independence of the judiciary.

Education

All education in Qatar is free, and scholarships are offered for study abroad. Primary and secondary school education in 1975/76 had 16,631 boys and 14,535 girls in 108 schools with 1,971 teachers.

PROSPECTS

Qatar is already a welfare state, in that such services as medical care and education (which is compulsory through the elementary level) are free. But it is a small country. Like Kuwait, the United Arab Emirates, and Saudi Arabia, its greatest shortage is of people—particularly skilled people. As elsewhere, a great emphasis is being placed on education, and this investment in human resources is beginning to bear fruit. But the labor pool is small. Thus, if Qatar is to maintain its current development and accomplish projected expectations, it will have to continue to depend on imported labor of various degrees of skill for many years.

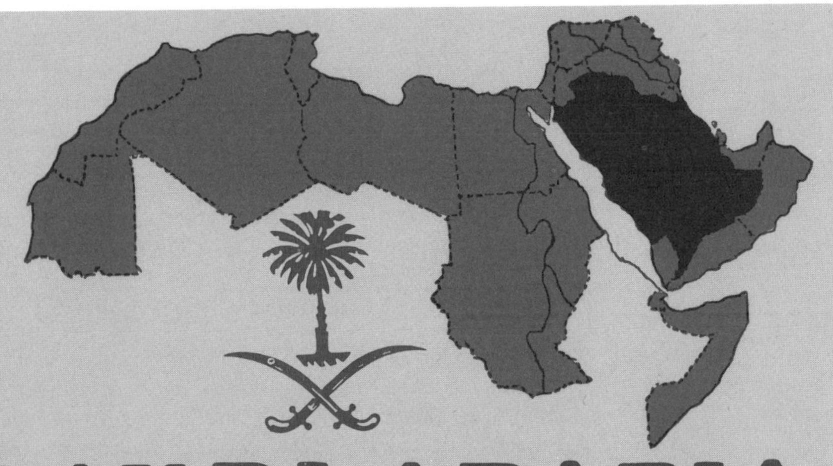

SAUDI ARABIA

المملكة العربية السعودية

PROFILE

Official Name: Kingdom of Saudi Arabia (Al-Mamlakah al-Arabiyyah al-Saudiyyah)

Head of State: H.M. Khaled ibn Abdul-Aziz Al Saud

Government: Monarchy

Area: 865,000 sq. mi. (= U.S. east of the Mississippi)

Population: 6,400,000 (est. 1976)

Population Density: less than 8 per sq. mi.

Capital: Riyadh (670,000)

Other Urban Centers: Mecca, Jidda, Medina, Ta'if, Abha, Dhahran, Damman, Al-Khubar

National Holiday: September 23

Currency: Saudi Riyal ($1.00 = 3.50 S. Riyal)

Sites of Interest: Mecca and Medina (Holy cities of Islam)

Main Airports: Jidda, Riyadh, Dhahran

Main Seaport: Jidda

Radio and Television: Programs in Arabic

Date of Joining the United Nations: October 24, 1945

Date of Joining the United Nations: October 24, 1945

Date of Joining the Arab League: March 22, 1945

SAUDI ARABIA

INTRODUCTION

During the 1960s, and especially during the 1970s, the Kingdom of Saudi Arabia experienced spectacular increases in income generated by its oil resources, and this increase in wealth generated profound changes in most sectors of the Kingdom. Traditionally conservative and inward-looking, Saudi Arabia is now at center stage in matters involving global commerce in oil, diplomatic maneuverings related to the Arab-Israeli conflict, Pan-Islamic developments and international economic aid.

PHYSICAL GEOGRAPHY

Topography

Saudi Arabia is the largest political unit in the Arabian peninsula. Its area is large by Middle Eastern and European standards, covering some 865,000 square miles (about the size of the United States east of the Mississippi River). The country forms part of a plateau which rises abruptly from the Red Sea and dips gently northeastwards toward the Arabian Gulf. The western scarp overlooks the Red Sea by 5,000 feet in the north and by upwards of 10,000 feet in the south. The water divide is only 25 miles from the Red Sea in the north and recedes to about 75 miles in the south. There is hardly a coastal plain, and the starkness of the scarp is broken by occasional dry river beds, or wadis.

Desert

In the west there are extensive surface lava flows and broken up volcanic material. The Rub' al Khali (Empty Quarter), the world's largest sand region, dominates the south and east and covers an area of a quarter million square miles, with 800-foot sand mountains. A smaller sand area, the Nafud, covers 22,000 square miles in the north central portion of the country. These two deserts are joined by a 900-mile sand arc, only 50 miles wide, known as the Dahna' and passing east of Riyadh. To the west of the capital there is a series of north-south cuestas, over 700 miles long. The most prominent is Tuwaiq Mountain, 3,500 feet above sea level and 800 feet above the general plateau surface. The Gulf shoreline is irregular and bordered by marshes and salt flats.

Climate

Saudi Arabia is almost entirely a desert; that is, the amount received from precipitation is less than what can be lost from the surface by means of evaporation and transpiration. Almost everywhere the annual rainfall averages less than five inches; 10 inches may fall in a short time, but then it may not rain again for two years. A narrow strip along the western highlands, southwards from Medina, receives fifteen inches or more annually, mainly during the summer months. Here, semiarid or steppe conditions prevail. There is not a single permanent stream in the country, or in the whole Arabian peninsula for that matter. The wadis carry water only when there is rain, and then only for a few days or weeks. There are, however, water bearing rock layers (aquifers) and springs which have made possible oasis settlement for thousands of years. Underground water resources have recently been tapped for irrigated agriculture in the eastern part of the country. The aquifers are supplied by the rains falling on the western highlands and central upland (such as Tuwaiq Mountain).

Temperature

January and February are the coolest months, averaging 74°F in Jidda on the Red Sea, 58°F in Riyadh in the interior, and 63°F along the Gulf in the east. Summers are hot and the temperature can exceed 100°F anywhere in the country. Warmest average monthly temperatures are 90°F at Jidda, 93°F at Riyadh, and 94°F at the Gulf. The greatest annual range is in the continental interior, where nights can be quite cool any day of the year. Humidity is oppressively high along either coast, but quite low in the interior.

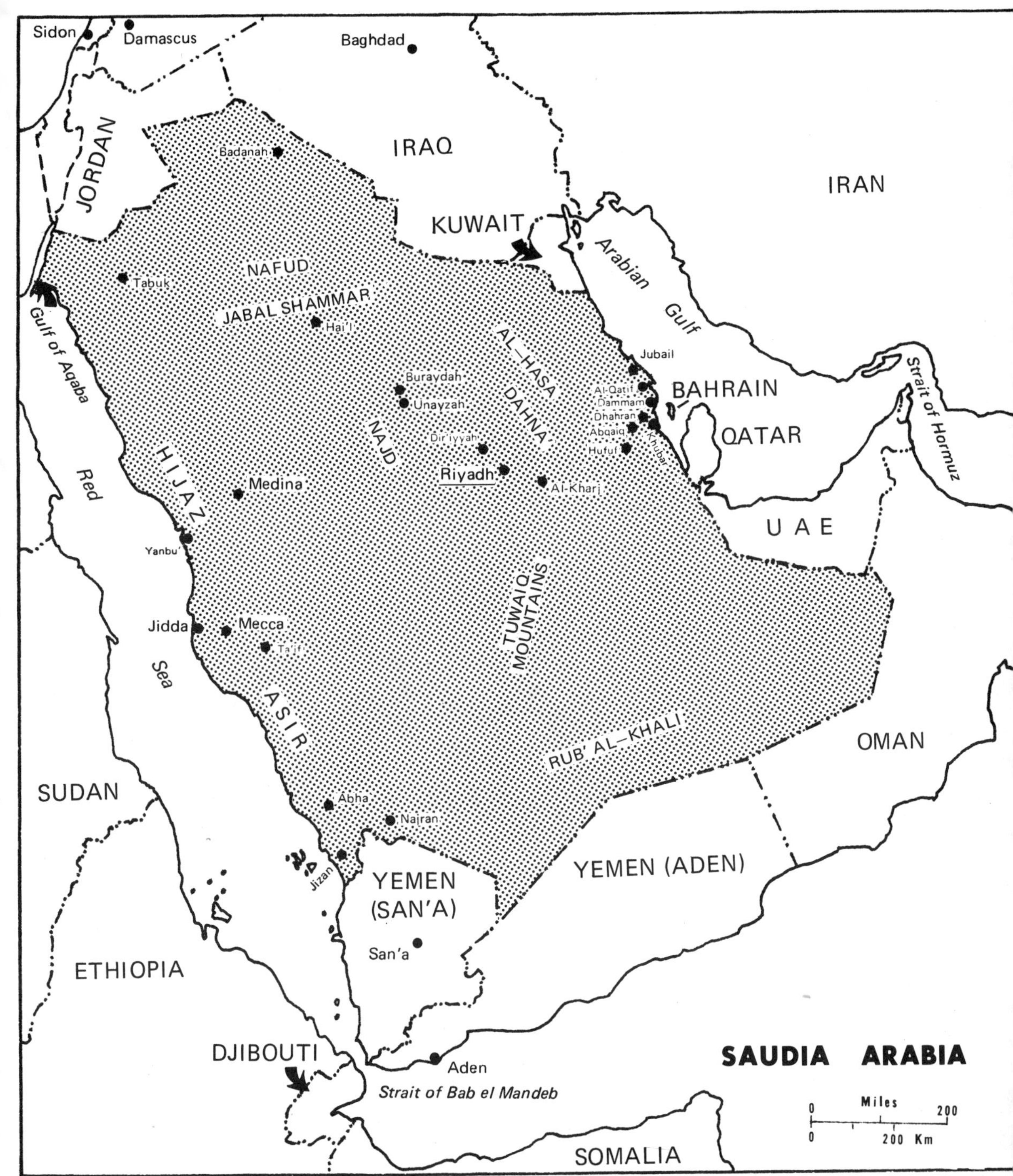

Sidon
Damascus
Baghdad
JORDAN
IRAQ
IRAN
KUWAIT
Badanah
Arabian Gulf
NAFUD
Tabuk
JABAL SHAMMAR
Hai'l
Gulf of Aqaba
AL-HASA
DAHNA
Jubail
BAHRAIN
Buraydah
Unayzah
Al-Qatif
Dammam
Dhahran
Abqaiq
Hufuf
Khubar
QATAR
Strait of Hormuz
NAJD
Dir'iyyah
Riyadh
Al-Kharj
HIJAZ
Red Sea
Medina
U A E
Yanbu'
TUWAIQ MOUNTAINS
Jidda
Mecca
Ta'if
ASIR
RUB' AL-KHALI
OMAN
SUDAN
Abha
Najran
Jizan
YEMEN (SAN'A)
YEMEN (ADEN)
San'a
ETHIOPIA
DJIBOUTI
Aden
Strait of Bab el Mandeb
SOMALIA
SAUDIA ARABIA
Miles
0 200
0 200 Km

SAUDI ARABIA

HUMAN GEOGRAPHY

People

Saudi Arabia is an Arab state and a Muslim state. Within the context of the Arab world it may be regarded as ethnically homogeneous, for here is where one expects to find "pure" Arabs. A closer look reveals a considerable heterogeneity, however. African influences are evident in the west, and Indian and Persian influences are found in the east. In the north there is a greater physiognomic affinity with eastern Jordan and western Iraq. Such variety reflects the millennia of settlement and movement within and around the peninsula, and the fact that the incorporation into one country of diverse tribes with long traditions of group individualism and assertiveness is only a twentieth century development. The name Kingdom of Saudi Arabia dates only from 1932.

Religion

The Kingdom's Islamic nature is as basic as its Arabism. It was here that Islam orginated, and it is the site of Islam's two holiest cities, Mecca and Medina. The law of Islam, the Shari'ah, is the law of the land. The late King Faisal actively pursued a policy of pan-Islamism, a movement which encompasses many more non-Arabs than Arabs. The world's half a billion Muslims face Mecca each time they pray, five times a day if they follow the ideal. Almost all Saudis adhere to the Sunni sect. The second main branch of Islam, Shi'a, is represented by perhaps 150,000, mostly in Al-Hasa and Al-Qatif in the east.

Two of the minarets of the Holy Mosque in Mecca

Young Saudis performing the traditional "sword dance."

Vital Statistics

The mid-1976 population is estimated at 6.4 million. The birth rate is a high 49 per thousand, and the death rate is 20 per thousand, giving an annual growth rate of 2.9 percent. If the growth rate is maintained, the population will double in 24 years and will reach 12.9 million in the year 2000. The infant mortality rate is 152 per 1000 live births per year. Forty-five percent of the population is under 15 years old, and the median age is a very young 17.6 years.

Regions

There are four traditional regions, Hijaz in the northern part of the western coastal highlands, Asir to the south, Najd in the interior, and Hasa in the east. Oil reserves and production are found in Hasa, commercial activity is centered in Hijaz (mostly in the Red Sea port city of Jidda, which is also the center of diplomatic activity), and administrative authority is centered in Najd (site of the capital, Riyadh). Asir is the least dry part of the country, where traditional agricultural activity is visible.

Population Distribution

Population densities are highest in southern Asir, exceeding 65 persons per square mile in Jizan near the Yemen border. In Riyadh province, Najd, the density is less than 10; it is below 5 in Hasa. Nafud and Rub' al Khali are uninhabited. Population density figures must be qualified in a country with stark contrasts between oases and barren areas, for the distribution is an especially noncontinuous phenomenon. Only 10 percent of the population is nomadic, and two-thirds of these nomads are in the northern and central regions. Thus there are thousands of square miles which are rarely utilized even by this group. The Bedouin population is estimated to be decreasing by 2 percent annually as a result of urban migration. The agricultural sector, only 28 percent of the national labor force, is estimated to be declining by almost 1 percent annually. Most of the decline is occurring in the Asir region. Cropped land, both irrigated and rainfed, amounts only to 0.2 or 0.3 percent of the national land area. In short, already two-thirds of Saudi Arabians live in towns, and the proportion increases every day. Riyadh is the largest city, with more than 670,000 people, followed by Jidda (575,000) and Mecca (370,000). Other major cities are Medina and Ta'if in the west, Buraydah, Ha'il, Unayzah and al-Kharj in Najd, and Dammam, Khubar, Hufuf, Abqaiq and Dhahran in the east.

Urban Centers

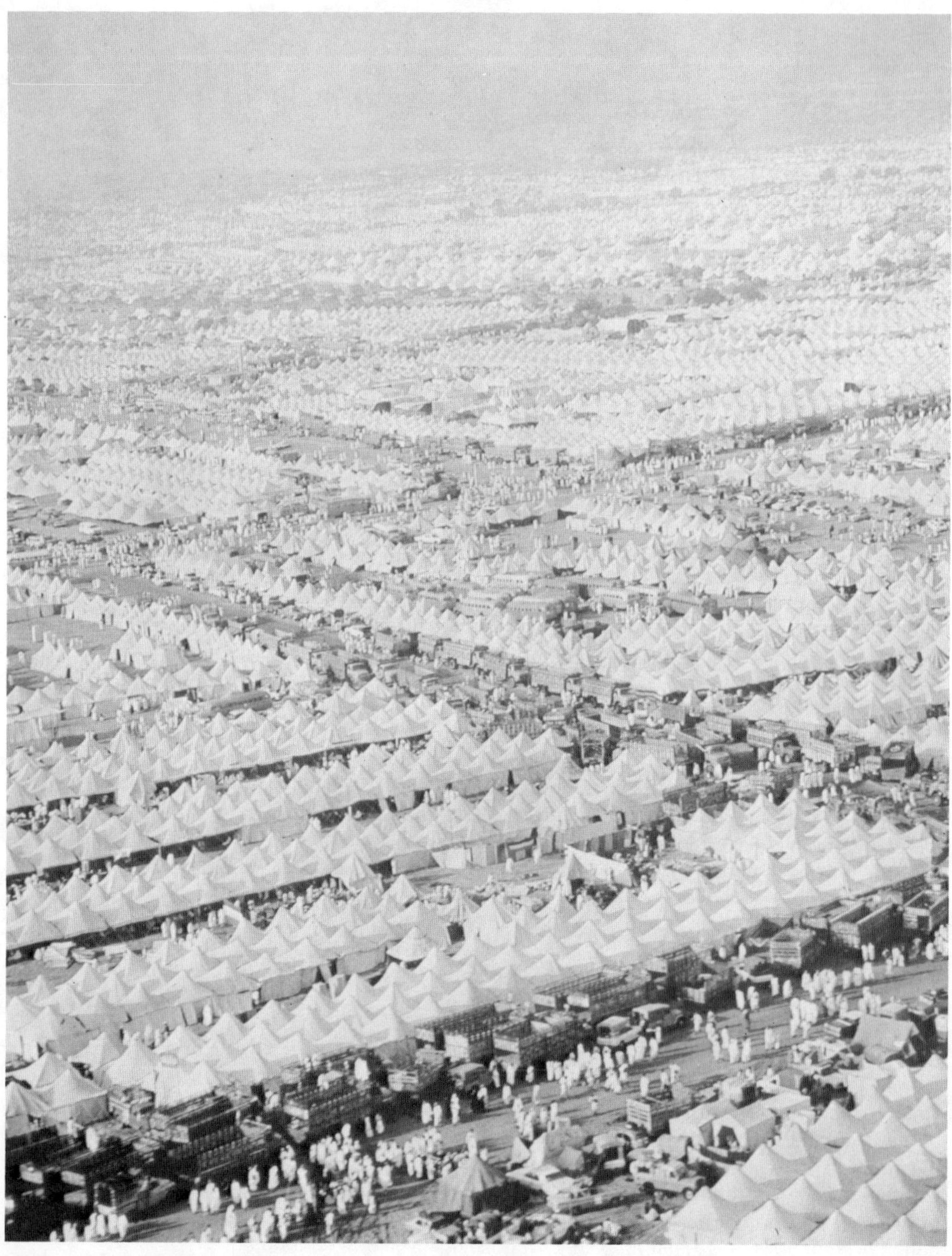

The pilgrim tent city on the Plain of 'Arafat.

ECONOMY

Oil

The national economy is overwhelmingly dominated by oil. In 1975 it accounted for about 70 percent of total domestic production, 99 percent of exports and almost 200 percent of the national budget. A Concession Agreement was signed in 1933 with Standard Oil of California, and the concession was assigned to what in 1934 came to be known as the Arabian American Oil Company (Aramco). Commercial production started in 1938, but it was not until after 1958, when Faisal (then Crown Prince) was asked by the King to handle fiscal matters, that financial stability was achieved. Saudi Arabia ranks first in the world in terms of known reserves, and in terms of production it is usually third, after the United States and the Soviet Union. Deposits are almost entirely in the east, along and underneath the Gulf, as well as in Rub' al Khali. Transportation of oil is by pipeline or tanker. Tapline, the Trans-Arabian Pipe Line, completed in 1950, crosses Jordan, Syria and Lebanon, terminating in Sidon on the Mediterranean. A $143 billion Second Five Year Development Plan was announced in May, 1975. The Plan aims to reduce the dependence on oil and increase national integration by distributing economic activity throughout the country. Industrial development will be based on two growth poles, Jubail on the Gulf and Yanbu' on the Red Sea. Other sites include Damman, Jidda, Buraydah (200 miles northwest of Riyadh), Riyadh, Jizan (on the Red Sea 40 miles north of the Yemen border) and Tabuk (325 miles northwest of Medina). The $17.2 billion allotted to industry will allow for the expansion of present refineries as well as the construction of new refineries, a steel and iron plant, a petrochemical complex and an aluminum plant. Other projects include a gasgathering plant, two oil products distribution centers, a car assembly complex, and six cement factories. New factories will produce automobile tires, soap, ceramics, clothing, glass, bricks and household utensils. Concessions have been granted to explore for lead, zinc, silver, copper, gold, nickel, iron, magnesium and phosphates. Seaport capacity will be expanded at Jidda, Yanbu' and Jizan on the Red Sea, and at Dammam and Jubail on the Gulf, with new ports at Yanbu' and Jubail.

Development Plan

Agriculture

Agricultural plans include a vast desalination program. Saudi Arabia imports 85 percent of its wheat and barley; this figure is expected to drop appreciably. An increase in date production will allow for export. Attention is also given to other crops and to meat and poultry.

Investment in vocational training centers will increase the labor supply. It is expected that by the end of the plan unskilled labor demand will be 446,000 compared with a supply of 296,000 (or 66 percent), and skilled labor demand will be 1,218,000 with a projected supply of 900,000 (or 74 percent).

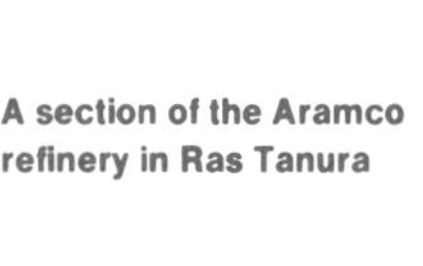

A section of the Aramco refinery in Ras Tanura

HISTORY

Early Tribes

Among the earliest known Arabian tribes is the Thamud, mentioned in Assyrian records (ninth to seventh centuries B.C.) and in the Quran. Thamudic inscriptions are found in much of central and northern Arabia, especially in northern Hijaz. The Lihyan tribe also flourished in northern Hijaz and adjacent parts of Arabia, and apparently still survived as a state by the 4th century A.D. By then the Lakhmids, the first group to adopt the Arabic language were dominant. Pre-Islamic Arabic poetry was developed under Lakhmid hegemony. A rival group, the Ghassanids, controlled northwestern Arabia and the Syrian Desert. They were Christians associated with the Byzantine Church. Both Lakhmids and Ghassanids were weakened by conflicts between Byzantium and Persia, and their political importance ceased with the spread of Islam in the seventh century.

Muslim Era

The Muslim era dates from 622 A.D., the year of Muhammad's migration (hijrah, or hegira) from Mecca to Medina because of his rejection by Mecca's leadership. Islam spread rapidly into Asia and Africa, and Mecca and Medina became Islam's two holiest cities. The political center of Islam moved out of Arabia in 661 (first to Damascus, then to Baghdad and Cairo). In 1517 Hijaz came under Turkish Ottoman control, while the interior was protected by its relative isolation. There, in Najd, the proselytizing Wahhabi movement for religious reform was founded by Muhammad ibn Abd al-Wahhab (1703-1792). He received the protection and active support of Muhammad ibn Sa'ud, amir of Dir'iyyah oasis near Riyadh, and founder of the dynasty which eventually became the ruling family.

Saudi Dynasty

The kingdom's founder was Abd al-Aziz ibn Abd al-Rahman al-Faisal Al-Saud (1880-1953), commonly known as Ibn Sa'ud or Abd al-Aziz. He was about eleven years old when his family fled Riyadh and sought refuge at the fringes of Rub' al-Khali, in Qatar, Bahrain and Kuwait. This experience gave him a greater understanding of different Bedouin groups and an appreciation of the political geography of the Arabian Gulf, where active competition was taking place among Britain, Germany, Russia and Turkey. In January, 1902, Abd al-Aziz and a group of sixty men captured Riyadh. During the following quarter of a century he conquered Najd in the interior (by 1906), Hasa in the east (by 1915), Jabal Shammar and its capital Ha'il in the north (by 1921) and the Hijaz in the west and north (by 1926). In the 1927 Treaty of Jidda, Britain recognized the sovereignty of the Kingdom of the Hijaz and Najd and Its Dependencies. The country was renamed the Kingdom of Saudi Arabia on September 22, 1932. A brief war with Yemen in 1934 confirmed Saudi Arabia's sovereignty over Asir in the southwest.

King Abd al-Aziz died on November 9, 1953 and was succeeded by his son Sa'ud, who ruled until November, 1964. The Royal Family, supported by religious leaders, the Council of Ministers and the Consultative Council, and acting within the precepts of the law of Islam, appointed his brother, Crown Prince Faisal, as King. Faisal was assassinated in Riyadh in March, 1975, and his half brother, Crown Prince Khalid (then 62 years old), was named King. Another half brother, Fahd, was appointed Crown Prince.

While most of Abd al-Aziz's preoccupation had been with the Arabian peninsula, he also became involved with international matters, especially during World War I. During World War II he maintained a neutral stance in favor of the Allies, and a cordial relationship with the United States evolved, highlighted by a meeting in February, 1945 with President Franklin D. Roosevelt on an American cruiser in the Suez Canal. The Kingdom's involvement with international matters increased rapidly thereafter. Saudi Arabia is a charter member of the United Nations.

Minarets and dome of the Prophet's Mosque at Medina

Aerial view of Riyadh, capital of the kingdom

GOVERNMENT AND SOCIETY

Administration

During the days of Abd al-Aziz, the person of the King combined legislative, executive and administrative functions, and he was clearly guided by the law of Islam, as interpreted by ulama (learned religious men). Each tribal chief was responsible for the behavior of his people, and the King's army was ready to act if needed. Since 1958, other institutions have acquired more responsibility and authority. The King appoints the prime minister, and the latter may propose the appointment of the deputy prime minister, the Cabinet ministers, and the ministers of State. The Council of Ministers is vested with legislative, executive and administrative authority, and has become a powerful executive body. The King has veto power, unless he fails to act within thirty days. Succession to the throne is not hereditary. The Crown Prince is designated by the Royal Family, with the support of the ulama, the Council of Ministers, and the Consultative Council. Together members of these groups are known as "the people who bind and unbind" (ahl al-'aqd wal hall), and it was they who persuaded King Sa'ud to abdicate in 1964, to be replaced by his Crown Prince brother, Faisal. There are seventeen administrative provinces *(manatiq idariyyah).* The governors of these are nominated by the minister of interior, approved by the Council of Ministers, and appointed by the King. A minister may not purchase or rent State property, sell or lease his property to the government, engage in commercial transactions, or accept the directorship of a company. Similar restrictions apply to governors and to lower level administrative officers in districts within their respective jurisdictions. The consultative principle applies at all levels of government.

Education and Welfare

Education for Saudis is free whether at home or abroad. Medical treatment, including medicine, is also free. A Social Security Statute provides aid to the aged, orphaned, widowed, unemployed and other needy individuals. By the end of the current development plan, university enrollment is expected to go up from 14,500 to 49,000 (a 238 percent increase). The number of hospital beds will increase from 4,100 to 11,400 (a 178 percent rise). The number of doctors will go up by 121 percent, from 1,900 to 4,200.

Communication and Transportation

By the end of the development plan color television will be accessible to 90 percent of the inhabitants. Radio broadcasting, printing facilities and the telephone and postal systems will also be expanded. There are international airports at Jidda, Riyadh, Dhahran, Medina, Ta'if, Jizan, Najran and Ha'il, and new ones are planned for Abha and Badana. Five domestic airports will be improved, and five others will be constructed.

To be granted a visa to Saudi Arabia, a person must be invited by someone, or some organization, within the country. The Kingdom is not actively encouraging tourism. Most visitors are for business reasons, although the country does afford much geographical and cultural variety. Archeological sites include the relatively recent Dir'iyyah ruins near Riyadh and the two thousand year old Nabatean rock settlements in the northwest. Unique to Saudi Arabia is the pilgrimage (hajj) to Mecca, undertaken by perhaps a million people a year. They come from Indonesia and the Philippines to the east, from Mauritania and Senegal to the west, from Soviet Turkestan to the north, and from Tanzania to the south. Until the advent of the oil era, the pilgrimage was the Kingdom's primary source of revenue.

PROSPECTS

Given the country's enormous wealth, acquired only recently (starting especially in the 1970s), one senses an overpowering impatience to get to tomorrow today. There is a commitment for the betterment of the life of the individual Saudi, as evidenced by the bewildering array of development projects. Long an important member of the Arab world and of the Muslim world, Saudi Arabia has been rapidly thrust into the forefront of world politics and economics. Its importance, and wealth, will surely continue through the rest of the twentieth century.

Overleaf: "The Sacred House" in Mecca with the Ka'ba in the center.

A composition in angular Kufic style in the shape of a mosque reading: "There is no god but God, and Muhammad is His Messenger."

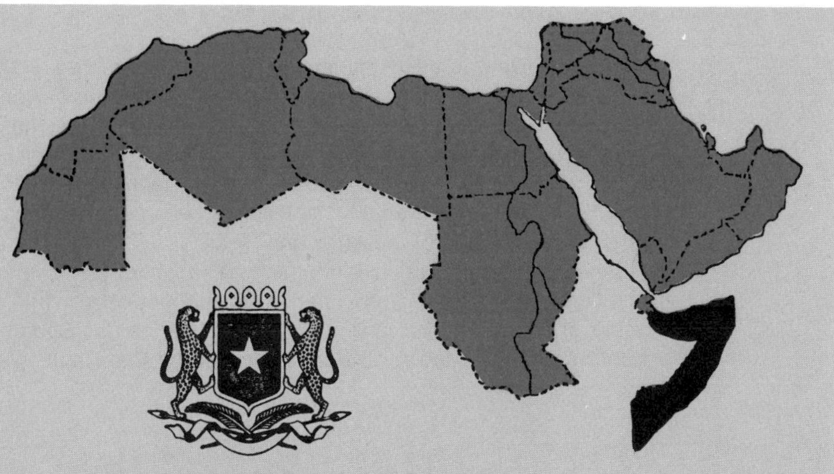

SOMALIA

جمهورية الصومال الديمقراطية

PROFILE

Official Name: Somali Democratic Republic (Jumhuriyyat al-Sumal al-Dimuqratiyyah)

Head of State: Mohamed Siad Barre

Government: Republic

Area: 246,200 sq. mi. (slightly smaller than Texas)

Population: 4,000,000 est.

Population Density: 16/sq. mi.

Capital: Mogadiscio (400,000)

Other Urban Centers: Kismayu, Hargeisa, Barbera

National Holiday: July 1

Currency: Somali Shilling ($1.00=6.25 SS)

Press: One daily, "Hidigta October" in Somali

Radio and Television: Radio transmissions in Somali, Arabic, English and Italian.

Main Airports: Mogadiscio and Hargeisa

Main Seaport: Mogadiscio

Date of Joining the United Nations: September 20, 1960

Date of Joining the Arab League: February 14, 1974

SOMALIA

INTRODUCTION

The Somali Democratic Republic is strategically situated on the African Horn jutting into the Indian Ocean. It dominates the Gulf of Aden and the entrance to the Red Sea with more than 1800 miles of coastline.

Two former colonies, the Italian and the British territories of Somaliland, were united to form the modern Somali Republic in 1960. Another part of Somaliland, the Republic of Djibouti, was under French rule until 1977 as the Territories of the Afars and Issas.

Although very young as an independent republic, Somalia is involved in building a viable and strong nation, and is active in world affairs. A member of the United Nations since independence, the Somali Republic is also a member of the Arab League and of the Organization of African Unity.

PHYSICAL GEOGRAPHY

Topography

Somalia occupies an area of 246,200 square miles (slightly smaller than Texas). The northern part (former British Somaliland) is hilly, and in many places the altitude ranges between 3,000 and 7,000 feet. The central and southern portions (former Italian Somaliland) are flat with an average altitude of less than 600 feet. Crossing the country to the south are two rivers, the Juba and the Shebelle, which rise in Ethiopia and flow south towards the Indian Ocean.

Climate

The prevailing climatic factors are seasonal monsoon winds, a hot and dry period followed by heavy but short rainfalls. The southwest monsoon, a cool sea breeze, makes the period from about May to October the most pleasant season in Mogadishu, the capital, and in the southeast coastal zones.

Crops

The southern portion, especially the inter-river region, is fertile and relatively well-watered. The principal crops in this region are sorghum, Indian corn, sesame, beans and fruit; sugar cane and banana are cultivated on a mechanized scale. The chief export crop is banana.

HUMAN GEOGRAPHY

Population

The population of the Somali Democratic Republic is estimated between 3,500,000 and 4,000,000. The Somali people, however, are a nation of roughly five million occupying a vast expanse of northeast Africa, facing Arabia. Their arid, sparsely populated territory extends around the eastern periphery of the Ethiopian highlands and reaches out to the Red Sea and Indian Ocean coasts south to the Tana River in northern Kenya. This area forms a natural geographical and ethnic unit but is currently split up into four political spheres: The Somali Republic, the Republic of Djibouti, the Ogaden region of Ethiopia and the northeastern province of Kenya. Merchant communities of Somali origin are also settled in various urban centers of East Africa, and in Aden there is a sizeable community of Somali merchants and traders.

The Somali form one of the largest ethnic groups in Africa, sharing a common language, heritage, culture and religion, Islam. Ethnically and culturally, they belong to the Hamo-Cushitic family of peoples including the Galla, 'Afar (Danakil), Eritrean, Saho, and Beja—all of these being peoples of the Ethiopian lowlands. Their closest kinsmen are the adjoining Galla to the southwest and the 'Afar in the Republic of Djibouti.

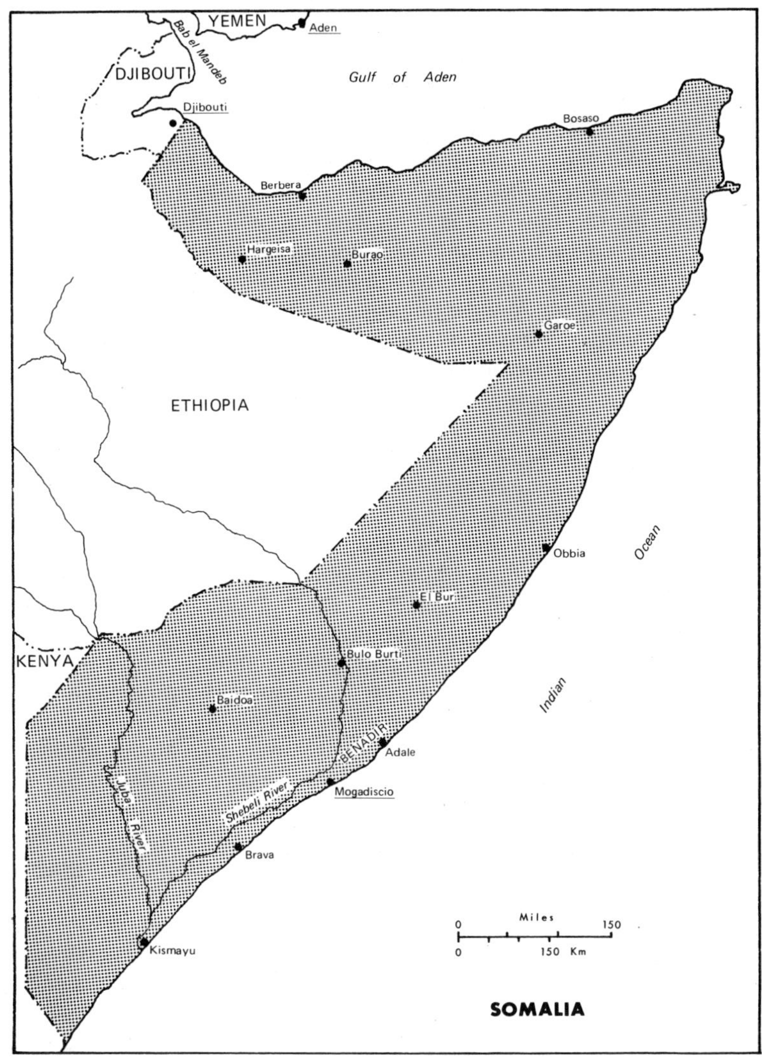

Urban Centers

The three largest cities and their approximate populations are Mogadishu (400,000), Kismayu (70,000) in the south, and Hargeisa (50,000) in the north.

Occupations

The great majority of the Somali are nomadic pastoralists. They maintain vast herds of camels and flocks of sheep and goats with which they are constantly on the move in search of pasture and water.

ECONOMY

Agriculture

The economy is the pastoral-agricultural type, the main form of wealth being livestock, principally camels, cattle, sheep and goats. Livestock and bananas account for 80 percent of the total exports. Sufficient meat and milk are produced to meet domestic needs.

Agriculture is pursued in the river regions, certain coastal districts and around Hargeisa. About one-eighth of the total area is suitable for cultivation. The principal cash crops are sugar, maize, sorghum, rice, beans, corn, sesame, groundnuts, fruits, and cotton for local consumption; bananas, grapefruit and coconut are exported.

Mineral Wealth

Mineral and ground water surveys have been carried out since 1963 by the United Nations Special Fund in cooperation with the government. One of the first major achievements was the discovery of over 50 million tons of iron ore near Baidoa (about 200 miles from the capital). The survey also discovered a very large quantity of uranium deposits over an extended area. The government has entered agreements with three foreign companies to exploit these valuable natural resources.

Thorium, appreciable deposits of bauxite, and rare earth-bearing minerals associated with radioactive materials have also been found. Iron ore deposits in the Bur Galan area are estimated to be in excess of 100 million tons. There is a reserve deposit of over 7 million cubic meters of sepilite. Encouraging signs of oil deposits have been obtained by some of the international oil companies which have Somali government concessions.

Industry

Heavy industry includes a sugar plant, a textile weaving mill, two meat packing factories, two fish processing and canning plants, leather tanneries and a milk processing plant. Some are joint ventures between foreign and Somali business interests. Current agriculture and livestock development programs envision a variety of processing industries. Most of Somalia's industry and large-scale businesses are publicly owned and managed.

Foreign Investment

Due to limited financial and technical resources, the substantial natural resources cannot be fully exploited without outside private investment. Consequently, the government has actively encouraged foreign investment. The existing foreign investment law allows especially favorable terms regarding taxation, protection of investments and repatriation of profits and capital. A number of investments from Italy, United States, and West Germany have already been established.

Foreign trade plays a key role in the economy. Trade is chiefly based on import-export. Somalia imports industrial and agricultural equipment, manufactured goods, foodstuff items and construction materials. Exports include livestock, canned meat, bananas, incense, hides and skins, canned fish, and several kinds of fruit. Transportation is conducted by air, truck and bus. There are no railways. The 9,000 miles of roads include 70 miles of all-weather roads.

A night scene of the main square of the capital Mogadiscio

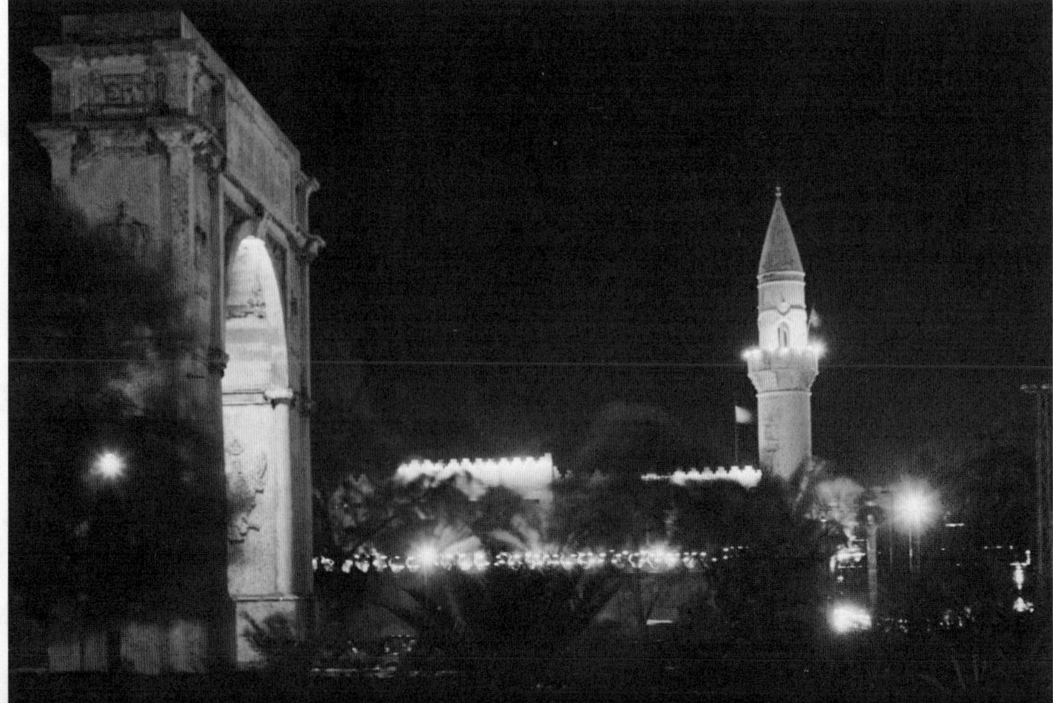

HISTORY

The history of Somalia is one of a great confederation of pastoral groups who in the course of several millennia developed into a homogeneous single entity united by language and other traditions. Like their Arabian counterparts of the pre-Islamic era, the Somali developed no centralized authority. Rather, authority tended to be based on clan aristocracy often with several lineages competing for political control. In the coastal centers political power was often dominated by religio-urban sheikhdoms which eventually developed into petty sultanates and spread their influence among the people of the interior. Despite the absence of highly centralized political authority, the Somali had in Islam a dominant unifying force which motivated them to develop and maintain a deep consciousness as a single nation reinforced by bonds of kinship. This was unbroken by the artificial colonial boundaries imposed during the last quarter of the 19th century.

Ancient

Somalia was known as the "Land of Punt" (God's land) to the ancient Egyptians whose merchant fleets plied the Red Sea coast as early as the second millennium B.C.

Islam

During the seventh century A.D. Persian and Arab merchants brought Islam to Somalia and other parts of Africa. The country appears in Arabic documents of the ninth century A.D., which describe Mogadishu and Brava to be important cities visited by traders of Arabia and the Far East. During this period, Mogadishu appears to have been one of the leading trade centers between Africa and Asia, frequented quite regularly by merchants of India and China.

Sultanates

The thirteenth century saw the rise of sultanates in various parts of Somalia. The most powerful was Adal, which emerged in the sixteenth century in present-day northern Somalia and northeast Ethiopia. Its charismatic leader al-Ghazi Imam Ahmed b. Ibrahim "Gurey" (1506-43) led the Muslims to resounding victories against the army of the Abyssinian Negus. Adal was probably more Islamic than Somali, but Somali contingents played a vital role in their victories and the Muslim chronicler of the period, Shihab ad-Din, mentions them frequently.

Modern

In the mid-nineteenth century European powers began to seek trade and naval concessions in the area. British interest centered around the twofold purpose of obtaining meat rations for its garrisons in Aden and a place to harbor its vessels without restrictions. The East India Company entered treaties of friendship with the sultan of Tajura as early as 1840. The British, however, did not move significantly in northern Somalia until 1884 when, following the withdrawal of the Egyptian garrisons from the area, they concluded treaties of protection with various Somali chiefs.

Meanwhile the Italians, recently united and feeling left out in the European scramble for African colonies, entered southern Somalia with a brisk interest. In 1885 Italy obtained commercial concessions in the Benadir coast from the sultan of Zanzibar. Through various painstaking treaties with diverse elements—the British, Somali chiefs, the sultans of Zanzibar—Italy extended her protection across the whole coast from Majeertinia to Kismayu by 1923. The Italians lost control of southern Somalia following their declaration of war on the United Kingdom in June, 1940, and from 1941 to 1950 the greater part of the Somali Horn was under British administration.

Independence

The period of transition toward self-government began in 1950. In December of that year Italy was appointed to a ten-year United Nations Trusteeship over its former colony. In 1960, both territories, the former British and Italian Somalilands, became independent and united to form the Somali Republic. On September 21, 1960, Somalia became a member of the United Nations.

GOVERNMENT AND SOCIETY

Administration

The Somali Democratic Republic is a unitary state whose head, the president, is elected by the national assembly for a term of six years.

Eight administrative regions and forty-eight districts are the responsibility of the Ministry of Internal Affairs, headed by a secretary of state. Each region is headed by a regional governor who also directs the Regional Revolutionary Council. District development affairs officers (DDAO), usually appointees of the central government, head the District Revolutionary Councils and, in general, conduct the management of the districts.

Social Unity

Like most African States, Somalia has devoted concerted national efforts to the problems of acculturation, urbanization and detribalization. Somalia has been highly successful in forging a national unity based on conceptions of citizenship, civic rights and obligations as well as equality before the law. The transition from tribe to nation has been facilitated by the existence of most of those characteristics which go into the making of a nation—common culture, religion, language, traditions and geographic contiguity. Indeed, Somalia is unique and favored in this respect, for Africa south of the Sahara is characterized by ethnic, cultural and linguistic plurality—a factor which all too often undermines national unity.

A Somali student at the Medical Center in Mogadiscio

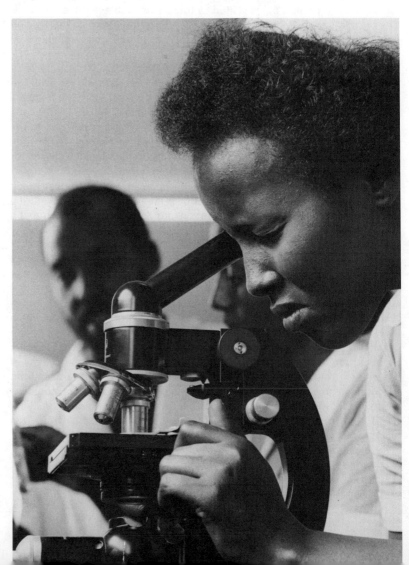

Education

In 1960, independent Somalia inherited two separate educational systems. The two colonial educational systems differed not only in the time allocated to each of the three stages, but also in content and language of instruction.

The most notable developments in education after independence were the unification of public schools and the adoption of the Latin script as an instrument for reducing the Somali language into writing. Credit for both achievements is due to the Revolutionary regime which has shown a special interest in public education since its assumption of political power in 1969.

In 1970-71 a unified curriculum, up to the secondary level, was applied to schools of the north and the south. There has been a dramatic expansion in enrollment. Elementary and secondary students totalled 42,156 in 1969-70; four years later enrollment jumped to 103,680, a 146 percent increase.

Defense

The armed forces consist of the National Army, which includes the Air Force, the Somali Police Force and the Custodian Corps, a group responsible for maintaining the prisons. The Somali National Army was created immediately after independence. It is fully mechanized and efficiently trained in land, air and sea operations. The joint services of the Somali Armed Forces are commanded by the Supreme Revolutionary Council.

Cultural Life

The Somali have been described as a "nation of poets." The poet plays a pervasive influence in society, similar to that of the bards of Arabia in the Jahili Age. Like the Arabian bard the Somali pastoralist lives in an extremely harsh environment, and their verses resemble each other both in form and thematic material. The creative genius of Somali oral literature was neglected by the colonial regimes, but government encouragement has brought new vitality and energy to the art form. The young generation of poets who have matured since independence dominate the national theater. Their themes of Somali national freedom, unity, peace and social progress intermingle with the traditional themes of love and war.

Traditional dances, songs and music are best preserved among the rural communities. Ritual dances have magico-religious significance and are an attempt to win the good will or at least the neutrality of the sinister forces of nature—disease, drought, marauding wild animals. Recreational dances are performed on all happy occasions—festivals, weddings, times of plenty, good rains. Popular music includes patriotic poems from classical poetry and songs with communal, political and love themes.

Tourism

Somalia still hides the secrets of bygone days. Ruins of ancient cities have been attributed to the time of the Queen of Sheba. Tourists can enjoy fine beaches and sea life as well as explore bushes and pristine caves. There are rich hunting grounds. The wildlife heritage includes a variety of species which will soon be protected in national game parks. Tourist facilities are being developed.

PROSPECTS

Though one of the less-developed countries of the Arab League, the Somali Democratic Republic is potentially rich in human and material resources. The challenge facing this nation and government is to harness these resources into productive channels that will bring about the political and economic emancipation of its people.

The years ahead will probably see a more forceful involvement of the Somali Republic in world politics, especially in Middle Eastern affairs. The Horn is so strategically placed that it can scarcely be disengaged from big power politics. The fact that it dominates the southern approaches to the Red Sea and the eastern coast of the Indian Ocean is reason enough to attract the attention of geopoliticians. Furthermore, Somalia's close proximity to Arabia and her common Islamic faith, deeply rooted in history and custom, and recently reinforced by its joining to the Arab League, are factors that are likely to bring it even closer to the Middle East.

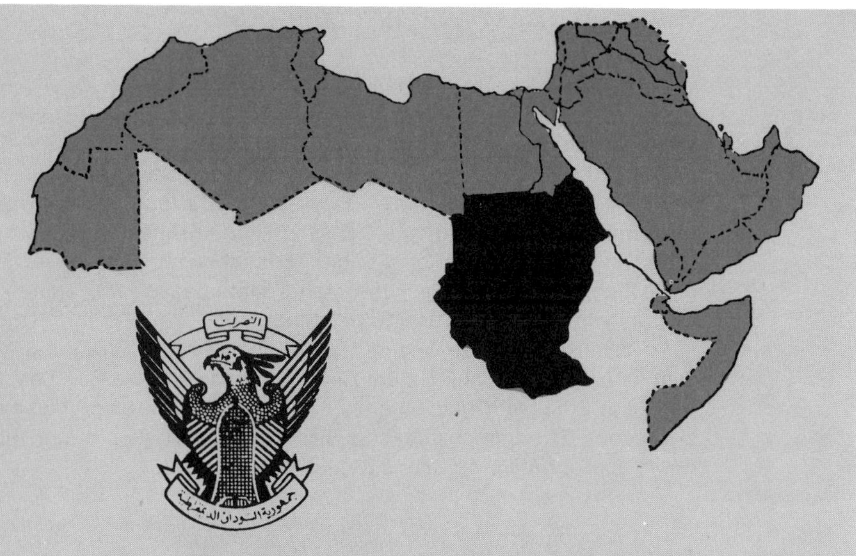

SUDAN

جمهورية السودان الديمقراطية

PROFILE

Official Name: Democratic Republic of Sudan (Jumhuriyyat al-Sudan al-Dimuqratiyyah)

Head of State: Jaafer Nimeiri

Government: Republic

Area: 967,499 sq. mi. (=United States east of the Mississippi)

Population: 16,300,000

Population Density: 17/sq. mi.

Capital: Khartoum (350,000)

Other Urban Centers: Khartoum North, Omdurman, Merowe, Dongala

National Holiday: January 1

Currency: Sudanese Pound (1 SP = $2.90)

Press: Al-Ayyam and Al-Sahafa, most important dailies

Radio & Television: Radio programs in Arabic, French, Italian Television network.

Sites of Interest: Ancient Nubian tombs and pyramids

Main Airports: Khartoum and Jubal

Date of Joining the United Nations: November 12, 1956

Date of Joining the Arab League: January 19, 1956

INTRODUCTION

Sudan, Africa's largest country, straddles a vast expanse of geography, history and culture. Its great diversity is a most prominent characteristic. While Sudan has not itself played a central role in world history, the great powers from the ancient Egyptians to the British imperialists have involved it in international affairs. However, it is often forgotten that Sudan once ruled Egypt during the height of the Kushites, that it was under Byzantine Christian rule for a longer period than under Islam, and that the great Sudanese nationalist, the Mahdi, defeated a joint Anglo-Egyptian military venture in the late nineteenth century.

To a certain degree Sudan may be likened to a structural keystone with its frontiers touching eight African nations and the Red Sea. Links to people in Ethiopia, Chad, Uganda and Egypt have often proved extremely significant. The immensely long Nile River and its two major tributaries are in appropriate proportions for this African giant.

PHYSICAL GEOGRAPHY

Topography

The Democratic Republic of Sudan is essentially a huge, shallow basin, mostly over 1500 feet above sea level, rimmed by highlands and mountains, and dominated by the Nile drainage system. Its area of 967,499 square miles is roughly equivalent to all of Western Europe, or to the United States east of the Mississippi River. In the far west in Darfur are the Jebel Marra highlands with the highest mountain reaching 10,070 feet. In the east, the Sudanese plains push all the way to the mountains which mark the border with Eritrea. Some of these mountains continue into Sudan as the Red Sea Hills which provide a relatively cool region above the hot, dry plains. A few prominent volcanic hills rise in the south, but most of the southern countryside is rather undifferentiated in terms of altitude.

Nile Valley

The most important region is the Nile Valley, particularly the extensive portion known as the Gezira which lies between the Blue and White Niles. It is in the irrigated Gezira that the agricultural wealth is concentrated. Once cotton was the monocrop, but more recently other cash crops like grains and sugar cane have become important. The country may be divided into three climatic zones. In the northern third there are extensive regions of virtual desert with very infrequent rains. The central third is characterized by savanna vegetation if the seasonal rainfall has been adequate. Blinding sandstorms may occur in this zone. The southern third is scrub forest with more regular summer rainfall, especially in the area along the frontier with Zaire and Uganda which contains flora typical of the tropical forest. The Red Sea coast is hot and humid.

In northern and central Sudan daytime summer temperatures may exceed 110°F, while winter nights may fall to 60°F. The range between day and night temperatures is often considerable.

Soil types reflect the climatic pattern. In the north the surface is either covered by shifting sands or is bare rock with no soil. As aridity diminishes southwards immature soils begin to appear. In central and southern Sudan alkaline clay soils are found, and along the Uganda and Zaire borders there is a belt of tropical lateritic soils. Alluvial soils are found along the rivers.

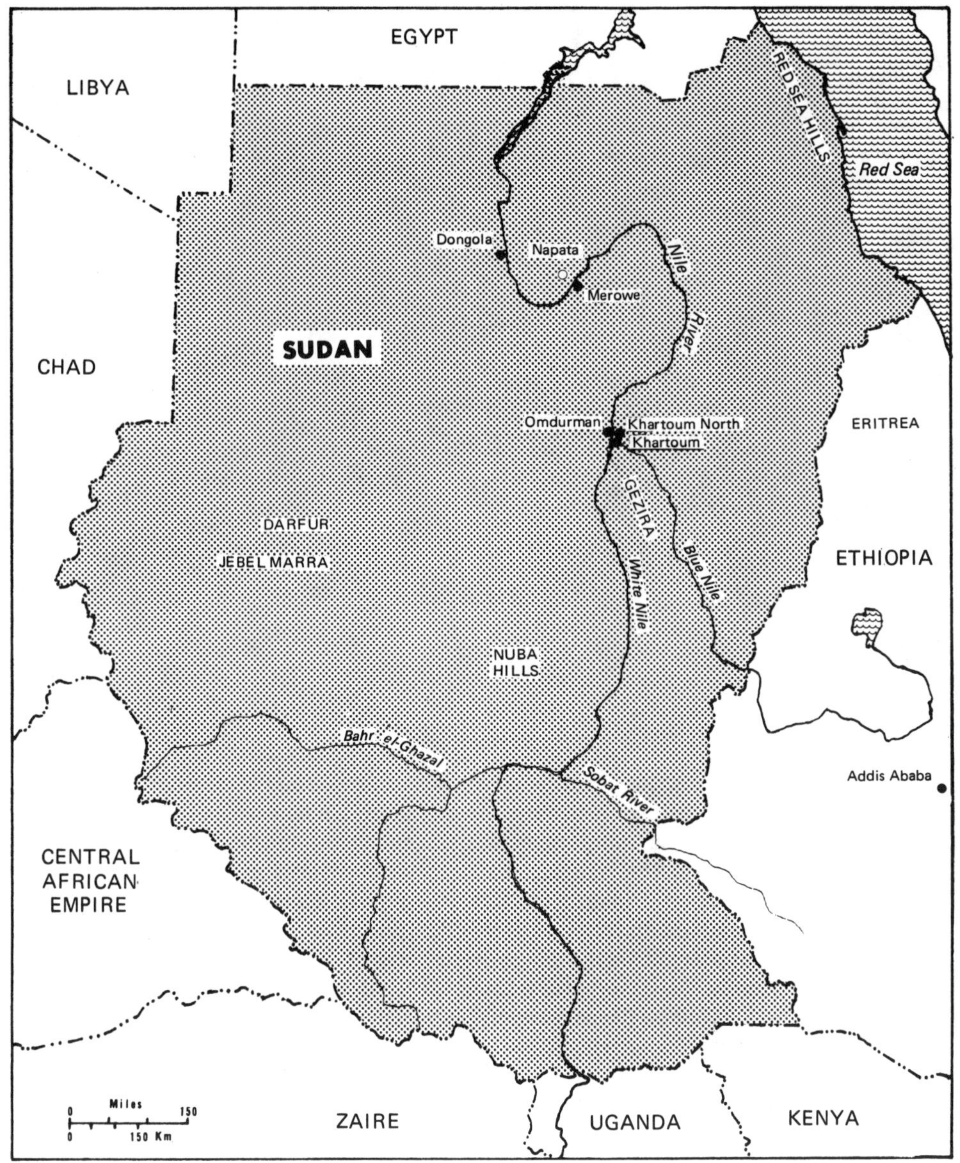

HUMAN GEOGRAPHY

The mid-1977 population is estimated at 16.3 million. Arabs predominate with about 40 percent, followed by Black Africans (such as Dinka and Nuer) in the south with 30 percent, mixed groups in the western Darfur region with 13 percent, Nuba in the Nuba Hills region with 6 percent, Beja in the northeast with 6 percent, and Nubians along the Nile near Egypt with 3 percent.

The boundaries of Sudan, like those of other colonies in Africa and the Middle East, were not drawn with much account taken of the peoples who would live within them. As a result Sudan is a highly heterogeneous state. In the northern regions the people are of mixed Arab and African ancestry—they are predominantly agriculturalists, Arabic-speaking, and followers of Islam.

Northern Sudanese women attend meeting in South.

People

In the eastern and western deserts there are a number of camel or cattle nomadic groups referred to by Sudanese as "Arabs," whose allegiance is more to their own ethnic groups than to the Sudanese nationality. The Niletic, Nile-Hamitic, and Sudanic peoples of the southern regions (Dinka, Nuer, Shilluk, Annuak, Zande) are either cultivators or cattle pastoralists who practice their own traditional religions. These groups are steadily being incorporated within the Sudanese system. Educated southerners, perhaps 0.5 percent of the southern population, follow various Christian sects, especially Catholicism.

Language

Over 70 percent of the population are Muslims. Islam came to the northern areas by way of Egypt and across the Red Sea from the Arabian peninsula. The people of western Sudan, in the Darfur region, were Islamicized by a different route, one coming from West Africa.

In the political and economic spheres the peoples of northern and central Sudan dominate, and their language, Arabic, is the official language of the country. Arabic is the first language of slightly more than one-third of the population, but Sudanese colloquial Arabic is the lingua franca. Educated Sudanese have considerable knowledge of English, the former colonial language.

Urban Centers

The largest urban concentration is the Three Towns area (Khartoum, Khartoum North and Omdurman), with a population of 800,000, comprising 5.6 percent of the national total. Khartoum is the center of politics, administration and transport, while Omdurman is the center of commerce and northern Sudanese culture.

The population is unevenly distributed over the often harsh landscape. More than 50 percent of the people are concentrated on about 15 percent of the land, primarily along the Nile and around Khartoum. Most of the rest are in the savanna areas west of the White Nile and south of Bahr el-Ghazal.

ECONOMY

Agriculture

The backbone of the Sudanese economy is agriculture. There are 617 million cultivable acres, but only 200 million are currently being used. Animal resources and forestry products each account for about 10 percent of the gross national product (GNP). Eighty-five percent of the work force is concentrated in primary production. Not only is the economy heavily weighted toward primary production but much of the agricultural wealth revolves around one cash crop—cotton. The irrigated Gezira cotton scheme began in 1925 and has more than 2 million acres under cultivation. Cotton alone has provided about two-thirds of the total export earnings. Instability in cotton prices and conversion to synthetic fibers have initiated a program which emphasizes sugar cane and grain production to diversify the economy and boost export earnings.

Industry

Industry is concentrated in the Three Towns area of Khartoum, Khartoum North and Omdurman where there are textile mills and chemical, beverage, tile, cigarette and leather industries. Legislation passed in 1972 provides incentives to foreign investors. Manufacturing industries contribute about 2 percent of the GNP.

Mineral Wealth

Mineral resources may include some petroleum reserves, but these have not been tapped. There is some gold in the Red Sea Hills and low grade iron ore in portions of the south. Copper, gypsum, manganese, chrome, lead and sulphur are found but are not exploited to any great extent.

While there are good international air connections, the internal road system is very deficient. There are only a few hundred miles of paved roads, although a rail system links most of the provincial capitals.

Marketplace in Khartoum.

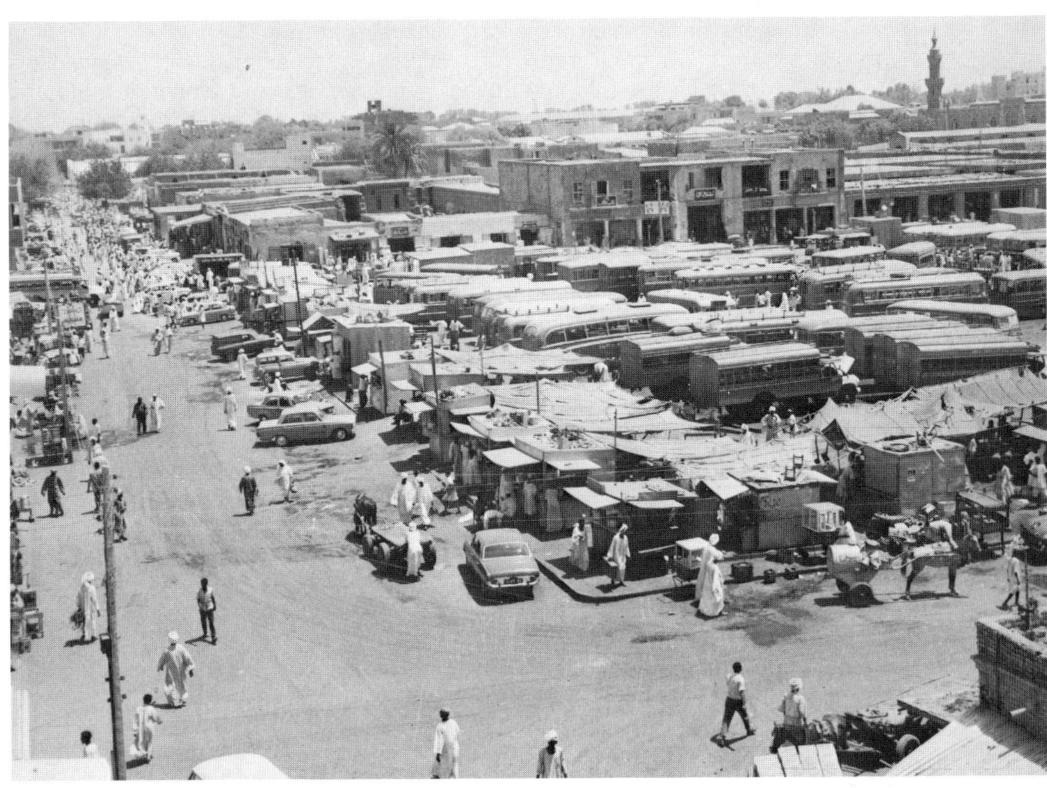

SUDAN

HISTORY

Ancient

For tens of thousands of years Sudan was populated by hunters, foragers and fishermen. Sedentary life began with the farming of the Nile floodplains. Some of the first recorded contact with other nations occurred when representatives of the Old Kingdom of Egypt (3200-2100 B.C.) arrived in search of gold, ivory, slaves, and incense and built rudimentary military outposts. During the Middle Kingdom (2100-1700 B.C.), northern Sudan was an Egyptian province, a source of slaves and rare minerals. The New Kingdom rulers (1570-1100 B.C.) brought an even greater Egyptian influence which penetrated as far south as Napata.

Kushites

The close links with Egypt began to erode during the rise of the Kushites (1100-750 B.C.), with their capital of Merowe, and a great sense of economic and political autonomy was evident. From 750 to 500 B.C. the Kushitic influence expanded to such a degree that a variety of Sudanese innovations made the Merotic culture significantly different from Egyptian patterns, including a unique form of writing. The Kushites occupied extensive areas of Egypt until Assyrians found them over-extended and seized Egypt for themselves. Merowe shrank in territory but lasted until 350 A.D. The high level of cultural achievement was in conjunction with the period of greatest political autonomy. The Merotic period saw Black Africa's first extensive trade network, an independent production of iron ore and the manufacture of iron implements.

Medieval

The ensuing contest among the great Mediterranean powers for influence in Sudan was resolved with the imposition of Byzantine and Coptic Christianity from 540 to 1504 A.D. The Christian period began to fade with the Islamic conquest in 1323 of the northern areas of Sudan; the southern Christian kingdom fell in 1504. Islamic expansion characterized the remainder of the medieval period with central Sudan coming under the influence of the Funj sultanates in 1504.

Mahdi

In 1821, the Turkish ruler in Egypt, Mohammad Ali, extended his control up the Nile into Sudan. A degree of improvement in trade and communication occurred, but brutal taxation, widespread corruption and persistent slavery made his rule unpopular. The Mahdiyya, a politico-religious movement with a fierce sense of nationalism, won a significant battle in 1881. Its leader, the Mahdi, gained control of much of Sudan by January, 1885, the year when General Gordon, leader of an Anglo-Egyptian military expedition, was killed.

Mahdi control was short-lived. By 1899 the Anglo-Egyptian force had succeeded in asserting its control. In that year the Anglo-Egyptian Sudan condominium was established, with Britain very much as the senior partner.

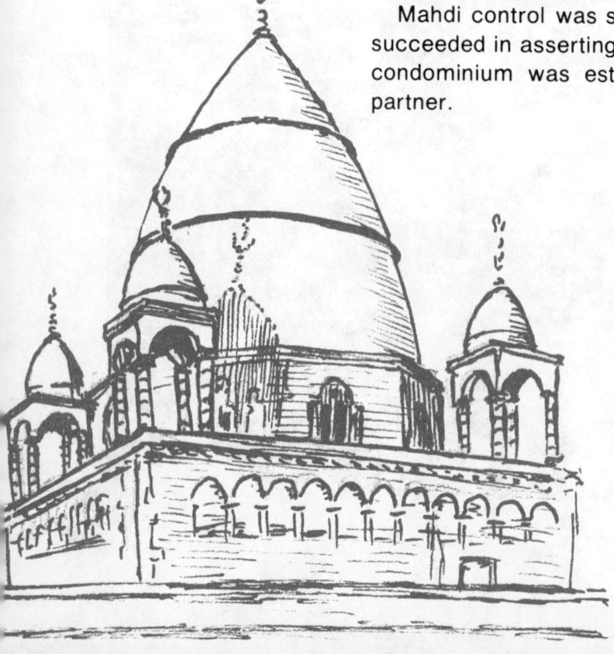

Mahdi's tomb at Omdurman

Independence

On January 1, 1956, Sudan became independent. In 1958 the parliamentary government was toppled by a pro-West coup under General Ibrahim Abboud, who was himself overthrown in the wake of a series of massive demonstrations in October, 1964. Secessionist disturbances in the south began as early as 1955 and were a constant dilemma for Khartoum. From 1965 to 1969 the country drifted with no decisive action taken on the pressing problems of the south and national development. On May 25, 1969 the second parliamentary period closed with a coup d'etat by Jaafer Nimeiri. The Nimeiri regime's initial strong leftist support deteriorated. After a three-day coup d'etat in July, 1971, Nimeiri turned to the West and relations with the Soviet Union chilled. The March 1972 Addis Ababa Agreement ended the civil war in the south.

GOVERNMENT AND SOCIETY

In May, 1969 the Democratic Republic of Sudan, committed to a policy of Sudanese socialsim, was proclaimed. The Sudanese Socialist Union (SSU) was formed in 1972 and is the only legal political party. After local SSU elections the People's Assembly was convened to form a new constitution.

Administration

The National Judiciary is comprised of a Civil Branch (including civil and criminal sections) and a Shari'a or Islamic Branch. The Shari'a is relegated to the domain of personal or family law only. People's Courts were instituted to combine national law with customary law at the local level. These courts are now referred to as Village Councils and are operated with SSU personnel. A High Judicial Council supervises legal affairs as provided by the SSU-promulgated constitution.

Education

Primary education is available on a mass level in the towns and cities. A smaller percentage of students go on to secondary school. Through the secondary school level the language of instruction is Arabic. At the University of Khartoum courses are taught in both Arabic and English. In the south, English and Arabic are used for education and administration. However, following the Addis Ababa Agreement there has been a commitment to expand the use of the languages of the south.

Social services account for 45 percent of the government budget; most services are free. Government health services provide the bulk of medical care.

Defense

The Sudanese Armed Forces occupy an important position, as military support has always been critical in influencing the course of national politics. In 1972 the Armed Forces numbered around 20,000, but since that time large numbers of former southern rebel troops from the Anya-Nya have been absorbed into the national army.

Tourism

Tourism has grown rapidly since the resolution of the prolonged civil war. The south has a number of game parks; the largest is Dinder National Game Park, 320 miles southeast of Khartoum. The capital's museums contains treasures from the ancient kingdom of Kush, from Pharaonic rule and from the Christian period. Historic sites in Omdurman give testament to the once powerful rule of the Mahdiyya. From Khartuom it is less than a day's travel to the archaeological ruins at the old Kushitic capital of Merowe.

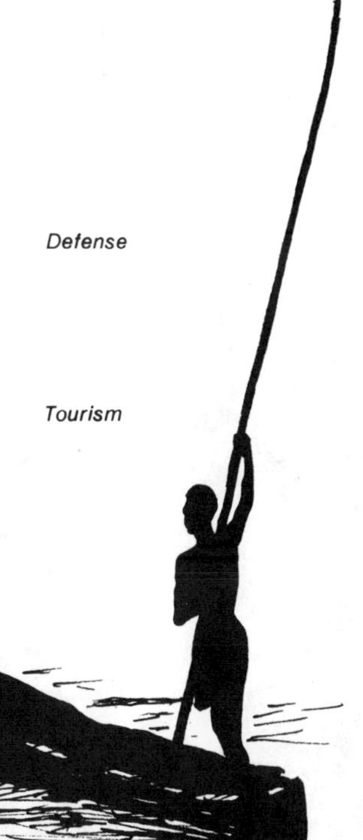

PROSPECTS

While foreign debts, a low per capita GNP and a reliance on imported manufactured items are serious handicaps to Sudan's development, there is an immense potential for future growth. Many of its human and natural resources have hardly been tapped. Hydroelectric power could be generated in vast amounts for internal consumption and for export. Proper water management could expand the irrigated lands to help raise foreign revenue by state-controlled agribusiness. Sudan is not yet suffering the intense population pressure that is so common in many Third World nations. Any development policy must have consistency and continuity and Sudan's several changes of government and oscillations from right to left have undermined the development program. The resolution of the southern problem which kept the nation divided for almost seventeen years is a most encouraging sign. Without national unity there can be no national development, yet it is only with a fair development of the resources of both the north and south that unity will be maintained.

A Sudanese singer accompanies herself on a lyre-like instrument.

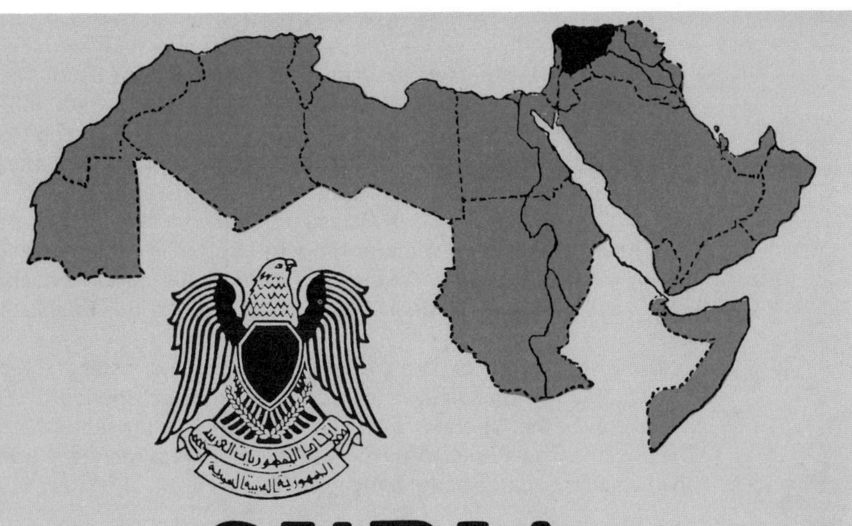

SYRIA

الجمهورية العربية السورية

PROFILE

Official Name: The Syrian Arab Republic (Al-Jumhuriyyah al-Arabiyyah al-Suriyyah)

Head of State: Hafez al-Assad

Government: Republic

Area: 71,498 sq. mi. (= N. Dakota)

Population: over 7 million

Population Density: 90/sq. mi.

Capital: Damascus (about 1,000,000)

Other Urban Centers: Aleppo, Homs, Hama, Latakia, Deir Ez-Zawr, Banias, Tartous

National Holiday: April 17

Currency: Syrian Pound ($1.00 = 3.9 SP.)

Press: Daily: Al-Baath, Al-Thawra, Tishrin, many periodicals

Radio & Television: Radio transmissions in Arabic, English, French, German, Spanish and Turkish. Television.

Sites of Interest: Damascus, Aleppo museums, Palmyra, Bosra, Crusaders Castles along Syrian coast

Main Airports: Damascus, Aleppo

Main Seaports: Latakia, Tartous

Date of Joining the United Nations: October 24, 1945

Date of Joining the Arab League: March 22, 1945

SYRIA

INTRODUCTION

Located at the eastern end of the Mediterranean, Syria has always been a geographic and cultural bridge linking Asia, Africa and Europe. The Syrian Arab Republic is crowded with vestiges of a long history reflecting the ebb and flow of empires and armies, of builders and traders, of prophets and poets. Its history and geography are intertwined with that of Jordan, Lebanon and Palestine. These modern states are part of Geographic Syria, an ancient territory referred to in Arabic as Ash-Sham, which extends from the Taurus mountains in the north to Arabia in the south and from the Mediterranean in the west to the Euphrates in the east.

The existing states in the area were created as a result of the defeat of the Ottoman Empire in World War I and the emergence of European control over the Ottoman province of Syria. The present boundaries of the Syrian Arab Republic were determined primarily by the French and the British mandates in the early twenties.

A water wheel "noria" on the Orontes River in the city of Hama.

PHYSICAL GEOGRAPHY

The Syrian Arab Republic lies on the eastern shore of the Mediterranean Sea with an area of 71,498 square miles. Its neighbors are Turkey (north), Iraq (east), Jordan (south), and Palestine and Lebanon (southwest). Along the coast a narrow strip of flat and hilly terrain has enough rainfall and spring-fed streams to be agriculturally productive. Paralleling the coast, a region of mountains and valleys extends the length of the country all the way to Mount Hermon in the south. Moving eastward, the next topographical feature is a strip of plains which produces most of Syria's crops and contains most of its cities. The plains gradually lead to a vast semi-desert (badiah) stretching east into Iraq and merging into the Syrian Desert which extends south across Jordan into Arabia.

The Orontes River (Al-'Asi) flows from Lebanon and runs north as far as Antioch before turning southwest to empty into the Mediterranean. The Euphrates comes from the Turkish mountains, traverses the flat semi-desert into Iraq and eventually merges with the Tigris which empties into the Arabian Gulf.

Winter rainfall is relatively abundant along the coast and diminishes gradually over the mountains and the eastern plains. It is scarce over the desert. Forests are found only in the mountains of Latakia along the coast.

HUMAN GEOGRAPHY

Population

The population is estimated at seven million. Throughout its long history Syria received many waves of migrations and conquerors, making the people a mixture of ethnic and religious characteristics. However, the predominance of the Arabic language after the Islamic conquest in the seventh century has branded the Syrians with a distinct Arabic cultural character. Small communities still speak languages such as Aramaic, Kurdish, and Armenian, but, in most of these cases, they also speak Arabic.

Religion

About 80 percent of the population are Sunni Muslims. Other Muslim sects, such as Shi'as, Alawites and Druzes also exist. Christians, although few in number, belong to a large variety of denominations. A small Jewish minority lives in Damascus.

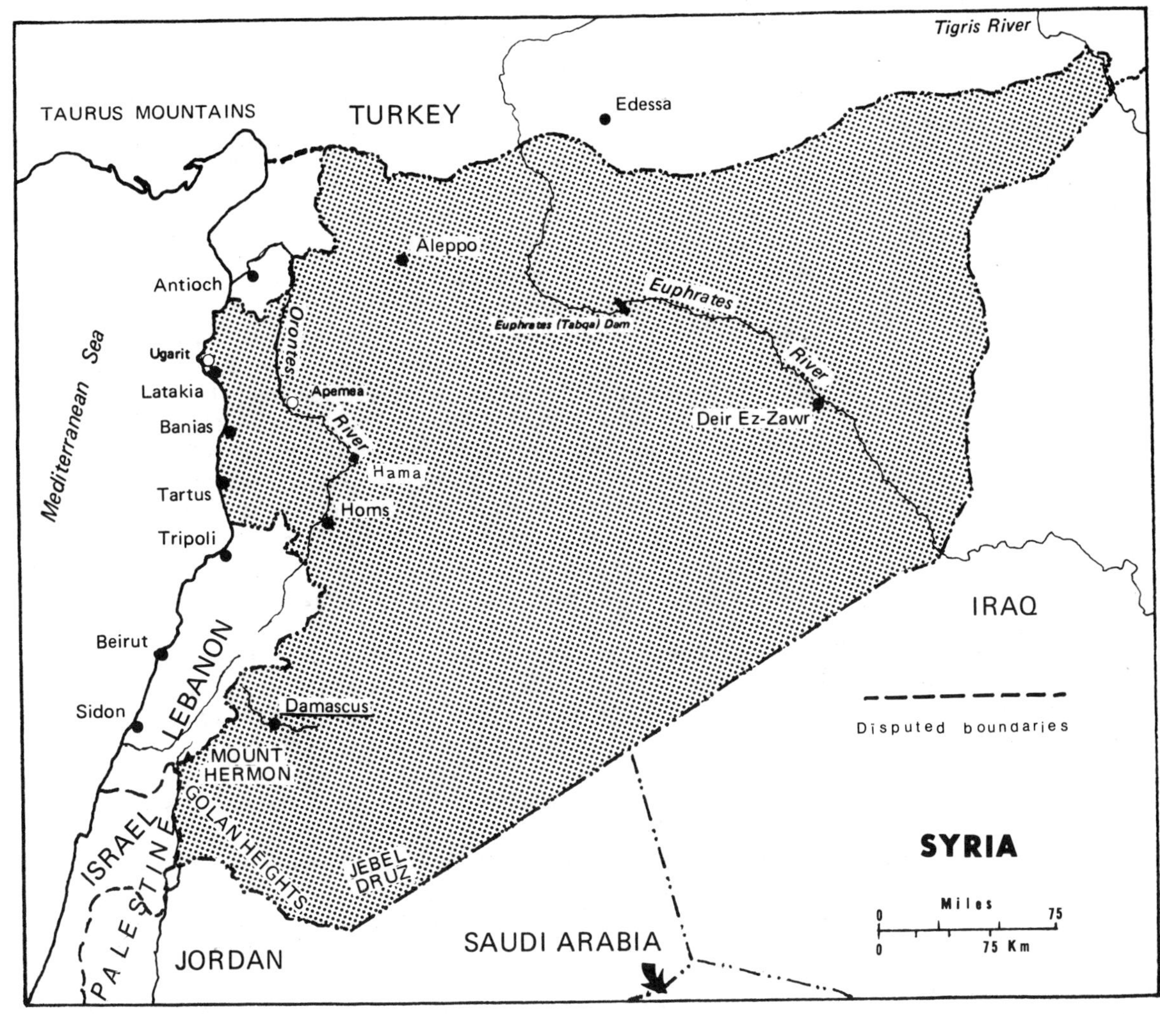

Migration from the rural communities and the nomadic interior is steadily swelling the urban areas, which now hold about 45 percent of the population. Syrian cities are among the oldest in the world. As in most of the Arab world, urbanism in Syria is a way of life that goes back to the dawn of history. Damascus, the capital, has streets that date back to biblical times and Aleppo is dominated by a medieval citadel. Yet both cities boast wide and modern boulevards with impressive private and public buildings.

Urban Centers

Mountain villages are clusters of houses in picturesque settings. In the plains of the interior some villages still display houses built of sun-dried mud bricks. The introduction of modern building materials, roads, and electricity is fast changing the appearance and character of the countryside.

Villages

The overall population density is about 90 per square mile (compared to overall U.S. density of about 50). However, only half of the area is inhabited. The rate of population increase is probably over 3 percent, thus the population will double before the year 2000. This rate of growth requires a fast increase in the rate of economic expansion if an improved standard of living is to be achieved.

Density

THE ECONOMY

Economic Policy

Since the early 1960s Syria has been steadily moving toward a centralized and regulated economy. Almost all large businesses, industrial firms, banks and insurance companies came under public control. In 1971 this trend was modified to provide greater encouragement to the private sector and stop the flow of Syrian capital out of the country. Gross fixed investment increased about 19 percent in 1971, but private investment rose 30 percent. Economic growth, which averaged less than 5 percent before 1971, has since tripled.

Agriculture

Syria remains primarily an agricultural country. An agrarian reform program has distributed about 3.7 million acres of land among 55,000 families. Agricultural cooperatives have more than 80,000 members. Agriculture accounts for one-third of the domestic output and more than a quarter of the national income. The total cultivable area is about 22 million acres, but only two-thirds of this area is under cultivation. There are nearly 5 million acres of irrigable land, but only 25 percent are irrigated. The most prominent government project, the Tabaqa Dam on the Euphrates, is expected to double the present irrigated area and to provide 800,000 kilowatts of electricity.

Cotton is the main cash crop. From only 12,400 tons in 1945, the annual yield has been increased to almost half a million tons. Cereals, especially wheat, are also important. When bad weather results in a poor harvest, wheat is imported. Fruits are abundant and some, such as apricots and nuts, are export crops. Olives, grapes and apples are grown in the mountains. High-grade tobacco is exported from the Latakia region.

Minerals

Syria is relatively poor in mineral resources. Oil has been discovered in the northeast corner of the country. Reserves are estimated at 300 million tons. Oil production in 1975 was 10.5 million tons, valued at $600 million.

Two oil pipelines run through Syria, one from Iraq and the other from Saudi Arabia, with a total annual capacity of 80 million tons.

Industry

Textiles and food processing industries are well established. Industrial growth amounted to about 95 before 1970 but a series of five-year plans has led to accelerated growth. In 1973 industrial output was valued at $225 million, an increase of 15 percent over 1972, and 1,993 permits were issued for new industrial projects in the private sector. Capital investment in these projects was estimated at $32 million. Diversification and the establishment of heavy industry are goals of the fourth Five-Year Plan (1976-80). The third Five-Year Plan concentrated on the ambitious Euphrates Dam.

The summer resort town of Bludan, near Damascus, with the snow-capped Mt. Hermon in the distance

Railways link the main cities of Aleppo, Homs and Damascus and connect with Lebanon, Jordan, Iraq and Turkey. New lines will link Damascus with Homs, and the port of Latakia with Deir Ez-Zawr on the Euphrates. A network of main roads (about 4,000 miles) connects Syrian towns and villages. Transit trucking moves goods from Syrian and Lebanese ports to Iraq, Kuwait, Jordan and Saudi Arabia.

The chief port is Latakia. Banias is an oil terminal. Tartus is developing as another port on the Mediterranean. International airports exist in Aleppo and Damascus. Syrian Airways provides air transport between Syrian towns, as well as into Arab and European cities. Major international airlines fly regularly to Damascus.

Palmyra, the remains of a desert capital that flourished in the 1st century A.D.

HISTORY

Ancient

Syria's location as a land bridge between Europe, Asia and Africa is the ritical factor in its history. Great empires arising in the Nile Valley, Mesopotamia and beyond have sought to dominate this vital area. Archeology confirms that Syria was one of the earliest areas in which man developed organized society.

Sargon of Akkad probably extended his Mesopotamian domain into Syria as early as the middle of the Third Millennium B.C. In the Second Millennium, the Hittites and the Egyptians vied for the area. Later, the Assyrians and Babylonians gained control. In the sixth century B.C. Syria became a part of the Persian Empire. Persian control ended with the conquest of Alexander the Great in 332 B.C.

During this long period, however, Syria kept its identity. Independent local states thrived, especially during the periods of decline of the imperial powers surrounding the area. The Amurru, Canaanite, Hebrew, and Aramaean Kingdoms had a profound impact on the development of civilization and religion. The earliest known alphabet comes from the city of Ugarit on the north Syrian coast as well as the oldest song with musical notation. The Canaanites contributed more to the development of navigation than any other people in history. The Aramaeans promoted inland trade and from about the middle of the First Millennium to the seventh century, Aramaic was the lingua franca of the whole Middle East, extending from Egypt to India.

"Krak des Chevaliers," a vestige of the Crusades and one of the best preserved of medieval castles

The Hellenistic period brought vigorous cultural and ethnic mixing. Many new cities were founded, the most famous of which are Antioch, Apamea, and Latakia. In 63 B.C. Syria became a Roman province, famous for its agriculture, industry and culture. When the center of the Empire shifted to Constantinople in 330 A.D., Syria was subjected to intermittent incursions and occupations by the Sassanian Persians. The spread of Christianity and the division of the Church into many sects, created religious and political unrest, which lasted until the Arab conquest in 635 A.D.

Arab Caliphate

The Arabs were not disruptive to Syrian life as they were not too alien from Syrian culture, language or religion. Within twenty-five years Damascus became the center of the Islamic Caliphate. The empire grew in power and wealth, extending from France to India and China under the Umayyad Dynasty (661-750 A.D.). The Arabization and Islamization of Syria progressed very slowly, but mostly without strife and strain.

The Abbasid Caliphs superseded the Umayyads and moved the capital to Baghdad in Iraq. The decline of the power of the Abbasids in the ninth century promoted independent states and dynasties in the empire. Syria was dominated by Tulunids and Ikshidids who were based in Egypt, and by Hamdanids, Seljuk Turks and Zangid rulers, mostly in the north of the country. A number of smaller local dynasties rose and fell in the tenth, eleventh and twelfth centuries, but the country was mostly under the control of the Shi'ite Fatimids of Egypt. During this period European Crusaders were able to establish military states in Antioch, Edessa (Urfa), Tripoli and Jerusalem. In 1174, Saladdin, having overthrown the Fatimids, captured Damascus and expelled most of the Crusaders. The country was devastated by Mongol invasions in 1260, 1270 and 1300.

Ottoman

The Ottoman Turks conquered Syria in 1516. During four hundred years of Ottoman control, the country's population dwindled, its commerce and industry were at a low ebb, and its cultural achievements were at a standstill.

In the nineteenth century, a literary revival, interest in education, improvement of communication with Europe, and the establishment of a few newspapers led to an awakening of Arab identity and pride. Some Syrian intellectuals (including Lebanese and Palestinians) migrated to other countries, especially Egypt which was relatively free of Ottoman rule. The Egyptian regime of Muhammad Ali occupied Syria for about ten years (1831-40). In 1860 the French intervened in Lebanon. Foreign missions established some schools and publishing houses. The Syrian elite began to agitate for reform. The movement for autonomy within the Ottoman Empire gradually changed to a movement of independence for an Arab state. The demise of the Ottoman Empire in World War I and the Arab revolution that helped this demise gave rise to a hope of finally having an Arab state comprising all of Syria as well as adjacent Arab lands. But Britain and France, who won the war, had other plans. Also the Zionist movement in Europe had made a deal with Britain for the establishment of a "Jewish National Home" in Palestine.

In March, 1920, Syrian nationalists with representatives from all geographic Syria (including Lebanon and Palestine) proclaimed an independent kingdom. But the San Remo Conference of 1920 granted France a mandate for the greater part of Syria. French troops moved to forcibly implement the mandate, and the nationalists were defeated at Maysaloun near Damascus. The French created five different states in the area to facilitate French rule. These states reflected different religious groups. However, the states of Latakia, Jebel Druz, Damascus and Aleppo were eventually unified as a result of Syrian pressure. The Lebanon was enlarged and remained separate.

In 1946, Syria gained its full independence. But before it could build an effective defense force, it was embroiled in the conflict that emerged in Palestine. The establishment of the state of Israel and the expulsion of large numbers of Palestinians created a burden for Syria and influenced its political life. After the 1948 war, a military coup toppled the president. This was followed by a series of coups, mostly bloodless.

Aleppo, Syria's second largest city and important commercial center. The medieval Arab citadel is on the left

In 1958 Syria and Egypt merged, but the United Arab Republic lasted only forty-three months. A coup by army officers dissolved the union. A new constitution was drafted. However, more coups occurred, and other attempts to recreate the union with Egypt failed to materialize.

Modern

In 1967 Israel attacked Syria and occupied the Golan Heights. On October 6, 1973, war was renewed as Syrian troops began to liberate the Golan at the same time the Egyptians were crossing the Suez Canal. The war went well for the Syrian army in the first few days, but the battle turned against them when the Israelis obtained fresh supplies of arms from the United States. On October 23, Syria conditionally accepted a cease-fire. The front remained active, however, until May, 1974, when, through mediation by the United States secretary of state, a troop-separation agreement was concluded. Syria insists on the recovery of all Arab territories and on granting the Palestinians their national rights.

A street in old Damascus with one of the ancient gates.

GOVERNMENT AND SOCIETY

Administration

Syria has a republican form of government. The president is elected for a term of seven years and has executive power. A Council of Ministers is nominated by the president. The legislative body is the People's Council which was formed in 1971. Its members are elected to four-year terms. The judicial power is independent. A High Constitutional Court considers the constitutionality of laws. The Constitution, adopted in 1973, declares that the "Syrian Arab Republic is a democratic, socialist, sovereign state" and that "it is a part of the Arab homeland," and that "its people are part of the Arab nation," and that "sovereignty belongs to the people."

Defense

The defense forces are officially estimated at 120,000 in the army, 2,000 in the navy, and 10,000 in the air force. National compulsory service lasts for two and a half years. Syria is a member of the Arab League Unified Military Command.

Free medical care is available in all state hospitals. There are over thirty government hospitals and fifty private ones. The law provides old age pensions and other benefits.

Education

Education in Syria is compulsory at the primary level, and free through the university level. There are about one million students in the primary schools, 350,000 in the preparatory and secondary schools, and more than 12,000 in the technical and trade schools. The universities in Damascus, Aleppo and Latakia have a combined student body of more than 50,000. The state school system is supplemented by private, religious and special schools. Adult education and literacy training have raised the literacy rate to about 50 percent. The language of instruction at all levels is Arabic.

Cultural Life

Teacher training and higher technical institutes include the Higher Industrial School in Damascus, the Damascus Oriental Institute of Music, the Damascus Institute of Technology, and the Aleppo Institute of Music. About 20 percent of the student enrollment in higher institutions are women. The National Theater was founded in 1960. That same year television was introduced. The development of the National Theater is now in progress. Syrian cinema is still in its infancy. However, some films have won international awards and recognition. Government schools encourage art and regularly sponsor art exhibitions.

Ma'lula, a picturesque village near Damascus, where the Aramaic language is still spoken.

PROSPECTS

The potential for future growth in Syria is promising. A significant increase in agricultural output is sure to follow the development of irrigation projects such as the great Tabaqa Dam on the Euphrates River, which will also produce hydroelectric power needed for industrial projects. This expansion in agriculture and in industry can, for the immediate future, keep up with the increase in population and probably sustain a moderate rise in per-capita income.

Another potential source of income, especially of foreign currency, can be found in an expanded tourist trade. Syria's antiquities of pre-Islamic as well as Islamic origin are many and spectacular, and its museums are rich and well-organized. The mountain resorts near Damascus and in the Latakia region by the Mediterranean can, with some development, attract many more tourists from all over the Arab world.

Development is being held back by the persisting state of conflict and preparation for defense arising from the confrontation with Israel. Funds that could be used for improved roads, services and projects are diverted to defense. As a "confrontation state," and lacking in significant oil resources, the Syrian economy has been improving, but at a slower rate than could be achieved with an extended period of peace.

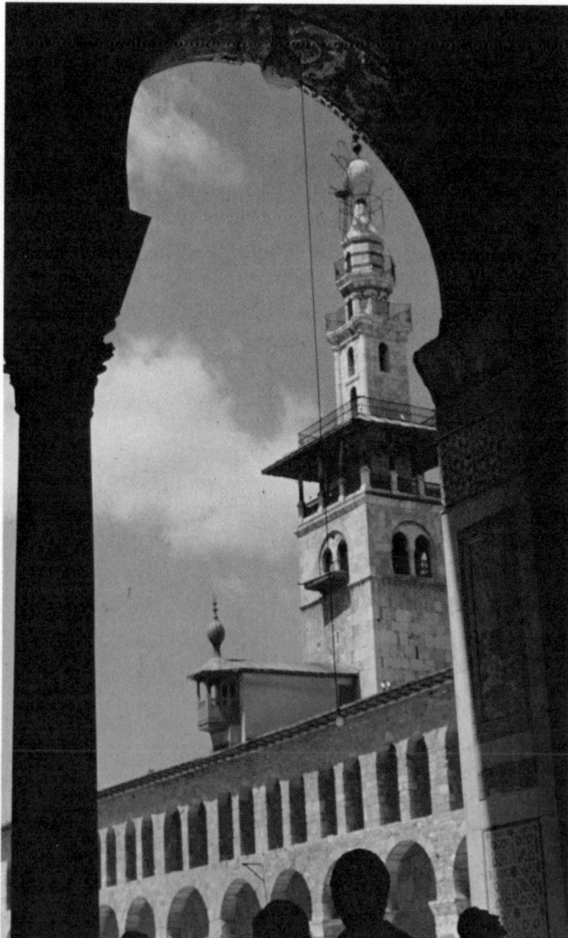

The 'Arous minaret of the great Umayyad Mosque in Damascus, one of the jewels of early Islamic architecture. Inside is the shrine of St. John the Baptist

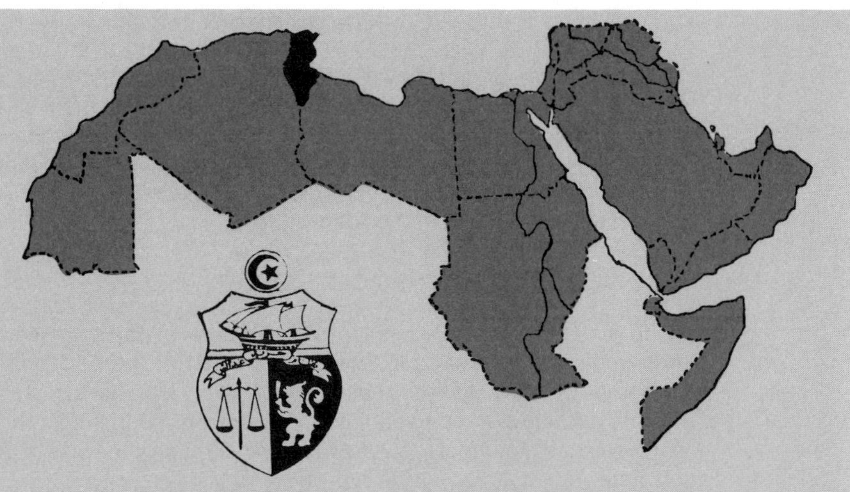

TUNISIA

الجمهورية التونسية

PROFILE

Official Name: Republic of Tunis (Al-Jumhuriyyah al-Tunisiyyah)

Head of State: Habib Bourguiba

Government: Republic

Area: 63,378 sq. mi. (= State of Washington)

Population: 5,900,000 (est. 1976)

Population Density: 93 per sq. mi.

Capital: Tunis (about one million)

Other Urban Centers: Sfax, Sousse, Bizerte, Kairouan

National Holiday: June 1

Currency: Tunisian Dinar (1 Dinar = $2.33)

Daily Press: Five daily papers in Arabic and French

Radio and Television: Radio broadcasts in Arabic, French and Italian. Full network

Main Airports: Tunis-Carthage

Main Seaports: Bizerte, Monastir, Sfax

Date of Joining the United Nations: November 12, 1956

Date of Joining the Arab League: September 1, 1958

TUNISIA

INTRODUCTION

No Humphrey Bogart movie was ever made there; it has practically no oil to speak of; and its leaders rarely attract the attention of the American mass media. Consequently, Tunisia has not achieved the kind of recognition among Americans enjoyed by its neighbors Morocco, Algeria and Libya. Nevertheless, its history, language, religion and customs make it an intrinsic part of the Arab world.

PHYSICAL GEOGRAPHY

Area

Tunisia is located in North Africa in the eastern part of a geographical area known as the Maghrib (the western part of the Arab world). It is bordered by the Mediterranean Sea (north and northeast), Algeria (west), and Libya (southeast). With an area of 63,378 square miles, it is the smallest country in North Africa and is roughly the size of Washington state.

Tell Region

There are three distinct geographical regions: the Tell highlands in the north, steppe plateaus in the center, and low-lying desert in the south. The Tell is by far the richest and in many respects the most important region in the country. Because of a relatively abundant winter rainfall, a main river valley and rich soils, a major portion of the country's agricultural output is produced there, including such major crops as wheat, fruits and vegetables. It is the site of the capital city of Tunis and some of the country's largest urban and industrial centers. Finally, a diversified landscape makes the Tell the most attractive and picturesque area in Tunisia. The country's two major mountain chains are in the Tell. The Kroumiries parallel the coral-rich northern shores of the Mediterranean and stretch from the Algerian border to the Gulf of Tunis. The Great Dorsale is to the south and runs in a northeasterly direction from near the town of Kasserine to the peninsula of Cape Bon. The Dorsale is part of the Atlas Mountains which stretch across all of the Maghrib, and it is the southern limit of the Tell.

Drainage

It is also in the Tell that Tunisia's major river system, the Medjerda and its tributary the Mellegue, is located. Both rise in Algeria and meet at the town of Jendouba (Souk el Arba); from there the Medjerda runs eastward across the whole width of the country towards the Mediterranean (Gulf of Tunis). While it is an important water resource with a year round, though variable, flow, it is not a navigable river. There is no other permanent stream.

Steppe Region

The central steppe region extends from the southern slopes of the Great Dorsale to a line approximately southwestwards from the coastal city of Sfax. In sharp contrast with the rolling green hills of the Tell, the terrain is monotonously flat, rocky and barren. The desert influence is moderated somewhat by the Mediterranean in the Sahel, thus allowing the cultivation of olive and almond trees and barley—all requiring only small amounts of water. Oases, on the other hand, do not rely on rain at all, but receive water from springs fed by natural underground reservoirs. A variety of fruits and vegetables are grown there, but the oases are most famous for the excellent dates produced by a great number of palm trees.

Sahara

Southwards, the rest of the country is part of the Sahara. This is the hottest, most arid, desolate and, except for the small al-Borma oil fields near the southern tip of Tunisia, most unproductive part of the country.

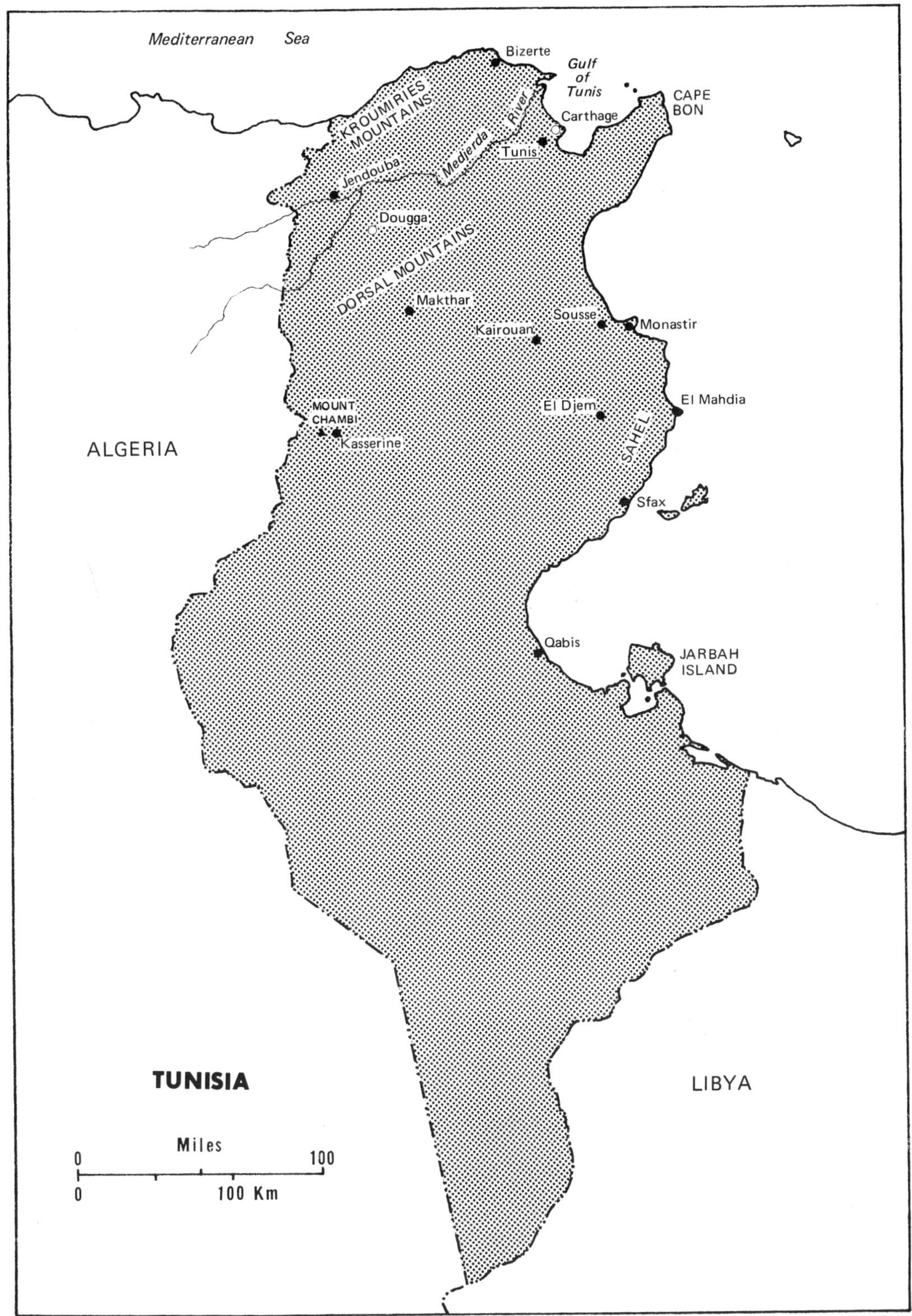
Mediterranean Sea
Bizerte
Gulf of Tunis
CAPE BON
Carthage
Tunis
KROUMIRIES MOUNTAINS
Medjerda River
Jendouba
Dougga
DORSAL MOUNTAINS
Makthar
Sousse
Monastir
Kairouan
MOUNT CHAMBI
Kasserine
El Djem
El Mahdia
SAHEL
ALGERIA
Sfax
Qabis
JARBAH ISLAND
TUNISIA
LIBYA
Miles
0
100
0
100 Km

TUNISIA

HUMAN GEOGRAPHY

People

The Berbers were among the earliest inhabitants of North Africa. They were characterized by curly red hair, blue eyes and fair skin. For a number of centuries, they were able to maintain their ethnic and cultural identity despite many foreign invasions. However, when the Arabs appeared in Tunisia in the middle of the seventh century, the Berbers began to intermarry with them, adopted their language and customs, and embraced their religion. As a result, most Tunisians today are Muslim, and all speak Arabic. In addition, the 75-year long period of French colonialism made French an important second language, spoken today by a third or more of the Tunisian population. Colonialism did not have any impact on religion.

Vital Statistics

The mid-1976 population is estimated to be 5.9 million. The birth rate is 38 per thousand, and the death rate is 13 per thousand, giving an annual growth rate of 2.4 percent. If the growth rate is maintained, the population will double in 29 years and will reach 10.9 million in the year 2000. The infant mortality rate is 128 per 1000 live births per year. Forty-four percent of the population is under 15 years old, and the median age is a very young 17.4 years.

Population Distribution

Seventy percent of the people live in the northern third of the country, and the bulk of the remainder are found in the central steppe region and in the coastal Sahel lowlands. This distributional asymmetry is related to the country's historic orientations across the Mediterranean and westwards into the Maghrib, as well as to the greater opportunities for livelihood in the north. This difference in opportunity in turn has brought about a south to north migration, as well as rural to urban. If current trends continue, it is estimated that the greater Tunis population will triple by the year 2000 to surpass the 3 million mark and account for more than 27 percent of the national total. The city itself has about one million people. The three next largest cities are also coastal: Sfax (about 110,000 inhabitants), Sousse (80,000), and Bizerte (70,000). Next is Kairouan (50,000), at the border between the coastal plain and the low steppe 35 miles west of Sousse.

Folklore music on the beach of Kerkennah

ECONOMY

Before independence, the economy was based on the production of a few agricultural and mineral commodities; these were exported to France in exchange for manufactured products and processed foods. In addition, the whole economy was firmly in the hands of French citizens. Thus, most of the rich lands of the north were owned by French settlers; most businesses, banks, railroads and shipping lines, were owned and run by Frenchmen.

Agriculture

After independence, modernizing the economy became the Tunisian government's major priority. Small farmers were encouraged to combine their plots into large farms so that modern production techniques became possible. Major investments were made to create irrigation projects, to increase yields through the use of fertilizers and pesticides, and to diversify production through the introduction of new crops.

These efforts have produced mixed results. On the one hand, production did increase in many areas. Between 1956 and 1971 olive oil production went from 100,000 to 160,000 tons; cereals from 632,000 to 765,000 tons; and fresh vegetables from 247,000 to 440,000 tons. On the other hand, agriculture remains quite inefficient, and its impact on the country's economic growth is still rather unsatisfactory. Even though farmers represent 47 percent of the population, agriculture accounts for only 22 percent of the nation's total economic output. As a result, Tunisia has had to import between one-third and one-fourth of its food requirements.

Industry

The industrial expansion has been much more dynamic, showing an annual average growth rate of 15 percent. The basis of this sector is the processing of mineral resources. Iron ore supplies the raw material for a steel industry. Phosphate, found in large quantities, is transformed into high-grade fertilizer; in 1974 it provided the country with some $150 million, compared with $20 million when it was exported in unprocessed form. The oil industry has expanded rapidly since the discovery of al Borma fields in 1964 and of promising off-shore resources. Production is small by Middle Eastern standards, but it is important to the economy, supplying an annual income exceeding $200 million.

Tourism

Industrial growth has led to the creation and rapid expansion of such services as construction, banking, transportation and education. It is expected that 50 percent of all jobs to be created in the coming years will be in industry. A very important part of this sector is the tourism industry. Thanks to its many historical sites, its miles of sandy beaches, its good resort weather and its proximity to Europe, Tunisia has been able to attract a large number of tourists. There are more than 200 hotels with a combined capacity of 56,000 beds, and in 1974 more than 716,000 tourists visited Tunisia. It is estimated that this industry has created 15,000 jobs in the last decade, and 2,000 new ones will be created annually for the remainder of the 1970s.

Communications

Tunisia undoubtedly has made important economic gains in its twenty years of independence. However, serious problems remain to be solved. A quarter of the active population is unemployed; agriculture is stagnating; the industrial sector depends on foreign markets to survive; and the average per capita income is still about $250 a year. Further economic growth depends on an improvement in the basic infrastructure, particularly communications. The road network connects all cities with much of the interior, though the quality can be improved and the density can be increased; most roads are very narrow. A railroad follows the coast from the Algerian border to the port city of Qabis (Gabes), with two extensions to the interior: one along the Medjerda River valley to Algeria, and the other from near Sousse to Kasserine. Train service is slow and not very comfortable. About half of the country's 80,000 telephones are in Tunis. The five main coastal cities also serve as harbors, and need improvement and an expansion of facilities. Almost all international air traffic is handled by the Tunis airport. Two new airports, at Munastir (near Sousse) and Jarbah (near Qabis), serve almost entirely for domestic and charter purposes. On the whole, the interior and south are less well served in terms of all facilities than the northern and coastal areas.

HISTORY

A nomadic people known as the Lybians, who first appeared in Tunisia around 5,000 B.C., are generally considered the earliest ancestors of the Berbers. In 814 B.C. Dido, a Phoenician princess, fled Tyre and started the new settlement of Kart Hadasht, the "new city." This later became Carthage. The people of the settlement were known to the Romans as Poeni, a word which has the same derivation as Phoenician and from which the adjective Punic is derived. Thus evolved what came to be known as the Punic Empire, the first major foreign occupation of Tunisia, to be followed by some eight others in the subsequent 2700 years.

Carthage

Carthage grew and prospered as a Mediterranean trade center. It soon controlled Phoenician trading posts in the Mediterranean, including those on the shores of Tunisia, and opened new ones in North Africa and southern Europe, especially Spain. In Tunisia, the Carthaginians expanded into the interior and imposed their political rule on the local Berber chiefs. Between 264 B.C. and 146 B.C. three bloody wars—known as the Punic Wars—pitted the two powers, Rome and Carthage, against each other. The Carthaginians were finally defeated, their city burned and covered with salt.

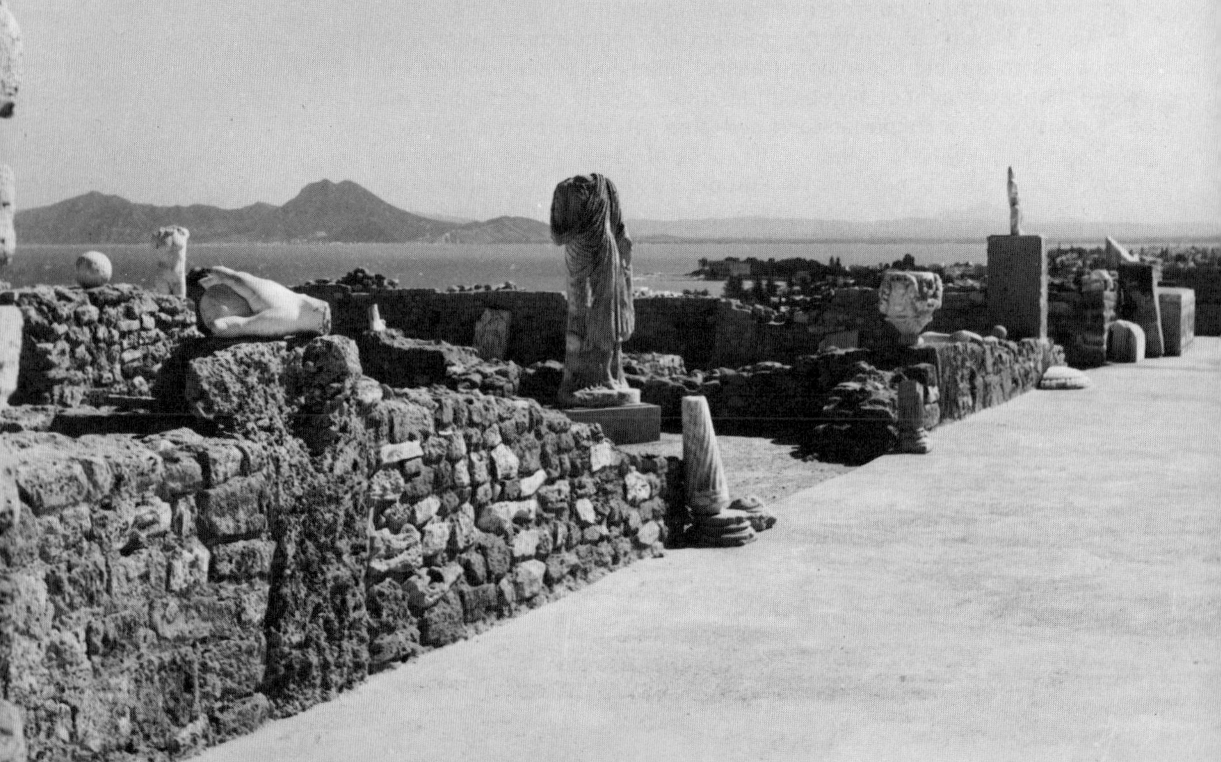

The remains of a Roman villa at Carthage. The city dominated Mediterranean trade in the 3rd century B.C.

Rome

Rome first established a protectorate, ruled indirectly through Berber kings. However, frequent revolts by these kings prompted Rome to turn its North African territories into provinces to be ruled by Roman governors. Africa, as Tunisia was then called, was the most important and prosperous of these provinces; Carthage was rebuilt in 44 B.C. and made its capital.

Roman rule continued until 439 A.D. when the Vandals took Carthage, after they had conquered southern France, Spain and modern Morocco and Algeria. Their empire lasted for less than a century and was easily taken over by the Byzantines. In 534, the latter occupied Carthage and much of Tunisia. But their 113-year rule was beset with constant challenges from the Berbers, so that when the Arabs reached Tunisia in 647 the Byzantines were in no position to stop them.

Arab

After they defeated the Byzantines, the Arabs returned home; but they came back twenty-three years later, this time with the intention of conquest. Their leader, 'Uqba ibn Nafi,' founded the city of al-Qairawan (Kairouan) in 670 and turned it into a powerful cultural, religious and political metropolis, and its mosque, which exists to this day, was famous throughout the Arab world. Following their conquest of Carthage in 695, the Arabs proceeded to bring the Berbers under their rule. A number of wars ensued, and the last major group, headed by Princess Kahina, was defeated in 702. Afterwards, many Berbers embraced Islam and helped the Arabs conquer the rest of North Africa and most of Spain.

Fatimids

In contrast to their ready acceptance of Islam, the Berbers were reluctant to accept Arab rule. At first, Ifriqiyah—as Tunisia came to be known—was ruled by governors appointed in Baghdad. But after 800, governors became more and more independent, and soon they created their own dynasties. The two most famous were the Aghlabiyun (Aghlabids) and the Fatimiyun (Fatimids), the descendants of the prophet Muhammad. The Fatimids moved the capital from al-Qairawan to a new city founded in 916 and named Mahdia. They also invaded Egypt in 969, and their caliph al-Mu'izz founded Cairo in 973-974 as the new Fatimid capital.

Mosque of Sidi Saheb in Qairawan

Between 1051 and 1159 Ifriqiyah was in complete chaos. No one could achieve political control; the country was attacked by the Pope (1087), the Normans (1148), and Moroccan Berbers. The latter waged a jihad (holy war) in 1159 and left one of their members, Abu Hafs, as ruler. This marked the beginning of the Hafsite period, which lasted for 350 years and was undoubtedly the greatest dynasty in Tunisian history. The Hafsyun (Hafsids) made Tunis their capital city, encouraged music, architecture and literature, and for the first time ambassadors appointed by the European powers were received. Complacency, however, soon led to weakness. Having neglected military affairs, the Hafsids became in the sixteenth century the victims of the imperialist designs of two emerging and antagonistic powers, Spain and Turkey. A Spanish protectorate was imposed on Tunisia in 1540, but it lasted for less than thirty-five years and was succeeded by a Turkish protectorate.

Hafsids

Turkish Rule

Rulers of Turkish origin were to remain in power until 1957, when Tunisia became a republic. Following a familiar pattern, the governors appointed by Turkey became increasingly independent and soon started their own dynasties. The last dynasty was started in 1710 by Husayn ibn 'Ali. In the middle of the nineteenth century, Tunisia ran into serious financial difficulties. Claiming that its many investments were in jeopardy, France decided in 1881 to turn Tunisia into a French protectorate. The Turkish bey (or king) was made a purely honorary figure.

French Influence

A nationalist movement began to emerge in the 1920s, but challenge to the French rule did not become serious until 1934 when Habib Bourguiba founded the Neo-Destour (new constitution) Party and led the country on the long road to independence. That independence was ultimately achieved on March 20, 1956. One year later, the Turkish monarchy was abolished, and Tunisia became a republic, with Bourguiba as its first president.

Independence

GOVERNMENT AND SOCIETY

President Bourguiba's term as first president was extended for life. Until recently, he was both head of state and head of government, but the latter function is now fulfilled by a prime minister. There is only one political party, the *Parti Socialiste Destourien* (PSD, the Socialist Destour Party), headed by Bourguiba. There is also a unicameral legislative body, consisting of 112 deputies elected every six years. The PSD has a monopoly over all political activities and has had an unchallenged control over all governmental institutions. In particular, the armed forces, with less than 27,000 men, have no political role whatsoever. The country is divided into thirteen administrative districts (wilayas) each headed by a governor appointed by the central government.

Administration

Well aware that sustained economic growth is difficult without education, the government has been spending an average of 8 percent of the gross domestic product and 25 percent of its annual budget on education. The number of students jumped from 450,000 in 1961 to over 1.2 million in 1971. A special effort is being made to provide at least a primary education to children between the ages of 6 and 14, who represent 28 percent of the population. In 1961, only 46 percent of them could be accommodated in schools, but facilities have been expanding rapidly since then, so that in the mid-seventies close to 75 percent of these children are in school, and it is hoped that in a few years every child will be able to attend school. A similar progress is being made at the secondary and university levels, which have upwards of 181,000 and 14,000 students, respectively.

Education

Mosque of the Turks in Djerba

There are major problems in making education conform to the country's economic needs. The educational system inherited from France tended to emphasize the humanities and the liberal arts, with the result that students today consider technical and vocational schools as inferior. There is an oversupply of unskilled high school graduates and of university students with degrees in law, literature and similar subjects, whereas the country needs mechanics, engineers and technicians. Government policies exacerbate the situation, because white-collar workers continue to be favored in terms of salary, job security and fringe benefits.

Health

Health services have been improved in the last twenty years, but they are still inadequate. There are only 15,000 hospital beds and less than 1,000 doctors, half of them foreigners. Nevertheless, major diseases have been practically eradicated; mortality rates have decreased from 21 per thousand in 1956 to 13 per thousand in 1976; and infant mortality has been similarly reduced.

These improvements, however, are problematic. The population is growing at an annual rate of 2.4 percent, which means that economic growth must at least equal that rate to provide the more than 100,000 people that swell the population each year with food, an education and a job. Because this is an awesome job for a country with limited resources, Tunisia adopted in 1966 a national plan for population control, which included encouraging the use of birth control methods, prohibiting marriages for women under 16 and men under 18, and legalizing abortion. It is hoped that the plan will lower the rate of population growth to about 1 percent by the end of this century.

Law

Another aspect of modernization has addressed itself to the Tunisian woman. More and more females are attending schools; they have been granted an equal status to men in such areas as the law and employment; they have the right to vote and to run for office. In addition, many aspects of the legal system, which was based largely on Muslim laws, have been changed. Polygamy is no longer legal, marriage and divorce have to be approved by legal and not just religious authorities, and corporal punishment of legal offenders is prohibited.

Cultural Life

Two totally different, and at times conflicting, cultures coexist—French-Western and Arab-Islamic. The former is of relatively recent origin, but it has created a social class that considers itself separate and even superior to the rest of society. Its members have usually been educated in France and are deeply influenced by its culture. In addition, the French have spread their language throughout the administrative and educational structures; that legacy has persisted and is likely to be perpetuated because, among other things, Tunisia still depends heavily on France for technical, economic and educational aid. Then there is the majority of the population which has not been affected by education and hence by the French culture. Their social and moral values continue to be influenced by Islam, family and village ties are still very strong, and government interference is resisted, if not rejected altogether. As a result Tunisia presents an interesting mix: radio and television programs broadcast in Arabic and French, newspapers and street signs written in both languages, mothers wearing the veil and daughters in miniskirts, fathers in their white *jebba* and sons in sports coats, and theaters showing Egyptian movies while others are featuring the latest French production.

Government policy had tended to moderate French influence by encouraging Tunisians to become aware of other African cultures and to rediscover, preserve and enrich their own. This trend has led to the creation of the National Institute of Traditional Arts, a theater company, a folk dance and music company, and the organization of annual festivals such as the Carthage Folk Festival and the Dougga Theater Festival.

Historical Sites

Tunisia has been called an "immense living museum" because of its more than one thousand historical monuments, some of them over three-thousand years old. Carthage is the most famous historical site, with a Roman amphitheater as large as the Rome Colosseum. Dougga, another ancient Roman city, has twelve temples, an amphitheater, baths, a Christian basilica and a Punic mausoleum. An imposing amphitheater built in the third century and capable of seating 30,000 spectators is found in El Djem, and Makthar has Punic, Roman and Christian ruins as well as pre-historic tombs (dolmen). Some of the world's best mosaics have been found in these sites, and many of them are kept in the Bardo museum near Tunis. Monuments from the Arab-Islamic period are an integral part of every Tunisian's daily life. These include the Kairouan mosque and the equally beautiful Zitouna mosque in Tunis.

PROSPECTS

After twenty years of independence, Tunisia has reached a crossroad. Major social upheavels have been avoided mainly because some economic progress has been made, and the current leaders have benefited from the cooperation of a population grateful to them for having achieved independence. At the same time expectations are being heightened but not always satisfied. One outlet, especially for those seeking work, has been to emigrate to Europe, and such migration often results in family disruption. Domestic employment opportunities need to be increased and improved, not only to reduce the out-migration of the skilled, but also to provide a greater sense of self-worth and participation in the national good for those unemployed but not able to emigrate.

Significant economic development will need continuing improvement in agricultural practices so as to reduce and perhaps eliminate the dependence on imported foodstuffs. Also helpful will be labor intensive projects needing relatively little capital. Tourism surely will continue to grow and will probably receive greater attention. The oil finds may prove substantial enough to generate a considerable income which can further fuel economic growth.

Minaret of the Great Mosque of Qairawan

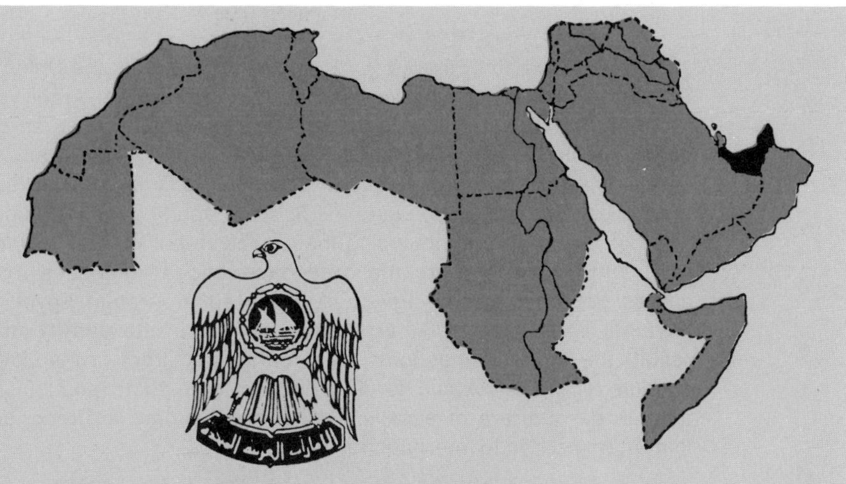

U.A.E.

UNITED ARAB EMIRATES

الامارات العربية المتحدة

PROFILE

Official Name: The United Arab Emirates (Al-Imarat al-Arabiyyah al-Muttahidah)

Head of State: SheikhZayed bin Sultan Al Nahyan

Government: Federation of emirates

Area: 33,000 sq. mi.

Population: 660,000 (est. 1977)

Population Density: 20/sq. mi.

Capital: Abu Dhabi

Other Urban Centers: Dubai, Sharjah, Ajman, Umm Al-Qaiwan, Ras Al-Khaimah

National Holiday: December 2

Currency: U.A.E. Dirham ($1.00 = 4 UAE.D)

Press: Daily: Al Ittihad and other periodicals. English: Emirates Nees

Radio & Television: Many radio transmitters. Color Television.

Main Airports: Ras Al-Khaimah

Main Seaports: Abu Dhabi

Date of Joining the United Nations: December 9, 1971

Date of Joining the Arab League: December 6, 1971

THE UNITED ARAB EMIRATES

INTRODUCTION

The United Arab Emirates (UAE), sometimes called the Union of Arab Emirates after its Arabic name, Ittihad Al-Imarat Al-Arabiyyah, is a federation of seven princedoms (emirates), proclaimed as an independent state in 1971. It is located in the eastern part of the Arabian peninsula along both the Arabian Gulf and the Gulf of Oman. For millennia this area's peoples were engaged in fishing, pearling and trading. Their strategic location contributed to their involvement in inter-regional matters, and over the years the area experienced influences from such places as India, Africa, Persia, Mesopotamia, Arabia, Egypt, Turkey, Portugal and England. Oil production started in the early 1960s. As a result, the desert princedoms were catapulted from pre-industrial to a satellite technology within hardly a decade. With a total population of less than three quarters of a million, UAE has become an important actor in matters related to international oil economics.

PHYSICAL GEOGRAPHY

Six of the emirates stretch along the Arabian Gulf; starting in the southwest they are Abu Dhabi, Dubai, Sharjah, Ajman, Ummal-Qaiwain and Ras al-Khaimah. The seventh, Fujairah, fronts the Gulf of Oman. The northernmost part of the Musandum Peninsula is an exclave of the country of Oman.

Area

The total area is estimated at 33,000 square miles. Boundaries with Saudi Arabia south and west and Qatar east are still not delimited. The boundaries between the emirates themselves resemble a jigsaw puzzle, with several enclaves and exclaves. In every case an emirate's capital has a coastal location and has the same name as that of the emirate.

Topography

The north is dominated by the northernmost part of Jabal Akhdar (Green Mountain), the prominent topographic feature in the eastern Arabian peninsula. The local range is known as Hajar Gharbi (Western Rockies). In the interior the plain is covered by alluvial outwash from the mountains and is fertile. Vegetation is sparse and consists of widely spaced desert shrubs. Southwards and westwards the sand dune belt merges into Saudi Arabia's enormous and forbidding Rub' al Khali (Empty Quarter), the world's largest sand dune region.

Climate

The UAE is in a hot desert zone. July and August are the hottest months, with a daily average temperature of 92°F. Daytime readings usually exceed 100°F and often reach 120°F. The coolest month is January, with a mean of 65°F and with daytime highs reaching 95°F. As in other tropical deserts, the daily temperature range is large throughout the year. It may be as high as 70 fahrenheit degrees. Humidity is uncomfortably high in summer along the coast, though airconditioned living is now the rule. Winters are comfortable and pleasant.

Rainfall

As much as 94 percent of total precipitation comes in December and January. Total amounts are not great, however. At Sharjah, the only location with a continuous climatic record since 1950 (and with an incomplete rainfall record since 1934), annual precipitation is 4.2 inches. Precipitation increases slightly northeastward towards Ras al-Khaimah, where the annual rainfall averages 6 inches and may reach 8 inches.

Daily sea breezes can cause the humidity to rise and the temperature to drop by as much as 10 fahrenheit degrees in less than half an hour. The effect reaches some forty or fifty miles inland. At night the flow of air is reversed, blowing from land to sea. The importance of these winds to the sensible weather (that is, the weather that is sensed or felt), is indicated by the fact that there are local names for eight different combinations of direction and intensity. In addition, there is the shamal (north), a strong wind which causes blowing sand. Sandstorms occur most frequently in March.

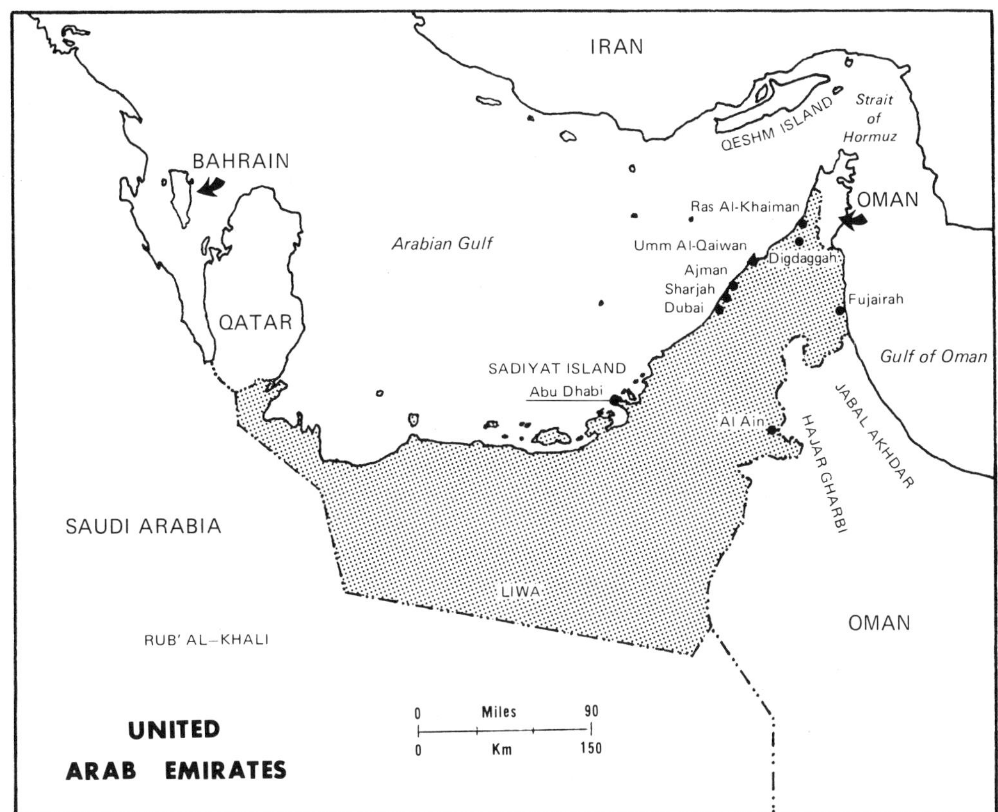

HUMAN GEOGRAPHY

Population

At the end of the eighteenth century, the seven emirates were inhabited by two main tribes, the Qawasim (sometimes referred to as Joasmee) and the Bani Yas. The Qawasim settled in the eastern part of the coast and on Qeshm island off the coast of Iran in the strategic Strait of Hormuz, and their descendants include the rulers of Sharjah and Ras al-Khaimah. The Bani Yas tribe, together with one of its branches the Al Bu Falah, inhabited the rest of the coast from Dubai to Qatar. These tribes, along with intermixtures from Iran, India, and Africa, comprise the indigenous population.

The 1977 estimated population is 660,000. Two-thirds of the federation's population live in Abu Dhabi and Dubai. Abu Dhabi alone accounts for 88 percent of the total area. It is the seat of government and the wealthiest and most populous emirate. Dubai ranks second in size, population and wealth.

ECONOMY

Pearling

For a long time the sea was the mainstay of the emirates. Pearling peaked in the late nineteenth and early twentieth centuries. About the year 1900 over a thousand boats and 22,000 men engaged in the activity. The industry collapsed in the 1930s, in part because of the worldwide economic depression and in part because of competition from cultured Japanese pearls.

Fishing

Fishing continues to be an important activity, and close to 10,000 persons engage in it. The many varieties of catch are an important source of animal protein, and a surplus is dried and exported to South Asia and East Africa, as well as to Saudi Arabia. Fishing is especially prominent in Ajman and Umm al-Qaiwain. Sharks are caught largely in Ras al-Khaimah. Dried shark fins and tails, used in the manufacture of medicine, are exported to Malaysia and Singapore.

Agriculture

Agriculture is a minor economic activity. Fujairah and Ras al-Khaimah have better natural conditions than the other emirates. In Ras al-Khaimah rain and underground water supplies are enough to support agricultural villages. There is a considerable variety of crops: dates, bananas, plantains, oranges, lemons, figs, grapes, pomegranates, mulberries and strawberries. Vegetables include tomatoes, eggplants, cabbages, cauliflowers, cucumbers, onions, radishes, turnips and parsley. Many of these products are exported to other parts of the federation. Alfalfa is used locally for animal fodder. This diversification followed the establishment in 1955 of the Agricultural Trials Station at Digdagga, ten miles south of Ras Al-Khaimah Town. An agricultural school now offers a three-year program. Dairy farming is being developed, and poultry farming is increasing. The possibility of self-sufficiency in fruit and vegetable products is enhanced by the successful Arid Lands Research Center on the island of Sadiyat, immediately northeast of Abu Dhabi. This project is supervised by the University of Arizona. Large polythene greenhouses are used, and entrance is through an air lock to assure control of atmospheric conditions inside.

A greenhouse of the Arid Lands Research Center on the island of Sadiyat.

Oases are important in agriculture. Al Ain oasis (a hundred miles east of Abu Dhabi, across the border from Oman's Buraimi oasis) in the Hajar foothills has plentiful spring water. It once supplied all the needs of Abu Dhabi Town. The latter need is now supplied by desalination. Al Ain's crops are dominated by dates and alfalfa, and there is a trend towards diversification in favor of vegetables and fruits. Liwa oasis is a hundred miles southwest of Abu Dhabi. Here, too, cultivation consists almost entirely of date palms, though some vegetables are being introduced. Water supply is less abundant than at Al Ain.

Oil

The federal economy is dominated by oil. Production began in 1962 in Abu Dhabi and in 1969 in Dubai. Exploration continues in the other emirates, excepting Fujairah. The oil industry directly employs only a small number of people, and the income it generates comes under the discretion of the government. The government in turn uses it mainly to provide social welfare services, such as education, health and housing. Secondly, oil income is used for a plethora of projects, many of which generate a considerable demand for construction labor, such as housing, roads, harbor expansion, airports and cement factories. Skilled and technical labor has had to be imported, almost entirely from Europe and the United States. In addition, the domestic labor pool has not been large enough to provide the needed unskilled and semi-skilled labor, resulting in a further influx of foreign workers. More than 40 percent have come from Iran and about 33 percent from India and Pakistan. At the same time, internal migration crowded into towns, so that by 1968 more than half the people of the emirates had become urban dwellers. Abu Dhabi and Dubai, by far the primary oil producers, have become the focus of most of the activity. In 1976 Abu Dhabi allocated 50 percent of its income to the federal budget.

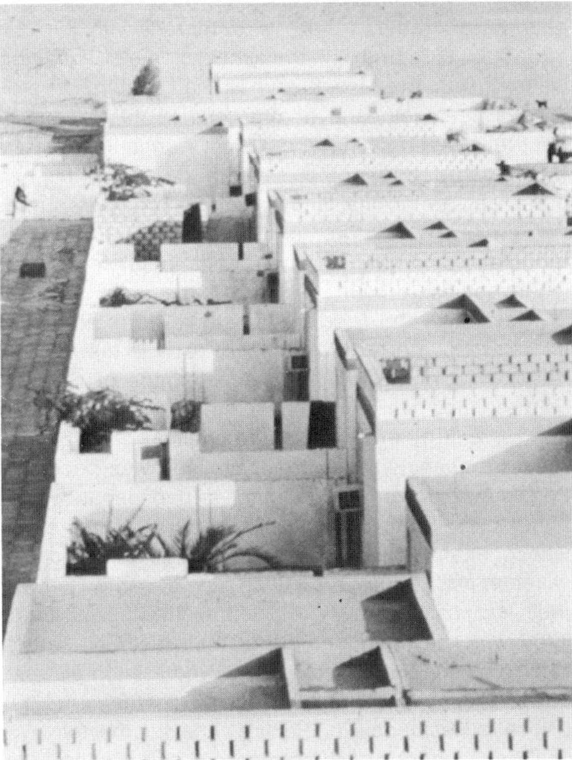

A typical housing project in the U.A.E. The goal is to provide a free house for every citizen.

HISTORY

Early Influences

The Gulf area has witnessed the ebb and flow of civilizations and empires. Like the Mediterranean Sea, it has served as an arena for interaction and not as an obstacle to movement. From time immemorial the local inhabitants have made their living from the sea, whether by fishing, pearling or trading. There was contact with the Phoenicians sometime after 3000 B.C. and with the succession of Mesopotamian civilizations, as well as with the Greek and Roman empires. Persian influences have always been felt, and commercial contacts have persisted with India, Southeast Asia, China and Africa. Continuing contact with Arabia, when Islam came during the seventh century A.D., was of profound importance. During the following thousand years there were various shifts in the centers of power and authority, and throughout all this time seafaring and commercial activity continued to dominate the livelihood of the local peoples.

The Europeans

The first of the Europeans to build forts and to establish settlements in the Gulf were the Portuguese, early in the sixteenth century following Vasco da Gama's rounding of the Cape of Good Hope in 1497. For a century they were in control, though occasionally challenged by the Turks. Local rulers were made obeisant. By 1600 when the British East India Company was founded, England was becoming active in the Gulf. Portuguese power was waning, in part because their country had been annexed by Spain in 1581 and in part because of the activity of Persia, whose Shah Abbas I had acceded to the throne in 1587. During the seventeenth century the Dutch also became involved in the Gulf through their increasing activity in Southeast Asia, but their influence ceased in 1765 with the abandonment of their last Gulf settlement on the Persian Kharg Island. There was a short-lived French presence, after the forming of the French East India Company in 1664. In 1763 Persia granted the British a Residency in Bushire, and for the following two centuries the Gulf came under British commercial and political supremacy.

To the European powers the Gulf was a small, though important, component of their far-flung intercontinental ventures. Its importance was secondary to and supportive of what lay beyond. To the Gulf's indigenous peoples, the Europeans were invaders who came to control them and who disrupted their own living habits. They retaliated by attacking the foreign ships. The Europeans, who alleged these acts to be a form of piracy, reacted with a greater force and eventually brought the local emirates under control. In 1853 a Treaty of Maritime Peace in Perpetuity was concluded with the sheikhdoms, or emirates, the terms of which were to be enforced by the British Indian government.

Maritime Truce

Earlier, in 1835, a Maritime Truce had been reached which led to the designation of the whole coastal area as the Trucial Coast and of the emirates as the Trucial States. Diplomatic and administrative matters were first handled by the East India Company, then by the government of Bombay. In 1873, the British Indian government took over until 1947 when India became independent and the Foreign Office in London became directly responsible. While Britain appropriated to itself responsibility for external affairs and for foreigners living in the Trucial States, it did not appropriate sovereignty. The Trucial States handled the conduct of internal affairs.

Independence

In the wake of the diminution of its imperial power, Britain announced in 1968 that it would withdraw entirely from the Gulf. In July, 1971 the United Arab Emirates was formed. At first it had only six members; Ras al-Khaimah joined in February, 1972.

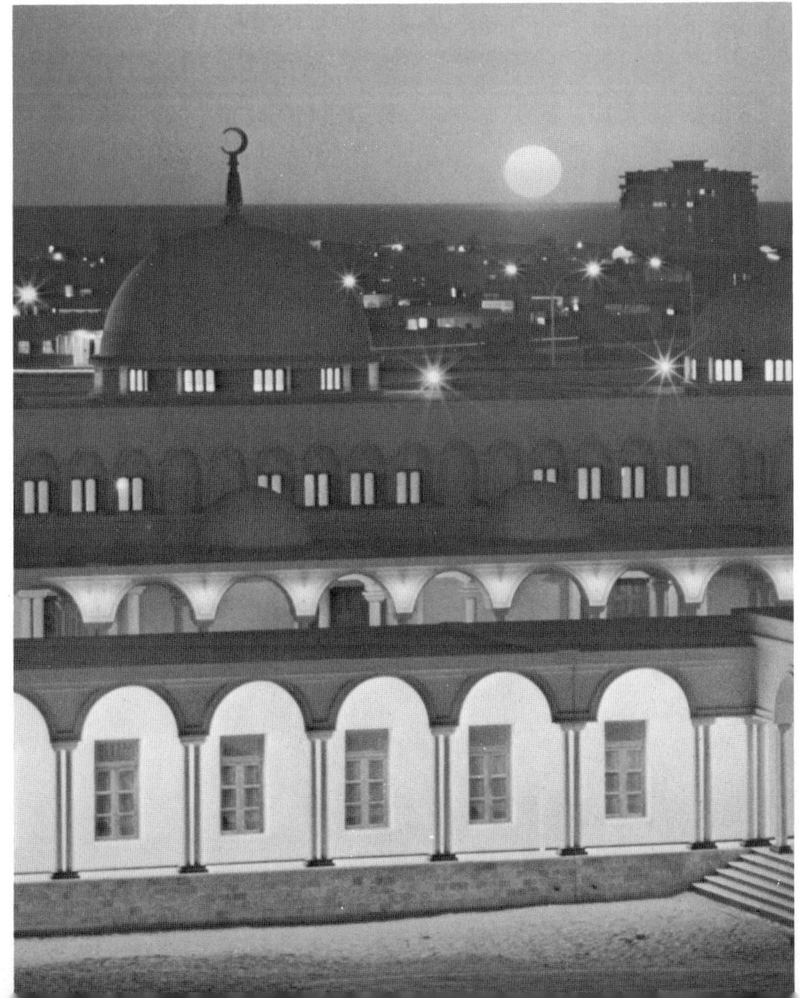

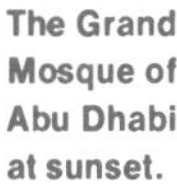

The Grand Mosque of Abu Dhabi at sunset.

GOVERNMENT AND SOCIETY

Education

Education in the Emirates is free. The Education Ministry is in the process of developing programs and facilities to cover the whole territory.

Health

Medical services are found mainly in Dubai, with hospitals and child welfare clinics. Hospitalization is free, and there is very little private medical practice. The government has set a goal of one doctor per 1000 people for the 1970's. At the present, most of the doctors come from outside the UAE.

Communications

Dubai has one Arabic weekly newspaper and two English daily bulletins. One radio station broadcasts in Arabic and English. Television programs originating in Kuwait are broadcast to all the union members.

Administration

Abu Dhabi was designated as the seat of the federal government, and its emir became the union's president. The vice president is Dubai's ruler. Dubai ranks after Abu Dhabi in area, population size, and wealth. The seven emirs comprise the Supreme Council of the Union. On matters of substance, decisions require the support of five members which must include the rulers of Abu Dhabi and Dubai. The Union National Council, or UAE's parliament, has 40 members chosen for a two-year term. The representation of each of the emirates is as follows: Abu Dhabi and Dubai, eight; Sharjah and Ras al-Khaimah, six; Ajman, Fujairah and Umm al-Qaiwain, four.

PROSPECTS

A traditional and essentially pre-industrial society in 1960, within a decade the United Arab Emirates experienced a dizzying transformation to a bustling community of international finance with one of the world's very highest per capita gross national products. The oil wealth will continue to fuel the frenzied and varied activity, at least for the balance of the century. What is lacking is an indigenous labor force which is large enough and skilled enough to manage the attendant industry and bureaucracy. It is not surprising that a great attention is being given to educational needs, and this human investment is beginning to pay dividends as educated nationals trickle back into the system. But the local population is so small that dependence on foreign nationals is likely to continue for many years. Thus, a symbiotic relationship is emerging between the United Arab Emirates and the West. The relationship may be strained by an occasional divergence of interest, but it likely will continue to be mutually beneficial.

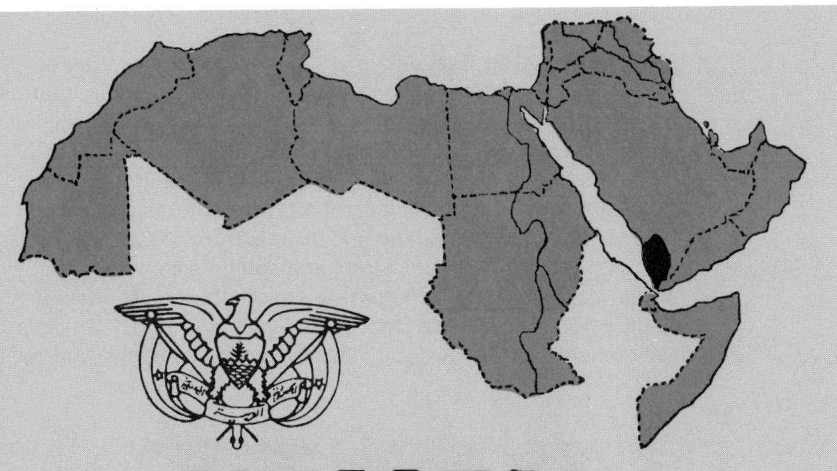

YEMEN

الجمهورية العربية اليمنية

PROFILE

Official Name: Yemen Arab Republic
(Al-Jumhuriyyah al-Arabiyyah al-Yamaniyyah)

Head of State: Ali Abdullah Saleh

Government: Republic

Area: about 60,000 sq. mi. (= Florida)

Population: about 7 million

Population Density: about 100/sq. mi.

Capital: San'a (125,000)

Other Urban Centers: Hudeidah, Ta'iz, Mukha

Currency: Yemeni Riyal ($1.00 = 4.5 Y.R.)

National Holiday: June 1

Main Airports: Al-Rahaba (San'a)

Main Seaports: Hudeidah

Radio and Television: 3 radio stations

Date of Joining the United Nations: September 30, 1947

Date of Joining the Arab League: May 5, 1945

YEMEN ARAB REPUBLIC

INTRODUCTION

The Yemen Arab Republic is a highland country located at the southwestern corner of the Arabian peninsula. It stands out in contrast to the rest of the peninsula in having a considerable amount of rainfall, a fairly large population and a long history of subsistence and some commercial agriculture. Its strategic location at the southern entrance to the Red Sea has contributed to its involvement with the interests of distant powers. Influences have come by land and by sea, from Arabia and Turkey on the one hand and from Europe, Africa and south Asia on the other. However, Yemen has been little affected by twentieth-century technological developments in agriculture, industry, health and social services. A 1973 development plan proposes to tackle communications and basic amenities.

PHYSICAL GEOGRAPHY

Topography

The interior boundary with Saudi Arabia has not been delimited. Estimates of Yemen's area range from 46,000 to 77,000 square miles. The country occupies the highest portion of the Arabian plateau, with a steep and highly dissected scarp descending to the Red Sea coast. The plateau edge ranges between 10,000 and 12,000 feet above sea level. The highest peak, Hadur Shu'ayb (12,336 ft.), is 40 miles southwest of the capital city of San'a. The narrow coastal plain (15-25 miles wide) is the Tihamah, a feature which extends northwards into Saudi Arabia. Its surface slopes up gradually to the foothills of the plateau escarpment where the rough terrain with deep valleys makes movement difficult and contributes to the isolation of the interior highlands. The plateau edge is about 75 miles from the sea. The landscape here consists of very rugged volcanic mountains. Eastwards the land dips gradually to the interior of Arabia. The lower eastern slope is known as the Meshreq (east) and eventually fringes the barren expanse of Rub' al Khali (Great Sandy Desert).

Climate and Temperature

In the Tihamah a Mediterranean climate is evident while in the highlands there is a distinct monsoonal effect. Along the coast winter is the rainy season, while in the highlands the maximum is reached in the summer. Rainfall increases with altitude, from 4 to 6 inches in the Tihamah to more than 40 inches on the western sides of the highest mountains. By comparison, Washington, D.C., also receives about 40 inches annually. San'a averages 24 inches. River valleys contain water all year long in the highlands, but by the time they reach the coast none has a year-round flow. Similarly, eastwards the river channels rapidly dry out. Springs are found along the foothills in the west, and wells are common in both the Tihamah and the eastern slopes. Temperatures are constantly high along the coast, with an annual average of 86°F (30°C). Along the western slopes the average drops to 64°F (18°C), and the frost line is at about 6700 feet. In the highlands the maximum and minimum temperatures average 82°F (28°C) and 18°F (−8°C), respectively.

Vegetation

Arid and semiarid steppe growth is found in the Tihamah. In the foothills and lower slopes plants include date palms, myrrh, mango, carob and fig trees. From about 4000 feet to the frost line euphorbia are dominant, eucalyptus, acacia, flowering shrubs, and perennial herbs are also found. Above the frost line are grassland and bush pastures.

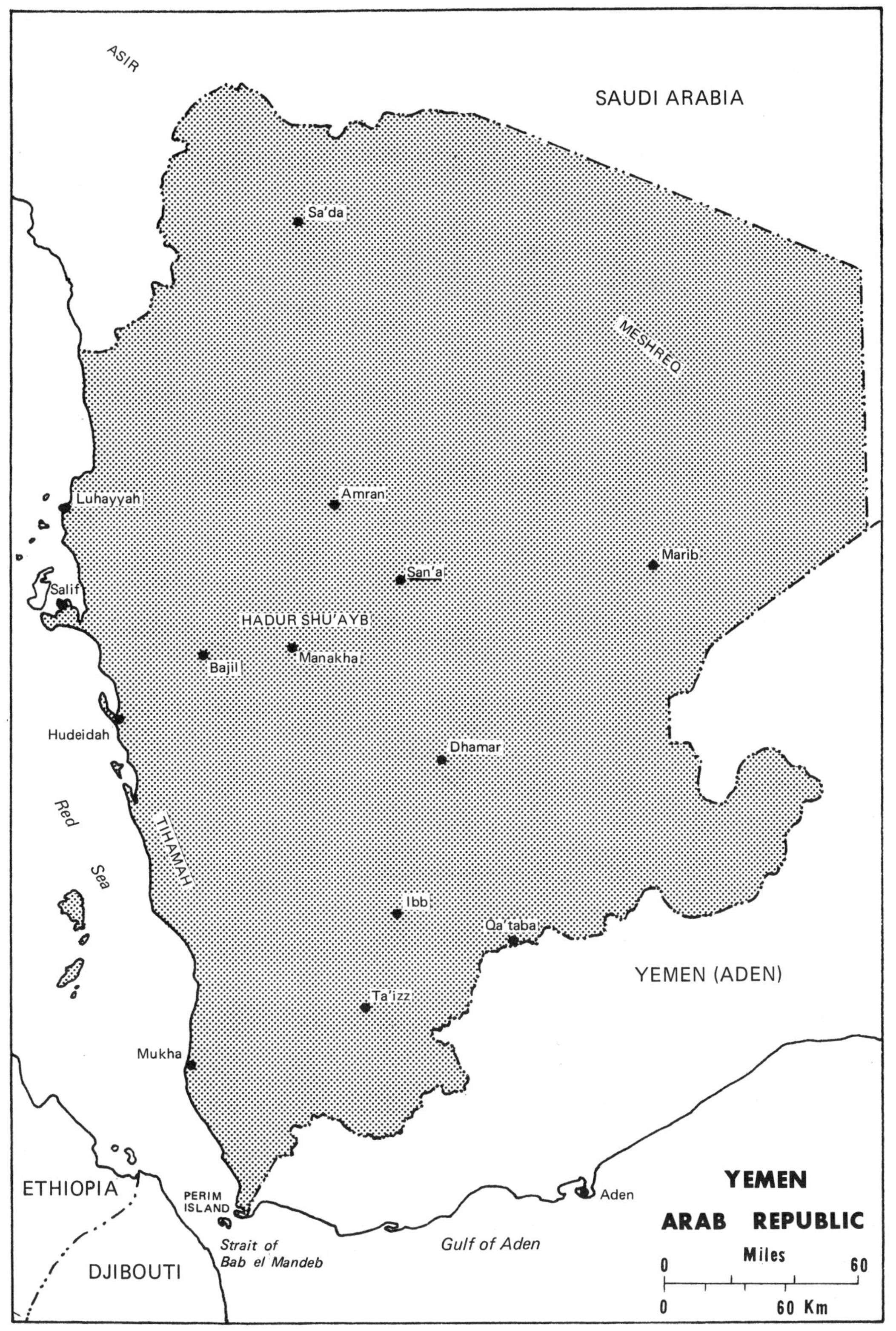
ASIR
SAUDI ARABIA
Sa'da
MESHREQ
Luhayyah
Amran
Marib
San'a
Salif
HADUR SHU'AYB
Bajil
Manakha
Hudeidah
Dhamar
Red Sea
TIHAMAH
Ibb
Qa'taba
YEMEN (ADEN)
Ta'izz
Mukha
ETHIOPIA
PERIM ISLAND
Aden
YEMEN
ARAB REPUBLIC
Strait of Bab el Mandeb
Gulf of Aden
Miles
0
60
DJIBOUTI
0
60 Km

Yemeni Children

HUMAN GEOGRAPHY

Vital Statistics

Since no census has been taken in Yemen, all population data are estimates. Total population is somewhat under 7 million (about the same as Saudi Arabia). Birth and death rates are 50 and 21 per thousand, respectively, giving an annual growth rate of 2.9 percent. Some estimates put the death rate higher than 30 per thousand. If the estimated rate of increase is maintained, the population will double in 24 years and will reach 13.8 million by the year 2000. Early marriages and large families are common. The median age is 17.6, and 45 percent of the population is under 15 years old. The per capita gross national product is U.S. $120.

Settlement

Only 7 percent of the population live in urban areas. The majority of the population are subsistence farmers. About 80 percent of the cultivated land is rainfed, and the rest is irrigated. Rural settlements are associated with the availability of water supplies and with defensive sites, and there is little connectivity between the villages. They are generally along the western (windward) slopes below the frost line. On the eastern slopes pastoral nomadism increases as population decreases. In the highlands stone and brick are used for housing, while in the Tihamah brick, mud, and grass are used.

In the lower foothills, the wet conditions provide breeding grounds for anopheline mosquitoes and other parasites, thus population densities are very low. Conditions are more favorable above 2,000 feet, and irrigation, using both streams and wells, allows for extensive terracing; the population density here is the highest in Yemen. Between 5900 and 8200 feet there is enough precipitation for rainfed agriculture. This plateau highland area contains most of the main urban settlements. Farther east, in the Meshreq, rainfall decreases rapidly, and agriculture is again dependent on irrigation, mainly by wells but also by means of small catchment dams. The latter practice was once quite common, and about eighty dams have been observed. The largest was at Marib, a hundred miles east of San'a; it broke down in the fifth century A.D. because of neglect. Current plans aim to reconstruct it and to vitalize several other dams.

Urban Centers

Most of the cities are along the western slopes of the central highlands. The largest is the capital of San'a, with about 125,000 people, followed by the main port of Hudeidah with close to 100,000. Ta'izz, the main city in the south, has a population of 85,000. Sa'da, Amran, Bajil, Dhamar, Ibb, Manakha, Qa'taba and Zabid are local market centers. In addition to Hudeidah there are two small ports, Luhayyah and Mukha, the latter is the origin of the name Mocha coffee.

Migration

While there is hardly any immigration to Yemen, emigration has been steady during the twentieth century. Many have gone to the neighboring People's Democratic Republic of Yemen (South Yemen) and account, by some estimates, for one-third of the latter country's population of approximately one and a half million. Others have gone to port cities in east Africa and the Arabian Gulf, and as far as Indonesia and Marseilles. Many are involved in the booming construction industry of the oil-exporting Arab countries, and many others have for long been involved in short term and seasonal employment migration: to Sudan for cotton picking, to Iraq for date harvesting, and to Dhofar in Oman for collecting myrrh and incense.

Bab Al-Yemen in San'a, Capital of Yemen, where the old and the new intermingle

ECONOMY

Modern Agriculture

Agriculture, the primary sector, has been little affected by technological innovation. For instance, dependence on animal power for plowing is the norm. In the Tihamah tropical crops such as bananas, mango, dates, cotton, and millet are found. On the extensively terraced slopes such Mediterranean fruits as citrus and grapes are grown. In the highlands cereals, vegetables, coffee and qat are the main crops. Qat is an evergreen shrub whose leaves are chewed and which seems to have a mild narcotic effect. Chewing qat is a major social pastime, practiced daily by the men during the afternoon and evening. Coffee, the primary cash crop, is grown, usually under irrigation, between 4300 and 6700 feet. The best variety comes from the San'a area and is known as Mocha because of its association with Mukha, the port of export. Cotton and qat also are cash crops, the latter is usually exported to South Yemen and Ethiopia.

Industry

Industry is limited to traditional small-scale activities—jewelry, basketry, leatherwork, glass and textiles. Larger scale manufacturing includes textiles, cotton cleaning and cottonseed oil. A rock salt factory at Salif on the coast about forty miles north of Hudeidah exports to Japan. Mineral wealth includes copper, iron, lead, zinc, silver, gold and uranium. However, their extent is not yet known and there is no production. Oil exploration is under way in the Tihamah.

Transportation

Communications are limited. In 1962 Chinese engineers completed a spectacular highway between San'a and Hudeidah; they also built a road northwards from San'a to Sa'da. U.S. aid helped in roads connecting San'a with Ta'izz in the south and Ta'izz with Mukha. Attention is being given to harbor facilities at Hudeidah, Mukha and Salif. International flights serve San'a, Ta'izz and Hudeidah.

Minaret of the mosque in San'a

HISTORY

The southwestern corner of the Arabian peninsula has witnessed a long succession of kingdoms and civilizations. It was the land of Sheba (the Sabaean kingdom, 950-115 B.C.) and its fabled queen, and of the Minaen civilization (13th to 7th centuries B.C.). The Himyarite dynasty, from whom the modern Imams claim descent, ruled from 115 B.C. to 525 A.D., when it was conquered by the Ethiopians. They in turn were overthrown by the Persians in 575. Islamic influence spread during the seventh century. The highlands came under the influence of the Zaidi branch of the Shi'a, and the Tihamah under the Shafi'i rite of the Sunni. Ottoman Turkey conquered Yemen in 1517, though its control was tenuous and repeatedly challenged by European powers.

Following World War I Yemen, under Imam Yahya, was involved in claims over Asir and the British Aden Protectorate, with some support from Italy. In 1934 the Treaty of Taif settled Yemen's northern boundary with Saudi Arabia. During the 1950s Yemen pressed a claim against Britain over the Aden Protectorate; some border incidents occurred. In 1958 Yemen joined the United Arab Republic (which linked Egypt and Syria) to form the United Arab States, but the federation was not workable and was dissolved by the United Arab Republic in December, 1961, three months after Syria had terminated its union with Egypt. Yemen was torn by a civil war from 1962 to 1969. The revolt was supported for a while by Egyptian troops, while the royalist side was supported by Saudi Arabia. A new constitution in 1970 resulted in elections in March, 1971, and a new Consultative Council incorporated former royalists. A rapprochement with Saudi Arabia was reached. Relations with revolutionary South Yemen (Aden) have fluctuated, and occasionally there has been talk of a union between the two. The prospects, however, appear increasingly dim.

The White Mosque of Al-Muatabiyah at Ta'izz, Yemen

Tall and decorative buildings are characteristic features of Yemeni traditional architecture

GOVERNMENT AND SOCIETY

Administration

A provisional constitution published in 1974 by the Military Command Council gives full legislative and executive power to the Council for a transitional period. The Chairman of the Command Council assumes the powers of Head of State and appoints a cabinet headed by a prime minister.

Education

The Republican regime initiated a state school system. Only few private schools had existed under the Imamate. By 1974 enrollment in primary, intermediate and secondary schools had reached 76,000.

The government is steadily establishing a system of social welfare and health care. By 1974 there were 180 doctors and pharmacists working in 40 hospitals and clinics with 4,000 beds.

PROSPECTS

Yemen has been referred to as Arabia's human reservoir. It has the peninsula's largest concentrations of peoples as well as the largest source of unskilled and semiskilled labor migrants. There were times in history when kingdoms and civilizations with far-flung connections were centered in the area—the present situation of poverty and isolation is by no means a historic norm. Political stability and administrative enlightenment seem to be emerging. Yemen has profited from the help of others, such as the Kuwait Fund for Arab Development and aid from the United States, the Soviet Union and the People's Republic of China. A very basic need is an inventory of human and other resources to permit meaningful planning on any scale and to enhance the prospect of improved educational, medical and other social amenities.

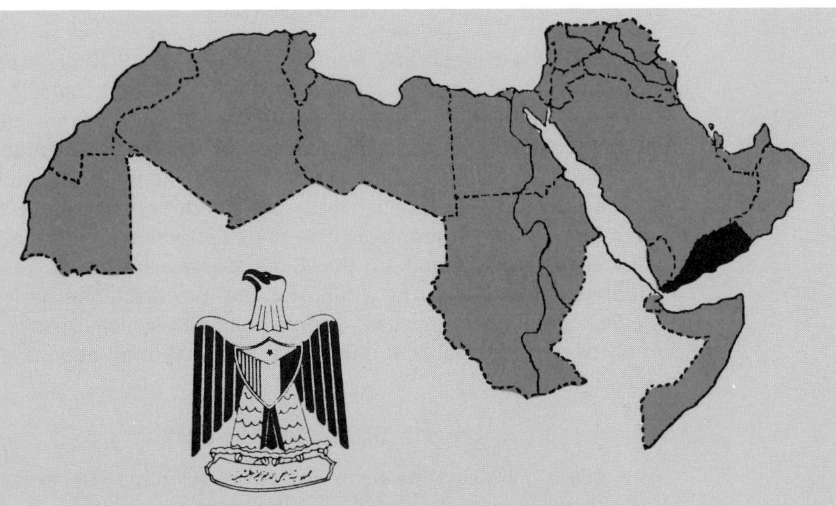

YEMEN

(PEOPLE'S DEMOCRATIC REPUBLIC)

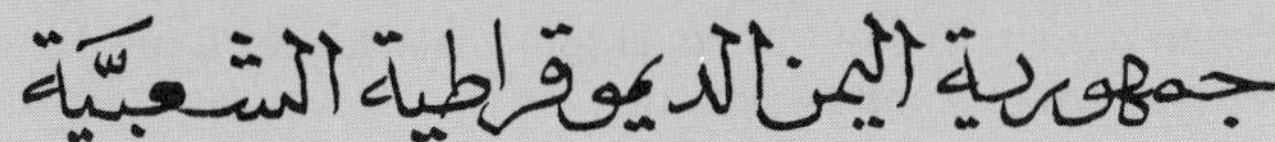

PROFILE

Official Name: People's Democratic Republic of Yemen (Jumhuriyyat al-Yaman al-dimuqratiyyah al-sha'biyyah)

Head of State: Ali Nasir Muhammad

Government: Republic

Area: 112,000 sq. mi. (=Nevada)

Population: 1,700,000 (est.)

Population Density: 15/sq. mi.

Capital: Aden (300,000)

Other Urban Centers: Mukalla, Say'un, Tarim, Shibam

Currency: Yemeni Dinar (1YD=$2.90)

Press: Daily: October 14, other periodicals

Radio & Television: One radio and one television station

Sites of Interest: Archeological sites in Shibam and Timma—The Valley of Hadramawt

Main Airport: Aden

Main Seaport: Aden

Date of Joining the United Nations: December 14, 1967

Date of Joining the Arab League: December 12, 1967

YEMEN (PDR)

INTRODUCTION

The People's Democratic Republic of Yemen (PDRY) is an upland country in southern Arabia. Historically its associations outside the Arab world have been with diverse and far-flung cultures and political powers in south and southeast Asia, eastern Africa, Turkey, and Europe. Aden, the capital city, plays a focal role in international trade and politics because of its pivotal location near the southern end of the Red Sea. Aden's fortunes have been sensitive to developments overseas, such as the closing and opening of the Suez Canal, and as a result have fluctuated dramatically. The country came into existence on November 30, 1967, and encompasses diverse subunits which usually had not formed part of one political unit. Thus, national integration is a primary task and goal.

PHYSICAL GEOGRAPHY

Area

The PDRY's boundaries have not been delimited. Its area of about 112,000 square miles (slightly larger than Nevada) includes the following islands: Perim (5 square miles), in the Strait of Bab el-Mandeb at the entrance to the Red Sea; Kamaran (22 square miles), 200 miles north of Perim and just off the coast of Yemen Arab Republic; and Socotra (1400 square miles), 600 miles east of Aden. PDRY also possesses the Kuria Muria Islands off the coast of Oman and 200 miles east of the PDRY-Oman border. These five small rocky islets, with a few fishermen on the largest, are claimed by Oman.

Topography

The coast stretches for 740 miles along the Arabian Sea. The scarp of the Arabian plateau rises virtually from the sea, with only a narrow sandy shore and a discontinuous coastal plain hemmed in by protrusions of the plateau. This gives the effect of mountain ranges along the coast. Altitude is highest in the west, approaching 10,000 feet, and decreases eastwards, reflecting the dip in the Arabian plateau. Beyond Ras Fartak (Fartak Headland), where the coast makes a right angle bend to the north, elevations are below 650 feet and a dozen eastward-flowing wadis produce a low-lying coastal region. In the interior are the fringes of Rub'al Khali (Great Sandy Desert) where elevations are down to about 2300 feet. Wadi Hadramawt is conspicuous and important physiographic feature in the east. It flows eastward parallel to and at a distance of about 100 miles from the coast before it bends southeastwards and reaches the sea 80 miles west of Ras Fartak. The lower (eastern) part of the valley is called Masilah.

Climate

The PDRY is mostly a tropical desert. Summer rain falls in the western highlands, and 30 inches annually may be received near the border with the Yemen Arab Republic. Rainfall diminishes eastwards to about 15 inches at the Oman border. The coast is hot and humid. Aden receives about 5 inches a year, primarily in winter (December-March), and its average January and July temperatures are 77°F and 90°F respectively. For Mukalla, 300 miles to the east, the equivalent figures are 73°F and 84°F. All along the coast summer daytime temperatures exceed 100°F. Eighty percent relative humidities are common.

Drainage

There are no permanent rivers. Most valley courses are wadis which carry water irregularly. Seasonal streams are found on the Gulf of Aden side of the western highlands, and the interior portion of the Hadramawt valley also has a seasonal flow. Springs and wells are important sources of water, and they are found on both the seaward and interior margins of the highlands.

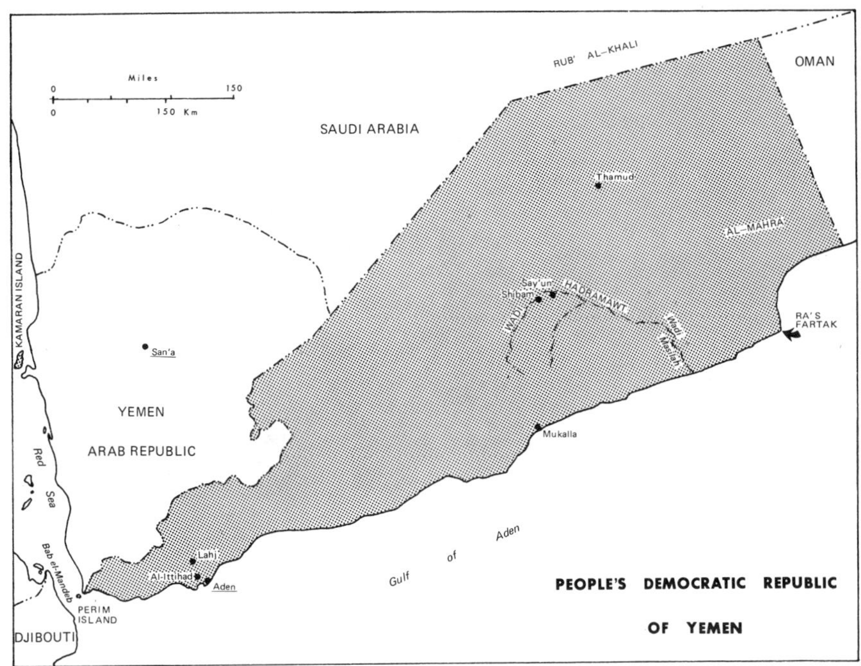

HUMAN GEOGRAPHY

Population

The population is estimated at 1.7 million. No census has ever been taken. Centuries of overseas trade links have resulted in a varied population mix. Some groups have physiognomic and cultural affinities with south Asia (India-Pakistan), and these peoples are sometimes referred to as Veddoids. There is a considerable African element, and in some coastal areas this component of the population exceeds 40 percent. Malay and Indonesian intermixtures are also to be found. The indigenous population itself is quite varied, because for centuries it was organized into numerous semi-autonomous states, and this separateness resulted in divergent cultural developments.

Language and Religion

The dominant cultural traits are Arab and Muslim. Arabic is the official language. In the easternmost part of the country, in Al-Mahra, the language is distinct from Arabic, though related in that both are Semitic. The dominant religious affiliation in PDRY is Sunni Muslim. Recent migrations from the Yemen Arab Republic have resulted in small urban communities, especially in Aden, of Zaydi Muslims.

Birth and death rates are respectively 50 and 21 per thousand per year, giving an annual growth rate of 2.9 percent. If these rates remain constant, the population will double in 24 years and will reach 3.4 million in the year 2000. Some 45 percent of the population is under 15 years old, and the median age is 17.6 years.

Population Distribution

About one-fourth of the national population is urban, with about 300,000 living in the Aden urban area. The second largest town is Mukalla, the eastern region's main city, with a population of nearly 100,000. The next largest cities are in interior Hadramawt: Say'un, Tarim, and Shibam, all have between 10,000 and 25,000 inhabitants. Otherwise the population is overwhelmingly rural and is largely in the west. Settlement is mostly along the narrow and rather discontinuous coastal plain, in the uplands where rainfall is relatively abundant, and in the upper (interior) portion of the Hadramawt valley.

A general view of Aden, capital of PDRY

ECONOMY

Low dams or barrages provide irrigation by impounding and diverting the occasional flow of water. The most productive agricultural area is Lahj, immediately north of Aden. The main crops are cereals, fruits, vegetables, dates, bananas and coconuts. Cotton and coffee are also grown, and qat is raised at higher elevations. Qat is an evergreen shrub whose leaves are chewed, akin to chewing tobacco, and which seems to have a mild narcotic effect. Frankincense trees grow above 3000 feet. Their sap, from which incense and myrrh are produced, is tapped before the start of the summer rainy season. These products were once traded regularly to the eastern Mediterranean, moving along a land Incense Route which passed through Medina. With increasing aridity, whether eastwards or towards the interior, pastoral activity replaces cultivation.

Agriculture

Fishing has always been a important activity along the coast, with shark, tuna, kingfish and sardines being the more common catches. The port of Mukalla is the main fishing center. Dried and salted fish is carried inland or exported to East Africa and to Sri Lanka.

Fishing

The coastal areas have traditionally traded with places across the waters rather than with the interior, and their fortunes have reflected developments overseas. This pattern is particularly well exemplified by Aden, which occupies a magnificent harbor resulting from a sunken volcanic crater. In 1276 Marco Polo found a bustling city of 80,000 with 360 mosques. It declined following the rounding of Cape of Good Hope by the Portuguese in 1497, and the loss of activity was compounded by the Ottoman Turkish conquest of Egypt. When the British attacked Aden in 1839 its population was down to 500. The opening of the Suez Canal in 1869 revived its prosperity, and during the following century its population increased rapidly. The closing of the canal in 1956-1957 and 1967-1975 was very damaging because of the overwhelming dominance of petroleum and its products in Aden's trade.

Trade

The free port status of Aden, its role as a major link in the lifeline of the British Empire, and the large British Petrol refinery opened in 1954 all contributed to attracting labor migrants from elsewhere, a process which had been going on for a long time. An estimated one-third of the population is from the Yemen Arab Republic. Indians, Indonesians, Somalis and others have also migrated to Aden.

YEMEN (PDR)

HISTORY

During the eighteenth century as well as in the days of pre-Islamic civilizations, there were times when southwestern Arabia, including today's PDRY and Yemen Arab Republic, was under one administration. But for much of its history the region was politically divided into small states.

British Occupation

The beginning of active British interest is related to the global competition between Britain and Napoleonic France. Following Napoleon's 1798 campaign in Egypt, Britain occupied Perim Island in 1799 and in 1802 concluded a commercial treaty with the Sultan of Lahj, north and west of Aden. The island of Socotra was occupied in 1834 and Aden was captured in January, 1839. In 1854 the Kuria Muria Islands were acquired from the Sultan of Oman. There were twenty-three autonomous Arab states in the interior; Britain negotiated protective treaty relations with their rulers between 1882 and 1914. Together these came to be known as the Aden Protectorate, though administratively they were divided into Eastern and Western Protectorate States.

Federation

During the 1950s a series of arrangements led to the formation in February, 1959 of the Federation of Arab Emirates in the South. The federal capital was the non-coastal city of Al Ittihad (The Union), six miles west of Aden. At first only six of the twenty states of the Western Protectorate were thus joined. By mid-1963 the number of member states had risen to fourteen. The name was changed in May, 1962 to Federation of South Arabia. Meanwhile, a liberation movement was in progress with the objective of ending British rule. Various national groups were involved, some reflecting the interests of other Arab countries, such as Saudi Arabia, Egypt and Yemen Arab Republic (YAR). One group sought a union with YAR.

Independence

Independence was secured on November 30, 1967 and that same year PDRY became a member of the League of Arab States and of the United Nations. On October 28, 1972 PDRY and YAR signed a peace agreement in Cairo which proposed eventual unification to form the Yemeni Republic, with San'a as the capital. Subsequent developments, such as a June, 1974 coup in YAR, have made the possibility of such union increasingly remote. In fact, when PDRY became independent in 1967 its name was People's Republic of South Yemen. The change to People's Democratic Republic of Yemen had been made in November 1970 and had reflected a growing ideological rift between the two Yemens. PDRY's foreign policy has been described as one of militant internationalism, and its leadership has indicated sympathies for anti-establishment revolutionary movements in other countries.

A palace in Aden displaying the traditional south Arabian architecture; tall and decorative.

GOVERNMENT AND SOCIETY

Administration

The constitution adopted in 1970 established a Provisional Supreme People's Council which took over legislative powers. The Council consists of 101 members selected from the ruling party, the National Liberation Front (NLF), the armed forces, the professions, the trade unions and other groups. The executive is composed of a head of state, a presidential council and a cabinet.

Judicial

The judicial system is a combination of secular codes for criminal and civil affairs (except in matters of personal status) and of Islamic Shari'a. The ministry of Justice is trying to coordinate the difference between the two systems.

Education

The educational system consists of primary, intermediate and secondary schooling, with more than 260 schools and a Technical Institute. Higher education is still sought abroad. This system is supplemented by private schools which are aided by the government.

PROSPECTS

With independence, the People's Democratic Republic of Yemen was confronted with a variety of problems. The Suez Canal had just been closed and remained so till 1975, thus further undermining an economy whose basis was at best meager. The Canal closing reduced Aden's trade by 75 percent. The British evacuation caused the unemployment of over 20,000 in supporting activities, and the termination of British aid cut national income by 60 percent. Domestic dissension exacerbated the burden of reconstruction. Aid has come from the Soviet Union to help the fishing industry and in support of the army, and from China in the form of medicine and highway construction. The Kuwait Fund for Arab Economic Development has financed agricultural projects as well as an economic survey of the whole country. Algeria, Libya and Iraq have also contributed development aid.

Primary needs include an active program to integrate the country in terms of communication and economic complementarity, a diversification of domestic economic opportunity to decrease the preponderance of Aden, and an ambitious and sustained educational program to help nurture a domestic resource of skilled and diversified labor. Before any of these ventures can be successful, a thorough census of human and physical resources is needed. With domestic stability and a reasonable international harmony, the People's Democratic Republic of Yemen should make steady progress in these directions.

Outdoor theater performers at Sahareej, PDRY.

APPENDIX

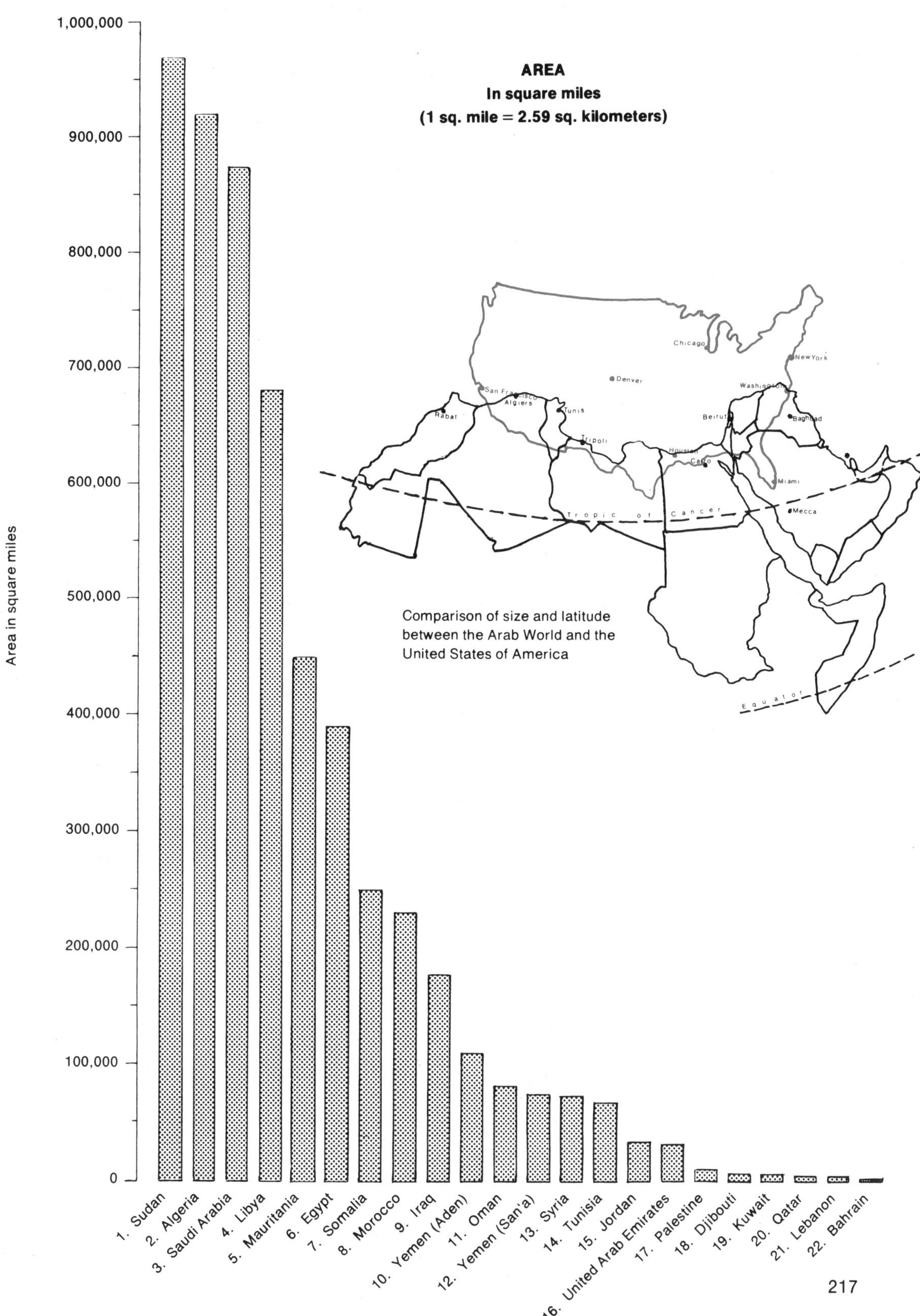
AREA
In square miles
(1 sq. mile = 2.59 sq. kilometers)
Area in square miles
1,000,000
900,000
800,000
700,000
600,000
500,000
400,000
300,000
200,000
100,000
0
1. Sudan
2. Algeria
3. Saudi Arabia
4. Libya
5. Mauritania
6. Egypt
7. Somalia
8. Morocco
9. Iraq
10. Yemen (Aden)
11. Oman
12. Yemen (San'a)
13. Syria
14. Tunisia
15. Jordan
16. United Arab Emirates
17. Palestine
18. Djibouti
19. Kuwait
20. Qatar
21. Lebanon
22. Bahrain
Chicago
New York
Denver
San Francisco
Algiers
Rabat
Tunis
Washington
Beirut
Baghdad
Tripoli
Houston
Cairo
Miami
Mecca
Tropic of Cancer
Equator
Comparison of size and latitude between the Arab World and the United States of America

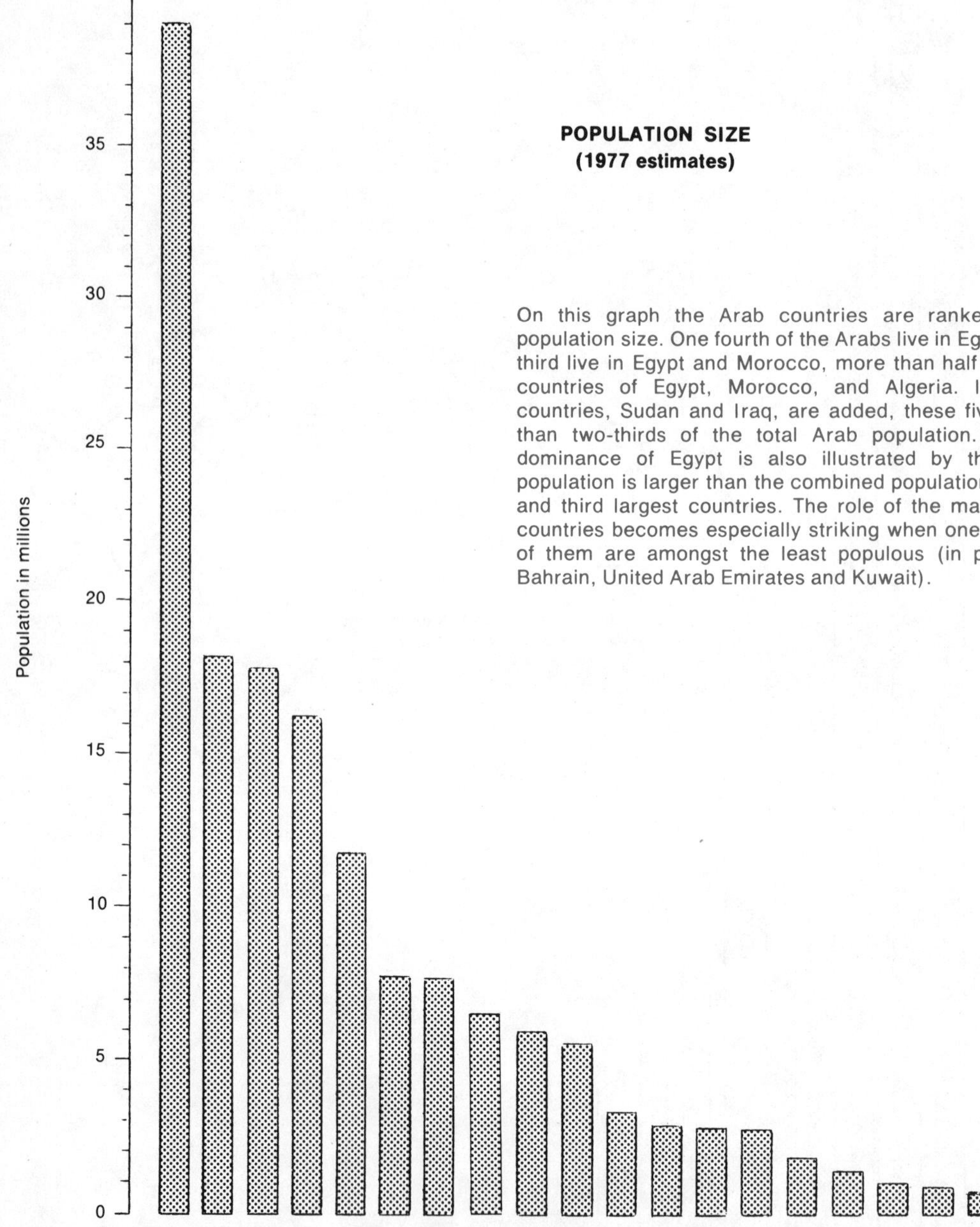

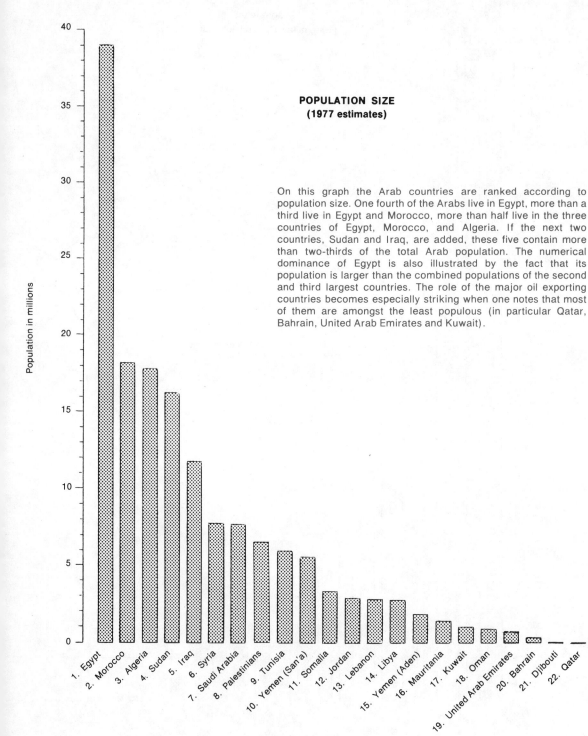

POPULATION SIZE
(1977 estimates)

On this graph the Arab countries are ranked according to population size. One fourth of the Arabs live in Egypt, more than a third live in Egypt and Morocco, more than half live in the three countries of Egypt, Morocco, and Algeria. If the next two countries, Sudan and Iraq, are added, these five contain more than two-thirds of the total Arab population. The numerical dominance of Egypt is also illustrated by the fact that its population is larger than the combined populations of the second and third largest countries. The role of the major oil exporting countries becomes especially striking when one notes that most of them are amongst the least populous (in particular Qatar, Bahrain, United Arab Emirates and Kuwait).

BIRTH RATES AND DEATH RATES
1975 estimates

(Djibouti and Palestine not included)

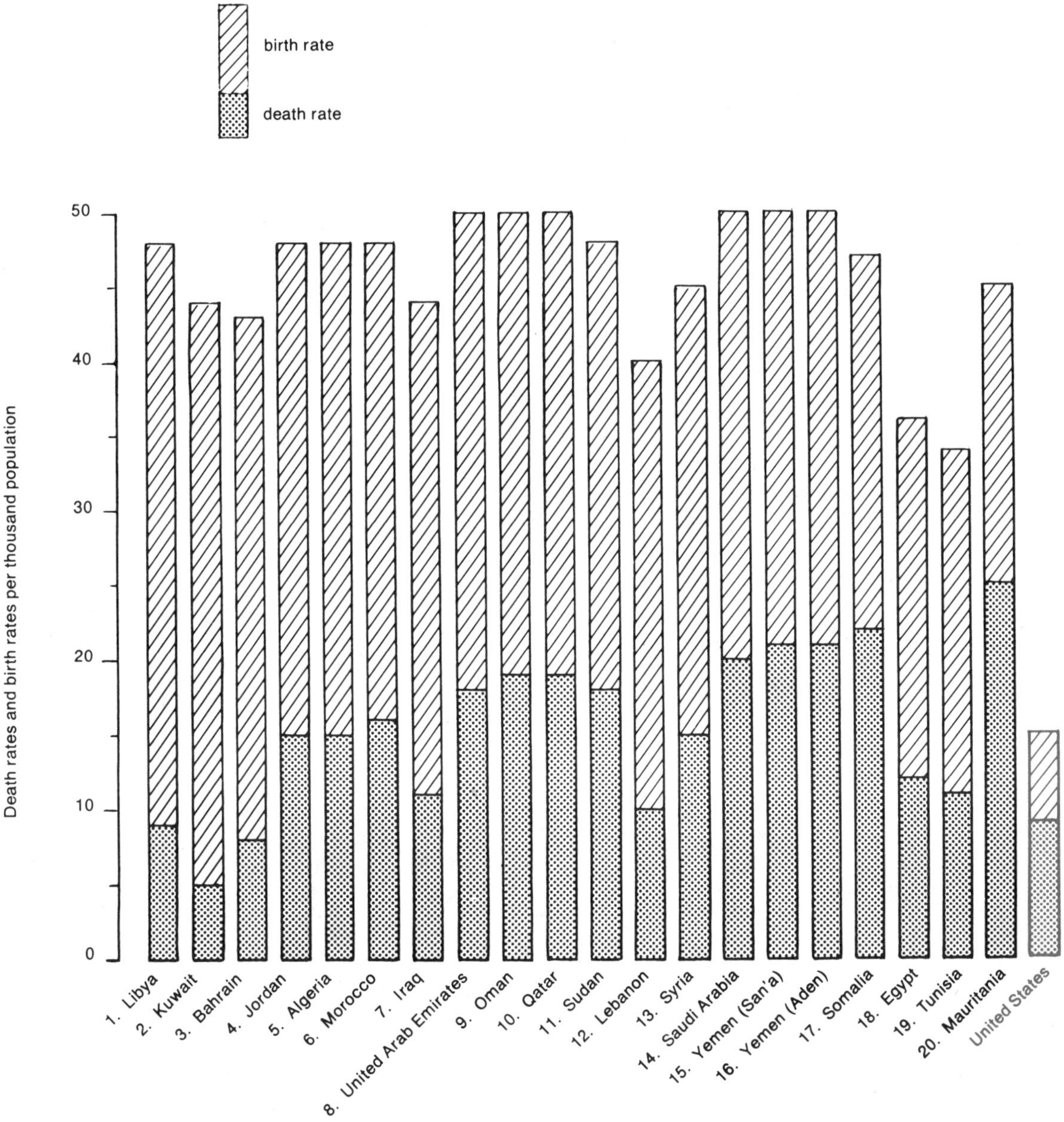

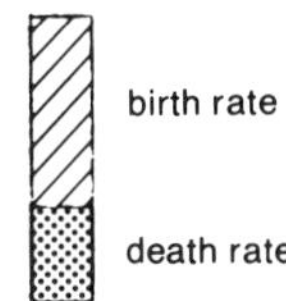

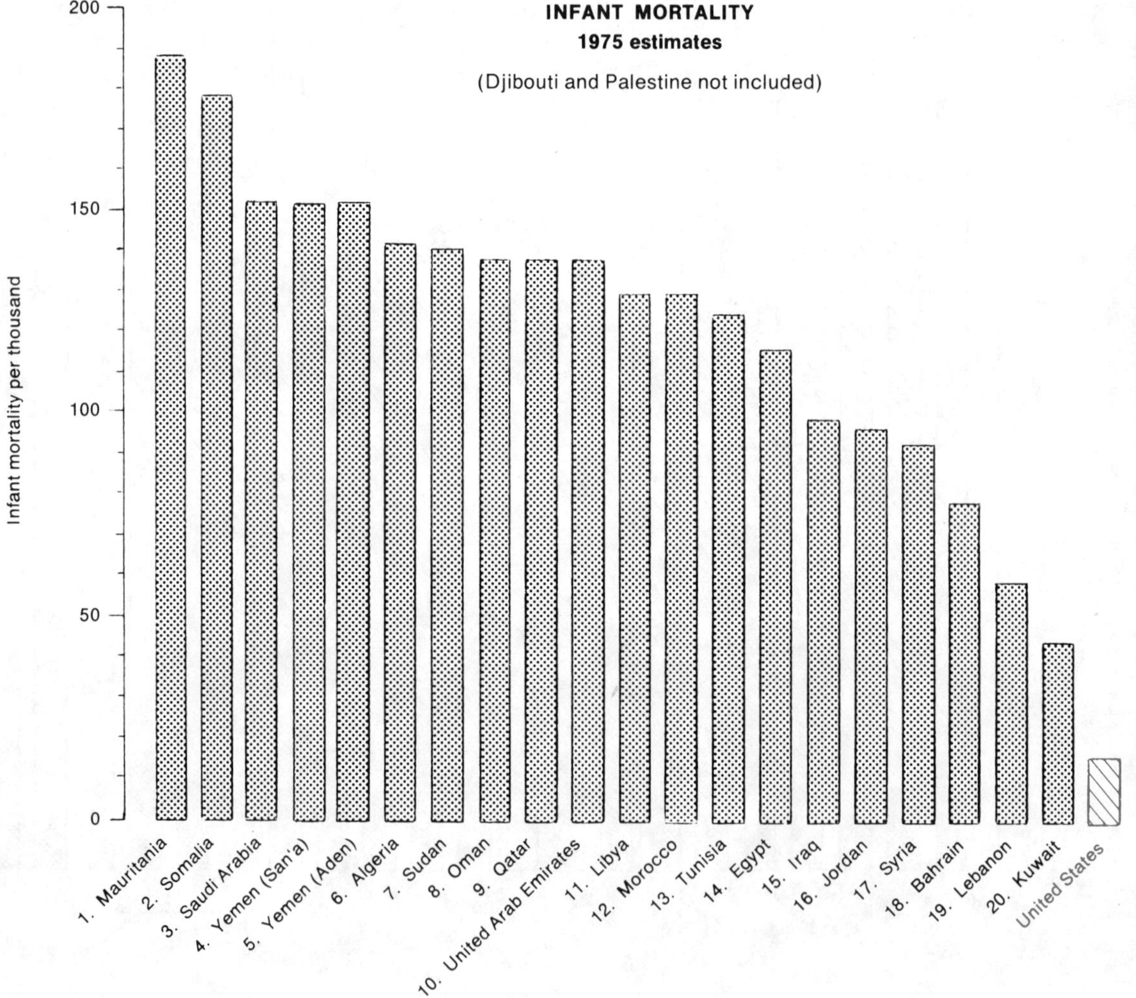
INFANT MORTALITY
1975 estimates
(Djibouti and Palestine not included)
Infant mortality per thousand
200
150
100
50
0
1. Mauritania
2. Somalia
3. Saudi Arabia
4. Yemen (San'a)
5. Yemen (Aden)
6. Algeria
7. Sudan
8. Oman
9. Qatar
10. United Arab Emirates
11. Libya
12. Morocco
13. Tunisia
14. Egypt
15. Iraq
16. Jordan
17. Syria
18. Bahrain
19. Lebanon
20. Kuwait
United States

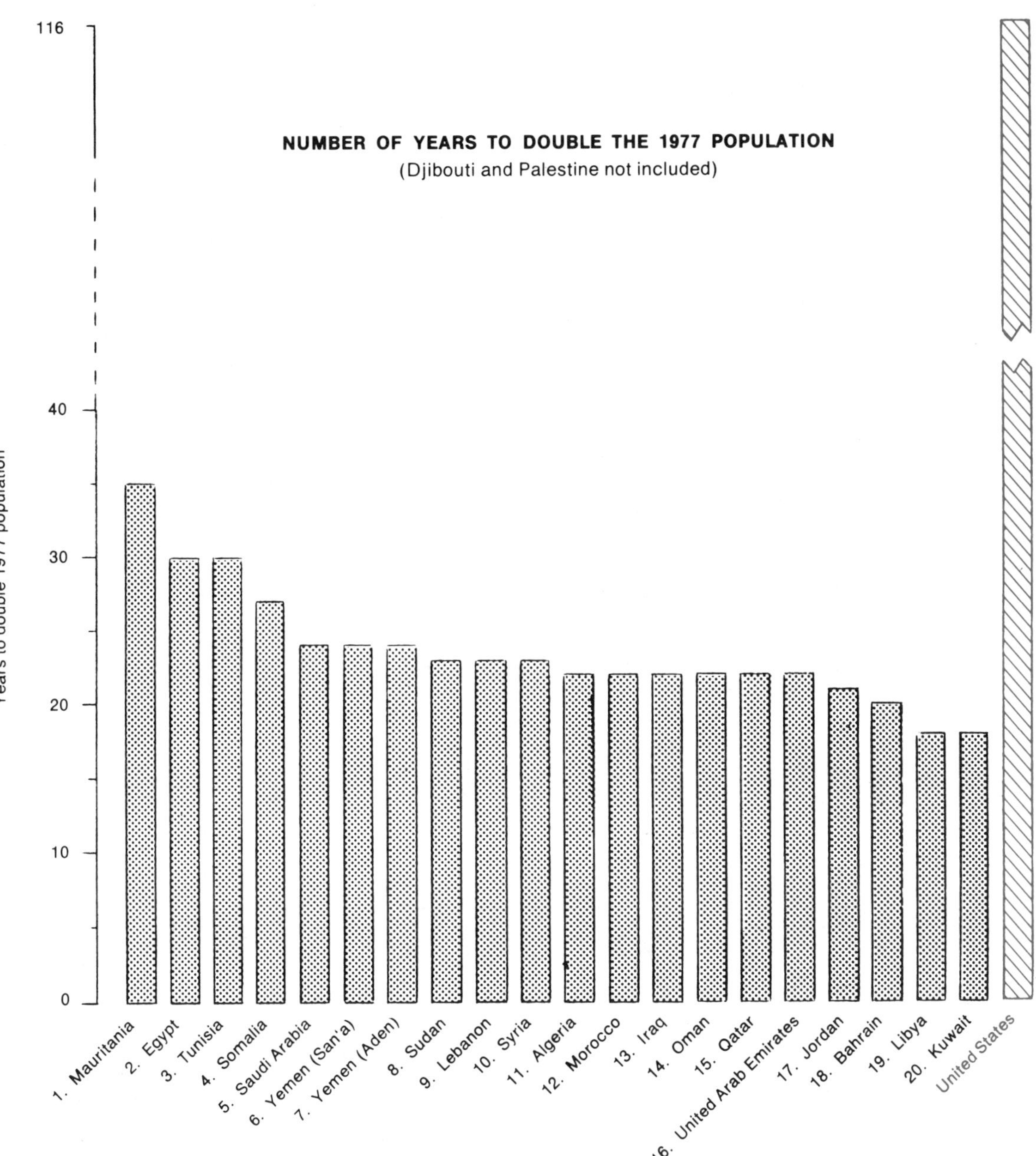
NUMBER OF YEARS TO DOUBLE THE 1977 POPULATION
(Djibouti and Palestine not included)
Years to double 1977 population
116
40
30
20
10
0
1. Mauritania
2. Egypt
3. Tunisia
4. Somalia
5. Saudi Arabia
6. Yemen (San'a)
7. Yemen (Aden)
8. Sudan
9. Lebanon
10. Syria
11. Algeria
12. Morocco
13. Iraq
14. Oman
15. Qatar
16. United Arab Emirates
17. Jordan
18. Bahrain
19. Libya
20. Kuwait
United States

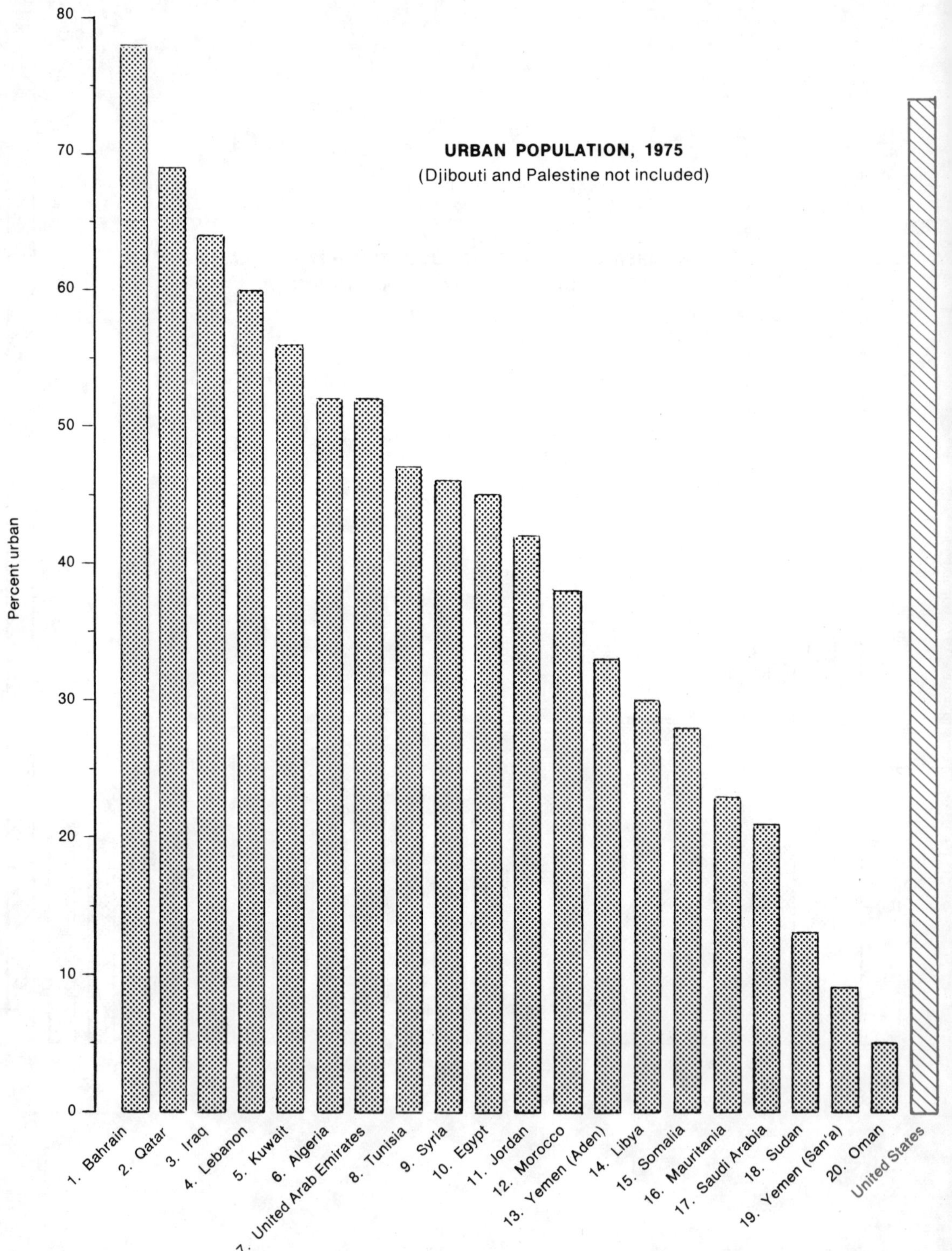
URBAN POPULATION, 1975
(Djibouti and Palestine not included)
Percent urban
80
70
60
50
40
30
20
10
0
1. Bahrain
2. Qatar
3. Iraq
4. Lebanon
5. Kuwait
6. Algeria
7. United Arab Emirates
8. Tunisia
9. Syria
10. Egypt
11. Jordan
12. Morocco
13. Yemen (Aden)
14. Libya
15. Somalia
16. Mauritania
17. Saudi Arabia
18. Sudan
19. Yemen (San'a)
20. Oman
United States

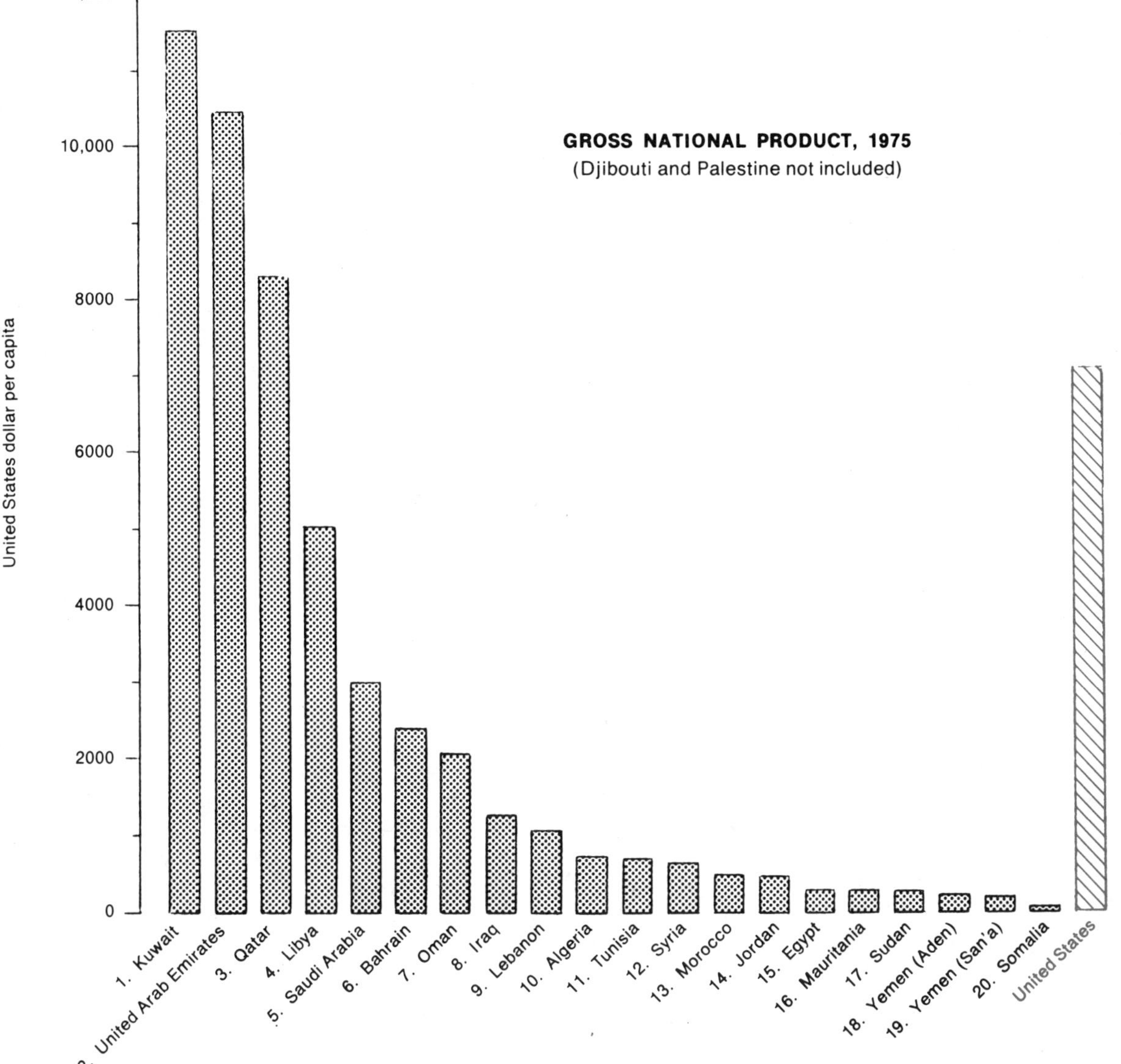
GROSS NATIONAL PRODUCT, 1975
(Djibouti and Palestine not included)
United States dollar per capita
12,000
10,000
8000
6000
4000
2000
0
1. Kuwait
2. United Arab Emirates
3. Qatar
4. Libya
5. Saudi Arabia
6. Bahrain
7. Oman
8. Iraq
9. Lebanon
10. Algeria
11. Tunisia
12. Syria
13. Morocco
14. Jordan
15. Egypt
16. Mauritania
17. Sudan
18. Yemen (Aden)
19. Yemen (San'a)
20. Somalia
United States

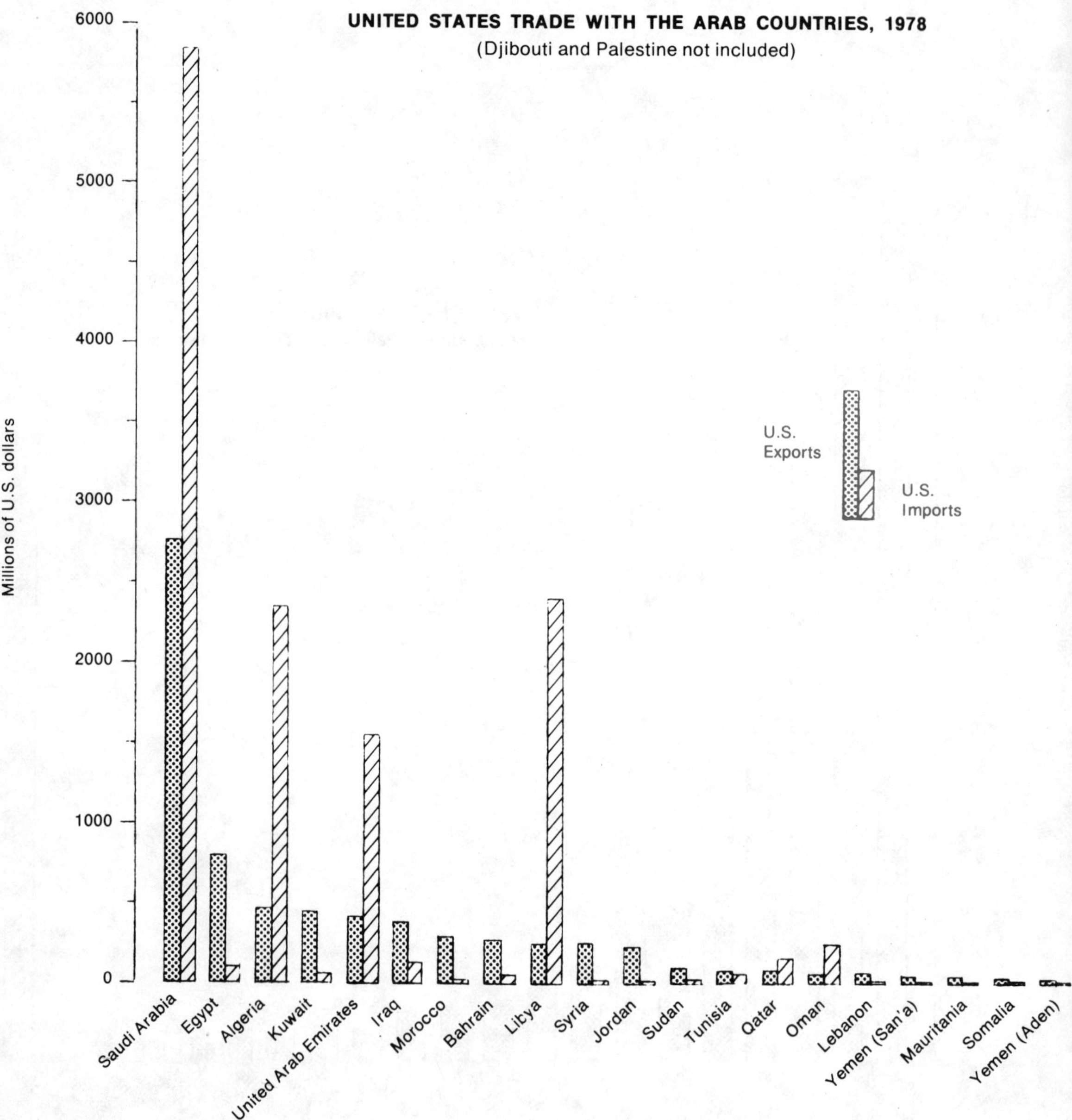

UNITED STATES TRADE WITH THE ARAB COUNTRIES, 1978
(Djibouti and Palestine not included)
Millions of U.S. dollars
6000
5000
4000
3000
2000
1000
0
U.S. Exports
U.S. Imports
Saudi Arabia
Egypt
Algeria
Kuwait
United Arab Emirates
Iraq
Morocco
Bahrain
Libya
Syria
Jordan
Sudan
Tunisia
Qatar
Oman
Lebanon
Yemen (San'a)
Mauritania
Somalia
Yemen (Aden)

CHRONOLOGICAL TABLES

I. FROM THE BIRTH OF MUHAMMAD TO WORLD WAR I

A.D.

560 Birth of the Prophet Muhammad.

622 The Hijra—Muhammad's flight from Mecca to Medina. Beginning of Islamic calendar.

628 Muslims capture Mecca.

632 Death of Muhammad. Abu-Bakr, first Caliph.

633 First Arab attack on Persia.

634 Omar becomes Caliph. Beginning of the expansion of the Arab Empire into Syria, Egypt, Iraq and Persia.

635 Arab armies enter Damascus.

637 Capture of Jerusalem.

641 The Persian Empire completely conquered.

641 Founding of Fustat in Egypt (Old Cairo).

643 Conquest of Tripolitania. Building the Dome of the Rock in Jerusalem.

649 Arab conquest of Cyprus.

655 Arab fleet destroys Byzantine fleet at Lycia.

656 Othman, 3rd Caliph, murdered. Ali becomes Caliph.

658 Mu'awiyah, governor of Syria, assumes Caliphate in Damascus. War between Ali and Mu'awiyah.

661 Ali murdered. Umayyad Dynasty in Damascus rules over Arab Empire until 750 A.D.

670 Arab armies in North Africa.

671 Arab siege of Constantinople fails.

674 Arabs at the Indus River.

680 Husayn, son of Ali, killed in Karbala.

694 Arabs overrun Armenia.

695 First Arab coinage.

700 Conquest of Algiers.

705 Walid I and the building of the Great Mosque of Damascus. The height of Arab military power.

710 Sugar planted in Egypt.

711 Tariq crossed into Spain at the rock later named after him (Gilbraltar=Gabal Tariq).

712 The Arabs in Samraqand. Learning the art of making paper.

715 Largest extent of Arab Empire—from the Pyrenees to China with Damascus as capital.

720 Arabs cross into France; conquer Sardinia.

720 Arab chemist, Abu Musa Jaffar, introduces sulfuric acid, nitric acid, aqua regia, and nitrate of silver.

732 Charles Martel stops Arab advance into France. Battle of Tours and Poitiers.

750 End of Umayyad rule.
Abbasid dynasty founded; based in Iraq.
Birth of Abu-Nuwas, famous poet (d.811).
Flourishing of medicine, astronomy, mathematics, optics, and chemistry begins.

755 Abdul-Rahman, Umayyad survivor, founds a separate Spanish state at Cordova.

760 Arabic numerals develop.

763 Founding of Baghdad, capital of the Abbasids.

774 Euclid's "Elements" translated into Arabic. Beginning of Golden Period of Arab learning.

785 Beginning of the building of the Great Mosque of Cordova.

786 Harun al-Rashid becomes Caliph.

813 Caliph Al-Ma'mun, patron of Arab learning. School of Astronomy in Baghdad.

826 Arabs in Crete and the Greek Islands.

827 Arabs in Sicily.

828 Almagest, Ptolemy's Astronomical Systems translated into Arabic.

830 Al-Ma'mun founds the Academy (House of Wisdom) in Baghdad.

850 Perfection of the astrolabe.

868 Tulunid dynasty in Egypt. The dismemberment of the Arab Empire continues.

869 Al-Jahiz, Arab literary figure, dies.

870 Al-Kindi, Arab philosopher, dies (b.813).

873 Death of the great physician, Hunayn ibn Ishaq.

878 Al-Battani begins his astronomical observations.

879 Building of Ibn Tulun Mosque, Cairo.

880 Ibn Qutayba, scholar and historian, dies (b.828).

900 The great physician Al-Razi (Rhases) discusses infectious diseases: plague, consumption, smallpox, rabies (d.923).

909 Rise of the Fatimid dynasty in North Africa.

915 Fatimids in Egypt.

915 Birth of al-Mutanabbi, one of the most quoted and celebrated Arab poets.

923 Death of Tabari, celebrated historian and theologian (b.838).

930 Cordova in Spain, seat of Arab learning.

940 Beginning of retreat from Spain.

950 Al-Farabi, Arab philosopher, dies (b.870).

963 Al-Sufi's "The Book of Fixed Stars" mentions nebula.

965 Birth of Alhazen (Ibn al-Haytham) who wrote more than 100 works on astronomy, optics, philosophy and medicine (d.1039).

968 Founding of the city of Cairo.

973 Birth of Al-Biruni, historian, mathematician and astronomer. He wrote on Indian philosophy and science (d.1048).

973 Born, Abu-al-'ala al-Ma'arri, blind poet, philosopher, and mystic. His writing was marked by rationalism and skepticism and influenced following generation. One of his works anticipates Dante's Inferno (d.1057).

975 Introduction into Europe of the present arithmetical notation (Arab numerals).

1009 Death of Ibn Yunis, astronomer (b.950).

1037 Death of the famous philosopher and physician Avicenna (Ibn Sina) (b.980).

1047 Seljuk Turks in power.

1059 Birth of al-Ghazali, philosopher and theologian (d.1111).

1096 The start of the Crusades.

1099 The Crusaders take Jerusalem.

1125 Almohades in Morocco.

1126 Birth of Averroes (Ibn-Rushd), Arab philosopher and physician in Spain. His work exerted great influence on development of European philosophy in the Middle Ages (d.1198).

1147 Second Crusade fails.

1154 Al-Idrisi's book of geography published in Palermo.

1176 Saladin (Salah al-Din) becomes ruler of Egypt and Syria.

1187 Saladin defeats the Crusaders at Hittin and takes Jerusalem.

1236 Cordova falls.

1258 The Mongols destroy Baghdad; the Abbasid Caliph takes refuge in Egypt.

1291 Remnants of the Crusaders driven out. End of Crusade.

1332 Ibn Khaldun, historian and philosopher, born. Considered founder of the modern science of sociology (d.1406).

1352 Travels of Ibn Battuta, famous geographer.

1401 Mongols under Timur Leng conquer Baghdad and Damascus.

1492 Fall of Granada. End of Arab rule in Spain.

1516 Ottoman Turks under Selim I begin conquest of Syria and Egypt.

1534 Ottomans capture Baghdad. Caliphate assumed by Ottomans.

1544 Sa'di Sharifs in Morocco.

1603 Revolt of Fakhr-ed-Din in the Lebanon.

1633 Defeat of Fakhr-ed-Din.

1665 French bombard Algiers and Tunis.

1798 Napoleon Bonaparte in Egypt.

1804 Wahhabis capture Mecca and Medina.

1811 Muhammad Ali consolidates his rule over Egypt; he wipes out the Mamluks.

1818 Ibrahim, son of Muhammad Ali, defeats Wahhabis in Arabia.

1830 The French occupy Algeria.

1832 Ibrahim conquers Syria.

1835 'Abd-el-Qadir of Algeria defeats French at Macta.

1839 Egyptian army under Ibrahim defeats Ottoman army at Nasibin.

1840 London conference to regulate Egyptian-Turkish relations. Egyptians leave Syria.

1843 Sanusiyah order founded in Libya.

1845 Capture of 'Abd-el-Qadir in Algiers.

1849 Wahabbis drive Egyptian troops out of Arabia.

1849 Controversy over the holy places in Jerusalem.

1860 Construction begins on the Suez Canal.
Sectarian trouble in Syria and Lebanon.

1869 Completion of the Suez Canal.

1870 Rise of the Mahdi in the Sudan.

1881 French occupy Tunisia. Arabi revolt in Egypt. British occupy Egypt.

1885 Mahdi attacks Khartum. Gordon killed. Mahdi dies.

1896 Kitchener defeats Mahdists at Omdurman.

1911 Italians begin conquest of Libya.

II. FROM WORLD WAR I TO 1977

1914 World War I. British land in Iraq.

1917 British take Baghdad.

1918 Damascus occupied by army of the Arab Revolt with Lawrence of Arabia.
Faysal becomes king of Syria.

1919 Nationalist upheavals in Egypt.

1920 French expel Faysal from Damascus.

1921 Faysal becomes king of Iraq.
Abdelkrim's revolt in the Rif of Morocco against Spanish rule.

1922 Constitution for Palestine under British Mandate.

1923 Fouad I declared king of Egypt. Wafd party dominates.
Transjordan becomes emirate under Abdullah.

1924 Ibn Saud occupies Mecca, Medina and Jidda.

1925 Marshall Petain in Morocco.
Syrian rebellion against French. Damascus bombarded.
Iraq Petroleum Company founded.

1926 Abdelkrim surrenders to the French in Morocco.
Abdul-Aziz ibn Saud becomes king of Saudi Arabia.
Lebanon proclaimed a republic.

1927 Saad Zaghlul dies in Egypt; Nahhas leads the Wafd Party.
Treaty between Britain and Iraq.

1928 Egyptian parliament dissolved.

1929 Restoration of Egyptian constitution. Hassan Banna forms Muslim Brothers organization.
Riots in Palestine.

1930 Passfield White Paper for Palestine.
New Syrian constitution.

1932 Iraq joins League of Nations; British Mandate formally terminated.

1933 Arabian American Oil Company (ARAMCO) founded.
Death of Faysal; Ghazi king of Iraq.

1934 British regularize their rule of Aden (treaty between Britain, India and Yemen).
War between Saudi Arabia and Yemen.

1935 IPC pipeline from Kirkuk in Iraq to Tripoli in Lebanon.

1936 Arab general strike in Palestine from April to October.
Farouk I becomes king of Egypt.
General Sidqi seizes power in Iraq.
Blum-Violette reforms in Algeria.

1937 Parti du Peuple Algerien (PPA) founded.
Capitulations abolished in Egypt.
Moroccan Unity Party founded. Economic Crisis in Morocco.
France agrees to give Syrian province of Alexandretta to Turkey.
Peel Commission Report on Palestine.

1938 Civil disobedience in Tunisia to protest French rule, organized by Habib Bourguiba.
Ferhat Abbas founds Union Populaire Algerienne (UPA).

1939 London Conference on Palestine.
British issue White Paper proposing partition of Palestine.
World War II begins.

1940 Italy attacks Sudan, occupies British Somaliland.

1941 British attack Italian Somalia and take Mogadiscio.
Kaylani's revolt in Iraq against British occupation.
British and Gaulist French forces invade Syria and Lebanon.
French formally relinquish mandate over Syria and Lebanon.

1942 Zionist Biltmore program for the formation of a Jewish State in Palestine.
Moncef Bey forms nationalist government in Tunisia.
Allies land in Algeria.

1943 Manifesto of the Algerian People demands independence.
French provisional Consultative Assembly in Algeria.
Declaration of Independence for Syria and Lebanon.
"Nationalist Pact" in Lebanon.
"Protocol of Alexandria" laying basis for Arab League.
Lord Moyne assassinated in Egypt by Stern Gang.

1944 Moroccan nationalists demand independence; Ahmad Belafrej arrested.
France allots 15 seats in the National Assembly for Algerian Arabs.

1945 Arab League created (March 22).
Uprisings against the French in Algeria and in Syria-Lebanon.
Anglo-American Committee of Inquiry formed to investigate future of Palestine.

1946 British propose creation of Greater Somalia under British trusteeship. Somali Youth League grows.
British troops begin withdrawal from Cairo and Alexandria to the Canal Zone.
Transjordan becomes kingdom under Abdullah.

1947 Egypt severs relations with Britain.
Riots in Tunisia.
Maghreb Office opened in Cairo to coordinate nationalistic movement in Arab North Africa.
Violence erupts in Palestine. United Nations Partition Plan for Palestine passed, November 27.

1948 Massacre of villagers of Deir Yassin in Palestine by the terrorist organization of the Irgun, April 10.
Zionist forces seize Haifa, April 22.
Imam Yahya of Yemen killed; Imam Ahmad succeeds him.
The establishment of the State of Israel declared, May 14.
Open Warfare between Arabs and Israelis.
Count Bernadotte, Palestine Mediator, assassinated by Stern Gang.

1949 Armistice between Israel and Egypt, Lebanon, Jordan, Syria.
Coup d'etat in Syria (Mar. 30, Aug. 14 and Dec. 20).

1950 Ben Bella, leader of OS (Organisation Secrète) in Algeria.
Jordan annexes the West Bank of Palestine.
Egyptians wage guerilla warfare against British in Suez.
Independence of Kingdom of Libya under King Idris I.

1951 King Abdullah of Jordan assassinated in Jerusalem, July 20.

1952 Tunisian uprisings in Bizerte and Ferryville. Bourguiba arrested, January 17-18.
Uprisings in Cairo, January 26.
Coup d'etat in Egypt, July 23. Farouk abdicates, July 26.
Sultan of Morocco demands restoration of sovereignty.
Riots in Casablanca, December 8.
Land Reform Act promulgated in Egypt.

1953 Egypt proclaimed republic; Ahmad Naguib, president, June 18.
Uprising in Morocco; French deport Sultan, August 20.
Israeli raid on Jordan, Qibya attacked, October 14.
King Ibn Saud dies, his son Saud proclaimed king, November 30.

1954 First all-Sudanese government, January 9, Sudanese parliament opens, March 1.
Nasser assumes power in Egypt, April 18. Anglo-Egyptian agreement on Suez Canal, July 27.
Internal autonomy for Tunisia, July 31.
United States establishes air bases in Libya.
Algerian revolt against French begins, November 1.

1955 Baghdad Pact formed, February 24.
Israeli raid on Gaza, February 28.
Sultan Muhammad V of Morocco restored to the throne, November 18.

1956 General Glubb dismissed by King Hussein of Jordan, February 29.
Sudan proclaimed independent republic, January 1.
Morocco's independence, March 3.
Tunisian independence, March 20.
Nasser President, June 3; British evacuate Suez Canal, June 18; America withdraws offer to finance High Dam, July 19; Suez Canal nationalized, August 12; Israel, France and England attack Egypt, October 29-31; cease fire, November 7.

1957 Suez Canal reopened, April 9.
Bey of Tunis deposed, Tunisia declared republic, Bourguiba president, July 25.
Sultan of Morocco adopts title of king, August 14.

1958 United Arab Republic (Egypt and Syria) proclaimed, March 5.
State of emergency declared in Aden, May 2.
Civil war in Lebanon, May; U.S. marines in Lebanon, July 15.
Coup in Iraq led by Qasim topples monarchy, July 14.
Faysal ibn Saud assumes power in Saudi Arabia, April.
Provisional Algerian government in exile in Cairo, September 16.
General Ibrahim Abboud leads coup in Sudan, November 17.

1959 Federation of Arab Emirates of the South inaugurated, February 11.
Somali Republic proclaimed, July 1.
Mauritania independent, November 27.
Meeting in Baghdad sets up OPEC (Organization of Oil Exporting Countries), September 10-24.

1961 Referendum in Algeria and France on Algerian independence, January.
Muhammad V of Morocco dies, Hassan II succeeds, February 26.
French military revolt in Algeria, April 26.
Kuwait declared independent, June 19.
Syria withdraws from the United Arab Republic, September 28.

1962 Algerian revolution ends, Algeria declared independent, July 3.
Muhammad al-Badr becomes Imam of Yemen, September 19. Beginning of Yemeni Civil War, Egyptian troops in Yemen, September.

1963 Colony of Aden joins Federation of South Arabia, January 18.
Coup in Iraq led by Col. Aref, February 8.
Coup in Syria led by Baath Party, March 8.

1964 Crown Prince Faysal assumes full power in Saudi Arabia, March 28, becomes king, November 2.

1965 Houari Boumedienne assumes power in Algeria, June 19.

1967 June War between Israel, Egypt, Syria, Jordan, June 5-10.
Israel annexes East Jerusalem, July 28.
President Sallal of Yemen deposed, November 5.
People's Democratic Republic of Yemen proclaimed, November 26. British troops leave Aden, November 30.
United Nations Resolution 242, November 22.

1968 Israeli attack on Karamah in Jordan, Palestinian organized guerillas and Jordanian troops resist, March 2.
General Hassan al-Bakr in power in Iraq, July 17.
General Hafiz al-Assad assumes power in Syria, October 26.
Israeli raid on Beirut airport, December 28.

1969 Yasser Arafat becomes head of the Palestine Liberation Organization (PLO), February 3.
War of attrition along the Suez Canal between Egypt and Israel, March to August, 1970.
Col. Ja'far al-Nimeiri seizes power in Sudan, May 25.
Mu'ammar al-Qadhdhafi leads coup in Libya, September 1; foreign military bases closed.
Cairo agreement between Lebanon and Palestinians, November.

1970 Aswan High Dam completed, July 21.
Qabus ibn Sa'id seizes power in Oman from his father, July 26.
Hijacking of airliners by Palestinian guerillas in Jordan, September 6. Fighting between Jordanian troops and Palestinian guerillas, September.
President Nasser dies; Anwar al-Sadat becomes president of Egypt, September 28.

1971 Sadat suspends Egyptian-Israeli cease-fire agreement, March 7.
Soviet-Egyptian Friendship treaty, May 27.
Coup d'etat in Sudan against Nimeiri fails, July 19-22.

1972 Israeli raids into southern Lebanon, February.
Soviet-Iraqi treaty of Friendship, April 9.
President Sadat orders Soviet advisors out of Egypt, July 18.
OPEC decides on 51% control in oil companies, October 5.

1973 Israel shoots down Libyan airliner over Sinai, February 21.
Air battle between Syria and Israel, September 13.
Egypt and Syria attack Israeli forces on occupied territories, October 6—beginning of the October War; Egyptian troops cross the Suez Canal.
United States begins airlift of arms to Israel, October 14.
OAPEC (Organization of Arab Petroleum Exporting Countries) announces embargo on oil shipment to the United States, November 5.
United Nations passes Resolution 338 to stop Arab-Israeli war, October 22. Kissinger begins shuttle diplomacy, November 6.
Cease-fire signed between Egypt and Israel, November 11.

1974 Disengagement agreement between Egypt and Israel, January 18.
War of attrition between Syria and Israel, March.
Unrest in Kurdish areas in Iraq, March.
Arab oil embargo against the United States lifted, March 18.
Disengagement agreement between Syria and Israel, May 25.
Arab League meeting at Rabat recognizes PLO as sole representative of the Palestinian people, October 28.
Yasser Arafat speaks before the UN General Assembly, November 13.

1975 Collapse of Kissinger's shuttle diplomacy, March 22.
King Faysal of Saudi Arabia assassinated, March 25.
Beginning of trouble leading to civil war in Lebanon, April 13.
Suez Canal reopens after eight years, June 5.
Interim agreement between Egypt and Israel, September 1.
United Nations General Assembly declares "Zionism a form of racism," November 10.

1976 Egypt terminates 1971 Soviet-Egyptian treaty, March 14.
Tall al-Za'tar Palestinian Refugee Camp falls after 54 days siege, August 12.
Elias Sarkis becomes president of Lebanon, September 23.
Cease-fire in Lebanese Civil War, October 21.

1977 Libya announces a new official name and administration.
The Palestine National Council, meeting in Cairo, adopts a 15-point political declaration.
Islamic Foreign Ministers Conference held in Libya, May.
Lebanese civil war takes a new form of fighting in the South.
President Sadat goes to Jerusalem to talk peace with Israeli premier, November.

THE ARAB LEAGUE

The League of Arab States is a voluntary association of sovereign Arab states designed to strengthen the close ties linking them and to coordinate their policies and activities and direct them towards the common good of all the Arab countries. It was founded in March 1945.

MEMBERS

Algeria	Lebanon	Palestine	Syria
Bahrain	Libya	Qatar	Tunisia
Djibouti	Mauritania	Saudi Arabia	United Arab Emirates
Egypt	Morocco	Somalia	Yemen Arab Republic
Iraq	Oman	Sudan	Yemen, People's Democratic Republic
Jordan			
Kuwait			

MEMBERSHIP AND FUNCTIONS

While it is a prerequisite that members must be Arab states that are fully independent, the activities of the League also often include Arab countries which are not independent. Palestine is considered an independent state, as explained in the Charter Annex on Palestine, and therefore a full member of the League.

The status of Palestine as a full member of the League was confirmed at a meeting of the Arab League Council in September 1976.

The Arab League itself is an international body with its own independent statutory powers and general objectives.

ORGANIZATION

COUNCIL

The supreme organ of the Arab League. Meets in March and September. Consists of representatives of the twenty member states, each of which has one vote, and a representative for Palestine. Unanimous decisions of the Council shall be binding upon all member states of the League; majority decisions shall be binding only on those states which have accepted them.

The Council may, if necessary, hold an extraordinary session at the request of two member states. Invitations to all sessions are extended by the Secretary-General. The ordinary sessions are presided over by representatives of the member states in turn.

Sixteen committees are attached to the Council:

Political Committee: studies political questions and reports to the Council meetings concerned with them. All member states are members of the Committee. It represents the Council in dealing with critical political matters when the Council is meeting. Usually composed of the Foreign Minister.

Cultural Committee: in charge of following up the activities of the Cultural Department and the cultural affairs within the scope of the secretariat; coordinates the activities of the general secretariat and the various cultural bodies in member states.

Economic Committee: complemented by the Economic Council since 1953.

Communications Committee: supervises land, sea and air communications, together with weather forecasts and postal matters.

Social Committee: supports cooperation in such matters as family and child welfare.

Legal Committee: an extension of the Nationality and Passports Committee abolished in 1947; studies and legally formulates draft agreements, bills, regulations and official documents.

Arab Oil Experts Committee: for study of oil affairs; also investigates methods to prevent the smuggling of Arab oil into Israel; and for coordination of oil policies in general.

Information Committee: studies information projects, suggests plans and carries out the policies decided by the Council of Information Ministers.

Health Committee: for cooperation in health affairs.

Human Rights Committee: studies subjects concerning human rights, particularly violations by Israel; collaborates with the Information and Cultural Committees.

Permanent Committee for Administrative and Financial Affairs.

Permanent Committee for Meteorology.

Committee of Arab Experts on Cooperation.

Arab Women's Committee.

Organization of Youth Welfare.

Conference of Liaison Officers: coordinates trade activities among commercial attaches of various Arab embassies abroad.

GENERAL SECRETARIAT

The administrative and financial offices of the League. The Secretariat carries out the decisions of the Council, and provides financial and administrative services for the personnel of the League. There are a number of departments: economic, political, legal, cultural, social and labour affairs, petroleum, finance, Palestine, health, information, communications, protocol. The most recently formed department deals with African affairs.

The Secretary-General is appointed by the League Council by a two-thirds majority of the member states. He appoints the Assistant Secretaries and principal officials, with the approval of the Council. He has the rank of Ambassador, and the Assistant Secretaries have the rank of Ministers Plenipotentiary.

DEFENCE AND ECONOMIC COOPERATION

Groups established under the Treaty of Joint Defence and Economic Cooperation, concluded in 1950 to complement the Charter of the League:

Arab Unified Military Command: Cairo; f. 1964 to coordinate military policies for the liberation of Palestine.

Arab Economic Council: to compare and coordinate the economic policies of the member states; the Council is composed of Ministers of Economic Affairs or their deputies. Decisions are taken by majority vote. The first meeting was held in 1953.

Joint Defense Council: supervises implementation of those aspects of the treaty concerned with common defense. Composed of Foreign and Defense Ministers; decisions by a two-thirds majority vote of members are binding on all.

Military Advisory Organization.

Permanent Military Commission: Established 1950; composed of representatives of army General Staffs; main purpose: to draw up plans of joint defense for submission to the Joint Defense Council.

OTHER INSTITUTIONS OF THE COUNCIL

Other bodies established by resolutions adopted by the Council of the League:

Academy of Arab Music.

Administrative Tribunal of the Arab League: Cairo; f. 1964; began operations 1966.

Arab Authority for Exhibitions: f. 1964 to coordinate the planning and holding of international exhibitions and fairs in the member states of the League; has a Council of representatives appointed by the member states.

Arab Centre for Industrial Development: created in 1968 in compliance with a decision of the League Economic Council; the Arab states are represented at the Centre by an official representative and an alternate; the secretariat includes departments for technical and economic studies and aid for the promotion of industrial information; began operations in 1970.

Arab Institute of Forestry: Latakia, Syria.

SPECIALIZED AGENCIES

All member states of the Arab League are also members of the Specialized Agencies, which constitute an integral part of the Arab League.

Arab Centre for the Study of Dry Regions and Arid Territories: Damascus, Syria.

Arab League Educational, Cultural and Scientific Organization (ALECSO); Cairo, Egypt; f. 1964; aims: to promote intellectual unity of the Arab countries by means of education; to raise cultural standards; to enable the Arab countries to participate in technical development; to establish specialized institutes; to train experts for research in Arab civilization. Each member submits an annual report on progress in education, cultural matters and science. The Arab League has a Permanent Delegation at UNESCO which may act on behalf of Arab states that are not members of the world body.

There are five institutions within the framework of the Arab League Educational, Cultural and Scientific Organization:

> *Institute for Arab Studies and Research Work:* f. 1953 for specialization by graduates of Arab universities; provides for studies in contemporary Arab affairs, including national and international affairs, economics, social studies, history, geography, law, literature and linguistics. A special department of the Institute is devoted to Palestinian affairs, to research into the Arab cause; the Institute aims to develop the understanding of Arab nationalism.

Arab Literacy and Adult Education Organization: f. 1966 to assist in the establishment and development of national institutions for literacy and adult education; to assist in formulation of national plans in these respects; to hold regional training courses, seminars and conferences; to coordinate research work; to grant scholarships and provide technical assistance; and to provide information.

Institute of Arab Manuscripts.

Permanent Bureau for Arabization: Rabat, Morocco.

Museum of Arab Culture: Cairo, Egypt.

Arab Health Organization.

Arab Institute of Petroleum Research.

Arab Labor Organization: established in 1965 for cooperation between member states in labor problems; unification of labor legislation and general conditions of work wherever possible; research; technical assistance; social insurance; training, etc.; the organization has a tripartite structure: governments, employers and workers. Publs. *Bulletin* (monthly), *Arab Labour Review* (quarterly).

Arab Organization for Administrative Science: set up with the approval of the League Council in 1961, commencing activity in 1969 soon after ratification of the agreement by four Arab states (Egypt, Iraq, Syria, Kuwait); to ensure co-operation in promoting administrative science, to improve the standard of administrative staff in the Arab states. Publ. Research series in administrative science.

Arab Organization for Agricultural Development: Khartoum, Sudan; proposed in 1969 by a decision of Arab Ministers of Agriculture, which was approved by the Economic Council in 1970 and ratified by the League Council; to contribute to cooperation in agricultural activities, and in the development of natural and human resources for agriculture.

Arab Organization for Standardization and Metrology: Cairo, Egypt; created 1965 after the Economic Council had approved an agreement for its creation by twenty Arab states as a specialized institution in the field of economic, commercial and industrial cooperation; began activity in 1968 to unify technical terms and standard specifications for products such as food, cloth, fertilizers, building materials, oil, minerals, electrical products; also deals with technical drawing and packaging; assists in the establishment of national bodies and collaborates with international standards activities. Publs. *Annual Report* (French and English), *Quarterly Bulletin* (Arabic and English), *Standard Specification* (Arabic, English and French) and information pamphlets.

Arab Postal Union: Cairo, Egypt; f. 1954; aims: to establish more strict postal relations between the Arab countries than those laid down by the Universal Postal Union, to pursue the development and modernization of postal services in member countries; Publs. *Bulletin* (monthly), *Review* (quarterly), *News* (annual) and occasional studies.

Arab States Broadcasting Union: Cairo; f. 1969 to promote Arab fraternity, to acquaint the world with the Arab nation, coordinate and study broadcasting subjects, to exchange expertise and technical cooperation in broadcasting. Mems.: 21 Arab radio and TV stations and four foreign associates. Publs. *Arab Broadcasts* (monthly, in Arabic), *ASBU Review* (quarterly, in English), *Broadcasting Studies and Researches* (irregular); *Broadcasting Reports* (irregular).

Arab Telecommunications Union: Cairo, Egypt; f. 1958; to coordinate and develop telecommunications between member countries; to exchange technical aid and encourage research. Publs. *Economic and Technical Studies; Arab Telecommunications Union Journal* (quarterly).

Civil Aviation Council of Arab States: Egypt; created 1965, began operations 1967; aims: to develop the principles, techniques and economics of air transport in the Arab World; to cooperate with the International Civil Aviation Organization and to attempt to standardize laws and technical terms; deals also with Arab air rates; Publs. *Air Transport Activities in Arab Countries, Lexicon of Civil Aviation Terminology* (Arabic); *Unified Air Law for Arab States* (Arabic and English).

International Arab Organization for Social Defense against Crime: f. 1965 at League Headquarters by the League Council to study causes and remedies for crime and the treatment of criminals; the organization consists of three bureaus:

International Arab Bureau for Narcotics: Cairo;

International Arab Bureau for Prevention of Crime: Baghdad;

International Arab Bureau of Criminal Policy: Damascus.

Joint Arab Scientific Council for the Utilization of Atomic Energy.

PUBLICATIONS

Information Department: *Information Bulletin* (Arabic and English); also bulletins of treaties and agreements concluded among the member states.

New York Office: *Arab World* (monthly), and *News and Views.*

Geneva Office: *Le Monde Arabe* (monthly), and *Nouvelles du Monde Arabe* (weekly).

Buenos Aires Office: *Arabia Review* (monthly).

Paris Office: *Actualites Arabes* (fortnightly).

Brasilia Office: *Oriente Arabe* (monthly).

Rome Office: *Rassegna del Mondo Arabo* (monthly).

London Office: *The Arab* (monthly).

New Delhi Office: *Al Arab* (monthly).

Bonn Office: *Arabische Korrespondenz* (fortnightly).

Ottawa Office: *Spotlight on the Arab World* (fortnightly), *The Arab Case* (monthly).

THE ARAB LEAGUE

THE PACT OF THE LEAGUE OF ARAB STATES

(March 22nd, 1945)

Article 1

The League of Arab States is composed of the independent Arab States which have signed this Pact.

Any independent Arab state has the right to become a member of the League. If it desires to do so, it shall submit a request which will be deposited with the Permanent Secretariat-General and submitted to the Council at the first meeting held after submission of the request.

Article 2

The League has as its purpose the strengthening of the relations between the member states; the coordination of their policies in order to achieve cooperation between them and to safeguard their independence and sovereignty; and a general concern with the affairs and interests of the Arab countries. It has also as its purpose the close cooperation of the member states, with due regard to the organization and circumstances of each state, on the following matters:

(*a* Economic and financial affairs, including commercial relations, customs, currency, and questions of agriculture and industry.

(b) Communications: this includes railways, roads, aviation, navigation, telegraphs and posts.

(c) Cultural affairs.

(d) Nationality, passports, visas, execution of judgments, and extradition of criminals.

(e) Social affairs.

(f) Health problems.

Article 3

The League shall possess a Council composed of the representatives of the member states of the League; each state shall have a single vote, irrespective of the number of its representatives.

It shall be the task of the Council to achieve the realization of the objectives of the League and to supervise the execution of agreements which the member states have concluded on the questions enumerated in the preceding article, or on any other questions.

It likewise shall be the Council's task to decide upon the means by which the League is to cooperate with the international bodies to be created in the future in order to guarantee security and peace and regulate economic and social relations.

Article 4

For each of the questions listed in Article 2 there shall be set up a special committee in which the member states of the League shall be represented. These committees shall be charged with the task of laying down the principles and extent of cooperation. Such principles shall be formulated as draft agreements, to be presented to the Council for examination preparatory to their submission to the aforesaid states.

Representatives of the other Arab countries may take part in the work of the aforesaid committees. The Council shall determine the conditions under which these representatives may be permitted to participate and the rules governing such representation.

Article 5

Any resort to force in order to resolve disputes arising between two or more member states of the League is prohibited. If there should arise among them a difference which does not concern a state's independence, sovereignty, or territorial integrity, and if the parties to the dispute have recourse to the Council for the settlement of this difference, the decision of the Council shall then be enforceable and obligatory.

In such a case, the states between whom the difference has arisen shall not participate in the deliberations and decisions of the Council.

The Council shall mediate in all differences which threaten to lead to war between two member states, or a member state and a third state, with a view to bringing about their reconciliation.

Decisions of arbitration and mediation shall be taken by majority vote.

Article 6

In case of aggression or threat of aggression by one state against a member state, the state which has been attacked or threatened with aggression may demand the immediate convocation of the Council.

The Council shall by unanimous decision determine the measures necessary to repulse the aggression. If the aggressor is a member state, his vote shall not be counted in determining unamimity.

If, as a result of the attack, the government of the State attacked finds itself unable to communicate with the Council, that state's representative in the Council shall have the right to request the convocation of the Council for the purpose indicated in the foregoing paragraph. In the event that this representative is unable to communicate with the Council, any member state of the League shall have the right to request the convocation of the Council.

Article 7

Unanimous decisions of the Council shall be binding upon all member states of the League; majority decisions shall be binding only upon those states which have accepted them.

In either case the decision of the Council shall be enforced in each member state according to its respective basic laws.

Article 8

Each member state shall respect the systems of government established in the other member states and regard them as exclusive concerns of those states. Each shall pledge to abstain from any action calculated to change established systems of government.

Article 9

States of the League which desire to establish closer cooperation and stronger bonds than are provided by this Pact may conclude agreements to that end.

Treaties and agreements already concluded or to be concluded in the future between a member state and another state shall not be binding or restrictive upon other members.

Article 10

The permanent seat of the League of Arab States is established in Cairo. The Council may, however, assemble at any other place it may designate.

Article 11

The Council of the League shall convene in ordinary session twice a year, in March and in September. It shall convene in extraordinary session upon the request of two member states of the League whenever the need arises.

Article 12

The League shall have a permanent Secretariat-General which shall consist of a Secretary-General, Assistant Secretaries, and an appropriate number of officials.

The Council of the League shall appoint the Secretary-General by a majority of two-thirds of the states of the League. The Secretary-General, with the approval of the Council, shall appoint the Assistant Secretaries and the principal officials of the League.

The Council of the League shall establish an administrative regulation for the functions of the Secretariat-General and matters relating to the Staff.

The Secretary-General shall have the rank of Ambassador and the Assistant Secretaries that of Ministers Plenipotentiary.

The first Secretary-General of the League is named in an Annex to this Pact.

Article 13

The Secretary-General shall prepare the draft of the budget of the League and shall submit it to the Council for approval before the beginning of each fiscal year.

The Council shall fix the share of the expenses to be borne by each state of the League. This share may be reconsidered if necessary.

Article 14

The members of the Council of the League as well as the members of the committees and the officials who are to be designated in the administrative regulation shall enjoy diplomatic privileges and immunity when engaged in the exercise of their functions.

The building occupied by the organs of the League shall be inviolable.

Article 15

The first meeting of the Council shall be convened at the invitation of the head of the Egyptian Government. Thereafter it shall be convened at the invitation of the Secretary-General.

The representatives of the member states of the League shall alternately assume the presidency of the Council at each of its ordinary sessions.

Article 16

Except in cases specifically indicated in this Pact, a majority vote of the Council shall be sufficient to make enforceable decisions on the following matters:

(a) Matters relating to personnel.
(b) Adoption of the budget of the League.
(c) Establishment of the administrative regulations for the Council, the Committees, and the Secretariat-General.
(d) Decisions to adjourn the sessions.

Article 17

Each member state of the League shall deposit with the Secretariat-General one copy of every treaty or agreement concluded or to be concluded in the future between itself and another member state of the League or a third state.

Article 18

(deals with withdrawal)

Article 19

(deals with amendment)

Article 20

(deals with ratification)

Annex Regarding Palestine

Since the termination of the last great war the rule of the Ottoman Empire over the Arab countries, among them Palestine, which had become detached from that Empire, has come to an end. She has come to be autonomous, not subordinate to any other state.

The Treaty of Lausanne proclaimed that her future was to be settled by the parties concerned.

However, even though she was as yet unable to control her own affairs, the Covenant of the League (of Nations) in 1919 made provision for a regime based upon recognition of her independence.

Her international existence and independence in the legal sense cannot, therefore, be questioned, any more than could the independence of the other Arab countries.

Although the outward manifestations of this independence have remained obscured for reasons beyond her control, this should not be allowed to interfere with her participation in the work of the Council of the League.

The states signatory to the Pact of the Arab League are therefore of the opinion that, considering the special circumstances of Palestine and until that Country can effectively exercise its independence, the Council of the League should take charge of the selection of an Arab representative from Palestine to take part in its work.

Annex Regarding Cooperation with Countries which are not Members of the Council of the League

Whereas the member states of the League will have to deal in the Council as well as in the committees with matters which will benefit and affect the Arab world at large;

And whereas the Council has to take into account the aspirations of the Arab countries which are not members of the Council and has to work toward their realization;

Now therefore, it particularly behoves the states signatory to the Pact of the Arab League to enjoin the Council of the League, when considering the admission of those countries to participation in the committees referred to in the Pact, that it should do its utmost to cooperate with them, and furthermore, that it should spare no effort to learn their needs and understand their aspirations and hopes; and that it should work thenceforth for their best interests and the safeguarding of their future with all the political means at its disposal.

SUGGESTED READINGS

PERIODICAL PUBLICATIONS

Adams, Michael, *The Middle East: A Handbook.* London; Blond, 1971.
Aramco World Magazine. New York: The Arabian American Oil Company. Monthly.
International Documents on Palestine. Beirut: Institute for Palestine Studies, and Kuwayt: The University of Kuwayt. Annual.
International Journal of Middle East Studies. New York: Middle East Studies Association of North America. Quarterly.
Journal of Palestine Studies. Washington, D.C., and Beirut: Institute for Palestine Studies and Kuwait University. Quarterly.
MERIP Reports. Washington, D.C.: Middle East Research & Information Project. Monthly.
The Middle East. London: International Communications. Monthly.
The Middle East and North Africa. London: Europa Publications. Annual.
Middle East Annual Review. Essex, England: The Middle East Review Co., Ltd., and New York: Rand McNally & Co. Annual.
Middle East International. London: Middle East International, Ltd. Monthly.
Middle East Journal. Washington, D.C.: Middle East Institute. Quarterly.
The Middle East Yearbook. Prepared by the Centre for Middle Eastern and Islamic Studies, University of Durham, England. London: The Middle East Magainze Ltd.
Muslim World. Hartford, Connecticut: Hartford Seminary Foundation. Quarterly.
Palestine Digest. Washington, D.C.: League of Arab States. Monthly.
Statistical Yearbook for Arab Countries. Cairo: Majlis al-Wahdah al-Iqtisadiyah al-Arabiyah.
U.S.-Arab Commerce. New York: U.S.-Arab Chamber of Commerce, Inc. Monthly.

THE ARAB WORLD—GENERAL

Abu-Loghod, Ibrahim. *Arab Rediscovery of Europe; A Study in Cultural Encounters.* Princeton, New Jersey: Princeton University Press, 1963.
Al-Qazzaz, Ayad. *The Arab World: A Handbook for Teachers.* Albany, California: NAJDA (Women Concerned About the Middle East), 1978.
Al-Qazzaz, Ayad. *Women in the Middle East and North Africa: An Annotated Bibliography.* Austin, Texas: University of Texas Press, 1977.
Antonius, George. *The Arab Awakening: The Story of the Arab National Movement.* Beirut: J. B. Lippincott Co., 1939.
Arberry, Arthur John. *Aspects of Islamic Civilization, as Depicted in the Original Texts.* Ann Arbor: University of Michigan Press, 1967.
Blunt, Wilfrid. *The Splendors of Islam.* New York: Viking Press, 1976.
Boullata, Issa J. *Modern Arab Poets, 1950-1975.* Washington, D.C.: Three Continents Press, 1976.
Boullata, Kamal, ed. *Women of the Fertile Crescent: An Anthology of Arab Women's Poems.* Washington, D.C.: Three Continents Press, 1978.
Bulliet, Richard W. *The Camel and the Wheel.* Cambridge, Massachusetts: Harvard University Press, 1975.
Cattan, Henry. *The Evolution of Oil Concessions in the Middle East and North Africa.* Dobbs Ferry, New York: Oceana, 1967.
Clark, J. I., and W. B. Fisher, eds. *Populations of the Middle East and North Africa: A Geographical Approach.* New York: Africana Publishing Company, 1972.
Cook, M.A. *Studies in the Economic History of the Middle East, from the Rise of Islam to the Present Day.* London and New York: Oxford University Press, 1970.
Cooper, Charles A., and Sidney S. Alexander, eds. *Economic Development and Population Growth in the Middle East. New York: American Elsevier Publishing Company, 1972.*
El-Mallakh, Ragaei, Barry Warren Poulson, and Mihssen Khadim. *Capital Investment in the Middle East: The Use of Surplus Funds for Regional Development.*New York: Praeger, 1977.
Fernea, Elizabeth Warnock, and Basima Qattan Bezirgan. *Middle Eastern Muslim Women Speak.* Austin: University of Texas Press, 1977.
Fisher, Sydney Nettleton. *The Middle East: A History.* New York: Alfred A. Knopf, 1971.
Gibb, Hamilton Alexander Rosskeen. *Mohammedanism; An Historical Survey.* 2nd ed. London and New York: Oxford University Press, 1954.
Gibb, Hamilton Alexander Rosskeen, and J. H. Kramers. *Shorter Encyclopaedia of Islam.* Ithaca, New York: Cornell University Press, 1965.
Gulick, John. *The Middle East: An Anthropological Perspective.* Pacific Palisades, California: Goodyear Publishing Company, 1976.
Hassouna, Hussein A. *The League of Arab States and Regional Disputes: A Study of Middle East Conflicts.* Dobbs Ferry, New York: Oceana Publications, and Leiden: A. Sijthoff, 1975.
Hitti, Philip Khuri. *The History of the Arabs from the Earliest Times to the Present.* 10th ed. London: Macmillan, and New York: St. Martin's Press, 1970.
Hourani, Albert, *Arabic Thought in the Liberal Age.* London: Oxford University Press, 1962.
Hudson, Michael C. *Arab Politics: The Search for Legitimacy.* New Haven: Yale University Press, 1977.
Karagolan, Aida. *A Gourmet's Delight: Selected Recipes from the Haute Cuisine of the Arab World.* Delmar, New York: Caravan Books, 1977.
Kazimi, Mujid S., and John I. Makhoul. *Perspectives on Technological Development in the Arab World.* Detroit: Association of Arab-American University Graduates, 1977.
Khadduri, Majid. *Political Trends in the Arab World: The Role of Ideas and Ideals in Politics.* Baltimore: Johns Hopkins University Press, 1970.

Littlefield, David W. *The Islamic Near East and North Africa: An Annotated Guide to Books in English for Non-Specialists.* Littleton, Colorado: Libraries Unlimited, Inc., 1977.

Mansfield, Peter. *The Arabs.* London: Allen Lane, 1976.

Mansfield, Peter, ed. *The Middle East: A Political and Economic Survey.* 4th ed. London and New York: Oxford University Press, 1973.

Nuseibeh, Hazem Zaki. *The Ideas of Arab Nationalism.* Ithaca: Cornell University Press, 1956.

Nutting, Anthony. *The Arabs: A Narrative History from Mohammed to the Present.* New York: Clarkson N. Potter, 1964.

Ostle, R. C., ed., and others. *Studies in Modern Arabic Literature.* Warminster, England: Aris and Phillips, Ltd., 1975.

Schacht, Joseph, and C. E. Bosworth, eds. *The Legacy of Islam.* Oxford: Clarendon Press, 1974.

Schulz, Ann. *International and Regional Politics in the Middle East and North Africa: A Guide to Information Sources.* Detroit: Gale Research Company, 1977.

Selim, George Dimitri, ed. *American Doctoral Dissertations on the Arab World, 1883-1974.* Washington, D.C.: Library of Congress, 1976.

Sweet, Louise Elizabeth. *Peoples and Cultures of the Middle East.* Garden City: The Natural History Press, 1970.

Tibawi, Abdul Latif. *Arabic and Islamic Themes: Historical, Educational and Literary Studies.* London: Luzac and Company, 1976.

Tuma, Elias H., ed. *Food and Population in the Middle East.* Washington, D.C.: Institute of Middle Eastern and North African Affairs, 1976.

Wilson, Rodney. *Trade and Investment in the Middle East.* New York: Holmes and Meier Publishers, Inc., 1977.

NORTHWEST AFRICA

Amin, Samir. *The Maghreb in the Modern World: Algeria, Tunisia, Morocco.* Harmondsworth, England: Penguin, 1970.

Gallagher, Charles, *The United States and North Africa; Morocco, Algeria and Tunisia.* Cambridge, Mass.: Harvard University Press, 1963.

Hill, Derek, *Islamic Architecture in North Africa: A Photographic Survey.* Hamden, Connecticut: Archon Books, 1976.

Knapp, Wilfrid, ed. *North West Africa: A Political and Economic Survey.* 3d ed. Oxford, New York: Oxford University Press, 1977.

Moore, Clement H., *Politics in North Africa: Algeria, Morocco, Tunisia.* Boston: Little, Brown, 1970.

Zartman, I. William, ed. *Man, State, and Society in the Contemporary Maghrib.* New York: Praeger, 1973.

Algeria

Lawless, Richard I. *Algerian Bibliography: English Language Publications, 1830-1973.* London: Bowker, in association with the Centre for Middle Eastern and Islamic Studies of the University of Durham, 1976.

Lazreq, Marnia. *The Emergence of Classes in Algeria: A Study of Colonialism and Socio-Political Change.* Boulder, Colorado: Westview Press, 1976.

Nyrop, Richard F., and others. *Area Handbook for Algeria.* Prepared for the United States Department of the Army by Foreign Area Studies, The American University. Washington, D.C.: U.S. Government Printing Office, 1972.

Ottaway, David and Marina. *Algeria; The Politics of a Socialist Revolution.* Berkeley: University of California Press, 1970.

Quandt, William B. *Revolution and Political Leadership: Algeria, 1954-1968.*Cambridge, Massachusetts: M.I.T. Press, 1969.

Libya

Allan, J. A., K. S. McLachlan, and Edith T. Penrose, eds. *Libya: Agriculture and Economic Development.* London: Cass, 1973.

Ansell, Meredith O., and Ibrahim Massaud Al-Arif. *Libyan Revolution: A Sourcebook of Legal and Historical Documents.* London: The Oleander Press, 1972.

Farley, Rawle. *Planning for Development in Libya: The Exceptional Economy in the Developing World.* New York: Praeger, 1971.

Gadallah, Fawzi, ed. *Libya in History.* Tripoli: The University of Libya, Faculty of Arts, 1968.

Johnson, Douglas L. *Jabal al-Akhdar, Cyranaica: An Historical Geography of Settlement and Livelihood.* Chicago: The University of Chicago, Department of Geography, Research Paper No. 148, 1973

Nyrop, Richard F., and others. *Area Handbook for Libya.* Prepared for the United States Department of the Army by Foreign Area Studies, The American University. Washington, D.C.: U.S. Government Printing Office, 1973.

Mauritania

Curran, Brian Dean, and Joann Schrock. *Area Handbook for Mauritania.* Prepared for the United States Department of the Army by Foreign Area Studies, The American University. Washington, D.C.: U.S. Government Printing Office, 1972.

Gerteiny, Alfred G. *Mauritania.* New York: Praeger, 1967.

Westebbe, Richard M. *The Economy of Mauritania.* New York: Praeger, 1971.

Morocco

Barbour, Nevill. *Morocco.* New York: Walker, 1965

Brown, Kenneth L. *People of Sale: Tradition and Change in a Moroccan City, 1830-1930.* Cambridge: Harvard University Press, 1976.

Dunn, Ross E. *Resistance in the Desert: Moroccan Responses to French Imperialism, 1881-1912.* London: Croom Helm, and Madison, Wisconsin: University of Wisconsin Press, 1977.

Hall, Luella J. *The United States and Morocco, 1776-1956.* Metuchen, New Jersey: Scarecrow Press, 1971.

Kininmonth, Christopher. *The Travellers' Guide to Morocco.* London: Cape, 1972.

Nyrop, Richard F., and others. *Area Handbook for Morocco.* Prepared for the United States Department of the Army by Foreign Area Studies, The American University. Washington, D.C.: U.S. Government Printing Office, 1972.

Tunisia

Reese, Howard C., and others. *Area Handbook for the Republic of Tunisia.* Prepared for the United States Department of the Army by Foreign Area Studies, The American University. Washington, D.C.: U.S. Government Printing Office, 1970.

Stone, Russell A., and John Simmons, eds. *Change in Tunisia: Studies in the Social Sciences.* Albany: State University of New York Press, 1976.

NORTHEAST AFRICA

Eygpt

Abu-Lughd, Janit. *Cairo: 1001 Years of the City Victorious.* Princeton: Princeton University Press, 1971.

Barbour, K. Michael. *The Growth, Location, and Structure of Industry in Egypt.* New York: Praeger, 1972.

Berque, Jacques. *Egypt: Imperialism and Revolution.* New York: Praeger, 1972.

Dawisha, A.I. *Egypt in the Arab World.* New York: John Wiley, 1976.

Fedden, Henry Romilly. *Egypt: Land of the Valley.* London: J. Murray, 1977.

Harris, J. R., ed. *The Legacy of Egypt.* 2d ed. Oxford: Clarendon Press, 1971.

Haykal, Muhammad Hasanayn. *The Road to Ramadan.* New York: Quadrangle, 1975.

Hurst, Harold Edwin. *The Nile; A General Account of the River and the Utilization of its Waters.* London: Constable, 1957.

Issawi, Charles Philip. *Egypt in Revolution: An Economic Analysis.* London: Oxford University Press, 1963.

Lacouture, Jean. *Nasser: A Biography.* New York: Alfred A. Knopf, 1973.

Little, Tom. *Modern Egypt.* New York: Praeger, 1967

Kinross, Lord. *Between Two Seas: The Creation of the Suez Canal.* New York: Morrow, 1968.

Mabro, Robert. *The Egyptian Economy, 1952-1972.* Oxford: Clarendon Press, 1974.

Mabro, Robert, and Samir Radwan. *The Industrialization of Egypt 1939-1973.* London: Oxford University Press, 1976.

Mansfield, Peter. *The British in Egypt.* New York: Holt, Rinehart, and Winston, 1971.

Mansfield, Peter. *Nasser's Egypt.* Baltimore: Penguin Books, 1965.

Nyrop, Richard F., and others. *Area Handbook for Egypt.* Prepared for the United States Department of the Army by Foreign Area Studies, The American University. Washington, D.C.: U.S. Government Printing Office, 1976.

Radwan, Samir. *Capital Formation in Egyptian Industry and Agriculture, 1882-1967.* London: Ithaca Press for the Middle East Centre, St. Anthony's College, 1974.

Richmond, J. C. B. *Egypt 1798-1952.* New York: Columbia University Press, 1977.

Sayyid, Afaf Lutfi Al. *Egypt and Cromer: A Study in Anglo-Egyptian Relations.* New York: Praeger, 1968.

Waterbury, John. *Egypt: Burdens of the Past-Options for the Future.* Hanover, New Hampshire: American University Field Staff, 1977.

Somalia and Djibouti

Andrzejewski, B. W., and I. M. Lewis. *Somali Poetry: An Introduction.* Oxford: Clarendon Press, 1964.

Contini, Paolo. *Integration of Legal Systems in the Somali Republic.* Ibadan, Nigeria: Institute of African Studies, University of Ife, 1964.

Kaplan, Irving, and others. *Area Handbook for Somalia.* Prepared for the United States Department of the Army by Foreign Area Studies, The American University. Washington, D.C.: U.S. Government Printing Office, 1977.

Lewis, I. M. *A Pastoral Democracy; A Study of Pastoralism and Politics Among the Northern Somali of the Horn of Africa.* London: Oxford University Press, 1961.

Lewis, I. M. *The Modern History of Somaliland: From Nation to State.* New York: Praeger, 1965.

Lewis, I. M. *Peoples of the Horn of Africa: Somali, Afar and Saho.* London: International African Institute, 1969.

Salad, M. K. *Somalia: A Bibliographical Survey.* Westport: Greenwood, 1977.

Somali Government. *Somali Culture and Folklore.* Mogadishu: Ministry of Information and National Guidance, 1974.

Thompson, Virginia, and Richard Adloff. *Djibouti and the Horn of Africa.* Stanford: Stanford University Press, 1968.

Sudan

Arkell, A. J. *A History of the Sudan: From the Earliest Times to 1821.* London: University of London, 1961.

Barbour, K. M. *The Republic of the Sudan: A Regional Geography.* London: University of London Press, 1961.

Bechtold, Peter K. *Politics in the Sudan: Parliamentary and Military Rule in an Emerging African Nation.* New York: Praeger, 1976.

Beshir, Mohamed Omer. *The Southern Sudan: From Conflict to Peace.* New York: Barnes & Noble Books, 1975.

Conte, Carmelo. Tr. by Richard Hill. *The Sudan as a Nation.* Rome: Giuffre Editore, 1976.

El-Mahdi, Mandour. *A Short History of the Sudan.* London: Oxford University Press, 1965.

Henderson, K. D. D. *Sudan Republic: Resources, Problems, Prospects.* New York: Praeger, 1965.

Holt, P. M. *A Modern History of the Sudan: From the Funj Sultanate to the Present Day.* New York: Grove Press, 1961.

Hurreiz, Sayyid Hamid, and Herman Bell, eds. *Directions in Sudanese Linguistics and Folklore.* Khartoum: Khartoum University Press, 1975.

Nelson, Harold D., and others. *Area Handbook for the Democratic Republic of Sudan.* Prepared for the United States Department of the Army by Foreign Area Studies, The American University. Washington, D.C.: U.S. Government Printing Office, 1973.

Rahim, Muddathir Abdel. *Imperialism and Nationalism in the Sudan: A Study in Constitutional and Political Development, 1899-1956.* Oxford: Clarendon Press, 1969.

Voll, John Obert. *Historical Dictionary of the Sudan.* Metuchen, New Jersey: The Scarecrow Press, 1978.

THE ARABIAN PENINSULA AND THE GULF

Anthony, John Duke. *Arab States of the Lower Gulf: People, Politics, Petroleum.* Washington, D.C.: The Middle East Institute, 1975.

Anthony, John Duke. *Historical and Cultural Dictionary of the Sultanate of Oman and the Emirates of Eastern Arabia.* Metuchen, New Jersey: The Scarecrow Press, 1975.

Arabian American Oil Company. *Aramco Handbook: Oil and the Middle East.* Dhahran, Saudi Arabia, 1968.

Clifford, Mary Louise. *The Land and the People of the Arabian Peninsula.* New York: J. B. Lippincott Co., 1977.

Halliday, Fred. *Arabia Without Sultans.* New York: Vintage Books, 1975.

Hay, Sir Rupert. *The Persian Gulf States.* Washington, D.C.: Middle East Institute, 1959.

Hopwood, Derek, ed. *The Arabian Peninsula: Society and Politics.* Totowa, New Jersey: Rowman and Littlefield, 1972.

Koury, Enver M. *Oil and Geopolitics in the Persian Gulf Area: A Center of Power.* Beirut: Catholic Press, 1973.

Nakhleh, Emile A. *Arab-American Relations in the Persian Gulf.* Washington, D.C.: American Enterpirse Institute for Public Policy Research, 1975.

Nyrop, Richard F., and others. *Area Handbook for the Persian Gulf States.* Prepared for the United States Department of the Army by Foreign Area Studies, The American University. Washington, D.C.: U.S. Government Printing Office, 1977.

Long, David E. *The Persian Gulf: An Introduction to its Peoples, Politics, and Economics.* Boulder, Colorado: Westview Press, 1976.

Osborne, Christine. *The Gulf States and Oman.* San Francisco: Four Corners Group, 1977.

Page, Stephen. *The USSR and Arabia.* London: The Central Asian Research Center (in association with the Canadian Institute of International Affairs), 1971.

Sadik, M. T., and W. P. Snavely. *Bahrain, Qatar, and the United Arab Emirates.* Lexington, Massachusetts: D. C. Heath and Company, 1972.

Stanford Research Institute. *Area Handbook for Peripheral States of the Arabian Peninsula.* Prepared for the United States Department of the Army by Foreign Area Studies, The American University. Washington, D.C.: U.S. Government Printing Office, 1971.

Stephens, Robert. *The Arabs' New Frontier.* Boulder, Colorado: Westview Press, 1976.

Tahtinen, Dale R. *Arms in the Persian Gulf.* Washington, D.C.: American Enterprise Institute for Public Policy Reseach, 1974.

Bahrain

Nakhleh, Emile A. *Bahrain: Political Development in a Modernizing Society.* Lexington, Massachusetts: D. C. Heath and Company, 1976.

Kuwait

Daniels, John. *Kuwait Journey.* Luton, England: White Crescent Press, 1972.

El-Mallakh, Ragaei. *Economic Development and Regional Cooperation: Kuwait.* Chicago: University of Chicago Press, 1968.

Shaw, Ralph. *Kuwait.* London: Macmillan, 1976.

Winstone, H. V. F., and Zahra Freeth. *Kuwait: Prospect and Reality.* London: Allen and Unwin, 1972.

Oman

Searle, Pauline. *Dawn Over Oman.* Beirut: Khayat Book and Pub. Co., 1975.

Skeet, Ian. *Muscat and Oman: The End of an Era.* London: Faber and Faber, 1974.

Townsend, John. *Oman: The Making of a Modern State.* New York: St. Martin's Press; and London: Croom Helm, 1977.

Qatar

Key, Kerim K. *The State of Qatar: An Economic and Commercial Survey.* Washington, D.C.: K. Key Publications, 1976.

Saudi Arabia

Assah, Ahmed. *Miracle of the Desert Kingdom.* London: Johnson Publications, 1969.

De Gaury, Gerald. *Faisal: King of Saudi Arabia.* New York: Praeger, 1966.

Katakura, Motoko. *Bedouin Village: A Study of a Saudi Arabian People in Transition.* Tokyo: University of Tokyo Press, 1977.

Nakhleh, Emile A. *The United States and Saudi Arabia: A Policy Analysis.* Washington, D.C.: American Enterprise Institute for Public Policy Research, 1975.

Nyrop, Richard F., and others. *Area Handbook for Saudi Arabia.* Prepared for the United States Department of the Army by Foreign Area Studies, The American University. Washington, D.C.: U.S. Government Printing Office, 1977.

Saudi Arabia, Kingdom of. *Guide to Industrial Investment in Saudi Arabia.* Riyadh: The Industrial Studies and Development Centre, 1974.

United Arab Emirates

Daniels, John. *Abu Dhabi: A Portrait.* London: Longman, 1974.

Fenelon, Kevin G. *The United Arab Emirates: An Economic and Social Survey.* London: Longman, 1973.

Hawley, Donald. *The Trucial States.* New York: Twayne Publishers, 1970.

Yemen (AR) and Yemen (PDR)

Doe, Brian. *Southern Arabia.* London: Thames and Hudson, 1972.

Gavin, R. J. *Aden 1839-1967.* London: Hurst, 1973.

Marco, Eric. *Yemen and the Western World Since 1571.* London: C. Hurst, and New York: Praeger, 1968.

Mordesir, Simone. *A Selected Bibliography of the Yemen Arab Republic and the People's Democratic Republic of Yemen.* Durham, England: Centre for Middle Eastern and Islamic Studies, 1977.

Nyrop, Richard F., and others. *Area Handbook for the Yemens.* Prepared for the United States Department of the Army by Foreign Area Studies, The American University. Washington, D.C.: U.S. Government Printing Office, 1977.

Wenner, Manfred W. *Modern Yemen.* Baltimore: Johns Hopkins University Press, 1967.

SOUTHWEST ASIA

Iraq

Khadduri, Majid. *Independent Iraq, 1932-58: A Study in Iraqi Politics.* London: Oxford University Press, 1960.

Khadduri, Majid. *Republican Iraq: A Study in Iraqi Politics since the Revolution of 1958.* London: Oxford University Press, 1970.

Khadduri, Majid. *Socialist Iraq.* Baltimore: Johns Hopkins University Press, 1978.

Nyrop, Richard F., and others. *Area Handbook for Iraq.* Prepared for the United States Department of the Army by Foreign Area Studies, The American University. Washington, D.C.: U.S. Government Printing Office, 1971.

Jordan

Aruri, Naseer. *Jordan: A Study in Political Development.* The Hague: Mortinus Nijhoff, 1972.

Al-Bukhari, Najati. *Education in Jordan.* Amman; Jordan Press Foundation, 1973.

Johnston, Charles. *The Brink of Jordan.* London: Hamish Hamilton, 1972.

Jordan, Hashemite Kingdom of, National Planning Council. *Five Year Plan for Economic and Social Development, 1976-1980.* Amman: Royal Scientific Society, about 1976.

Nyrop, Richard F., and others. *Area Handbook for the Hashemite Kingdom of Jordan.* Prepared for the United States Department of the Army by Foreign Area Studies, The American University. Washington, D.C.: U.S. Government Printing Office, 1974.

Toni, Y. T., and Suleiman Mousa. *Jordan: Land and People.* Amman: Ministry of Culture and Information, 1973.

Lebanon

Barakat, Halim. *Lebanon in Strife: Student Preludes to the Civil War.* Austin, Texas: University of Texas Press, 1977.

Buheiry, Marwan R., and Leila Ghantus Buheiry, eds. *The Splendor of Lebanon.* Delwar, New York: Caravan Books/American University of Beirut, 1977.

Hitti, Philip K. *Lebanon in History.* London: Macmillan, 1967.

Hudson, Michael C. *The Precarious Republic: Political Modernization in the Lebanon.* New York: Random House, 1968.

Salibi, Kamal S. *Crosswords to Civil War: Lebanon 1958-1976.* New York: Caravan Books, 1976.

Salibi, Kamal S. *The Modern History of Lebanon.* New York: Caravan Books, 1977.

Sayigh, Yusif Abdullah, *Entrepreneurs of Lebanon: The Role of a Business Leader in a Developing Economy.* Cambridge: Harvard University Press, 1962.

Smith, Harvey H., and others. *Area Handbook for Lebanon.* Prepared for the United States Department of the Army by Foreign Area Studies, The American University. Washington, D.C.: U.S. Government Printng Office, 1974.

Suleiman, Michael W. *Political Parties in Lebanon.* Ithaca: Cornell University Press, 1967.

Syria

Abu Jaber, Kamel S. *Arab Ba'th Socialist Party: History, Ideology, and Organization.* Syracuse: Syracuse University Press, 1966.

Nyrop, Richard F., and others. *Area Handbook for Syria.* Prepared for the United States Department of the Army by Foreign Area Studies, The American University. Washington, D.C.: U.S. Government Printing Office, 1971.

Shorrock, William. *French Imperialism in the Middle East: The Failure of Policy in Syria and Lebanon, 1900-1914.* Madison: University of Wisconsin Press, 1976.

Tibawi, A. L. *A Modern History of Greater Syria, Including Lebanon and Palestine.* London: Macmillan, 1969.

Zeine, Zeine N. *The Struggle for Independence. Western Diplomacy and Fall of Faisal's Kingdom in Syria.* Beirut: Khayats, 1960.

Palestine

Abu-Lughod, Ibrahim, ed. *The Arab-Israeli Confrontation of June 1967: An Arab Perspective.* Evanston: Northwestern University Press, 1970.

Abu-Lughod, Ibrahim, ed. *The Transformation of Palestine: Essays on the Origin and Development of the Arab-Israeli Conflict.* Evanston: Northwestern University Press, 1971.

Aruri, Naseer, ed. *Middle East Crucible: Studies on the Arab-Israeli War of October 1973.* Wilmette, Illinois: Medina University Press Internaional, 1975.

Bull, General Odd. *War and Peace in the Middle East: The Experiences and Views of a UN Observer.* Boulder, Colorado: Westview Press, and London: Lee Cooper, 1977.

Burns, E. L. M. *Between Arab and Israeli.* New York: I.Obolensky, 1962.

Cattan, Henry. *Palestine and International Law: The Legal Aspects of the Arab-Israeli Conflict.* London and New York: Longman, 1976.

Cattan, Henry. *Palestine, the Arabs, and Israel: The Search for Justice.* London: Longmans, 1969.

Davis, John H. *The Evasive Peace: A Study of the Zionist-Arab Problem.* Cleveland, Ohio: Dillon/Liederbach, Inc., 1976.

Hirst, David. *The Gun and the Olive Branch: The Roots of Violence in the Middle East.* London: Faber and Faber, 1977.

Hurewitz, J. C. *The Struggle for Palestine.* New York: Norton, 1950.

Hutchison, Cmdr. E. H. *Violent Truce.* New York: Devin-Adair, 1956.

Jiryis, Sabri. *The Arabs in Israel.* Beirut: Institute for Palestine Studies, 1968.

John, Robert, and Sami Hadawi. *The Palestine Diary.* Two Volumes. Beirut: Palestine Research Center, 1970.

Khalidi, Walid, ed. *From Haven to Conquest: Readings in Zionism and the Palestine Problem until 1948.* Beirut: Institute for Palestine Studies, 1968.

Khouri, Fred J. *The Arab-Israeli Dilemma.* Syracuse, New York: Syracuse University Press, 1968.

Langer, Felicia. *With My Own Eyes: Israel and the Occupied Territories 1967-1973.* London: Ithaca Press, 1975.

Lilienthal, Alfred. *The Other Side of the Coin: An American Perspective of the Arab-Israeli Conflict.* New York: Putnam, 1961.

Menuhin, Moshe. *Jewish Critics of Zionism: A Testamentary Essay.* Detroit: Association of Arab-American University Graduates, 1976.

Quandt, William B. *Decade of Decisions: American Policy Toward the Arab-Israeli Conflict, 1967-1976.* Berkeley: University of California Press, 1977.

Rodinson, Maxime. *Israel and the Arabs.* Harmondsworth, England, and Baltimore, Maryland: Penguin Books, 1969.

Sharabi, Hisham B. *Palestine and Israel: The Lethal Dilemma.* New York: Van Nostrand Reinhold, 1969.

Sykes, Christopher. *Crossroads to Israel.* London: Collins, 1965.

Taylor, Alan R., ed. *Palestine: A Search for Truth.* Washington, D.C.: Public Affairs Press, 1970.

Tibawi, A. L. *Anglo-Arab Relations and the Question of Palestine, 1914-1921.* London: Luzac & Co., Ltd., 1977.

Van Arkadie, Brian. *Benefits and Burdens: A Report on the West Bank and Gaza Strip Economies Since 1967.* New York: Carnegie Endowment for Internaional Peace, 1977.

Van Horn, Maj-Gen. Carl. *Soldiering for Peace.* London: Cassell, 1966.

Zogby, James J., ed. *Perspectives on Palestinian Arabs and Israeli Jews.* Wilmette, Illinois: Medina Press, 1977.

INDEX

AAUG MONOGRAPH SERIES

No. 1. *The Arab-Americans: Studies in Assimilation,* edited by E. Hagopian and A. Paden. (out of print)

No. 2. *The Palestinian Resistance to Israeli Occupation,* edited by Naseer Aruri. (out of print)

No. 3. *The Arab World: From Nationalism to Revolution,* edited by Abdeen Jabara and Janice Terry. (out of print)

No. 4. *Settler Regimes in Africa and the Arab World: The Illusion of Endurance,* edited by I. Abu-Lughod and B. Abu-Laban.

No. 5. *Middle East Crucible: Studies on the Arab-Israeli War of October 1973,* edited by Naseer Aruri.

No. 6. *Arabs in America: Myths and Reality,* edited by Baha Abu-Laban and Faith Zeadey.

No. 7. *Perspectives on Palestinian Arabs and Israeli Jews,* edited by James Zoghby.

No. 8. *Perspectives on Technological Development in the Arab World,* edited by Mujid Kazimi and John Makhoul.